An Introduction to Man and His Development

ANCIENT
INDO-EUROPEANS
3000 B.C.

EUROPE

CELTS

SCYTHIANS

DORIANS

HITTITES

ETRUSCANS
Rome

GREECE
Troy
Mycenae

Knossos
CRETE

Byblos
Tyre
Jericho

Nineveh
Jarmo
Babylon
SUMER
Susa
Ur

PERSIA

SAHARA

DESERT

Memphis

EGYPT
Thebes

ARABIAN

DESERT

AFRICA

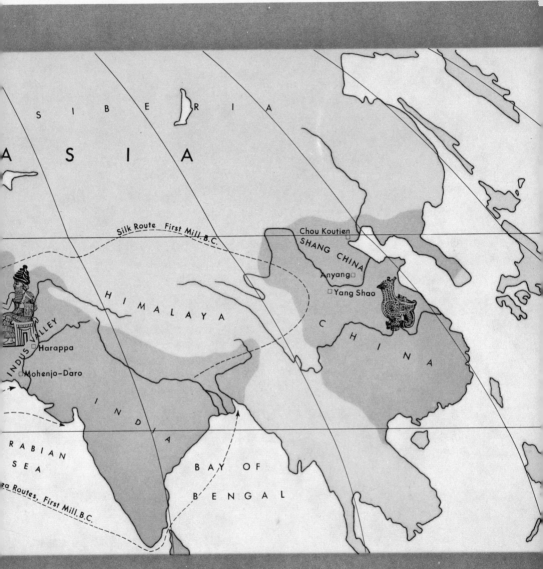

S I B E R I A

A S I A

Chou Koutien□

SHANG CHINA

Anyang□

□Yang Shao

H I M A L A Y A

C H I N A

INDUS VALLEY

□Harappa

□Mohenjo-Daro

I N D I A

ARABIAN
SEA

BAY OF

B E N G A L

...a Routes, First Mill. B.C.

CIVILIZATION UNTIL A.D. 400

An Introduction to Man and His Development

DAVID RODNICK

New York

APPLETON-CENTURY-CROFTS

DIVISION OF MEREDITH PUBLISHING COMPANY

For
Elizabeth
(who wanted me to write this book)
and for
Amie
(who I hope will read it)

Preface

This book is designed to present a point of view, one for which I am greatly indebted to the field of cultural anthropology. But because it is also a book designed to introduce the beginning student to the even larger field of the social sciences, I have borrowed heavily from the observations of the paleontologist, the classical archaeologist, the biologist, the sociologist, the psychologist, the historian, the economist, and the political scientist.

The hero of this book is Man. To the beginning student, understanding such a broad subject may appear formidable indeed. Yet it has been my experience that most beginning students are curious to understand at least the broad outlines of the world that have come down to them at the start of their maturity. I believe that an anthropological framework can help allay some of their curiosity by providing them with a point of view toward Man—what he has accomplished in the past, what he is doing now, and what we can reasonably expect him to do in the near future, assuming that the future never becomes the present but always remains "near." I believe that most students would like answers, no matter how incomplete, to these three questions: Where did we, as human beings, come from? Where are we now? and Where are we going?

Most textbooks in anthropology give a good answer to the first, but a very poor one to the second and no answer at all to the third. Perhaps I shall not succeed any better, but I nonetheless offer in the pages to follow some tentative replies to the second and third questions. These are based upon my own interests and field work in modern scientific, industrial, metropolitan civilization.

With this frame of reference in mind, I have designed the book for those students who would like to know what the social sciences, reflected here by an anthropological point of view, have to offer in their brief passage toward a first degree. It is also for those students in engineering schools who would like to understand the contribution of the field without becoming bogged down in a mass of detail that is irrelevant and unusable in their own professional careers. It is also intended for those instructors in junior, senior, and teachers colleges who are not anthropologists or social scientists, but who must double as teachers in areas in which they may have had only enough professional training to make them wish to know more.

In general, I can say that the book is intended for those who would like a concise, coherent story of what is known so far about the development of man and his works. The amount of information about both early and contemporary man is scanty indeed, but it is still possible to discern some order in the information that is available.

D. R.

Contents

II
Who We Are

III
Where We Are Going

Introduction

Although primitive man is important for having provided us with a perspective on the different varieties of belief and behavior that mankind has developed, I have not overemphasized his role as the central hero of my story. (In the present interpretation, neither minority nor majority beliefs about any form of human interaction are really pertinent.) Within the context of time, the preliterate man is a marginal man. He will soon disappear under the onslaught of our urbanized scientific and industrial Tertiary civilization. Information about him should help us understand our past behavior a little more clearly, as well as the behavior of individuals who are confused by new norms and insecurities.

In utilizing anthropology as a point of view, we must cut across disciplinary lines in order to consider our hero, Man, in a unified and coherent manner. Anthropological field work, though basic, is somewhat restricted in its vision because it deals only with certain phases of man's development and leaves out others. I have combined data gathered through such field methods with illustrative materials taken from the tremendous amounts that other disciplines have gathered about our contemporary mixed civilizations—mixed in the sense that they display varying degrees of development from the simple to the complex.

It seems obvious to me that our contemporary modern civilization, despite its evolutionary origins, is completely distinct from any form of civilization that we have known so far; and I do not believe that we shall gain insight into its complexities through intensive studies of preliterate or peasant societies. It can best be understood in its own terms by studying the huge bureaucracies that make up our industrial, commercial, governmental, and academic worlds. Although I do not attempt to undertake this enormous task, it is an approach that I have attempted to clarify in the second part of the book.

Although I am convinced that the new civilization emerging in the more industrialized and populated areas of the world is of an order so different from the old that it will change mankind more in the future than it has been changed in the past, still I think that we can imagine what some of these future trends will be by visualizing what has happened and what is happening today in the United States. The United States is the first complex nation that is perhaps now ready to step across the threshold separating the old Secondary civilization of farmers and industrial labor from the new Tertiary civilization of highly educated, innovating populations engaged in problem solving as a new form of primary industry. Since the students who will take courses in the social sciences will play more important roles as educators and innovators in the future than most of us have played in the past or present, I believe that it is necessary to introduce them now (though incompletely) to the dim outlines of the coming civilization in which they will make important decisions. I have thus attempted in Part III to deal with some of the important trends today that are leading to the Tertiary civilization of tomorrow.

The book contains a good deal of speculation on my part concerning the huge voids that exist in human history. I have, however, attempted to base these speculations on the latest available scholarship in both prehistory and recorded history. Some points may seem to repeat ones made in previous chapters, but these duplicating statements generally serve as connecting links or threads in a story that I hope will give the curious student a meaningful and coherent picture of himself and his fellow human beings.

Finally, I have tried to write the kind of book that I wish someone had written for me when I was an undergraduate and graduate student.

Where
We Came From

1

1

The Beginnings of Man: The Lower and the Middle Paleolithic Ages

Around five billion years ago the earth, its sister planets, and the sun were born of nebular gases that had previously filled interstellar space. These gases had existed for untold aeons, and the sun and the planets were neither the first nor the last star and its satellites to be born in space.

After its birth the earth required some two billion years in which to cool enough to permit simple unicellular forms of life to develop in its widespread primitive seas. The simple algae forming on top of the waters, feeding on sunlight, may have been the first of the early varieties of plant life. These may have assumed new shapes as time slowly began the changes that made the simple structures of invertebrates more complex. And these in turn eventually changed into even more complicated shapes.

Life Begins

During the course of perhaps a billion and a half years, the simple forms of invertebrate life began to evolve into jellyfish, into infinite varieties resembling plants, and into primitive shellfish. Some 400 million years ago (slightly before the age when the coal fields were laid down), the first vertebrates, the simple fish of the ancient seas, began to dart back and forth seeking food. A little over 300 million years ago, land plants began to cover the surface of those areas freed from inundation. Over 200 million years ago, amphibians took over the swamps and tidal areas. These were followed by land reptiles, and later by dinosaurs, who ruled unchallenged until a little more than 60 million years ago.[1]

[1] All dates are somewhat speculative; future decades may see more exact dating of these eras.

The Dinosaurs

The last cold-blooded dinosaur disappeared before the first man-ape appeared on the scene. Comic strips and television programs that put both forms of life on earth at the same time are guilty of the most extreme poetic license. (This juxtaposition may make prehistoric life somewhat more interesting to those moderns who prefer to judge the past from the point of view of the present; but since about 57 million years may separate the last of the dinosaurs from the first of the borderline men, the truth on the subject might be even more interesting to them than the distortion.)

With the end of the reptile age, the warm-blooded mammal, bearing its young and suckling them with milk from its mammary glands, came to prominence. More intelligent than the reptiles that they displaced, these mammals had already shared the earth for at least 100 million years with the dinosaurs. They had grown from diminutive, ratlike mammals, which scurried from sight whenever the larger reptiles came into view, into the massive whale and mastodon. For millions of years the nonprimate mammals predominated as the chief forms of warm-blooded animal life.

The Primates

Some 70 million years ago, the earliest of man's ancestors, the insectivores (small, insect-eating shrews), began to develop. From these came the predecessors of monkeys, the earliest forms of lemurs, which were small nocturnal animals with prehensile tails and hands with fingers that could grab and hold. The more advanced primates (including man) may, however, have stemmed from a species whose last extant representative is a small, nocturnal, owl-eyed animal living in Borneo, genus *Tarsius,* which is no larger than a small squirrel.

Man as a hominid comes from a long line of unknown primates, some of whose fossil bones have been found in Europe, Asia, and Africa. Although some present-day apes, such as the chimpanzee and perhaps the gorilla, may share many of the fossil pithecus (or ape) ancestors with us, their line of evolution has gone in a different direction. If man were suddenly to be destroyed by a nuclear war, the apes that might survive could not turn into men millions of years hence: their evolution has undoubtedly carried them past the point of no return on a different evolutionary road.

One early ancestor of modern-day apes may have been a small Dryopithecine ape, a fossil named Proconsul, after a chimpanzee in the London Zoo. Its bones were uncovered in East Africa in 1933, and it lived some

25 million years ago. Proconsul was halfway in size between a chimpanzee and a gorilla and may have looked somewhat like a baby chimpanzee. Other fossil apes have been found in southern Italy, India, Africa, and China; but the early genealogy of man has very wide gaps, and closer blood relatives may be found in coming decades.[2]

The Australopithecines

The first primate that moved across the border separating the apes from the hominoids may well have been an intermediate ancestor of the Australopithecines, some of whose remains have been found in Africa and Asia, in varying numbers, from 1924 to the 1960's. Evidently the separation between the lines that led on the one hand to the chimpanzees and gorillas, and on the other to the early hominoids, may have taken place about 5 to 10 million years ago. Australopithecus, one of the first hominoids, may have lived from about 3 million years ago to roughly 600,000 B.C. or later. A more specialized variety of Australopithecus, Zinjanthropus (African Man, or *Australopithecus robustus*), was discovered by Dr. Louis Leakey in Tanzania in 1959. Two University of California geologists, utilizing the Potassium 40 dating process, placed this Australopithecine specimen at 1,750,000 years old. (Over a period of hundreds of millions of years, radioactive Potassium 40 in the skeletal bones breaks down completely into Calcium and Argon 40. The small amounts of Argon 40 in the fossil bones of Zinjanthropus indicated that it was from 1,500,000 to 2,000,000 years old.) [3]

We are not on very sure ground when we talk about the Australopithecines, of whom Zinjanthropus was a later type. There is a good deal of uncertainty as to how human they were and as to whether they led to later lines of humans—*Homo erectus* (upright man) and *Homo sapiens* (thinking man).

The first Australopithecus, the skull of an infant, was found in 1924 in a limestone quarry some 200 miles southwest of Johannesburg, Repub-

[2] See Bibliography at end of Chapter 1. Some physical anthropologists (e.g., Lasker, pp. 76–77) believe that Oreopithecus, whose bones were found in a coal mine in Tuscany, Italy, and who may be 100 million years old, is perhaps closer to the later lines of hominid development. Leakey (*Adam's Ancestors*, p. 179) doubts that Dryopithecus led to the development of man. He looks upon Dryopithecus as a side line that led to the chimpanzee and gorilla.

[3] *The New York Times* of March 18, 1964, reported the discovery of other Australopithecine fossils that may also be as much as 1,750,000 years old. Between 1961 and 1963, Dr. Leakey found bone fossil remnants of a pre-Zinjanthropus small-brained pygmy hominid, to which he has given the inexact name of *Homo habilis* (able man) It is quite possible that *Homo habilis* made windbreak shelters for himself, as well as a variety of very primitive pebble tools. Dr. Leakey believes that this small-brained pygmy was more in the line of man's ascent than the Australopithecines with whom he co-existed at that time.

lic of South Africa. In succeeding years, four other Australopithecine sites were found within a radius of 300 miles by three South African paleontologists (those who study fossils) named Dart, Broom, and Robinson. A great many fossils were found in broken condition, all seeming to indicate that Australopithecus and his younger relatives were man-apes. Some anthropologists are of the opinion that, although Australopithecus' head may have looked rather apelike, he may have had a human-looking body.

Zinjanthropus, or *Australopithecus robustus,* is somewhat of a puzzle. If he is as old as 1,750,000 years, then we must move much further back in time the threshold over which some apes must have stepped in order to become the first hominoids. We would need to assume, then, that man as a tool-using primate goes back at least three million years. Further archaeological work during the next decade or two will undoubtedly clarify the picture. So far we know very little about *Australopithecus robustus.* Two remnants had been found by 1962: the first was the skull of a seventeen-year-old youth who evidently died of natural causes at the shore of an extinct lake; the second consisted of parts of a skull, some teeth, and fragments of leg bones found in 1960. To make the picture even more interesting and confusing, Dr. and Mrs. Leakey also found parts of an eleven-year-old child who was certainly ancestral to Australopithecus and who had a brain capacity of 700 cubic centimeters, half that of modern man but greater than that of the ape.

Some small, rudely chipped stones were found near the Zinjanthropus discovery, indicating that this early type of hominoid was a tool maker. Evidence also suggests that Zinjanthropus ate gritty roots, which he dug up with his primitive tools (his teeth were well worn for his young age); that he had a taste for meat; that he killed small, slow animals by driving herds of them into swamps and there slaying the young and those easily caught; and that he used skins (among the tools found with parts of the second skull was a bone skin-polisher, used perhaps to smoothe the surface of pelts).

Whether Zinjanthropus had speech we have no way of knowing, but we can assume that tool making must have required either the use of some form of rudimentary speech or visual learning. Yet Zinjanthropus' brain was only half that of modern man and a little larger than a female chimpanzee, which makes us uncertain whether he had complete speech. Certainly Zinjanthropus and the later Australopithecines were closer to men than to apes, but at the present time their position in the evolutionary line leading to modern man is quite cloudy. Further study and excavations are needed before a clearer description can be made.

In 1961 another Australopithecus skull was found, in the Republic of Chad in Africa. In the same year some fragments of a skull and a tooth were found in Israel near tools that could be roughly related to the tools that had been associated with Zinjanthropus in Africa. Some possible but still undetermined Australopithecus finds uncovered in Java in 1941 and 1952, plus the discovery of some possibly related teeth in China, indicate that this species of early man-apes may have been quite widespread in ancient times.

The Pleistocene, or the Period of Man

Before we describe any more of man's ancestors, it is necessary to digress for a series of insertions that will help us later to place man against a proper time perspective. About one to three million years ago the climate of the earth gradually became colder, and the first of the Ice Ages began to spread its glaciers across northwestern Europe, parts of Asia, and the top half of North America. This span of Ice Ages and warmer intervening periods extending through the present is called the Pleistocene.

There are various theories to explain why the climate of the earth suddenly became colder at that time, why it warmed up during three intervals, and why each warming period was followed by a colder one. The easiest theory to believe is the one proposed by Sir George Simpson, who suggested that at this time the sun began to emit more heat, causing more evaporation from the seas, which created greater cloudiness. The increase in cloud cover caused the temperature of the earth to fall a few degrees, thus leading to snows that melted very little and that led, over a period of thousands of years, to the formation of glaciers. South of the glaciers were rain belts. As the sun became hotter, the earth became cooler; but as the sun later gave out less heat, there was less cloud cover, and the earth became warmer, thus causing the various Interglacial, or warm, periods. (In the second half of the twentieth century, we are in the fourth Interglacial, or warming period.)

Some of the glacial periods lasted as long as 70,000 years. The first Interglacial, or warming period, lasted perhaps 190,000 years. The first cold spell, or Ice Age, is referred to as the Günz, the second as the Mindel, the third as the Riss, and the fourth as the Würm. This means that the first Interglacial, or warming period, is referred to as the Günz-Mindel Interglacial, the second as the Mindel-Riss, and the third as the Riss-Würm. This classification makes it possible to place early men and the tools they made in a time sequence, which tells us how long both man and his tools have existed. Roughly, one can say that the last Ice Age, or Würm Glacial, lasted about 92,000 years before it ended some 16,000 years ago.

A further digression must point out that the earlier Pleistocene is concurrent with the Paleolithic, or Old Stone Age (referring to the type of tools, mostly of chipped flint, lava, or stone, which were made by early men). The greatest part of the Paleolithic is called the Lower Paleolithic, which should be remembered as the earliest and oldest part. The Lower Paleolithic lasted at least 500,000 years, the Middle Paleolithic around 100,000 years, and the Upper Paleolithic about 60,000 years. (The Upper Paleolithic ended 10,000 years ago.)

If the date given for Zinjanthropus is the correct one, one can say that the Australopithecines (the earliest types of hominoids) lived in the beginning of the Pleistocene and the Paleolithic, and that they survived well into the middle part of the Lower Paleolithic. The more man-like primates, who are called hominids (as compared to the previous hominoids), men such as *Homo erectus,* hunted during the Lower Paleolithic. Future archaeologists and paleontologists may discover even earlier specimens of *Homo erectus* than those we know now who might have lived in the Paleolithic or the Pleistocene. The gaps in our knowledge are great and the number of fossil bones pitifully small.

Later Australopithecus

Australopithecus hunted over a wide range of territory extending from South Africa and Morocco to Java and southern China. His brain was somewhat larger than that of the other primates, and his tools indicate that he may have had a primitive type of social structure (and perhaps a rudimentary language) to permit him to make the same tools generation after generation in almost the same way. This implies that Australopithecus, unlike the other lower primates, had a simple form of culture (or behavior based upon thought), which—if we can speculate about him with little evidence—may have permitted him to use his rudimentary language to express simple ideas, such as directions where good hunting could be found, how tools should be made, and perhaps his fears and hopes, using means of communication other than screams and grunts. With language, the man in Australopithecus was slowly evolving while the ape in him was slowly receding.

Since early Australopithecus was able to invent tools to help compensate for his physical weakness, perhaps his primitive intelligence may also have told him that it was easier to kill slow-moving animals when two or more men hunted together. Perhaps it was easier to keep men working together when the young ones were not driven out of the small group by the jealousies of the older adults (as occurred among the apes) but were encouraged to make the group stronger by taking their mates from the young of neighboring families—thus stilling the pangs of jealousy in the elders and strengthening each small family by tying it to other families, and perhaps at the same time creating the incest taboo.

Whether all this developed as early as Australopithecus, we do not know. But it is possible that man was able to survive this early period by developing symbolic ideas and interconnections between ideas (both of which are part of what we call culture). Perhaps he discovered rather early in his existence that it was easier to hunt in small bands of interconnected families than in isolation. And perhaps even the discovery of fire was an important social force in bringing families together. Man was not yet the lord of all he surveyed, and many carnivores existed that were in an advantageous position to contest their supremacy with Australopithecus. (It would be a long time before man would cease to fear the dangerous carnivores that lurked near his camping sites hoping to make meals out of relatives when juicier morsels were not available.)

Homo erectus

Somewhere in the Old World more than 600,000 years ago, a new type of hominid, *Homo erectus,* arose to displace hominoid Australopithecus. This new man could have lived side by side with Australopithecus during a period of tens of thousands (or even hundreds of thousands) of years. Certainly his early tools were no better than those fashioned by Australopithecus. We do not know if he had learned to make fire when we first find him displacing the earlier types of ape-men, although it is possible that he had.[4]

Like his Australopithecine predecessors, *Homo erectus* roamed a large part of the Old World, from North Africa and Europe to Java and China. It is not difficult to imagine the life he may have led. He may have used the furs of small animals to protect himself from the intense cold of the glacial periods and to make it possible to sleep in primitive lean-tos during the long, cold nights. His sleep must certainly have been disturbed by the noises of the carnivores. Perhaps he had no fire to protect him from his animal enemies until about 400,000 years ago. Many of the young and old members of his band, and even those in their prime, may have been surprised by some carnivorous animal or pack of animals both at night and in the daytime. In the process, he may have discovered that he himself was a source of food for other animals. His clubs and primitive cutting tools must have been poor protection against the packs of lions, tigers, leopards, and wolves that roamed the earth's surface looking for something to eat. Sleeping huddled together with

---

4 In November, 1964, Chinese archaeologists announced the discovery of a complete skull cap and orbital, nasal, and temporal bones in the village of Kung Wangling in Lantion County in Shensi Province. The skull, thought to be about 500,000 to 600,000 years old, is assumed to be an early specimen of *Homo erectus.*

their slumbers continually interrupted by fears that they were being attacked, early men may have considered the night not as a time of repose and relaxation, but as a fearful interval between twilight and dawn when they could again see their attackers from far off and thus make provision for defending themselves.

The goals of early man must have been almost entirely concerned with food. He was no physical match for the carnivores, the warthogs, or the large animals that have since become extinct. He was intelligent enough, however, to get them to do what he wanted by learning to cooperate with his fellows. He could drive large animals off cliffs or into swamps and marshes, where he could catch the young or even the large ones that were immobilized.

It is doubtful that early man, even in cooperation with others, would have dared to attack dangerous animals in the open. Perhaps his way of surviving was to travel in small bands of many families, keeping close together and, making discretion the better part of valor, attacking only those animals that were smaller, trapped, outnumbered, or unable to fight back effectively. In turn, it would have taken a brave predator to attack a group that was ready to fight together.

When we consider how many millions of ape-men and early non-Sapiens men wandered over the continents of Eurasia [5] and Africa searching for their scanty food supplies, it is interesting to note that few fossils of early men have been found by the mid-twentieth century. The sum total embraces only a little over one thousand separate parts of ancient men, including pieces of their skulls, jawbones, teeth, leg bones, and fingers. A few almost complete skeletons have been found, but most fossils have been only small, scattered fragments of bone.

This scarcity of fossils is understandable since ancient man did not bury his dead but left them where they died. Their remains were eaten by scavengers and their bones left to disintegrate and scatter with the wind. The digging tools of the archaeologist have thus far uncovered remains only from those few who died along the shores of lakes (where the rising water and soft mud covered their bodies, eventually turning their bones to limestone) or in caves (where their skeletons were covered with garbage, dirt, and rubble and were then permeated by the slow drip of dissolved limestone from the ceiling, which over a period of thousands of years turned their soft bones into rock-like fossils).

Between 600,000 and 20,000 B.C. few men existed at any time in any specific part of Eurasia or Africa. Men hunted in small bands over an area of about a hundred square miles. If the area was rich in game, it could provide a living for twenty to thirty persons. But most areas probably supported fewer than these. Around 500,000 B.C., then, early man took

[5] For all anthropological and historical purposes Europe is only a peninsula of Asia. Its existence as a continent was created by ancient Greek ethnocentrism.

enormous risks in his attempt to survive against uncertainties and dangers of all kinds. For his protection he had only a few cutting tools of chipped flint or stone, a sharpened stick (and perhaps fire), a handy club probably made from a bough, few if any containers, and some tattered, poorly prepared skins for cover in cold weather or for padding on the rough ground at night.

It is even doubtful that early man used caves for shelter until he discovered the use of fire. With its discovery, he was able to keep deadly carnivores away and to sharpen his digging sticks and perhaps his wooden spears. We do not know when early *Homo erectus* began to make wooden spears, since wood, unlike flint or stone hand-cutting tools, is highly perishable. On the other hand, his stone-core hand axes and his flaked cutters, which have survived to this day, have helped us to date the sites of early man. Other than these tools, Lower Paleolithic man carried few possessions with him as he and the members of his band moved about looking for game.

Pithecanthropus

Pithecanthropus, an early *Homo erectus* (misnamed Ape-Man), lived some 500,000 years ago in Java, where he hunted many animals that have since become extinct. Parts of only nine Pithecanthropus individuals have been found, in the form of skull caps, teeth, and thighbones. It is now assumed that these men lived over 500,000 years ago and that they might have survived until about 50,000 years ago. Pithecanthropus may, however, have had an extensive ancestry as a Homo before this time.

Pithecanthropus had a brain capacity only one-third greater than that of the Australopithecines who preceded him. But this quantitative difference was evidently qualitative enough to permit him to hold his own with the animals that disputed his territorial rights. His tools were not much better than those of the Australopithecines; but he might have had a primitive social structure and the use of language, which would have permitted him to teach others how to make wooden spears with primitive cutting tools and how to sharpen them so that they would continually have their points renewed. The later varieties of Pithecanthropus (Sinanthropus, for instance) learned to tame fire and to "feed it" so that it would not go out. With the use of fire, dangerous animals could be kept at bay at night, caves could be explored and used for living and storage purposes, and nights were made less fearful—perhaps becoming more pleasant for storytelling, comradeship, dancing, and warmth. It is possible that *Homo erectus* may also have used fire to cook, thus softening his meat for chewing (though we have no evidence for this at present).

Sinanthropus

About 350,000 years ago, in the northern part of China near the present city of Peking, another variety of Pithecanthropus called Sinanthropus (Chinese Man) hunted, used fire, and ate either his own dead (perhaps during time of famine) or the dead of neighboring groups. Thighbones that seemed to have been split open by human tools were found in the 1930's in the famous cave of Choukoutien, which suggests that Sinanthropus probably ate bone marrow.

At least forty separate individuals have been found in the collection of skull caps, teeth, jawbones, thighbones, and other parts of the human anatomy that survived disintegration.[6] The skulls had been smashed to reach the brains, a human custom that later man, including the twentieth century inhabitants of New Guinea and Borneo, has continued. Sinanthropus must also have been fond of venison, for most of the bones in the Choukoutien cave were those of small deer.

Sinanthropus lived in a fairly warm interval between the second and third glacial periods. (There were few glaciers in northern Asia at any time because of the low rainfall.) Although Sinanthropus is generally depicted as being in the nude, it is possible that he used a few skins of animals (especially the deer, which he killed in large numbers) either as clothing or as cover at night. Sinanthropus may have been more inured to cold weather than man is at present. It is also possible that he used deer skins to hang in front of his cave as a windbreak and to keep out wild animals, as later men did.

We know nothing about Sinanthropus' social life. He may have hunted in small bands composed of related families. We do not know whether he supported his parents or put them out of the way when they became too old to fend for themselves. He must have been somewhat solicitous of his young; otherwise human beings would not be living today. The men in the band would certainly have done the hunting, with the hunters perhaps eating the choicest cuts of meat before they divided the rest with the band. Perhaps a lone hunter would eat the entrails and other tidbits before dragging the remainder back to his family. Whether or not he cooked his meat we will never know. The chances are that he may have enjoyed eating his food raw, since he may have been too impatient to wait for it to cook, or he may not have known any better.

[6] As Professor Carleton Coon has pointed out in *The Origin of Races* (p. 432), if one were eaten and his bones were tossed on a garbage heap in a cave, he would have a better chance to be preserved for the future edification of the archaeologist than if he had been abandoned as dead on a prairie for carniverous animals to eat. In the latter case, his bones would have turned to dust within a few decades and been scattered. On a garbage heap, the effect of water seepage mixed with limestone from the ceiling would eventually transform his bones into a fairly hard cement.

Like Professor Franz Weidenreich, who studied the Sinanthropus bones for many years before his death in 1949, Professor Carleton Coon of the University of Pennsylvania believes that Sinanthropus may have evolved into later Mongoloid man after mixing with some primitive ancestors of *Homo sapiens* who might have wandered into his territory. At any rate, *Homo erectus* was closely enough related to *Homo sapiens* to be able to exchange genes freely over a period of time, which implies that sexual attraction may have gone hand in hand with making the acquaintance of the stranger easy and interesting. It should be pointed out, however, that early man had a certain amount of physical variation just as modern man does and that the genetic possibility of further evolution may have developed in some individuals sooner than in others. One can easily assume that certain individuals within the Sinanthropi may have passed across the threshold into *Homo sapiens* without help from any outside source of genes. One can also postulate the existence of a primitive *Homo sapiens* living side by side for a long period of time with an advanced *Homo erectus*.

Certainly travel 300,000 to 400,000 years ago must have been restricted, and a good deal of inbreeding probably took place within those geographic areas that were isolated by high mountains, deserts, or large bodies of water. Each small band may have had a hunting territory ranging from less than 1,000 to more than 30,000 square miles, which would have been respected by neighboring bands. The number of individuals that a *Homo erectus* saw, visited, and interacted with in his entire lifetime may not have been more than a thousand at the most. Distant varieties of men would thus have become even more specialized in their physical traits because of thousands of years of interbreeding, with only rarely a chance meeting with men of new and different physical characteristics. On the other hand, men did not evolve in complete isolation within a period of 500,000 years or more; if they had, modern men would be far more differentiated than they actually are. We must postulate, then, an interconnected and interrelated body of genetic lines in which almost all men over the Old World during a period of hundreds of thousands of years accepted genes even from those who at some time or other were isolated and even physically different from themselves.

We must make this assumption if we are to create some sort of coherent story to explain man's slow development. All we have to work with are a few clues here, some mementos there, a few widely scattered fragments of bone, some charred earth, and some crudely chipped stone tools. We need to see the broad, though admittedly vague, paths that man has followed, rather than seek specific genetic genealogies tying millennium to millennium. Our knowledge of early man will surely become more complete in succeeding decades, just as we have a more coherent picture of his beginning and development today than we had even a quarter of a century ago. But we shall probably never know the specific details of the fascinating story of man as completely as we might wish.

Heidelberg Man

Although our story in the Far East is still vague and incomplete, we must now turn our attention to the West. The time is still 400,000 to 500,000 years ago. A primitive hominid with his few relatives roams western Europe hunting small game. All that is left of him is a jaw found in 1907, which is large, primitive, and possesses almost a full set of teeth. This single lower jaw was found in the village of Mauer, a few miles southeast of the city of Heidelberg. For this reason Mauer becomes interchangeable with Heidelberg as the name of the jaw of this contemporary of Sinanthropus. We know very little about him, since we have never seen him complete, although he may be associated with the chipped-core, stone hand axes found at the same time in Europe (referred to as Abbevillian or Chellean, after the sites in France where they were first found). There is, however, no direct evidence connecting the two. We do not know whether he used fire—as the distant Sinanthropus did—for no other evidence besides his jaw has ever come to light. He has not been found in large numbers of fragments in any cave, as Sinanthropus was, or even in more than one site, as was true of Pithecanthropus.

Dr. Coon believes that the teeth of Heidelberg man show more kinship to the later Europeans than to his contemporary, Sinanthropus, or the later Mongoloids.[7] If this assumption is accepted by other physical anthropologists, then one can suppose that Heidelberg man was perhaps one of the earliest European men, although he was a *Homo erectus* rather than a *Homo sapiens*. We have no idea how large his brain was or whether it was evolving in a *Homo sapiens* direction, as Dr. Coon believes.

Chellean Man

In 1960, Dr. Leakey, who also discovered Zinjanthropus, found a human skull at Olduvai in Tanzania, which he named Chellean (after the Chellean, or Abbevillian, hand axes found nearby). Potassium 40 analysis gave its age as 360,000 years, which makes Chellean man a contemporary of both Heidelberg man and Sinanthropus. His tools are similar to those found in Europe during the era of Heidelberg man, although they appear to be slightly cruder. Chellean man's brain capacity was between 1,100 and 1,200 cc, which is considerably higher than the 700 cc of Zinjanthropus and the 900 cc of Pithecanthropus though in the same range as Sinanthropus.

[7] *Ibid.*, pp. 491–92.

Steinheim Woman

If we now return to Europe, we shall make the acquaintance of a woman who died while she was still young. A large part of her skull (though little else) was found in 1936 at Steinheim, a few miles north of Stuttgart in Germany. She is considered to be about 250,000 years old, which makes her a little younger than either Heidelberg or Sinanthropus.

Swanscombe Woman

Parts of the skull of another young woman, who died near Swanscombe along the Thames River in England some 250,000 years ago, were found at different times between 1935 and 1938. Her skull capacity of about 1,300 cc is within the range of modern woman, and although her bones are a bit thicker than those of modern Europeans, many anthropologists consider her one of the earliest of the *Homo sapiens* fossils.

Fontéchevade Man

The Steinheims and the Swancombes were followed by the Fontéchevades, who lived in southwestern France 150,000 to 200,000 years ago. Only parts of two individuals have been found, with the skull fragments of the second one being somewhat more complete than those of the first. His brain capacity was large, around 1,470 cc, which puts him definitely in the category of modern man (he had double the brain form of ancient Zinjanthropus). His skull was smashed, and his bones were charred after death.

Perhaps Fontéchevade may have been suddenly attacked while eating his evening meal. Perhaps he furnished a meal for someone else who feasted on his brains, liver, and kidneys, but considered the rest of him too tough and scrawny.

Other Early Europeans

Following Fontéchevade man, who resembled Swanscombe, other types of early Europeans who crossed the threshold to become a higher form of thinking and talking man began to appear. A number of fragmentary remains of men who lived over 100,000 years ago were found in Ehringsdorf, Germany, in 1925. Other bones of early men living 150,000 to 200,000 years ago have also been found in Yugoslavia and in Italy. Two skulls found outside the Roman walls in 1929 and 1936 (named Saccopastore after the site) indicate a type of man who was similar to Steinheim, who was definitely early *Homo sapiens,* and who lived between 150,000 and 200,000 years ago. These finds indicate that the European population of that time, though primitive, may have been as varied physically as the peoples who live in that area today.

Man even in his early days had a good deal of individual variation. Since at that time there were no artificial barriers of religion, language, or nation, much interbreeding, based more upon propinquity than upon any conscious social distance scales, may have taken place.

Neanderthal Man

Time moves inexorably forward, and now we find ourselves again in Europe and the Middle East about 100,000 years ago. In Europe, the population seems suddenly to have shifted and changed. New men have come on the scene, beetle-browed and large-nosed, with flattened foreheads and heads and short, heavy, broad-shouldered bodies. If we were to meet them after having spent some time with the Fontéchevades, the Swanscombes, the Steinheims, and the Saccopastores, we would feel that, although the newcomers appeared to be more intelligent, better hunters, and family men, still they seemed to have regressed quite a bit physically. These new arrivals had larger brain capacities than the men who lived before them; in fact, their brains were even larger than those of modern men. But despite this, they have consistently been the most misunderstood and most maligned of all early men. They have been drawn as ape-men, and the impression given by many writers on early man is that these men disappeared, as they deserved to, because more advanced humans came on the scene and, not liking their looks, proceeded to exterminate them.

These newcomers are known as the Neanderthals, from the site where the first of their group was found, along the small, slow-moving river called the Neander in the western part of Germany. When the first Neanderthal fossil was discovered a little over 100 years ago, he was believed to be an abnormality, an idiot, or some strange malformation of man, rather than a human being in his own right. From that time to the present, fossilized bones of Neanderthal man have been found in large numbers in France, Italy, Greece, Czechoslovakia, Russia, Morocco, Israel, Iran, and Central Asia.

As a result of the finding of an almost complete skeleton in 1911, Neanderthal man was reconstructed as a bowed, apelike man, unable to stand erect, who seemed to be a throwback to some prehuman ape-man. But this reconstruction, according to Professor Coon, was based upon the abnormalities of a man between forty-five and fifty years old who was found in a cave at La Chapelle-aux-Saints in the southwestern part of

France and who had evidently been crippled with arthritis and was senile and toothless for many years before his death. Recent physical studies indicate that his bones were normally as straight as those of modern man.

In Israel, two caves in Mount Carmel near Haifa were excavated between 1929 and 1934, bringing to light five almost complete skeletons, which were dated at about 115,000 years old. One of them, though normal, appeared to be similar in features to the old Neanderthal man in La Chapelle. The other four seemed to bear more resemblance to modern man.

Many of the Neanderthal jaws found thus far have well-developed chins (this is especially true of the four from the Mount Carmel caves); some have not, indicating only that Neanderthal man was mixed and varied even during the height of his period of predominance. He certainly came closer to a modern European in appearance than to an ape, and the chances are that if he were fully dressed in present-day clothes, he might not even command a second look. The most unusual aspect about him would be the stockiness of his frame and his large, fleshy nose, perhaps larger than that of modern European man. Neanderthal man was between 5'4" and 5'6" in height, very heavily built, with shorter, broader hands, heavier bones, a more sloping forehead, and a more muscular frame than modern European man. His feet had wide soles and perhaps no instep.

Neanderthal man disappeared a little over 40,000 years ago, having been the main occupant of Europe and the Near East for almost 100,000 years. There has been a good deal of speculation about his extinction, with many popular writers imagining him as a gentle but somewhat stupid man who was finally wiped out by invaders from the north who became the ancestors of modern European man.

Some evidence suggests that Neanderthal and Upper Paleolithic men (the ancestors of modern European man) worked and lived side by side in Europe, southwestern Asia, and northern Africa for thousands of years. The area was big enough for both of them, and it is quite possible that both groups are ancestral to us. Neanderthal and Upper Paleolithic men may have taught one another a good deal, may have had intense friendships, and may have sealed their amity by taking mates from one another's groups. Both may even have found the other side fair to look at and agreeable to know. (Contemporary speculation leans to the theory, proposed by Professor Coon, that Neanderthal man was absorbed by the new *Homo sapiens* hunters, descendants of the pre-Neanderthals, who returned to Europe from central or southwestern Asia during the intervals of mild weather in the last Ice Age.)

Just as a small migration of early European men could have moved slowly into eastern and central Asia in pursuit of game and there mixed with the Sinanthropi to develop a new mixture that evolved into the highly capable and intelligent Mongoloid *Homo sapiens* (a theory proposed by Professor Coon), so a small migration in reverse may have come from eastern Asia to northern Africa and Europe over 200,000 years ago. They may have found the pre-Neanderthals in Europe, northern Africa, and southwestern Asia friendly, intelligent, and attractive—thus giving rise to a new racial mixture, which may well have been Neanderthaloid man in the varied forms in which we know him, with his greater intelligence, courage, and sense of compassion.

Having been reared on a diet of science-fiction and conquistadores novels, many of us tend to assume that all contacts between different peoples are bound to be hostile (like two unfriendly leopards first circling one another suspiciously, before closing in for a death struggle). This pessimistic point of view about man's innate hostility toward strangers who are different from him may derive from our knowledge of the early warring civilizations with their need for loot, human slaves, and sacrificial victims, rather than from any knowledge we have of man during the long period of time in which he did not live under conquering empires, whether of the ancient or the modern varieties.

The initial contacts between Europeans and the American Indians were not necessarily hostile, nor did the early French and Spanish explorers in America experience unusual difficulties in wandering through thousands of miles of Indian-held territory. Similarly, if explorers from Asia had come into Europe at the time of the Renaissance, they might not have found an unfriendly reception—unless they came as hostile conquerors. Even the Crusaders saw the Saracens as worthy of friendship and emulation, and Marco Polo at the end of the thirteenth century had a very friendly reception at the court of Kublai Khan in China.

There is no reason to believe that early men behaved as a group of brutal members of some primeval criminal gang. Neanderthal men and even Sinanthropi may have been quite gentle with one another. The cannibalism that may have been practiced by men before Neanderthal (and even by Neanderthal) may have been similar to that of the Aztecs, the Plains Indians, the Maori, and perhaps ancient Europeans—ceremonies in which one consumed parts of a worthy relative or a brave foe in the hope of absorbing his virtues. In many ancient religious rites, part of the god or gods was consumed by the followers. (Or, perhaps early men consumed other men only when game was scarce and hunger was in the land. This form of cannibalism has been practiced even in modern times by those faced with dire need.)

Neanderthal Man's Social Life

Although we cannot return with any time machine to the caves or shelters of Neanderthal man, we may be permitted to make certain conjectures about his social life. First of all, Neanderthal seems to have been the earliest man to bury his dead rather than to throw them on a nearby garbage heap. This implies that Neanderthal man may have had some primitive ideas about life and death.

Neanderthal man also seems to have been compassionate; he may have felt pity, and he may have also had a sense of respect. The old man of La Chapelle-aux-Saints was crippled with arthritis of the joints and so obviously could not participate in the hunt. His teeth were gone. Yet someone had kept him alive for years. This would have entailed bringing him food, chewing the tough pieces of meat for him, and pounding the wild vegetables and seeds so that he could eat them as mush.

In 1957 in a cave in Iraq, the skull of a 45-year-old man was found, crushed by a limestone slab that had fallen from the ceiling of a cave. This Neanderthal man had been born with a withered right arm, which would certainly have prevented his being as good a hunter as he would have been with a normal arm. Yet he was kept alive. His useless arm had been amputated later on above the elbow, an operation that he survived successfully. He was also blind in his left eye from wounds he had received. But he survived this too and died in his cave many years later. If Neanderthal man was an unfeeling and unthinking brute, would we find these evidences of speculation on the need for certainty about posthumous existence and of a compassionate human concern for those who were old and crippled?

Perhaps there was a good deal of individual variation in temperament and personality even at that time. Depending upon the warmth of the family life and the care given to the growing child, there may have been marked differences between a Neanderthal family in one part of Europe and another somewhere else. Perhaps the cases of human compassion may have been exceptional rather than normal. But whatever the facts may have been, the evidence seems to indicate the definite humanity of certain Neanderthal men.

Since Neanderthal men must have lived in small bands, perhaps an elder served as leader to hold the band together, possibly by his knowledge of magic, his superiority in hunting, his ability to rekindle a fire, his cleverness in learning from his own experiences and those of others, or his skill in using traps to catch the huge animals that competed with Neanderthal man for living space.

It is clear that Neanderthal man was not a lone hunter, for one man could have been no match for the giant cave bear (twice as large as the grizzly), the huge mammoth, the woolly rhinoceros, or the large cave lion that hunted where Neanderthal man also sought his game.

In recent years, Neanderthal man's social reputation has improved enormously. We are now beginning to believe that he did extremely well with the very little he had to work with and that we may have done him a disservice by our past ignorance of him. As we get to know him better, we may find that he was a fairly admirable individual, despite his human failings and, of course, his mistake in picking 100,000 years ago as a time in which to be born.

The Contemporaries of Neanderthal Man in Asia

Homo erectus was a contemporary of Neanderthal in southeastern Asia, where a large number of his bones have been found near the Solo River in central Java. Solo man, though a contemporary of Neanderthal, was by no means his intellectual equal; in many ways he appears to have been closer to Pithecanthropus. He was more underdeveloped physically, and his tools were not as well made as Neanderthal's. We know nothing about his social life, but the chances are that he may have been a rather nice person for other Solo individuals to know, perhaps cooperative, helpful, and friendly. He may have been somewhat slow-witted, but he was certainly more highly developed mentally than the Pithecanthropi who had preceded him by a few hundred thousand years.

Early Man in Africa

In 1945 Professor Arambourg of France found some human fossils in Algeria that have been tentatively dated around 200,000 years old and characterized as *Homo erectus*. In the development scale they were placed later than Sinanthropus and earlier than Neanderthal. They could have been the early *Homo erectus* men who mixed their genes with the primitive pre-Neanderthal peoples of Europe to produce Neanderthal man. In 1953, on the other hand, skull fragments were found in a cave in Morocco which seem to be ancestral to those discovered in Algeria. They have been dated at about 400,000 years old, which would make them contemporary with Heidelberg man and the Sinanthropi of China. Other fossil fragments found in North Africa between 1933 and 1960 indicate tentative relationships to the Australopithecines as well as to the Sinanthropi.

One of the most complete fossil skulls found in Africa is that of Rhodesian man (*Homo rhodesiensis*), discovered in 1921 in a mine in Northern Rhodesia. Dated at about 25,000 years old, it is a curious mixture of both ancient and modern man. The skull capacity measures about 1,280 cc, which is only slightly less than that of modern man but certainly greater than that of many of our Australoids of today. In many ways Rhodesian man resembled Neanderthal man with his flattened forehead and superorbital ridges (bony brow ridges above the eyes), but in the shape of the lower face he more nearly resembled modern man. It is possible that Rhodesian man may be a comparatively late survivor of only one of the many ancestral types of the African Negro and that he may also have been a contemporary of Neanderthal, just as Solo man was. In 1947 a human jaw, 40,000 years old and similar in form to that of Rhodesian man, was found in the Transvaal.

Summary

We have now reported most of the sparse number of fossil sites discovered thus far, covering the beginnings of man from the Australopithecine Zinjanthropus to the emergence of *Homo sapiens* in Europe during the Upper Paleolithic era some 40,000 years ago.

There is little doubt that some sort of tenuous relationship exists between all the early men whose bones we have commented on. Although there was a good deal of local variation in physical detail, mankind appears to have developed mentally at about the same pace and at about the same time. Early man was primarily a hunter and a gatherer of seeds and wild roots. His tools were few; and although a certain amount of regional variation is evident in their structure, the invention of a new shape by one eventually became the possession of others. Everywhere *Homo erectus* wandered in his search for game, he met other men who, though underdeveloped, were still men, primarily because they possessed that most remarkable of all human talents, language.

With language early men could describe their tools and instruct others in how to make them. They could point out where game could be found. They could plan together the destruction of the largest and the most ferocious of the land animals. With speech they could rear their children to live as they had lived. They could discuss the spirit world and the spirits that men have within themselves. They could teach their sons how to fracture flint—that a series of sharp blows would break the stone into a cone and slivers of flint—and then how to use the core or cone to cut off branches that could be fashioned into spears for throwing or thrusting. With language man became conscious of his own defects and his lack of power. With language as thought he could devise ways to overcome his physical weaknesses. His mental superiorities stressed the discovery of principles and their application to forms of improvement and the invention of new tools and weapons. Throughout the hundreds of thousands of years of man's development, there must have existed tens of thousands of thinking men who became the heroic, unsung innovators who taught their descendants how to work and hunt more efficiently, and how to make sense out of a world that had previously appeared disordered.

Thus far we have covered only the Lower and Middle Paleolithic ages (named after the stone tools that their inhabitants made). The earliest tools of the Paleolithic (the pebble tools of *Australopithecus robustus* are previous to this time) were the stone, or flint, hand axes. To make these, one stone was used as a hammer to fracture another stone in such a way that only the interior part, or core, was left. This core could then be struck again and again in such a way as to obtain the proper sharpness for a cutting edge that could be used on wood, pelts, or flesh. The cores were then used to make other tools or weapons. The cores could not be made without the flint stone's being struck at such an angle that it would fracture into the parts needed. Although this technique was used primarily to get at the flint within the limestone nodules (the flint being as sharp as glass), it was also used later on to fracture other kinds of stone. When this technique is used, we refer to its products as Abbevillian or Chellean tools of the Lower Paleolithic.

During the Middle Paleolithic (250,000 to 40,000 years ago), men learned to use a bone to strike the nodule of stone in order to reach not only the core but also the flakes or strips that could then be used as flint knives, scrapers, chisels, and other primitive tools. The early part of this period is referred to as the Acheulian or the Clactonian, from the names of the sites in France and England where the more finished hand axes and flint strips were first found. The Middle Paleolithic is also the period of time in which the Swanscombes, Steinheims, Fontéchevades, and North African forms of related Sinanthropi lived. The Middle Paleolithic also includes the later Mousterian period, during which men learned to work the flakes more carefully and to fashion the cores more skillfully. The Mousterian is the period of Neanderthal man. With his disappearance and the entrance of *Homo sapiens* into Europe and southwestern Asia, we come into the Upper Paleolithic, one of the first great revolutionary epochs in man's history. The Upper Paleolithic is 40,000 years away from our present time and is the stage when man everywhere was dimly and feebly seeking to make his life more satisfying so that he could survive more successfully in the world around him.

Selected Bibliography

Bibby, Geoffrey, *The Testimony of the Spade* (New York, Knopf, 1956).

Childe, V. Gordon, *Man Makes Himself,* rev. ed. (New York, New American Library, 1961).

Coon, Carleton S., *The Story of Man* (New York, Knopf, 1955).

————, *The Origin of Races* (New York, Knopf, 1962).

Dobzhansky, Theodosius G., *Evolution, Genetics and Man* (New York, Wiley, 1955).

Gladwin, Harold Sterling, *Men out of Asia* (New York, McGraw-Hill, 1947).

Hawkes, J., and Woolley, L., *Prehistory and the Beginnings of Civilization* (New York, Harper & Row, 1963).

Hibben, Frank C., *The Lost Americans* (New York, Crowell, Apollo Edition, 1961).

Howells, William, ed., *Ideas on Human Evolution* (Cambridge, Harvard University Press, 1962).

———, *Mankind in the Making* (Garden City, N.Y., Doubleday, 1959).

Lasker, Gabriel Ward, *The Evolution of Man* (New York, Holt, Rinehart and Winston, 1961).

Leakey, L. S., *Adam's Ancestors* (New York, Harper & Row, Harper's Torchbooks, 1960).

MacGowan, Kenneth, and Hester, Joseph A., *Early Man in the New World* (Garden City, N.Y., Doubleday, Anchor Books, 1962).

Mongait, A. L., *Archaeology in the USSR* (Baltimore, Penguin, 1961).

Montagu, Ashley, *Man: His First Million Years* (New York, New American Library, 1962).

von Koenigwald, G. H. R., *The Evolution of Man* (Ann Arbor, University of Michigan Press, 1962).

2

The Upper Paleolithic

With the Upper Paleolithic, some 40,000 years ago, we arrive at more familiar ground. The people who inhabited both the Old and the New Worlds possessed roughly the same variations that they have today. (Man was now starting to move across the Bering Sea over the land bridge that at that time joined eastern Siberia and the westernmost tip of Alaska.)

North Africa was inhabited by a Bushman-like variety of people. As far as we know, the ancestral Negroes, who were also *Homo sapiens* at this time, occupied the grasslands and forests of western Africa.[1] The Australoids were in eastern India and southeastern Asia; the Mongoloids covered Asia, stretching from northeastern Siberia to the islands of Indonesia (sharing them with the Australoids); and the Caucasoids covered Europe and Asia as far as middle Siberia and the borders of India. During most of this period in Europe, only the western part was inhabited—large glaciers covered northwestern and central Europe. The climate was cold and rainy in southern Europe and its connected land mass of southwestern Asia, and it was snowy and bitterly cold in the more northerly parts. Siberia was cold, but because of the scanty precipitation, the ground was barely dusted with snow. The western part of Alaska was free of glaciers, although Canada and the northern part of the United States were covered with ice up to a mile high, leaving only a relatively narrow strip east of the Rocky Mountains free of ice. Through this pass between the glaciers early man (a composite perhaps of Australoids, Caucasoids, and Mongoloids) came, following the herds of mammoths, large-horned bison, and giant deer by way of Alaska into the grasslands of North America. About 30,000 years ago, he left his mark in several caves in New Mexico and in sites near Mexico City. He had made himself at home in the southernmost

[1] Negroids were evidently widespread at this time in Asia, indicating that there were Negroes inhabiting areas other than Africa. At present, the connections are not clear.

tip of South America almost 10,000 years before three small ships left Portugal to seek a new trade route between Europe and the East Indies.

The Age of Innovation and Invention

Great changes took place during the Upper Paleolithic, which ran parallel to the last of the Ice Ages (Würm I and II). A fairly small human population moved along the rim of the advancing glaciers, hunting the large animals that fed on lichens and mosses (these grew only where the weather was cold).

The Upper Paleolithic was an age of innovation and invention. Man's tools were more varied and more skillfully made. Clothes of skins and fu.ら were now tailored and sewn with leather thongs in form-fitting garments and perhaps decorated with bone or shell ornaments of various kinds. Men wore warm boots of fur and skin. They used bone harpoons, fishhooks, thrower-sticks, and spear launchers (small, hand-held platforms for the spears, which gave them a greater thrust, speed, and distance). Men learned to cooperate in hunting, erecting large traps and pounds for the mammoths, wild horses, and bison. By means of cooperative action among entire bands, they could induce herds of animals to kill themselves by jumping off cliffs in frightened attempts to escape their human tormentors. Men still remained the hunters, while the women served as housekeepers, seamstresses, preparers of hides, and collectors of wild roots and seeds.

Population

In Paleolithic days a plentiful supply of food meant security; but more often there may have been hunger and even famine.[2] Epidemics undoubtedly decimated the small bands, but perhaps there was enough space and even isolation between groups of men to allow an epidemic to run its course without spreading through all the human campsites. Along the peripheries of human habitation men may not have seen their neighbors for many months at a time. The birthrate could have been high, perhaps over fifty per thousand (as against twenty in the United States today, and forty to forty-five in Central and South America). The death rate may almost have equaled the number of births, causing the population to grow very slowly. Perhaps for hundreds or even thousands of years, various peoples may even have diminished in numbers. We can speculate that

[2] We have no documentary sources concerning the way Upper Paleolithic men lived, so the following pages must be taken as speculation.

nowhere was there enough security in the supply of food, or enough children to grow to adulthood to hunt for their elders when the latter became old. Death must have come early to adults, for few could hope to live beyond fifty, and at sixty one may have been truly ancient.

Yet *Homo sapiens* had come a long way by the Upper Paleolithic. He had now won mastery over the animal world and was over the threshold of making himself master of the natural and physical worlds as well.

Religion

(Upper Paleolithic man was now also seeking to control the unseen world, largely through a newfound interest in magic. He expressed his deep-seated desires through such art forms as amulets and became increasingly interested in the spirit worlds, which had the power to reward or deprive him of his needed food. He developed his art forms not for aesthetic enjoyment, but perhaps to clothe his wishes in concreteness. For example, the Gravettians, who hunted the mighty mammoth in central Europe and southern Russia more than 30,000 years ago, made little ivory statuettes showing exaggeratedly pregnant women—perhaps to indicate their strong desire for more children and to increase the fertility of their wives. The Lower Perigordians, who lived in France and Spain at the beginning of the Upper Paleolithic (and who may have resembled the western Europeans of today), made amulets and carvings in their caves of pregnant women as fertility figures. The Aurignacians, who are also known as Cro-Magnons and who differed little physically from the Lower Perigordians (or Combe Capelle man, whom they superseded), were also much concerned with guaranteeing the fertility not only of their women but also of the animals that they hunted. The Solutrean and the Magdalenian epochs saw the creation of cave murals and bas-reliefs, in which men manufactured reality for a world they were attempting to understand and control.

We do not know when man first began to use magic in his quest for security. As he developed, he may have had a strong need for knowledge to help him fulfill his goals. Even before Neanderthal man he may have known and feared death. By creating a pleasant world where the spirits of the dead could go, he could perhaps prepare himself more easily for the sudden termination of his earthly life. At the same time, he may have hoped to encourage the spirits of the dead to go to their world where they could act as guardians for man rather than as his feared enemies. It was preferable to have the spirits in a place separate from their former habitations because if they stayed close, they could be an unknown and perhaps uncontrollable force.

Upper Paleolithic man buried his dead in or near his living place. He painted them with red ocher to give them a future life (even before this time men had undoubtedly associated the color red with fire, warmth, and life) and gave them food supplies for their long trip to the spirit world. Neanderthal man had also buried his dead in a sleeping position and in some cases built fires over the grave to warm them or to give them new life. (Even Neanderthal man saw the connection between life and warmth.)

Upper Paleolithic man made dramas out of his rituals. To ensure a plentiful supply of bears, reindeer, horses, and bison, he made images of them in clay or paint within his deeply recessed caves. He then danced in front of or around these images while praying to their spirits not to be hostile or angry with men, but to provide them with food as good parents should. At the end he symbolically killed the animals, either by sticking spears into the soft clay or perhaps by throwing weapons at those that were painted. The reality of the dance and the rituals thus became a cause-effect relationship that would create a future supply of food. Bison and herds of deer and horses were painted as if early man were driving them off the tops of cliffs or trapping them in marshes or within narrow, high-banked streams. By depicting what had taken place in the past, man hoped to ensure the duplication of it in the future.

By painting images or molding clay forms in the deepest recesses of caves (where one sometimes had to crawl on his stomach for many yards in order to reach them), Upper Paleolithic man may have thought that he was not only figuratively but actually creating these animals in the deep wombs of the earth. The artist and the shaman (or medicine man) may thus have seen themselves as the creators of new life in these objects.

Because of the continuous insecurity caused by periodic famines and the ever-present threat of death, early man may have been preoccupied with increasing both human and animal fertility. He may also have been the first to use the phrase "Be fertile and multiply" as a chief goal in life for both humans and animals.

Perhaps it was Upper Paleolithic man who first began to placate the spirits of the bear in a ceremony carried on until recently by the Ainus of Japan and the Indians of both western and eastern America. This may have occurred when the large *Ursus spelaeus,* or cave bear (an easy prey during the winter months), became extinct and it became necessary to seek smaller hibernating bears. Upper Paleolithic man might have hoped to prevent the extinction of all bears (and thus ensure a good supply of food for himself) by apologizing to the spirit of the dead bear for having killed it, urging it to understand that he did this only because his family and he needed food badly. He might have hoped that the spirit bear would not hold this against his band and him but would help them find enough bear meat in the future when other forms of hunting became difficult. Upper

Paleolithic man may have hoped that the spirits of the dead bears would be compassionate and understanding and would not prevent the flesh of their descendants from being eaten by man. Thus man may have put himself in the position of being as dependent on the bear spirits for food as children are dependent on their parents. This need of man to use analogies from his own life in understanding the unknown world of the spirits has continued even to this day: man can only describe what he knows, and the unknown must be clothed in the familiar if it is to become comprehensible.

The ritual drama and dance were certainly present during the days of Upper Paleolithic man, perhaps accompanied by simple songs and music. To give reality to their fantasy, men had to act out their deepest wishes and strongest desires, to depict them in art forms, to recite them in poetry, or to create imagery through folk tales. These devices were developed by man to ease the void he felt as a helpless, puny primate unable to influence his fate. With art as communication he found the ability to change his destiny, to control a previously frightening world, and to make himself into an all-powerful figure. Man could provide himself with a new confidence in mastering his inner fears. By means of imagery, masks, and dances, he could put himself in the place of the spirits and thus say, "There go I." He could then appeal to them, appease them, and obtain concessions from them in terms that he could understand. The unknown became familiar, friendlier, more understanding, and easier to control through proper cause-effect relationships.

Upper Paleolithic Housing

In the popular mind, Upper Paleolithic man is associated with caves primarily because of the beautifully executed mural paintings, which indicate that he lived in caves when they were available. But in most of Europe, Asia, Africa, and even the New World, there were never enough caves to go around. Caves restrict the hunter to the immediate vicinity; flat grasslands are more inviting to large herds of herbiverous animals than rocky crags and difficult precipices. If there were as many as 2 million to 5 million men living at any one time during the Upper Paleolithic, most of them would undoubtedly have found the caves and their immediate hunting territories preempted. Many probably followed the large herds of mammoths, bison, deer, and horses as they migrated for pasturage. Perhaps it was this steady pursuit of large herds of food on the hoof that brought Upper Paleolithic man to the New World.

Since the climate in Europe and northern Asia was cold during much of the Upper Paleolithic, men needed more than primitive windbreaks as shelter from the elements. Archaeological excavation indicates that men living in the plains of Europe built square or round semisubterranean houses, which were roofed with boughs, stones, and dirt. Tents were evidently in use throughout the entire Upper Paleolithic; and those Gravettian hunters of southern Russia who pursued mammoths and reindeer appear to have built fairly large tents of skins, which they weighed down with mammoth tusks to keep them from blowing away during winter storms. In summer long windbreaks with more than one hearth inside may have been used to keep the sleepers safe from prowling carniverous animals and high winds. In winter families may have slept close to the hearth fires, wrapped in furs to keep warm.

Social Organization

We can assume that the bands became specialized in their labor: there was man's work and woman's work, as well as work for the children. The cripples, the old, and the infirm may also have had allotted tasks, or perhaps they were left to die when they were unable to keep up with the migrating band (as was done among the Eskimos and some of the North American Indians). The specialization of labor within the band may have been further divided. Some may have directed the hunts, deciding what each was to do and how he was to do it. Others may have been skilled artists who made portraits and carvings of the animals to be killed. The artists may have learned their skill from relatives, or they may have been picked out as apt pupils because of some talent they displayed when youngsters in imitating the designs and forms made by their elders. Perhaps one or two who had epileptic fits or hysterical seizures were chosen to solicit the help of the spirit world in curing illnesses, in talking to the dead, or in appeasing the various spirits to prevent misfortune from befalling the band.

Perhaps specialists or a few ingenious individuals made the chipped-stone tools that preceded most of those we use today: the chisel, the awl, the knife, the saw, and the various bone tools that were turned out in a much greater variety than ever before. By the time the Upper Paleolithic period came to an end 10,000 years ago in western Europe (and 14,000 to 16,000 years ago in southwestern Asia), the bone needle with an eye had been invented and thread was made of twisted sinew. Possibly the bow and arrow had also been used toward the end of the era. Fire was made with flints and iron pyrites; lamps were fashioned of stone and used with a wick and animal oils. Certainly the intricate paintings and carvings made in the deep, recessed caves of southwestern France and northern Spain during the latter part of the Upper Paleolithic—called the Magdalenian Period—could never have been executed without artificial light from the stone lamps that have been found in these caves.

Upper Paleolithic Art

Among the ivory carvings that have been found is a delicately produced head of a young girl with braids on top of her head. Most of the murals and carvings were concerned with fertility rites, but a certain number were caricatures of men and women that were drawn on the inside of cave walls and indicate that the people in Europe looked very much as they do today. One wall painting from the Trois Frères cave in southern France portrays a possible deity who may have been one of the chief protectors of the hunters. This figure is shown with reindeer antlers, the head of an owl, the forepaws of a bear, the body of a deer, the tail of a wolf, and the legs and genitals of a man. (The drawing is generally listed as being that of a sorcerer, but I can see no reason for this assumption since it is very possible that Upper Paleolithic men were more interested in invoking spirits of animals than in portraying themselves.)

Upper Paleolithic Culture

Upper Paleolithic man was a man in the fullest meaning of *Homo sapiens*. He possessed a vocabulary extensive enough to tell myths and legends from the past, to describe the animals he saw or hunted, to carry on his magical incantations and formulas, to deal with events of day-to-day life, to explain the unknown world about him in words that were meaningful, and to communicate his thoughts, feelings, and wishes. Today our symbols, goals, and varieties of technology and information are on a different level, but we could understand his way of life if we should discover some Upper Paleolithic hunter, say, who had been able to survive in some isolated valley. (Men can still be found in the desert regions of central Australia whose way of life may be similar to that of Upper Paleolithic man. Although they lack his developed technology, they speak a complicated language, they have a complex kinship system, an intricate ritual, and a religious organization, and they keep in their memories far more detailed genealogies than we do.)

Upper Paleolithic man inhabited all the known continents, including the New World and Australia. He had become an artist and a skilled craftsman, and he made a large number of inventions that benefited those who came after him. He hunted and exterminated the mammoth both in Eurasia and in North and Central America. In the New World his bones have been found with those of the giant sloth and the mammoth. His remains have been found at sites in Minnesota, Texas, New Mexico, Mexico, and the tip of South America—indicating that like Kilroy in World War II, Upper Paleolithic man was also there, though some 10,000 to 30,000 years before. His way of life, which derived from what he had received from the Middle Paleolithic, made possible the improvements found in the Mesolithic. In this respect he was very human: man, whether *Homo erectus* or *Homo sapiens,* did not (and still does not) have to reinvent everything he needed in every generation. He is bequeathed the immortal treasures of the human mind, which can be used as foundations for improvements and still further innovations. Upper Paleolithic man was both the ancestor and the mentor of Mesolithic man, who now comes on the scene.

Selected Bibliography

Braidwood, Robert J., and Willey, Gordon R., eds., *Courses Toward Urban Life* (Chicago, Aldine, 1962).

Childe, V. Gordon, *Man Makes Himself* (New York, New American Library, 1955).

——, *What Happened in History* (Baltimore, Penguin, 1961).

Coon, Carleton S., *The Story of Man* (New York, Knopf, 1955), Chapter 3.

Hoebel, E. A., *Man in the Primitive World* (New York, McGraw-Hill, 1958), Chapter 6.

Kühn, Herbert, *On the Track of Prehistoric Man* (New York, Random House, 1955).

Piggott, Stuart, ed., *The Dawn of Civilization* (New York, McGraw-Hill, 1961).

Singer, Charles, Holmyard, E. J., and Hall, A. R., eds., *A History of Technology,* Vol. I (New York, Oxford University Press, 1958).

Washburn, Sherwood L., ed., *Social Life of Early Man* (Chicago, Aldine, 1961).

White, Leslie A., *The Evolution of Culture* (New York, McGraw-Hill, 1959).

3

The Mesolithic, or the Middle Stone Age

About 10,000 years ago, the last Ice Age came to an end in Europe. The rains slowly advanced northward from the subtropical regions to areas previously occupied by glaciers and to the climatic belt of severe cold. Through the following centuries, the weather became progressively warmer.

The Paleolithic, or Old Stone Age, also came to an end and was followed by a period of more efficient food organization, the invention of many important tools, the use of complex traps of various kinds, and the development of fishing as a substitute for hunting meat. (Although we have today improved our techniques for catching fish, the ways in which they are caught are still similar to those invented thousands of years ago.) The brief Mesolithic period provided the basis for the later Neolithic, which was to prove even more revolutionary in its changes than the Mesolithic.

Fishing

Although the Mesolithic was still a hunting and food-collecting stage, men now learned to hunt new forms of life. In the coastal and lake regions of Europe they constructed semipermanent sites where they hunted along the peripheries and fished intensively along the shores. (Spearing fish seems to have been engaged in during the Upper Paleolithic also.) New kinds of fishhooks were devised, the barbed harpoon was brought to a new level of usage, fish traps and weirs were constructed to catch large quantities of fish, and the process of smoking both fish and meat was evidently also discovered.

Along the shores of the North Sea huge shell heaps were left by the

Mesolithic dwellers of Denmark. Generation after generation over a period of 2,000 to 3,000 years ate oysters, clams, and other forms of shell-fish and threw the shells on the nearby garbage heaps. These eventually became covered with drifting sand to form small hills.

Mesolithic Inventions

Fishing weirs required the plaiting of flexible, slender branches either from trees or bushes. Fishing nets, also a Mesolithic invention, were made out of twisted fiber strands of plants, which proved to be stronger and finer than animal sinews. Baskets and other plaited objects were made by the same techniques used for the weirs, but they were finer in weave and were decorated with animal and geometrical designs. The bow and arrow came into its own, although it was originally an Upper Paleolithic invention. The bowstrings were now made of twined plant fiber strong enough when pulled to exert a tremendous force on the arrow, thus representing a new, miniature version of the stone-headed spear.

The arrow became a necessity for hunting the large geese and ducks that flew over the marshes of western and central Europe. Perhaps the feathers may have first been added to the arrow as a touch of magic to help bring down the birds. Later, their true purpose of keeping the arrow steady on its flight may have become apparent. Mesolithic man was now able to add to his diet of fish and game the large birds that came in great flocks to feed in the marshes and swamps.

Mesolithic man partially controlled the forest by developing special adzes and axes through placing sharpened flints into antler-bone sleeves and hafting (or tying) these onto wooden handles. With his axes he was now able to cut down timber for use in his housing and his dug-out canoes.

The dug-out canoe was made by cutting down a large tree and digging out its interior or by burning it out by placing lighted slivers into the parts that had already been chopped out and then scraping out the burnt remains. Mesolithic man may have used his canoes (maneuvered with large wooden paddles roughly similar to those used today) primarily for fishing purposes and for transporting the game and fowl that he killed in the marshes around the lakes and inland seas. Barbed spears and arrows made of small pieces of flint set in pitch and hafted made their appearances in Europe. The mattock (predecessor to the hoe) was now made of a reindeer shoulder blade tied at right angles to a shaft and was used to dig out edible wild roots. Farther east, about 10,000 years ago, in the mountains of southwestern Asia, Mesolithic women supplemented the food supply provided by their men's hunting and fishing by collecting wild seeds that appear to have been ancestors of wheat and barley. These seeds were cut with a sickle edged in small flints and were then apparently ground into flour with mortars and pestles.

The Domestication of the Dog

During the Upper Paleolithic the dog was probably a scavenger that belonged to a group of small, wolflike animals accustomed to hunting in groups under a leader. A few may have found themselves detached from their groups and, being leaderless, hovered around the outskirts of the semipermanent villages of men, feeding on what men threw away as inedible. Because of their natural friendliness and dependency, the young dogs may have become pets for the women and children. Thus may have begun the relationship between man and dog that has continued throughout the ages. From his early role as scavenger, the dog graduated to that of hunting companion and watchdog, warning his master of strange animals lurking near the village or of strange men loath to make themselves known. Certainly no animal has found it easier to live intimately with man than the medium-sized species of wolf or jackal (now extinct) whose descendants became one of man's closest companions.

Religion and Social Organization

The Upper Paleolithic fertility statuettes of clay or ivory (showing women with exaggerated sexual characteristics) were as common during the Mesolithic as during the Neolithic. The concept would later become transformed into the earth-goddess or the mother-goddess figure. (Though some men may be innovators, most are traditionalists in their daily lives, preferring the accepted and plausible to the exploration of more imaginative meanings.)

The Upper Paleolithic division of labor and its system of ranking men, women, and children according to their social importance undoubtedly continued into the Mesolithic. In the Natufian sites of 10,000 years ago in ancient Palestine, the Mesolithic chieftains were buried under the hearths of their large, domed, mud-brick huts and were given more goods than the commoners to take with them to their spirit world.

Anthropomorphic gods may have been unknown in the Mesolithic and even in the late Neolithic. Mesolithic man's cosmogony may have been a world of complex spirits and embodied power manipulated by magical rites, sacrifices, and flattery, as it was for Upper Paleolithic man. Perhaps the world of ghosts, peopled by spirits less intelligent than living men, may have been derived from the Mesolithic, or perhaps even from the Upper Paleolithic. The sun and the moon may also have begun to play more important roles in the mythology of the Mesolithic people. They may have been considered the dwellings of the most important spirits, or life forces, and they may even have embodied power in themselves. At least the beginnings of this otherworld view may have started in the days when easier food conditions gave Mesolithic man more time to speculate about the physical world and its periodic calamities that made his life temporarily uncomfortable.

Housing

During the Mesolithic, man's shelter was much improved. In summertime in northern and western Europe, rounded huts of willow and thatch were constructed; and in winter perhaps men lived in semipermanent subterranean houses, roofed with logs, dirt, and large stones. Skin tents in the form of tipis (made famous by the American Plains Indians) may have been common among the hunters of Eurasia. Sunbaked, mud-daubed wattle huts may have been more prevalent than tents in southwestern Asia and northern Africa.

The Domestication of the Goat

We have no evidence that any animals other than the dog and goat were domesticated during the Mesolithic period. The goat and the dog are associated with the early Natufian settlements of Palestine. The Natufians, a small-boned Mediterranean people, constructed the world's first permanent community, Jericho in Palestine, 9,000 years ago. They may have come down earlier from Anatolia, hunting and collecting food. No evidence appears thus far to indicate that the goat was found elsewhere between 8,000 and 10,000 years ago.

The Mesolithic as a Transitional Period

The Mesolithic must be understood as part of a development linking the Upper Paleolithic with the Neolithic. Toward the end of the Mesolithic, stone axes in antler sleeves became prevalent, housing improved, and the dog and perhaps the goat were domesticated. In the hilly and mountainous areas along the borders of present-day Iran, Iraq, Syria, and perhaps Turkey, the first patches of wild grasses were cultivated in a rudimentary way, ultimately leading to the development of agriculture still hundreds if not thousands of years away. Mesolithic men hunted and fished where they could, while the women and children sought out wild vegetables, tough roots, seeds, fruits, nuts, and small animals, as other women and children had been doing for hundreds of thousands of years.

In western Europe, the Mesolithic lasted until about 3,000 B.C., and in northwestern Europe it lasted about 600 years longer, when it was gradually superseded by the Neolithic. The Mesolithic ended earlier in southwestern Asia, and the Neolithic (in which most of the world's inhabitants still lived until the twentieth century) began about 6,700 B.C.

Until recently, the Eskimo lived in a Mesolithic stage of culture, as did many of the North and South American Indians. When viewed from our vantage point of thousands of years, the Mesolithic appears as a period of change. But to one living in Europe around 5,500 B.C., few changes would have been noticeable from one generation to the next.

Human change must be viewed as a development that is slow and spotty, with a good deal of conservatism and allegiance to traditional ways of doing things. Much recent peasant mentality may well go back to the Mesolithic in its origins. Fears of the stranger and of the Evil Eye are very old and may be pre-Neolithic in Europe and southwestern Asia. (A man who is unaware that he possesses an Evil Eye can bring misfortune to those whom he praises by calling them to the attention of hostile, vindictive spirits, who delight in showing man that they still have the last word as to whether he is to enjoy a life free of misfortunes.)

How much of the nature worship that preceded Christianity in Europe goes back to the Mesolithic we shall never know. We can tentatively assume that a religion of a preliterate period, which has taken 2,000 years to develop, is still only in its infancy. Festivals devoted to the winter and the summer solstices and to the spring equinox (which have come down to us as syncretic religious festivals) might also be of Mesolithic origin.

For Selected Bibliography, see end of Chapter 4.

4

The Neolithic

The heavy rains of the Ice Age, which had signaled its existence to those far east of the Mediterranean, now moved west and northward. Game became somewhat scarcer, and the population increased far beyond the capacity of the hunting areas to support it. The population of human beings may have doubled from about 5 million at the end of the Upper Paleolithic to about 10 million a few thousand years later at the beginning of the Neolithic. Men were ever on the move away from the marginal desert and arid mountainous areas seeking to increase their diminishing food supply.

Southwestern Asia is surrounded by mountains and deserts, and access is easiest by sea. But it would be thousands of years before men would be able to unfurl sails and move to areas where land was more plentiful. When the water level rose as the receding glaciers poured their locked water into the seas and oceans, the few land bridges connecting southwestern Asia to Europe were inundated. Men could cross from island to island, however, with their crude dug-out canoes, coiled reed boats, and skin coracles.

The Beginnings of the Neolithic

The stage was now set for the greatest revolution in food production in man's history. Somewhere on the sides of hills near streams in southwestern Asia during the Neolithic period, man learned to take the wild grasses that he had been collecting for tens or perhaps hundreds of thousands of years and to cultivate them. (As in the New World, he then learned to cultivate maize.) For this purpose he needed mutations of wild grasses that would not open their pods automatically when ripe (thus letting the wind scatter their seed), but ones that would perish unless man opened their pods mechanically (thus permitting the species to survive and multiply only at man's will).[1]

Somewhere in southwestern Asia near the present borders of Iran and Iraq around 7,000 B.C., the Neolithic age was born. The high hills of this area are watered by winter rains from the Mediterranean and are covered by a mixture of weeds and grassy plains. From this region came the wild ancestral grasses of wheat, barley, and their weedlike relatives and the wild ancestors of sheep, goats, pigs, and cattle. The domestication of these wild plants and animals was destined to change the surface of the earth by encouraging the establishment of settled agricultural villages. The increased food supply of these villages and the more varied specialization of skills within them would soon lead to the development of primitive administrative centers. The Neolithic revolution, then, consisted of the invention of agriculture, the domestication of all the animals we have today, the development of pottery, the rudiments of all the tools we use, and the continued proliferation of stone- and mud-housed populations who would till their lands, keep their animals, and live in settled areas.

Increase in Population

The most revolutionary aspect of the Neolithic was not in the rudimentary forms of the tools we use today, but in the great increase of man's basic food supply. It was possible for a large population to live on land that heretofore would have sustained only a small number of people through hunting and food collecting. Although fishing would continue to support a large population along the coastal regions for thousands of years, it was agriculture and its related pastoral economy that quintupled the population of the world, from 10 million to more than 50 million, during the 4,000 years that it took for the peasants to become the basic foundation for the large empires and city-states that came into existence before the Christian era. By that time, world population had increased another five times to 250 million.

The Earliest Agricultural Villages

The incipient growth of agriculture and the pastoral economy may have taken place during a time span of about 2,000 years, from 11,000 to 9,000 years ago. By the latter date, an elementary agricultural village life with

---

[1] The evidence seems to indicate that agriculture and the domestication of animals developed in a broad band between Greece and Afghanistan during the ninth and eighth millennia B.C.

some domesticated animals seems to have been established both along the high hills and mountains of the Zagros (on the eastern side of the valleys of the Tigris and Euphrates rivers, which run along the borders of Iraq and Iran) and on the hilly eastern side of the Fertile Crescent (which runs from the eastern Mediterranean to the Persian Gulf).

Here on this crescent of land running from contemporary Israel and Lebanon through Syria down to Iran and Iraq, we find the nucleus of the Neolithic age and the growth of permanent villages that had both farming and hunting as a way of life. By 6,700 B.C., the villages of Jarmo, Kermanshah (in present northeastern Iraq), and nearby Tepe Sarab cultivated wheat and barley, and kept domesticated dogs, goats, and perhaps pigs, sheep, and cattle. A little earlier (around 7,000 B.C.), the Natufians (in present-day Israel, Lebanon, and Jordan) were founding permanent villages, such as Eynan on the upper Jordan River and Jericho, the oldest continuously inhabited town in the world with a Carbon 14 date of 9,000 years.

In these Natufian villages, traces of domesticated barley and primitive wheat have been found, which indicates that some agriculture might have existed around 6,000 B.C., although there is little evidence that there were domesticated animals in Palestine as early as in the Iraqi and perhaps Irani highlands. The early Natufians hunted and fished in Mesolithic fashion, and their descendants gradually took over the cultivation of cereals from their neighbors to the immediate northeast. By 6,000 B.C., a simple cultivation had evidently been established along the Mediterranean plain of present-day Israel and Lebanon. The presence in Palestine of obsidian, or volcanic flint, from Anatolia (present-day Turkey) indicates that through the trade of obsidian for cereals, cultivation had also spread to Anatolia by 6,000 B.C. There were also Neolithic farming villages in Syria at this time, evidently connected with the Natufian settlements.

Within a thousand years, from 6,000 to 5,000 B.C., farming villages had spread to Anatolia, Cyprus, and perhaps to mainland Greece. Sites in Lebanon, Syria, and Israel show that by 5,000 B.C. they were covered with regular villages with rectangular huts of mudbrick or stone with plastered floors. They also indicate the existence of pigs, sheep, and cattle as well as dogs and goats.

The Invention of Pottery

Pottery was another important Neolithic invention. Although Upper Paleolithic and Mesolithic men made clay figurines that were sometimes hardened by being dropped in a fire, they had made no attempt to fashion clay into synthetic stone pots, primarily because they had no use for heavy and breakable pottery. With the establishment of agriculture and settled village life, men needed impermeable containers that could be used for cooking as well as for storing liquids. By 6,500 B.C. primitive pottery without slip or glaze was made in large quantities in southwestern Anatolia, and some pottery has even been found at sites that may go back to about 7,000 B.C. Until further evidence is found, we may assume that the present southern borders of the highlands of Anatolia may have been the home of the first pottery makers.

The Diffusion of Early Neolithic Ideas

Seminomadic tribes that wandered with their few domesticated animals between the settled agricultural villages of the Fertile Crescent may have been the agents who spread the domestication of animals and the cultivation of cereals to Egypt, North Africa, the Anatolian plateau, Cyprus, and perhaps Greece. By about 5,500 B.C. there were permanent villages with houses of brick in both Anatolia and Cyprus. There is some evidence that agriculture, domestication of animals, and pottery making were in existence in Greece by this time. By 4,000 B.C. the Neolithic culture had been carried by migrants to central Europe, and by 2,500 B.C. to England and Scandinavia. The eastward diffusion of the Neolithic culture may also have occurred by way of seminomadic peoples who wandered over the highlands of Iran, seeking pasturage for their flocks and temporary agricultural plots. Spreading eastward, agriculture came to northwestern India and northern China between 4,000 to 3,000 B.C., to isolated parts of southeastern Asia and to the New World by 3,000 B.C.

Early Trade

We do not know how the Neolithic age came to southeastern Asia or to the New World from its original center around the bordering highlands of the Fertile Crescent. In agriculture, perhaps it was concepts and symbols that were diffused rather than actual products. Although seminomadic peoples may have taken various processes with them, we must assume that a well-developed trade in obsidian and flint existed, even during the Mesolithic period, between the highlands of Anatolia and the Balkan area. Perhaps early Neolithic traders, traveling by canoe up the rivers, carried goods to Greece and as far as the head of the Adriatic.

It is quite possible that by 5,000 B.C., a well-organized trade may have been developed from the Persian Gulf to the coastal regions of India and to southeastern Asia. Perhaps by 4,500 B.C. the invention of sails and outriggers and the production of larger boats may have helped to carry trade artifacts even further than southeastern Asia; and perhaps over a period of still another 2,000 years, trade goods and the ideas of cultivation and domestication may have been extended even further east.

We are now in the realm of speculation; but rather than assume a series of similar independent discoveries made among peoples isolated from one another, I prefer to postulate that these discoveries developed through adaptive inventions that were made by different peoples but based on basic ideas transmitted from others who had seen the inventions in distant parts of the world or had been told by others how these things were done elsewhere.

The Inventions of the Neolithic Age

The Neolithic age was an extremely inventive one. Clothing was no longer made only of skins and bark (the lining from the inside of the bark, worn until recently in Polynesia and elsewhere), because new substitutes came upon the scene. Flax may have been the earliest vegetable fiber grown. Perhaps the plant was first used for its oil seeds, and only later was it discovered that the fibrous inner lining could be made into a type of cloth. The Mesolithic basket, or fishing net, with its plaited weaves may have been the basic model for the primitive loom, which was made somewhere, sometime before 5,000 B.C. Goat's hair may have come next. (Wool is a later development, based on the selective breeding of those sheep where a mutation had taken place from straight hair to curly wool. Wild sheep when first domesticated apparently had no wool.) Cotton was not used until about 3,000 B.C., when it evidently came to India from the Red Sea coastal area of Egypt. From India it spread back to southwestern Asia. (Here we have another great gap in our knowledge of early man, for a cotton plant identical in chromosome structure was found at a site in Peru that is dated at 2,500 B.C.)

Wool was not used in Europe until about 2,000 B.C., and cotton was not available even to the wealthy until the late Middle Ages. Silk was of Chinese origin and perhaps was not traded with Rome until a century or so before the time of Christ. The European Neolithic peasants must have used bast, or the inner bark fiber, for clothing and footwear. (The Russian peasant made his footwear out of bast until long after the Russian Revolution.) Ramie, a vegetable fiber now used in making sacks, was also grown and used for coarse textiles during the late Neolithic period in southwestern Asia.

The Diffusion of Agriculture through the Rest of the World

The concepts of agriculture and the domestication of animals spread by word of mouth from one tribe to another or were carried far afield by newly migrating people. Agriculture and domesticated animals had spread to Egypt by 5,000 B.C.; to the Sudan, Ethiopia, and Kenya by 4,000 B.C.; to India by 4,000 to 3,500 B.C.; and to northern China by 3,000 B.C. From these areas the southwestern agricultural complex spread farther to southeastern Asia by 2,000 B.C., where there was an independent horticultural complex in which millet and rice were cultivated. From there it spread to India and China, adding the two cereals of these areas to the original stock of cereals from southwestern Asia. The Neolithic was in full swing in central Europe by 4,000 B.C., and in northern and eastern Europe by 3,000 B.C.

Agriculture in the New World evidently developed independently. By 1,500 B.C. lands were evidently being cultivated in the southwestern parts of the United States and in Peru. The cereals were different, and there were not many varieties of wild animals that could have been easily domesticated.

In China the goat, the pig, and the cow (though not for milking) were domesticated early. In southeastern Asia a native pig and chicken (with its eggs) became diffused back to Eurasia. Our contemporary pig originated in southeastern Asia, although pigs of European and southwestern Asian origins were raised in the first part of the Neolithic. By 2,000 B.C. the southeastern Asian pig, chicken, and eggs were known in southwestern Asia and Egypt; by 1,000 B.C. they were also eaten in Europe. The migrating Malayans of the first millennium B.C. may have brought the chicken to Africa. (The turkey was domesticated in the New World and not brought to the Old World until the sixteenth century.)

The Neolithic age spread to most parts of Africa after the first millennium B.C. The cereals, vegetables, and fruits that were cultivated in western Africa were evidently native to the region (okra and watermelon, for instance, are two of the products that came to us from western Africa via the slave trade). In eastern Africa, agriculture evidently preceded domesticated animals. They were seemingly carried by different peoples, with later conquerors introducing the domesticated animals. (Until recently, the cattle peoples in eastern Africa considered themselves socially superior to those engaged in agriculture.)

In Europe also, the agricultural settlers rather than the pastoralists came first, migrating up the Danube from the Balkans to central Europe around 5,000 to 3,000 B.C. Another group of farmers and potters came up from northern Africa via Spain and France at this time. Both met in the area of northern Germany. They were followed by pastoral peoples coming out of the plains of southern Russia and reaching the Netherlands, Belgium, and northeastern France by 2,400 B.C. By 1,000 B.C., the Celtic peoples began to move out of the East in large numbers to central and western Europe. Other peoples moved up from northern Africa to Spain, France, and the British Isles from 2,500 B.C. to 1,500 B.C. Europe and Asia were so underpopulated during Neolithic times that it was possible for a peaceful invading people to settle among established groups without disturbing them unduly. There is no doubt that the successive migrations of peoples added both to the techniques of cultivation and to the improvement of tools and breeds of domesticated animals.

Neolithic Housing

All over Europe, permanent villages were being established, with houses made of wood, clay, or stone. In Switzerland by 2,000 B.C., wooden houses were built on piles along the shores of large lakes. In Poland by 1,000 B.C., palisaded villages with long log cabins were in existence. In the Hebrides at this period, stone houses contained beds and furniture that were also fashioned from slabs of stone. In Germany, northern France, and England, houses were constructed of timber and clay, with thatched roofs, and looked roughly the same as they did during the Middle Ages. In Scandinavia and in the great woods and plains of Russia, houses were mostly subterranean structures, with roofs of logs and thatch; and a few log cabins were built after the introduction of improved tools. (Three thousand years later, this type of log cabin would come to Delaware with the first migrating Swedes and Finns.)

Neolithic Foods

Most of the foods we eat and the animals we domesticate originated in the Neolithic. A list of the more important foods derived from the Neolithic would include the following from the Old World: leafy cabbage (the head variety was not known until the Middle Ages), lettuce, spinach, cress, carrots, radishes, wheat, barley, oats, rice, rye, lentils, broad beans, pulses (a variety of pea), olives, apples, pears, plums, and cherries. From southern and southeastern Asia came sugar cane, lemons, oranges, and coconuts. From the New World came maize, beans of most varieties, potatoes, tomatoes, squash, chocolate, and vanilla. From Africa came a large variety of fruits and vegetables, the best known being the previously mentioned okra and watermelon. Melons proper may have come from the highlands of central Asia. Tea came from China, but it was evidently not known there until after the Neolithic period, and its introduction to Europe did not take place until the seventeenth century. Coffee was originally grown in the highlands of Ethiopia, but it is doubtful whether it was used as a beverage until the later Moslem period. The animals domesticated in the Neolithic were goats (these along with the dog may also have been domesticated in the Upper Paleolithic and the late Mesolithic), reindeer, sheep, pigs, cattle, chickens, turkeys, and llamas (in the New World).

The Neolithic Peoples

Most of the preliterate people of Africa, Polynesia, and Asia and an over-whelming number of North and South American Indians (with the exception of those living in the civilizations of Mexico, Central America, and Peru) were living in the earlier Neolithic period until the eighteenth century. The post-Neolithic, as it developed later in southwestern Asia, represented the stage in which most villagers of India, China, northern Africa, southwestern Asia, and eastern and southern Europe lived until the impact of the Scientific-Industrial Age began to affect them in the twentieth century.

The Neolithic as a Village Economy

The Neolithic age is associated with permanent or semipermanent villages dependent almost entirely for their food supply on cultivated plots or fields and on domesticated animals. In southwestern Asia, the Neolithic became more complex (largely through the invention of the plow pulled by oxen) than it did in the preliterate areas of northern Asia, North America, Africa, and Polynesia. Most of the cultivation of agricultural products in these four areas was done with the digging stick and the hoe, rather than the plow, and little surplus food was available to encourage the growth of large settlements.

In the great civilization of the Americas, towns were few and far between; and even the settled villagers had to rely as much upon hunting as upon their small crops. With the possible exceptions of the turkey and the llama, no domesticated animals were available for food. The presence of these two, however, could suggest to us that the idea of domestication may have come to the aboriginal settlers of the New World from elsewhere, but that there were no animals, such as existed in the Old World, that lent themselves to taming and domestication. (Later colonization from Europe would bring them.) In Negro Africa, the cow, goat, and chicken all arrived after the first millennium B.C. from the northeast and from Malaya via Madagascar (which was settled by Malayans from Indonesia during the first millennium B.C.).

In the older Neolithic villages of Africa, the New World, and Polynesia, all labor was human labor. The women cultivated plants by using the dibble stick (a primitive type of hoe), while the men hunted or assisted in gardening. In Mesopotamia in southwestern Asia, men had learned to utilize the strength of the ox to pull a wooden plow, which could make a deeper furrow than was possible with a hoe and a digging stick. More land could then be cultivated and greater supplies of food grown—thus freeing surplus labor for specialized jobs.

The Beginnings of Irrigation

When men came down from the hills east of the Fertile Crescent in the seventh and eighth millennia B.C., they found that the land along the Tigris and Euphrates rivers was fertile but that the rainfall was too scanty to grow crops in all seasons of the year. In the incipient stage of agriculture, crops were therefore planted near the river edges so that the periodic overflow of the river would water the plants. Sometimes the ground below the high water mark was scooped out so that later flood waters would fill it. A dam of mud was then built to keep the contents from flowing back into the river when the level dropped again. Small channels were cut from this reservoir to conduct the water to the fields when the rainfall was low. Here were the beginnings of irrigation, which enabled men to live in the semiarid areas that produced the first great temple civilizations.

In Egypt after 5,000 B.C., agricultural villages began to proliferate along the Nile River. Egypt receives almost no rainfall, and only the annual overflowing of the Nile from July to the end of October provides water for the rich silt brought down from the two sources of the river, the mountains of Ethiopia and Uganda. Each village built dikes around its borders so that it could stand above the flood. Later on this developed into basin irrigation whereby canals were dug through the various dikes to carry water to the areas that needed it.

In Mesopotamia, the Tigris and Euphrates rivers—unlike the Nile— do not overflow at a specific time each year, but vary in accordance with the extent of the rainfall and snow cover in the mountains of Anatolia and Iran. This means that the population probably learned early how to build dikes and reservoirs to impound the surplus water until it was needed and to prevent damage to property and life by flash floods.

The Rise of Government

The need for cooperative work in building irrigation ditches, reservoirs, and dikes and in draining swamps and marshes near the rivers led to the appointment of various village (and later, district) officials, who had the authority to order whatever labor was needed for the public works. Here we have the first indication of the importance of government, which may have come into existence not because of tyranny or the conquest of one people by another, but primarily because of the increased need for cooperative services when populations and villages grew larger. Someone had to regulate the relations between villages and to be responsible for seeing that necessary communal functions were performed—including proper sacrifices to the gods whose goodwill the villagers needed in order to survive.

Specialized Division of Labor

In the delta of the Tigris and Euphrates rivers near the Persian Gulf, various Neolithic villages bound themselves loosely to one another in order to increase the supply of specialized labor. Most men farmed and cared for their animals. A few planned the irrigation ditches and the reservoirs. Others became the priestly intermediaries between the world of spirits (now taking anthropomorphic forms) and the world of men. Some became spokesmen for tradition as judges, deciding suits that arose because some men, for personality reasons, tended to ride roughshod over the self-esteem of other men. Some became skilled craftsmen and taught others how to make better tools, sow new plants, or handle their animals more efficiently.

The simple division of labor that had existed in the Upper Paleo-lithic between the men, who were the hunters, and the women and children, who were the food collectors, progressed in Mesolithic days to a division between those who fished, hunted, built canoes, made specialized tools, made fishing nets and weirs, and propitiated the spirits to ward off disease and danger.

In the Neolithic villages of southwestern Asia some 7,000 years ago, the division of labor had gone even further. Some now specialized in making pottery; others wove cloth out of hemp, ramie, linen, or wool; some made tools and worked the wood for plows; and others may have made the brick for their beehive-shaped or square huts. Although each villager was in some ways a jack-of-all-trades (as he was in eighteenth and nine-teenth century rural America), a few had now become specialized crafts-men. Some had even become traders who traveled great distances to obtain obsidian, flints, shells, colored stones, and pigments, which village men needed for personal ornament and for religious and cosmetic pur-poses.

The Fertility Cults and Religion

Paleolithic man was concerned with increasing the number of hunting animals so that, with the extra food, his women would become fertile and bear children who would survive. Enough food and children constituted the good life for Paleolithic man, and he asked little more than that from his fertility statuettes and murals. In the Neolithic, man assumed that crops required magic in order to grow and flourish. The good earth was viewed as analogous to woman. Seed was placed in the earth so that she could become fertile and produce bountiful crops. The sex act was seen as similar to the workings of nature. The mother figure now became transferred to the symbol of the earth goddess, and the pregnant statuettes of women in the Paleolithic now became the presence of the spirit of fertility that made all things grow. Later on, the agricultural earth goddess would give birth to a son, who became the grain god. He died every year in the late fall and was resurrected in the spring. It was he, as the early sun god, grain god, or king of fertility, who died so that man could live.

The interpersonal relationships of the living thus became the basis for peopling the supernatural world with male gods who acted as fathers, chiefs, punishers, dispensers of justice, regulators of labor, and givers and curers of disease. The female gods brought death as well as life, hunger as well as food. In general, however, the latter were compassionate mother figures to whom one could appeal for sympathy, food, and affection. The world of the living thus became transferred to the world of the gods. Worship of the latter reflected how complex social organization and institutional beliefs had become by 5,000 B.C. The Neolithic age in Mesopotamia was slowly evolving into the temple city-states with their kings, temples, merchants, and priests.

By about 5,000 B.C., the early hunting bands in southwestern Asia had evolved into tribes of closely knit villages with subdivisions and clans. The single tribe was based on common descent from an ancient ancestor, while related tribes shared the tradition that they were descended from a common ancestor. The spirits of the ancestors kept the tribes together and watched over their former villages benignly, eventually becoming their founding gods. The sacred chieftain combined authority over the village with the obligation of performing needed rituals and gift-giving to the gods (which thus induced rivers to rise, crops to grow, children to be born, and rain to fall). The Neolithic gods also gave that greatest of all gifts, life itself, which was bestowed upon man on condition that he give them life in return—either that of his needed animals or that of his firstborn child. Later on, human beings would be captured through warfare to satisfy the insatiable desire of the gods for life that strengthened their own immortal lives and gave life to their worshippers. The sacred village chieftain later became the chief priest of the temples, who at first governed in the name of the gods but in time became the secular power whose authority over persons and property was in itself a gift from the gods.

The Neolithic Age Evolves

Villages spread from Mesopotamia in all directions, and with them went the advanced technology and the new agricultural deities. Boats of reeds, made waterproof with bitumen, became larger; and soon, fixed sails were attached so that wind, instead of human labor at the oars, could be employed for energy. Since there was no flint, obsidian, or special wood along the Tigris-Euphrates valley, boats sailed in all directions to exchange products of the soil for the stones, pigments, tools, and decorations that were needed for daily life. Merchants carried their trade by ship through the Persian Gulf to the island of Bahrein, Africa, and India, and overland to Anatolia, Armenia, and Iran.

As the villages increased in number, their ideas were adopted by some of the nomadic hunters and early shepherds. They in turn became carriers of the culture of the Mesopotamian center, extending their concepts to the peripheries of their known world. Although there were no large towns during the Neolithic (they came at a later period), the large village with its surrounding agricultural and pasture lands—possibly fortified against invading nonagricultural people—became the memorial of the age. If the village was prosperous enough to have a large surplus of food, workers could then be spared to build walls, canals, irrigation ditches, large trading boats, and equipment. One building may have been constructed larger than the others and dedicated to the ancestors of the village (now deified), whose spirits were then invited to come and live among their people to advise as well as protect them.

Neolithic man may now have been more confident in his ability to produce enough food and to manage his life to provide the economic security he wanted. He knew what relations his fellowmen were to him, what symbols of obligations and tokens of respect were native to his group, and what each man's gradations in kinship, and thus in status, might be. For Neolithic men and women, life in the village was the only life they knew. They were members of an important village, which in turn was related to others nearby. The village had food most of the time. The local gods were sometimes protective, often provided bountiful crops, and even increased the number of domestic animals. From the villager's point of view, his housing was as comfortable as he could make it. The many religious and hunting occasions also served as holidays, when he could feast with his fellowmen, talk of the latest gossip in the village and its surroundings, and take part in the general entertainment. (There was no interest in outsiders. The most important and most interesting people were those who belonged to his village, who were related to him, and whom he could place in his kinship system.)

A man was born and went through the various rites of passage. He was initiated into the tribe as an adult, married, became the father of many children, and was regarded with respect by the rest of his village. He could expect cooperation and mutual aid from his relatives whenever he requested it. He could become old at fifty with dignity, respected by his kinsmen and his children. Although he would die, he would still be remembered by his descendants and the rest of the village. His residence would be transferred to another existence where he could watch over his family, listen to their prayers and requests, and with the help of others in this transitional world of the spirit, live even longer than on earth. Farther than this, Neolithic man was not concerned. The Neolithic men and women in the villages of Mesopotamia, in the growing settlements of northern Africa, Europe, and Asia, and later in North America and Africa, could readily ask themselves what other life could be better than this. What else could bring more satisfaction and happiness than the conviction that man's wants were simple and if they could be satisfied even in part, he could die content that he had lived his life to the full.

This was the spirit of an age that continued from the sixth millennium B.C. to the twentieth century of our own era. It is disappearing now as a way of life, and it may not survive the next hundred years. But as an age, it lasted far longer than has our contemporary scientific and industrial civilization. It was the age of the common man, of the peasant with simple wants, simple pleasures, and simple goals. Neolithic fathers could only hope that their sons would live and believe as they did. Mothers could only wish that their daughters would relive their routine lives.

The Neolithic peasant had no desire for change. Education in the village was based upon continuing the ideas, the technology, and the beliefs of the older generations and their ancestors. Though never truly idyllic, village life would eventually be hazily regarded as a golden age by those later generations who would be harassed by warfare, tyrannical kings, overlords, and poverty caused by the inability to call one's labor or product one's own. Prophets and soothsayers (some founding important world religions) would arise to urge a return to the simple truths and the democratic equality of the Neolithic villager and pastoral nomad. They would cry out against the development of the towns and city-states as abominations in the sight of the righteous gods. The alienation of large numbers of people from themselves and from their relatives would be viewed as oppression of the weak and poor. Men would be urged to free themselves of their urban ambitions and worldly desires for gain, and to return to the simple pleasures and wants of the ancestral husbandman and nomad.

We move on then to the end of this phase of man's development, when he begins to build towns out of his villages, learns to make tools of copper and bronze, introduces organized warfare and slavery, and makes human sacrifices to his gods (who in turn will inform him arrogantly that he has been created only to serve and flatter them).

Out of Mesopotamia around 4,000 B.C the Primary city-state civilization was born, and like the Neolithic village, which also arose in this region, it would spread until it too would influence the ways of life of most men. Like the Neolithic, Primary civilization would also have a lasting influence and effect, both for good and for evil.

Selected Bibliography

Alimen, H., *The Prehistory of Africa* (London, Hutchinson, 1957).

Braidwood, Robert J., and Willey, Gordon R., eds., *Courses Toward Urban Life* (Chicago, Aldine, 1962).

Childe, V. Gordon, *Man Makes Himself* (New York, New American Library, 1955), Chapter 6.

————, *What Happened in History* (Baltimore, Penguin, 1961), Chapter 3.

Coon, Carleton S., *The Story of Man* (New York, Knopf, 1955), Chapters 3 and 4.

Hawkes, J., and Woolley, L., *Prehistory and the Beginnings of Civilization* (New York, Harper & Row, 1963).

Linton, Ralph, *The Tree of Culture* (New York, Knopf, 1955), Parts 5 and 6.

Mongait, A. L., *Archaeology in the USSR* (Baltimore, Penguin, 1961).

Piggott, Stuart, ed., *The Dawn of Civilization* (New York, McGraw-Hill, 1961), Chapter 2.

Shapiro, H., ed., *Man, Culture and Society* (New York, Oxford University Press, 1956), Chapters 4, 6, and 14.

Singer, Charles, Holmyard, E. J., and Hall, A. R., *A History of Technology*, Vol. I (New York, Oxford University Press, 1958).

Wittfogel, Karl A., *Oriental Despotism* (New Haven, Yale University Press, 1957).

5

The Beginnings of Primary Civilization: The Sumerian Towns

Beginning in 4,000 B.C., the social changes that took place in southwestern Asia were not in the villages themselves (which continued to live as they had in 5,000 B.C. and still would in 1,000 B.C.), but in the ties that kept neighboring villages together. To regulate and protect the lives of the villagers, various officials had to be appointed to fulfill such tasks as collecting taxes in grain, seeing that the irrigation ditches were kept in repair and clear of obstacles, organizing a temporary military force, acting as judges in disputes between the villages, and carrying on trade, with surplus food exchanged for raw materials that could not be obtained locally.

In addition to their own efforts, the villagers needed the help of the supernatural world to ensure good crops, to multiply their herds, and to ward off sickness and misfortune. To propitiate the local gods who protected each village, animals were sacrificed, grain was offered, and proper obeisance and humility were shown to those with power. (This seems to me to reflect the authoritarian and patriarchal organization of the earlier Mesopotamian village, which fashioned its deities in the images of its own head men. If gentleness had been the rule in the family and in the village, the gods would have been portrayed as benign rather than as aloof, arbitrary, and difficult to please. Perhaps the Mesopotamian villager during the late Neolithic period was not accustomed to egalitarianism and personal freedom. Otherwise a more dignified human adjustment in appealing to supernatural authority would have been made; the gods would not have been depicted as insisting upon servility and humiliating meekness on the part of those asking assistance. Human freedoms have evidently been in the process of growth and development throughout the ages. Perhaps the dream of a golden age should be seen in the still distant future rather than in an innocent and Elysian past.)

The abodes of the gods in the villages demanded caretakers and servants, who were expected to account to the gods on what was received and what was expended and who now owned the goods, the crops, and even the labor of the people under their sway. Thus the first building of significant size in the village may have been the large mud-brick and plaster abode of the chief god or gods, which later became the temple. Near the temple lived the servants of the gods and the merchants who came to trade their pottery, linen, flint, and obsidian under the watchful eyes of the village gods who punished those who cheated, perjured, or were dishonest in other ways.

The village temple soon became the social as well as the industrial center of the new towns, as workshops staffed by artisans made the tools and implements required for the tasks of the peasants, warriors, and priests. The temple itself began to receive gifts of food, animals, and even labor from those who had benefited from the various favors of the gods. It also became the center for the officials who were concerned with the building and repairing of the large number of irrigation canals (now owned by the gods), which increased rapidly as the food supply encouraged the growth of the population and the establishment of new satellite villages. With the increase in population, conflicts developed between the various new temple towns over their land, the amount of irrigated land that was theirs, and their water rights. The conflicts that arose from an inability to adjudicate these disputes or to find effective compromises, which would let those in authority keep "face" with one another and their subjects, led to an increase in the authority of the head men and in the organization of warriors so that decisions could be carried out by force.

With the organization of a semiprofessional or professional military force, the towns came into a transitional stage in the development of the first civilization. This stage was characterized by control over the village peasant, who worked for the religious authorities—officials who occupied a higher social rank than he and who exercised authority over him. In return for the services rendered by the priestly city-state, the village was expected to supply the city-state with food, with servants for the temple and the priests, with labor for the public works, and with recruits for the military force.

The military conflicts between the various religious town-centers and their village satellites led not only to the enormous improvement of Neolithic technology, but also to the search for stronger tools and weapons. It is quite possible that the use of copper (and later, bronze) tools from the fourth millennium B.C. on as replacements for flint, obsidian, and polished-stone tools (used during the later Neolithic) may have stemmed from the growing need for sharper and more durable spearheads and arrowheads. This need would have encouraged Sumerian merchants to explore the mountain areas of Anatolia, Armenia, and Iran for sources

EGYPT AND MESOPOTAMIA

of copper. In return, the merchants traded surplus copper and bronze tools, weapons, cloth, jewelry, and pottery that the Sumerian cities on the lower reaches of the Tigris and Euphrates rivers were now able to manufacture in large quantities through the growing number of skilled temple craftsmen. As the copper and tin sources became scarcer, merchants fanned out in ever-widening areas seeking the ores that were nonexistent in the vicinity of the Sumerian city-states.

Thus far in these few pages we have been describing the slow development of the world's first civilization, that of the loose bond of Sumerian city-states, each with its individual temples, military forces, bureaucracy of temple and government officials, skilled workmen, and supervisors. All other ancient civilizations in the Old World developed and grew from this first source, each adding its bit to the organization and knowledge originally learned from the Sumerians. The priestly ruling groups of the latter, through trial and error, had organized the labor and ideas of men more efficiently than had been done before. Over a period of 2,000 years they built up codes of civil and military law based on precedent, or the past judgments of the priestly leaders and administrators. The Sumerian temple towns also laid the foundations for most of the beliefs that later became part of religious dogmas concerning man's origins, the purposes of his existence, and the destiny to which he was subject.

The Development of Human Slavery

During the latter part of the Neolithic period, men learned to utilize the strength of the ox to pull a digging stick or plow through the earth so that seed could be sown in furrows. Then flocks of animals were driven over the ground to trample the seed down. With the beginning of Sumerian civilization, still another source of energy was added to that of the animals: slave power. After military conflicts between the various city-states, defeated soldiers were no longer killed but were brought as prisoners to the temples for the gods to decide what should be done with them.

Perhaps in the beginning of slavery, prisoners were sacrificed to the gods, who needed life in return for the life they gave to the community. Later on, perhaps their lives were spared so that they might become the slaves of the gods. Soon a surplus of slaves might be sold at auction to the highest bidder and the proceeds used for the gods' more pressing needs— the purchase of new ingots of pure copper (to be mixed with tin to make bronze), gold, and jewels—or whatever it was that the gods desired. Later still, the subjects of a defeated village or city could be sold into slavery and their property and lands confiscated. Today we pity the fate of those captured in war who temporarily lose their personal freedom, but such has been the destiny of the captured or weak in an almost unbroken progression, from the days when the Sumerians first began to codify the rules of warfare to the succession of traditionalists who have followed them all the way to our own era.

The Sumerian Cities

We do not know the populations of the temple towns that in the fourth millennium B.C. became part of the first civilization fashioned by man. We know the cities themselves only through archaeological excavations. Their layers of pottery, bone, mud-brick walls, and temple floors have given us a detailed description of how these people lived. The clay tablets have given us insights into their thinking. Some indication of their beliefs has come down to us through the story of the world's creation as given in Genesis, a story of distant Sumerian origin, and in that of Noah and the flood. The latter story makes more sense against the background of the flat surfaces of land between the Tigris and Euphrates rivers (with their mud flats and unpredictable, rampaging floods and no natural walls or cliffs to stem the raging waters) than it does against a background of the rolling hills and the semiarid rocky promontories of ancient Israel with its few streams and narrow green Mediterranean plain. (Though the Biblical patriarch Abraham was traditionally thought to have left the Sumerian city of Ur, it is more probable that he departed from the Hurrian city of Huran.)

Archaeology has given us, however, a great amount of detail about Eridu, Ur, Larsa, Umma, Uruk, and Lagash. (In the latter city, the ruler Gudea, who lived around 2,000 B.C., had realistic portraits of himself made in stone to commemorate the services he had performed for both the gods and his people.) None of these towns evidently had more than 10,000 inhabitants. It was in the temple town of Uruk that writing was first invented to give the gods a means of recording what they owned and what was owing to them, and of keeping an account of the transactions that were carried out in their behalf by the temple priests. Since there were too many records to be memorized, the early priests learned to depict on clay the number of cattle, the jars of oil, the slaves, and the other objects that were bought, sold, or retained.

The first writing was pictographic. Later it became symbolic, the symbols representing the sounds of the words that stood for cattle, copper, oil, or captives, with other notations being understood for numbers. Finally, the symbols were made even more abstract and given a wedge shape (from the shape of the stylus that made them), which then made them known as "cuneiform," or "wedge-shaped."

The City of Uruk

Uruk has left us good examples of the temples built by the Sumerians to their gods. In the beginning, around 3,800 B.C., a plastered mudbrick temple was built almost on ground level. After a few centuries it was torn down, a mound made of its mudbrick, and a new temple then erected. The new temple was later destroyed and rebuilt, and the process took place time and time again until finally a mound more than a hundred feet high remained, upon which still another temple was finally built. This architectural design of the temple would be taken over by the Egyptians and 2,000 years later (with modifications) by the Greeks.

Although some other Sumerian towns were older than Uruk and started building their temples before 3,800 B.C., Uruk was the first where the pattern of the temple town developed. At Uruk, the gods were first represented by realistic sculpture. Large mudbrick walls were built to protect the town, whose center was dominated by the great abode of the chief god. The main part of this abode, or temple, started from a platform that was in itself over forty feet high. Surrounding the temple was a square and then an inner wall, followed by concentric circles of walls between which were built the residences of the artisans, accountants, merchants, and workers. Finally, toward the outer wall lived the peasants, who formed the majority of the town's inhabitants. Each morning they went out to till and irrigate their fields and to tend their flocks, returning with their animals and tools at nightfall. Thus at Uruk began a peasant way of life that would continue well into our time. (The true urban civilization, a consequence of the industrial and agricultural revolutions, occurs when whole cities are populated by those who toil in workshops and offices, while only a minority raise the food.)

In ancient Uruk, the way of life was still rural for at least 90 percent of the population. Most of the population worked in the fields surrounding the town rather than in the town itself. The priests kept cows in sheds near the temple and either had them taken out to pasture in the mornings or had fodder brought to them. The cows were milked as the goats had been. Perhaps a soft cheese was made from the curds of milk, or the latter may have been left to ferment to make a sort of pot cheese. We are not sure that the churning of butter was known during Sumerian times.

The Temple as the Town Center

The temple was the center of learning and of craftsmanship. Here, writing was a chief occupation and was taught to apprentice scribes. The principles of arithmetic and geometry were also discovered here. And the pseudoscience of astrology was created here (to influence later generations of newspaper readers and to be used to determine dates for betrothals, construction of houses, and other matters, especially in India and China). In the temples the Sumerians learned to use the number 60 as a unit—60 seconds in a minute, 60 minutes in an hour, 360 minutes as a quarter of the day, and 360 days in the year, as well as 360 degrees in a circle.

The Sumerian Concept of the Importance of Man

Man, according to Sumerian belief, was born to serve the gods, to be dependent upon their whims, and to be as nothing in their eyes. This concept the Sumerians also bequeathed to us. Sumerian man, who fashioned his way of life, who learned to use language to express his thoughts, who was curious to know the consequences of his acts, who sought the relationships between things, who employed his culture to mold the associations that existed between his gods and himself, stood in abject fear before the creations of his own mind. He created roles for the gods and goddesses in which they were wrathful, jealous, envious, petty, continually pulling rank on one another, and insisting on receiving more privileges than the gods in neighboring towns. They quarreled with one another, were dishonest, and lived only for the fine foods, jewelry, clothing, and drink that they received as their due from those who were put upon the earth only to serve them. The gods and goddesses of the ancient Sumerian cities may have been reflections of their contemporary secular lords and ladies—the nobles who insisted upon special privileges as their right (as they would continue to demand even thousands of years later both for themselves and for their descendants).

The Sumerian Social System

The Sumerians organized society as never before. They ranked men in a hierarchy from the lowly peasant through the artisans, merchants, scribes, and priests and finally to the lords of the cities. The peasant received his seed, tools, and clothing from the temple workshops; and in return he seeded and harvested the grain, which belonged to the gods. The merchant traded grain, wine, dates, oil, and textiles, which he received from the temples, for the precious metals that came from the mountains to the north and the west (to be used by the temple workshops). Although all men were theoretically equal before the deities, some men were obviously more privileged than others. Depending upon their social function within this graded hierarchy, some received special foods, clothing, jewels, and higher social rank.

Sumerian Attitudes Toward Themselves

It is difficult to know how the Sumerians visualized themselves. We do have some inklings, however. From the mass graves of the lords and ladies of Ur during the third millennium B.C., we can surmise that the main patterning was resignation to one's fate. Men did what they were told: they lived not for any future rewards or for any hope of a better life, but because life was in the living. Death was not looked upon as a release from the fullness of life. According to Sumerian belief, the souls of the dead lived a miserable existence, eating clay and drinking ashes and enduring an eternity of shadowy and meaningless passage through time.

The Tombs of Ur

In 1923, on the outskirts of ancient Ur, the British archaeologist Leonard Wooley found tombs of the town's lords and ladies, who had been buried in stone crypts, surrounded by court attendants, soldiers (with their chariots, copper helmets, and spears), onagers (a wild ass domesticated by the Sumerians), and scores of musicians and servants. All were arrayed in their best finery and placed in orderly rows by others, after they had taken poison so that they could accompany their lords and ladies to the next world. In one mass grave, half of the court ladies had gold circlets in their hair, and half had silver. (One girl, evidently late for her funeral, kept her circlet in her pocket for she had no time to put it on.) All seemingly went to their deaths apathetically, perhaps because it was their duty and no other alternative was open to them. We have here an indication of the general frame of mind of those who lived in the Sumerian towns of 5,000 to 6,000 years ago. They lived in a social world that they did not make and that they evidently felt they could do little to change.

Similarities of Sumerian Towns

Although the Sumerian towns, or small cities, differed from one another (for example, they all had different deities to protect them), their way of life was roughly similar. They all learned from one another. Their social systems, institutionalized beliefs, military organization, temple and palace architecture, plus their indifference to one another, were clearly similar. Though loosely united, these cities fought with one another, made their prisoners into slaves, and saw to it that the meaning of the slogan "To the victor belongs the spoils" became an inflexible rule both of warfare and of political organization.

The Peasants

The peasants, on the other hand, gained little from the development of temple-centers. They did benefit, however, from the engineering works that kept the periodic floods of the Tigris and Euphrates rivers in check, and from the impounded water of the basin reservoirs, which irrigated their lands during seasons of low rainfall. Perhaps the temple artisans improved the shape of the primitive plow or increased the efficiency of the tools used in cultivation, but the increased surplus from the peasant's proceeds was taxed as rent and royalties.

The vast majority of Sumerian peasants lived as peasants had in Neolithic times, and roughly as they would thousands of years later (even in the twentieth century, in Iraq, Iran, Syria, Jordan, Pakistan, and India). Their lives consisted of work, a frugal diet, a stoical, uncomplaining (and unthinking) acceptance of their lot, and simple pleasures of social interaction with their families and peer group. The chances are that peasants died young and that both the men and the women were gnarled and disfigured by the time they were fifty or sixty. Peasant women in Sumerian times must have been treated more like domesticated animals than human beings worthy of being protected against humiliation (which is what we should mean by the "dignity of the individual").

The Nobles

The copper tools and weapons, gold and silver ornaments, precious jewels, fine wine goblets, linens, large houses (some built of stone, which had to be transported from the mountains at great expense), wooden carvings, and musical instruments (such as the harp, double flute, and lute) were not created for the pleasure of the peasants: these were designed for the satisfaction, needs, and desires of the nobles, for whom this first civilization was developed. This small accumulation of luxuries was made possible only by having 90 percent or more of the population—the peasants —grow the food and raise the fruits, vegetables, and animal fibers so that the small remaining 10 percent could be brickmakers, construction workers, craftsmen, scribes, priests, nobles, and kings. As one ascended in the social hierarchy, status went hand in hand with the right to become a greater consumer and enjoy more wealth than those in the lower ranks. On the bottom were the slaves, the widows and orphans, and those aged who had no strong family ties. Individuals in this first temple civilization benefited from the wealth of the community in the following descending order: the kings and nobles, the court attendants, the temple officials, the supervisors, the architects, the contractors, the merchants, the scribes, the warriors, and finally the craftsmen.

Sumerian Interactions

It was not easy to live in this Sumerian world where each strong man's hand was raised against both the strong and the weak. The man without power or strong family ties invited his many enemies to drag him down as defenseless, the same thing evidently happening to those who were considerate or trusting. Cities fought one another for extra lands, for captives, for water rights, for proof that one's war god was mightier than another's. One had to prove one's right to possess the privileges of the powerful through incessant struggle against others who were trying to demonstrate the same thing to themselves and others.

Perhaps the Sumerian boy was reared to be aggressive about asserting his virility and honor so that no one would place him in the category of the weak and powerless. Perhaps he considered as his greatest satisfaction in life proving that he was not weak (even though he died in the attempt). One could not live feeling defeated and contemptible in the eyes of others.

Patterns of hunting behavior, which developed early in the time of Paleolithic man, received new social meaning when most men could no longer hunt but had to cultivate the soil and perform the rounds of daily work in the temple towns, as tradition and authority ordered them to do. Warfare thus became the medium whereby the former hunter could prove his virility and lack of submissiveness to the female earth. Although he had to submit to those who led him, he could win the approval of his superiors (men like himself though older) through acts of bravery and thereby enter their ranks to rule over those weaker than himself.

One became a nobleman or even a king through expressing this traditional male dominance. One could also become wealthy in doing so, for the victors had all rights over the labor and property of those weaker than themselves. (The peasant male in Sumeria probably felt in his turn that he had the right to the labor and property of his wife and children.) "To the strong belong the weak" was the essence of the slogan taken over by those who improved the methods of warfare. When the Semitic peoples from the north and west conquered the Sumerian cities and took over their civilization, they organized the subject population even more efficiently and effectively than before. And so began another page of the history that was to be written by the Semitic-speaking invaders from the west, by the Indo-European-speaking invaders who came into India from central Asia, by the various invaders of China, by the Persians, by the Macedonians, by the Romans, by the Germanic and Ural-Altaic-speaking hordes, by the Aztecs and Incas of the New World, and more recently by the crop of would-be conquerors in Europe, Asia, and South America.

The Advance of Sumerian Civilization

As the cities in Sumeria continued to fight one another during succeeding centuries, new dynasties of kings built ever larger and more luxurious palaces and temples to themselves and to their gods. Warfare became more efficient (the Sumerians invented the war chariot with its solid wheel and domesticated the onager, or wild ass, to pull it), with more skilled craftsmen making better spears, arrows, bows, battle-axes, helmets of copper (gold for kings and top nobles), and lighter war chariots. More and more sculptors and scribes made mementos and records that would keep their local sovereign's name from ever vanishing from men's minds. Literature was born as court poets and musicians recited and sang long epics in praise of the gods, weaving into the contents the names and deeds of their employers so that future generations would be as impressed by their exploits as the nobles' retainers were. One could prepare for one's place in the realm of the dead, but memorials while one was still alive were prized even more.

The Sumerians as People

No one knows from what region the Sumerians originally came. The Sumerians referred to themselves as the "black-headed people," which indicates that they originally came from a region containing a blonde mixture. In a black-headed population no one notices that his hair is black: it becomes the norm. The Sumerians may have come from the other side of the Zagros mountains in Iran, from the direction of Armenia, or from the regions of the Persian Gulf. No one knows.

The physical appearance of the Sumerians depicted in the faces of their sculptured gods, of their rulers (such as that of the later Gudea, ruler of Lagash), of the scribes, and of the women and in the engravings on cylinder rolls shows a population with characteristics similar to those considered Hebrew, Lebanese, Syrian, Armenian, or Persian. In other words, they resembled the physical stereotypes we think of as Levantine. The Sumerians would not be out of place in any Mediterranean population of the twentieth century.

The Elamites and the Akkadians

In the meanwhile, struggles between Sumerian city-states encouraged the people occupying the peripheries of the Sumerian areas to try their hand at the power game of the strong taking over the weak. To the east, the Elamites from their town of Susa (Iran) invaded the Sumerian cities and received as spoils of war the benefits of Sumerian craftsmanship, military organization, and priestly knowledge.

To the north and west, Semitic-speaking tribesmen came out of the mountains and deserts after 3,000 B.C. to settle peacefully in Sumerian towns, intermarrying with the Sumerians and adopting their way of life. (Semitic is a linguistic term and should be used only to refer to those who spoke a language of the Semitic branch of the Hamito-Semitic family of languages, for example, Akkadian, Assyrian, Aramaic, Ethiopic, Arabic, Babylonian, and Hebrew. It does not refer to any race of people or any special type of individual. Most Semitic-speaking people were Caucasoids and were physiologically related to their neighbors who spoke non-Semitic languages.)

By 2,400 B.C. the Sumerian cities and the Elamite towns were conquered by the first empire builder, Sargon, from the northern town of Akkad in Babylonia. Sargon was a Semitic-speaking king who claimed a childhood similar to that of Moses. He too was cast into the river in a basket by his mother, where he was later found by a "water carrier." Subsequently the goddess Ishtar "smiled on him and gave him fame and fortune." Sargon also conquered other parts of southwestern Asia, and his empire lasted for 200 years.

The Successors to the Sumerians and Akkadians

Through the Akkadians, the Sumerian cuneiform method of writing spread to other areas, but the Akkadian language became the language of diplomacy and business. When the Akkadian empire was overthrown in 2,200 B.C., power again reverted to the two Sumerian military towns, Ur and Uruk. By 2,000 B.C. further invasions by the Elamites of Iran and the Amorites [1] of Syria finally destroyed the power of the Sumerian cities for good. By 1,800 B.C., or within 200 years, the Babylonian empire was fashioned from the Sumerian and Akkadian cities of the north, and the temple civilization inched forward again, spreading its craftsmanship, writing, and bureaucratic organization further to the east and west and keeping its elite in power by setting up an even more efficient soldiery. For the next 1,500 years various Semitic- and Indo-European-speaking empires would collide against, conquer, and influence each other, finally suffering defeat at the hands of even better organized armies from afar who brought their rule, language, architecture, laws, and way of life to those they conquered. The Indo-European-speaking Hittites defeated the Babylonians, and in turn were conquered by the Phrygians. These were defeated by the Assyrians,

---

[1] Abraham, though from Ur, was evidently a descendant of one of the Amorite invading tribes.

who were then conquered by the Medes and Persians, who in turn were crushed by the Macedonians, whose descendants would finally bow to the Romans.

The Unchanging Peasants

Meanwhile, the peasants would go on tilling their plots of land as their forefathers had done aeons before; craftsmanship would be carried on by those who learned their trades from their fathers; writing would continue; the knowledge and beliefs of the past would live on in new, modified forms; and the vast majority of village inhabitants would continue to try to propitiate their gods and goddesses in order to avert the same calamities that had been occurring generation after generation to their fathers and forefathers. In the temple towns some men, through visions, would try to find causal factors to explain these calamities; out of their efforts new ethical and moral codes and more abstract religious ideas would be born to explain why events happened as they did. As in the past people would continue to be compassionate, cruel, kind, envious, generous, and hostile and in general to exhibit a great variety of organized and disorganized behavior. Among them would be a few who in their own small ways would try to build up some kind of knowledge about man and his behavior, which could encourage him in the always new belief that there were choices to be made other than those that had been handed down by tradition and the laws of one's forefathers. Unfortunately for every age, these individuals would continue to be few.

For Selected Bibliography, see end of Chapter 6.

6

The Nile River Valley
Civilization of Egypt

Primary civilization with its writing, craftsmanship, towns, temples, slavery, warfare, and organized government slowly spread westward from the Sumerians to the Egyptians. The latter spoke a Hamitic language, which was part of the Hamito-Semitic family of languages, and lived in a land that received little rain and was saved from being a desert only by the yearly overflow of the Nile River from July to October. It was the Greek historian Herodotus who made the famous remark that Egypt was chiefly the gift of the Nile. Five thousand years ago hundreds of thousands of peasants may have lived within the thin green belt extending no more than ten miles on either side of the river. By the mid-twentieth century more than 25 million lived there.

Ten thousand years ago, Egypt had sufficient rainfall to enable grass to grow hundreds of miles from the Nile. In these prairies, the Paleolithic and Mesolithic ancestors of the Egyptians hunted wild ox, gazelle, hippopotamus, and buffalo. As the rainfall lessened, men and animals moved closer to the Nile where the grass still grew and water was available to quench their thirst.

Early Egyptian Villages

For thousands of years the early Egyptians hunted and fished along the shores and marshes of the Nile. But sometime in the sixth millennium B.C., nomads from Syria-Palestine, from the areas bordering the Tigris and Euphrates, and from the semiarid wastes of southwestern Asia wandered in with their flocks of cattle, goats, and sheep. When they came to the lush grasses along the Nile, they settled in the empty spaces between the older Egyptian encampments, pasturing their animals on the rich prairie grass and planting their small crops of wheat and barley (with wild edible weeds in between) along the mud banks.

These settlers brought agriculture and a pastoral economy with them. Over a span of years they influenced their Mesolithic neighbors (especially when the latter's hunting became poorer and the supply of game and animals could not keep pace with the existing population) to adopt their settled way of life. By 5,000 B.C. we find Neolithic villages along the Nile that were carrying on a mixture of hunting, primitive agriculture, and stock raising. Their inhabitants lived in reed-reinforced mud huts or in small, rounded reed shelters. They buried their dead in shallow graves and supplied them with clay pots containing spiritual food for their afterlives. Each village was run by its head man, whose chief role was to appease both the benign ancestral ghosts and the hostile spirits of the crocodiles and other man-harming spirits.

Even at this Neolithic stage of growth, Egyptian craftsmanship in stone and in earthenware pots, ivory carvings, flint knives, and tools was on a high level; but nothing in either the artistry or the organization of human labor on the village level at this time indicated the incipient civilization that was to come 2,000 years later. When the first temples were going up in the Sumerian city-states and the various local rulers were inventing new bureaucratic processes and skills, the Egyptian villagers were still basking and working under their desert sun, fishing in the Nile, cultivating their small plots of land by hand, harvesting their grains with flint sickles, and in general living and working as the tribes of East Africa did until recently.

The Spread of Civilization from Sumeria

About 3,500 B.C., the technical ideas and thinking of Primary civilization came to Egypt from the Sumerian cities. These concepts may have arrived first in the south of Egypt, the area closest by boat to the Persian Gulf and the Sumerian city-states, rather than in the north of Egypt over the Palestinian-Syrian land route. Knowledge about early architecture, boats, metallurgy, and writing evidently came from the East. Although there was some diffusion from Palestine, Lebanon, and Syria, the greatest influences apparently came directly by boat from the Sumerian cities or from the islands of the Persian Gulf that the Sumerian merchants used as transient stopping places.

Within a period of 300 years after 3,500 B.C. the old Neolithic culture of the villages along the Nile was changed by new ideas coming from the outside, and these changes later became part of the way of life of the small village elites. The latter grew to be more powerful and numerous as they utilized the Sumerian concepts of organizing human labor in a bureaucratic hierarchy. Scribes in the district temples now began to keep detailed and intricate records of how much food was grown, how many taxes were collected, and how much surplus labor was available for building large public works.

The organization of large numbers of workers and resources and the recording of activities and supplies by use of symbols are the two foundation stones of Primary civilization. Until the nineteenth century, urbanism as a way of life was rare even in western Europe; it was even rarer in the Ancient World. Early Primary civilization was peasant-based. The peasant and his village were ruled by a bureaucratic hierarchy centered in small districts or in a small city, only a fraction of whose inhabitants made the goods or provided the services for the governing officials and their assistants. The remainder were peasants who tilled the land and pastured their flocks outside the towns.

Early civilization rewarded the rulers or those who performed valuable services for them. The greatest recompense of all went to the rulers and to the military commanders who helped keep them in power. Their incomes consisted of the services and labor of the peasants and artisans, who were owned by their rulers as property and could be transferred to the service of those whom their masters wished to compensate. The labor that turned a rough stone into a gem was considered part of the finished product. The artistry and brains of those who possessed enough talent to fashion a precious stone in its setting were considered as much the personal property of the powerful as the handiwork the artisans created.

The First Egyptian Dynasty

By 3,200 B.C. all the villages of both upper (southern) and lower (northern) Egypt were united under the rule of a southern king, Narmer, who had learned his arts of warfare from the East and had used his power to make himself the first master of the country. The Primary civilization that developed after this date was Egyptian in spirit and innovation, although, as has already been pointed out, it owed much of its original framework to the Sumerians and other neighbors, and to the ancient Neolithic Egyptian villagers, who had worked in stone and ivory centuries before Primary civilization arrived to organize labor and services for the benefit of the ruling elites.

The luxuries of Egyptian civilization were for the benefit of the rulers and nobles and their retainers and relatives. More than 95 percent of the population, the peasants, gained little from the birth of this Primary civilization, although their labor was more effectively organized for the advantage of the other 5 percent. Gradually the percentage of peasants became reduced to about 90 percent as more skilled officials, craftsmen, workers, priests and soldiers were needed to keep government services functioning. Taxes levied upon the village headmen demanded more and more grain, foodstuffs, and raw materials, forcing the headmen to exert greater pressure upon the peasants to produce more and consume less. Grain and manufactured goods were sent out of the country to pay for metallic ores, timber, and other resources that were not present in Egypt. This trading created new classes of craftsmen, merchants, and sailors.

The Gods and the Kings

As in the Sumerian cities, the peasants and lower classes in Egypt were considered to exist largely to serve the gods, the goddesses, and the kings, who acted as intermediaries between the deities and man. Each year (so regularly that a new yearly calendar of 365 days was based upon this event) the Nile overflowed its banks for more than three months and thus permitted irrigation of the land and cultivation of the crops. Agriculture provided the foundation for the kingdom of Egypt. The king stored the surplus grains to provide for those few years when the Nile failed to flood its banks sufficiently, thereby causing famine and death. The gods gave the Nile floodwaters to the peasants of Egypt. It was to ensure the continuance of this phenomenon that the early kings were descended from the gods to rule the people in the gods' name.

Until the third millennium B.C. only kings, nobles, and their relatives had immortal souls; the souls of all others ceased to exist at death. As a result of priestly reactions to the existing standards of justice, equality, and ethical behavior, every man was soon endowed with an immortal soul; but the nobles and the wealthy would continue to live better in the next world than the peasants, who could do nothing to escape a fate that would be theirs for eternity. Master and slave would remain, as would ruler and ruled, warrior and captive, district governor and peasant, and all the other social gradations that divided society more and more minutely into a scale from the most important to the least important.

The Organization of Men and Resources

At an early date, the labor of the peasants was drafted during the dry season to build hundreds of miles of canals, reservoirs, and dams, which impounded the precious floodwaters of the Nile at its height so that later its contents could be spread over the greatest possible expanse of land for the longest possible period of time. Since there was no rainfall, the Egyptian had to learn to adapt to the substitute of irrigated land. This required either self-discipline or a discipline imposed from without. For most of the world's population and throughout most ages, men have required that rulers impose the discipline of public works. (Only in some golden age of the far distant future will men through their own education and knowledge be able to impose this cooperative self-discipline upon themselves.)

Discipline from the outside required intellectuals, or men of disciplined thought, to invent the organization and the techniques of work so that the floodwaters could be used to their maximum. In the temples, early intellectuals anticipated the flood by observing the heavens to determine when certain stars would come again to the positions they had occupied during the last flood. By utilizing the stars to measure time on earth, they could determine when the flood waters would come down, how long they would last, how much land would be covered, when the crest would be reached, and when it would begin to recede. By keeping careful records of past years, they could know when the dam gates had to be opened and closed, how to trap the flooding water by erecting basin reservoirs to impound the excess, and how to use this water when the river level had receded.

The Rise of Engineering and Centralized Planning

In the third millennium B.C. construction of huge pyramids required civil engineering, means of transportation, production methods, mathematics, sculpture, and ceramics on a scale never before visualized. For example, the Great Pyramid, built shortly after 2,600 B.C., was 750 feet long on each of its four sides and almost 500 feet high. It contained 2,000,000 blocks, each weighing more than two and a half tons, and the entire structure was oriented to within one-twentieth of a degree to the true north. The blocks were cut so expertly that not even a thin knife blade could have been inserted between them when they were in place. They were transported by raft and primitive boat 600 miles down the Nile River from quarries near the present Aswan Dam. The entire structure was surfaced over with polished white limestone (which was removed by the Arabs a little over 1,000 years ago, just as the wealthy citizens of Rome during the Middle Ages stripped their ancient monuments of marble and stone facing to use it again in new churches and palaces).

This huge edifice is not so much a monument to a dead Pharaoh as a memorial to those geniuses of management and intellectual innovation who planned the work of tens of thousands of men who had to be organized, fed, motivated, taught, and supervised. Materials and men of widely varying skills had to be brought together to build the Great Pyramid, which housed the embalmed body of a forgotten king. Copper tools were invented on the spot to cut the limestone and the granite blocks. Accurate measurements were devised to assure that each block was cut to fit in its proper place. The blocks had to be transported on rollers to the banks of the Nile to await the yearly flood tide, which would take them 600 miles north. On the site, mathematicians devised techniques for measuring what had already been completed and the size of those stones yet to be cut. Surveying had to be made into an accurate profession and the stones had to be transported and put into place without knowledge of the wheel or the block and tackle, but with knowledge only of the primitive lever, the inclined plane, and the roller. All this had to be invented and put together only fifty to one hundred years after men had first learned to cut stone for building purposes!

At this time, there was a need for innovation; and innovators were rewarded, encouraged, and given freedom to solve the problems faced in building a structure never before attempted. Fortunately for the innovators, there were no traditions to act as obstacles to their efforts.

The Great Pyramid was a monument to the human mind and to man's ingenuity, to the importance of language and culture, and to the ability of man to solve his problems when encouraged and permitted to do so. It was also a fitting memorial to the profession of the intellectual, the oldest and most human of man's professions. Only during the height of the Roman Empire 2,600 years later would such an original and efficient use of human energies be surpassed.

Evaluation of Egyptian Civilization

Egyptian civilization reached its apex of development more than 5,000 years ago, after a trial run of only a few hundred years. By that time it had reached a level of technical achievement in metallurgy, architecture, sculpture, painting, ceramics, and glass-making that would not be surpassed for at least 2,000 years. But after that, the civilization became static and fossilized, producing little that was new and surviving generation after generation according to traditional ways in which the rules and regulations governing each aspect of daily life were almost unchangeable.

It was as if a great genius with enormous promise had grown up being less productive at fifty than at fourteen. By twenty he had run out of originality and after that was conscious only of the past and his childhood. Such was the fate of Egyptian civilization, the second oldest on the world scene—wonderfully inventive in its earlier centuries, reaching its heights of development around 2,400 B.C., and then remaining stagnant technically and socially for thousands of years afterward. It was a remarkable achievement in that a few minds reached heights of intellectual endeavor never before visualized; but when all was said and done, it was a civilization that mainly benefited the few: those who ruled. The village peasant who grew the food and engaged in the laborious work of building the pyramids, the canals, the dams, and the huge temples to the gods, gained little. His life continued to be one of drudgery, illiteracy, malnutrition, and disease through countless generations up to the twentieth century.

On the other hand, the intellectuals gained, through the pleasure involved in solving problems and being creative. The nobles, Pharaohs, and their retainers gained, for theirs were lives of leisure, luxury, and enjoyment of all the pleasures that other human minds could devise for them. Perhaps 5 percent of the population from 3,200 to 2,400 B.C. gained from the fruits of a few human talents, while 95 percent were no better off than they had been during the precivilized Neolithic age. Under the rule of their kings they ate no better, feared the unknown no less, and were no safer from the ever-present evils of hunger, disease, violent death, and man's cruelty to man.

Egyptian Religion

As is the case in modern India with its contradictory theologies all included in the pantheon of Hinduism, ancient Egypt gave a triple inheritance to her descendants: what she had received from her own preliterate sources, what she had borrowed from her neighbors, and what she had received from the various waves of immigrants at different periods. (The immigrants may have brought with them the seeds of change, but the Egyptians themselves wanted to change nothing that they had received from tradition.)

Rē and Osiris

The Egyptians saw no contradiction between Rē, the sun god, and Osiris, the god of death. The sun made possible a deliverance from darkness, and its rays brought life to the watered earth. In the cloudless skies of Egypt the sun shone day after day. Each evening it settled in the west, where it was devoured, but each morning it was resurrected, a miracle that indicated a continuing victory over death. As a result, the dead were also buried in the west, and like the sun they too fought their battles with death and were resurrected.

Osiris was concerned with the creation of the world. He was the son of the earth god and married his sister Isis. He became the first ruler of the Egyptians. He governed wisely but aroused the envy of his brother Set, who killed him and scattered the remains of his body. Isis, with the help of the other gods, sought out the parts and found them all except the genitals, which were hidden from view at the bottom of a deep river. Osiris was then reassembled; but because he had no genitals, he could not reproduce the living, and for this reason he was restricted to being the god of the dead. Horus, the son of Osiris, sought out Set, and killed him, and ascended the throne of Egypt. The Pharaohs of Egypt thus considered themselves the descendants of both Osiris and Horus, and so were both gods and kings.

The worship of Rē, the sun god, was carried on by the Pharaohs with the help of an intellectual priestly class. The Osiris-Isis-Horus cult was the religion of the common man and may have had part of its origins in the fertility sects that developed with agriculture and stock raising. The early Neolithic Egyptian sacred chiefs may have been killed when their powers waned in order that new and younger energies could come to their people. The dying chiefs entered the world of the ancestral spirits where they continued to protect the living. The Osiris cult may also have received some of its origins from this ancient ritual.

Egyptian Art

Like the Upper Paleolithic hunters, the ancient Egyptians felt that reality could be recreated. Their arts were not intended to serve as exhibits in museum galleries, any more than the mural art of the Magdalenian period 12,000 years before was intended to satisfy the aesthetic pleasures of later viewers. Both were created not to be seen but to become realities. The lifelike sculptures and mural paintings found in the tombs of the ancient Egyptians were physical alternates for the embalmed body, placed there for the soul to enter in case the body disintegrated over a period of millennia. They were not intended to be seen by human eyes.

Reality was also recreated in the scenes of the life of the deceased—his estate, his workers, and his soldiers—all of which could serve him in the next world by being modeled or painted in their actual images. Unlike the Sumerians and the later Shang emperors of China, there were no human sacrifices in the eighty or more pyramids built to house the embalmed bodies of the various Pharaohs and their furniture, jewels, and other valuable possessions.

Though intended for eternity, the tombs were robbed within a few centuries after death, the bodies scattered and the possessions redistributed among the powerful and wealthy. As noted earlier, the tombs are now monuments not to the dead Pharaohs but to the minds of unknown thousands who planned and executed their detailed work. These left a heritage in the arts and crafts and in the foundations for mathematics, engineering, and technology that would not be eclipsed for generations to come. What these unknown but talented men created in these useless and temporary tombs became the foundation for a later technological and organizational civilization.

Egyptian Rule

Egyptian civilization also left a small heritage of moral norms to succeeding ages. Although a good deal of harshness and cruelty existed toward those who did not pay their taxes or disobeyed the orders of the rulers and their administrators, the goals of the later Pharaohs (as stated on their memorials) were not to impress their subjects with fear, but to govern justly, kindly, and compassionately. Most Pharaohs were certainly not as kindly, as just, or as considerate of the peasants and underlings as their memorials indicated; nonetheless, they had standards at which they could aim.

Social Interactions

Temple priests speculated about the injustices that existed on earth—perhaps because they felt themselves to be victims. In consequence, they wrote detailed instructions from the gods dealing with the ruler's responsibility to dispense justice, to consider the necessities of his fellowmen, and to interact kindly with his social inferiors.

Women in the upper classes were evidently treated considerately by their husbands. Tomb paintings show wives and husbands with their arms around each other. Although men continued to be the rulers, the administrators, and the scribes, a good many queens ruled through their husbands. One, Hatshepsut, even became a Pharaoh. Paintings of the period also indicate a good deal of affection between parents and children among the upper classes. (We know little about the peasants except that they were brutally treated by the administrators who came to collect their grain and animals.)

There were many classes of officials, and the surest route to high social standing was to be born a noble, a member of a Pharaoh's family, or the son of a petty official who was sent to the temple school to become a scribe. (As in the case of the later Chinese, the route up the administrative ladder came mainly through education.) Artists and artisans were considered as workers, far beneath the level of scribes, administrators, and nobles. Only a few artisans were available to make the small number of items that the peasant often found less expensive to make himself.

The Egyptians were conquered by foreigners after 1,700 B.C., when mixtures of nomadic tribes from Palestine, Lebanon, and Syria, and perhaps ancestors of the Hebrews, took over the northern half of Egypt and governed it for over one hundred years. Egyptian civilization, however, remained a vital force in the Mediterranean area until the first centuries of the Christian era. It endured longer than the Sumerian and other ancient civilizations. Like the Sumerian, it helped set the patterns for later civilizations—the Greeks and Romans would be deeply in its debt.

Although we speak of Egyptian civilization as urban, it was not urban in our sense of the term. Most of the population was composed of peasants living in villages. It was in essence an opportunity for luxurious living on the part of a few at the expense of the poverty-stricken many. But it could not have been otherwise since the technological basis for agriculture and the crafts was not developed enough to permit greater productivity and thus a higher standard of living for the peasants. If the social classes of nobles, administrators, scribes, priests, and others with specialized skills had not existed, there would have been no canals, public works, or intellectual knowledge to influence later civilizations of the Mediterranean.

Selected Bibliography

Aldred, Cyril, *The Egyptians* (New York, Praeger, 1961).

Childe, V. Gordon, *What Happened in History* (Baltimore, Penguin, 1961).

———, *New Light on the Most Ancient East* (London, Routledge, 1952).

Coon, Carleton S., *The Story of Man* (New York, Knopf, 1955).

Davidson, Marshall B., ed., *The Horizon Book of Lost Worlds* (New York, Doubleday, 1962).

Emery, W. B., *Archaic Egypt* (Baltimore, Penguin, 1961).

Frankfort, Henri, *The Birth of Civilization in the Near East* (Garden City, N.Y., Doubleday, Anchor Books, 1960).

Kramer, Samuel N., *Sumerian Mythology* (New York, Harper & Row, 1961).

Linton, Ralph, *The Tree of Culture* (New York, Knopf, 1955).

Piggott, Stuart, ed., *The Dawn of Civilization* (New York, McGraw-Hill, 1961).

7

The Harappan Civilization
of the Indus Valley

We now turn farther east, to the third river-valley civilization—the Indus, or the Harappan. For a thousand years (between 2,500 and 1,500 B.C.), a great civilization, centered in two large urban areas, stretched more than a thousand miles north and south from the northern reaches of the Indus River to 500 miles below its mouth. Each of the two urban centers had a population of about 50,000 inhabitants with a large scattering of satellite villages surrounding it. Harappa was on the northern end of the river; Mohenjo-Daro was 400 miles away on the southern end. The political boundaries of this civilization covered most of western Pakistan and northwestern India, extending to the border of Iran on the west, the coastal region along the Arabian Sea to the south, and the ancient village sites near New Delhi and Bombay on the east.

Like the Nile and the Tigris and Euphrates rivers, the Indus River in its southern course flows through an arid, desertlike country with too little rainfall to permit either agriculture or an extensive pastoral economy. The river starts in the green foothills of the Himalayas where torrential rains during the monsoon season and melting snows in spring give rise to numerous tributaries. The Indus overflows its banks each year; and large lakes, marshes, jungles, and swamps are left as residues along its middle course. As the river moves toward the Arabian Sea, it cuts across large areas of desert. Its waters have permitted men to live along its banks from earliest times and doubtless were an important factor in the growth of a great technical civilization in this area more than 4,500 years ago.

By sea, the Indus delta is only a little more than 1,500 miles from the mouth of the Tigris and Euphrates rivers and roughly 2,500 miles from the nearest Egyptian ports. Thus it is nearer to the location of the Sumerian cities than to the Egyptian settlements.

The Beginnings of Indus Civilization

Civilization is the end product that comes from organizing human skills. With the centralization of authority, writing and reports become absolutely essential if rulers and administrators are to know what is happening. The necessity of having a convenient center where the ruler and his family, his administrators, their assistants, and the priests can live within reporting distance created small urban clusters of houses. The latter then began to attract the workers and artisans, who left the villages where they were surplus part-time peasants to live in the administrative centers where they could receive work and food by supplying the needs of the ruling bureaucracy. Over a period of time a small middle class of traders, merchants, bankers, goldsmiths, and small-scale entrepreneurs built larger houses in the centers, began to emulate the standard of living of the lesser nobility, and thus required even more workers and their families to move to the urban complexes. These became the servants, carpenters, brickmakers, builders, cabinetmakers, weavers, dyers, jewelers, producers of cosmetics, and keepers of shops. The slow accretion of these functions lasted over a few hundred years, but by 2,500 B.C. Harappa and Mohenjo-Daro were both well-established cities of 50,000 each, with small administrative centers between them containing populations of 2,000 to 6,000.

The Origins of the Civilization

We know almost nothing of the origins of the Indus valley civilization. We can assume that the urban ideas and knowledge of technology, political organization, metallurgy, irrigation, canal building, and writing of the Sumerians moved eastward by sea (the Sumerians traded in large reed boats, waterproofed with bitumen and driven by square sails of hemp or ramie cloth) or across the arid highlands and deserts of Iran. The Elamites and seminomadic peoples to the east may also have acted as traders and diffusers of ideas. Probably influences came from both sources, with the greater coming by sea. Or perhaps the creators of the Indus valley civilization were indigenous people who influenced the Sumerians as much as the Sumerians influenced them.

It is also possible that sailors and colonists from Sumeria may have settled along the Indus valley, marrying in the villages there, and on return trips bringing artisans and petty administrators back with them. Perhaps these colonies attracted members of the Sumerian lower classes, who may have felt that there was little opportunity for them to advance at home because of their lack of influence and their low family position.

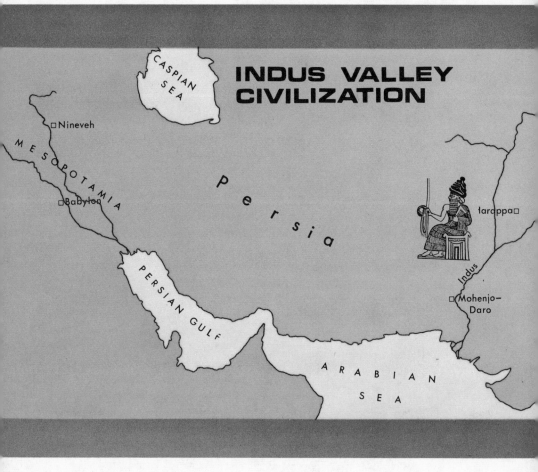

In the villages along the Indus River, on the other hand, they may have found a receptivity to their knowledge and skills.

These immigrants from Sumeria would certainly have known how to smelt copper and how to cast bronze (the Bronze Age began around 3,500 B.C., and copper was known in the Middle East from 5,000 B.C. onward). They would have been able to grasp the principles of writing by symbols, even though they were not professional temple scribes, and would thus have been more inclined to invent new writing symbols. They could have brought with them from Sumeria the skills of the carpenter, the weaver, the brickmaker, and even the jeweler. Not being priests, however, they could not have brought their gods or temple abodes. If temples existed in the Indus valley cities, they have not been identified so far.

These last paragraphs are speculation of course, but there are no archaeological layers beneath the ruins of these Indus valley cities to indicate a developmental period similar to those in Mesopotamia or in Egypt.

If we speculate further, we might wonder whether the villages to which the Sumerian colonists were attracted were recently founded or were established when the colonists took wives from the nearby area, thus deciding to settle down and encouraging their wives' kinsmen to move to the new centers. Perhaps the lower Indus valley was similar enough to the arid valley of the Tigris-Euphrates to make the settlers feel at home and to permit them to use their newly established trading posts as a base for further trips by boat—up the Indus River to the Himalayas or along the long coastal area of India to Indonesia, the Philippines, and the coast of China—in their quest for metals, timber, jewels, obsidian, and building stone.

The Indus civilization may have prospered for more than 1,000 years (until it was destroyed by invaders from the northwest) because the two cities organized the peasants in their areas to produce grain and to manufacture goods and cloth, which could then be traded to areas beyond the sailing range of merchants and seamen from the mainland Sumerian cities or from the trading islands in the Persian Gulf.

The Technical Level as Indicated by Housing and Sanitation

The cities of Harappa and Mohenjo-Daro reached a high level of technical civilization. The average resident in both cities may have had better housing and sanitary facilities than the urban dwellers of the Tigris-Euphrates or the Nile valleys. While the Sumerians used sun-dried mud-brick for buildings, the towns of the Indus valley used baked brick. The urban plan for both Harappa and Mohenjo-Daro contained similarities to the Sumerian cities, but there was none of the unplanned chaos of the Sumerian towns. The houses (especially those of the administrators and the small middle class) were made of plastered baked brick, were large and roomy, were two stories tall with bathrooms and latrines on the upper floor, and had semiopen drains leading down to clay barrels in the alleys for sewage disposal.

In both cities long, straight streets intersected each other at right angles in a grid plan. In the center of each city was a large citadel, or fort, next to another large building identified as a granary. Nearby was a large bathing pool, used perhaps for ritual cleanliness. There appeared to have been no other public buildings in the form of either temples or palaces.

Indus Valley Government

Harappa and Mohenjo-Daro did not have a primitive totalitarian rule, as many of the early archaeologists working on the ruins believed, but probably had an administration governed by councils of equals or an oligarchy in which the overlords as trustees did not function as gods. We simply do not know what sort of oligarchy governed. A council of elders may have been composed of the richest merchants, the nobles, or the warriors, or it may have been a combination of all three.

All of this implies that the rulers did not build palaces equal to those of Sumeria or Egypt. Even the gods themselves may have been shaped from images of ancestral head men who were benign and free of arrogance and condescension.

Both Harappa and Mohenjo-Daro were large settlements, at least three miles in circumference. The citadel in Harappa was almost 1,400 feet long and 650 feet wide and was surrounded by a high wall 45 feet wide, with bastions, ramps, and gates. The citadel at Mohenjo-Daro was somewhat similar. Both cities seemed to share the same civilization and way of life, which makes it appear that some kind of federation rather than an empire governed the two cities and the intervening towns and villages.

Craftsmanship and Artistry of the Indus Valley Cities

The level of craftsmanship in bronze work, jewelry, and other artifacts indicates that high standards were set and achieved. The seals that have survived cannot be read, and no other form of writing appears. Perhaps writing was done on some kind of perishable materials rather than on clay tablets, as in Sumeria. But intricate records must have been kept because the population contained large numbers of artisans and traders. The two great cities imported manufactured goods from Sumeria; silver, copper, and jewels from Afghanistan; gold from southern India; turquoise from Iran; and timber from the upper reaches of the Indus River. They also exported finished copper and bronze, stone, ivory, wood, and animals. As befitted a trading people, the Indus valley civilization also had an efficient system of weights and measures. For accounts both decimal and binary systems were used, rather than the unit of 60, which was the Sumerian practice.

Religion

Indus valley religion may have been similar to twentieth century Hindu beliefs, with a trinity consisting of a first creator, a god who protected man, and a god who brought death by disease and warfare and required continuous propitiation. Under these three gods, there may have been tribal or village spirits, ancestral spirits, household deities, and the special gods who protected various crafts and callings. There may also have been fertility cults, but no signs have been found indicating this type of worship. Although the gods may have been important, there is no indication so far that they were jealous and arrogant, which would have demanded large temples and shrines like those found in the Sumerian cities.

Agriculture

The Indus valley people are the first ones known to have used cotton, although it appears that their cotton plant may have come originally from southern Egypt. They grew cotton, wove it into cloth, and exported both to Sumeria. Their traders and sailors may also have been the intermediaries who brought cotton to southeastern Asia. From there (though there is no evidence for this) it may perhaps have traveled by unknown hands and means to the west coast of South America, where cotton of the same genetic structure and dated at about the same time as that in the Indus valley has been found.

The peasants grew wheat, barley, peas, sesame, melons (from Iran), and perhaps dates (from Sumeria). Domesticated animals, other than the dog, included humped Indian cattle, water buffalo, asses, pigs, camels, and possibly goats. The community as a whole not only provided for the peasants' needs, but may also have insisted upon receiving grain and barley in return. The peasants may have been lent seed, tools, and even animals. Perhaps, like the ancient villages of Egypt, the land was held communally and labor was pooled to divert the floodwaters of the Indus into reservoirs behind high dams.

Indus ideas about irrigation may have come from Sumeria with some modifications made to meet the special conditions of the raging Indus River at floodtide. Under some sort of bureaucratic direction, the people built tall brick dikes along the river, in addition to canals, reservoirs, and dams. Both Harappa and Mohenjo-Daro, as well as the smaller towns and villages, were constructed on mounds of earth, which put them above the crest of the floodwaters.

Social and Political Organization

The Indus civilization had the high level of cooperation and communal effort necessary to tame the Indus River and to build the neat urban centers with their straight streets, drainage system, night soil collection, and watchmen in the citadels.

The large bathing pools also suggest the existence of some sort of communal ritual cleanliness—much as in twentieth century India where Hindu temples are surrounded by ritual bathing pools. Extensive irrigation systems require tireless watching and supervision plus detailed planning and coordination: indifference could bring about their destruction in a matter of years.

The Indus civilization also required coordinated military action. The Indus River, which brought boats from the cities to the Himalayas and to the Arabian Sea, could, by the same token, bring invaders along these routes. There could have been many visitors, who might have watched with envy the growth of wealth in the cities and towns: the surplus of grains, the large number of trading boats going up and down the river, the well-being and prosperity of the inhabitants, their cotton clothing, their jewels, and their high level of craftsmanship. For over a thousand years (longer than the age of any modern European nation, including England), the Indus civilization endured, prospering and undoubtedly attracting to its population the younger members of distant villages and numerous nomadic tribes who preferred a life of assured food to a life of insecurity. It was an efficiently organized civilization, governed perhaps by a staff of disciplined administrators and planners performing for the good of its various parts. Its influence may have extended over a territory of 500,000 square miles.

If Indus civilization had been governed by kings or emperors, it is likely that some ruins of palaces might have remained. No evidence of any such buildings has come to light. Only a few stone statues have been uncovered. One is of a stern, bearded man in his fifties, of Caucasoid visage, who could have been one of the great administrators, a chief planner, or even a god (though this is unlikely). He is dignified, wears no jewels, has no warlike helmet, and is not shown towering over kneeling figures. Perhaps he may have played a role similar to that of Gudea, governor of Lagash in Sumeria, who attempted to rule justly but did not call himself king.

Contemporaries of Indus Civilization

The Indus civilization lasted for more than a thousand years. For hundreds of years it was a contemporary of the mixed nomadic invaders known as the Hyksos, who had overthrown the royal rule in Egypt. It lived past the age when Sumeria had ceased to exist. It was on the decline when the Babylonians were at the height of their power. And it was approaching extinction when the Cretans saw their port cities destroyed by a combination of earthquakes, fire, and Mycenaeans. By 1,500 B.C., when it ceased to exist, the Chinese civilization was beginning to flower, and agricultural settlements were being established in Central and South America.

Stagnation in Indus Civilization

Once their form of civilization had reached its apex, the Indus valley centers stood still. Their leaders and citizenry were evidently satisfied with what their hands and minds had wrought. They could see no need to change or improve what to them was apparently perfection. For generation after generation everything went along smoothly, and the leaders and most enlightened public undoubtedly wanted to keep it that way. For hundreds of years, perhaps, there was enough to eat, clothing was plentiful, housing was comfortable, and life was good. If one took no risks, one chanced no losses.

There must have been family gatherings to celebrate births and marriages, and occasions to commemorate deaths. There was undoubtedly a close sense of interrelationship and of belonging. The administrators were undoubtedly efficient, the soldiers courageous, and the individual had a preordained destiny that he felt he could not change. One lived as well as he could, expected no more from life than what he got, learned to take happiness and sorrow in his stride, and perhaps hoped for greater rewards in the next life. Perhaps most, however, wanted no more in the next life than they had in the present.

The steady pattern of life as it went on for more than a thousand years indicates a mechanism that kept change at a minimum and evidently made men content with their lot. Perhaps there was divination and even a highly developed astrology, derived from the Sumerians, in which one was able to ascertain what destiny had in store for him.

One could not revolt against what one could not change, and one could not be discontented if no alternatives were apparent. Perhaps life in the Indus valley over 3,500 years ago was carried on in an interdependent milieu in which each individual knew from childhood what was expected of him and what he in turn could expect from others.

The Disintegration of Indus Civilization

During the last few hundred years of its existence, the city of Mohenjo-Daro showed a deterioration of its housing standards. The population expanded gradually as more and more people came in from the outlying areas. Rooms became smaller as they were divided and subdivided (as in the slums of modern cities), and construction itself became shoddier. The skills of the earlier ages became standardized, and perhaps the earlier vigilance of the bureaucracy became dulled as individual judgment was overruled by a mass of laws and regulations that were developed from precedents of the past.

Perhaps the engineering of the earlier ages deteriorated when individuals took over these tasks as birthrights from their fathers. Possibly the administrators inherited their positions as a function of their status at birth. The continued yearly inundations of the cities by the Indus River meant that the building and rebuilding of Harappa and Mohenjo-Daro became routinized tasks over the centuries. The canals and dams may have deteriorated as later generations decided that repairs could wait. Timber for repairs of caved-in protective banks may have been more and more difficult to obtain except by raft from the upper reaches of the river.

The End of Indus Civilization

By 1,500 B.C. Indus valley civilization had become a tired one. The fortified citadels and the soldiers were perhaps unable to stem the ferocious invading nomads from Afghanistan who were under the leadership of Indra, the "fort-destroyer" (whose name was given to the entire subcontinent). It is believed that after a siege of many months the men, women, and children in Mohenjo-Daro were slaughtered wherever they were found by the invading warriors. No mercy was evidently shown to the conquered by these nomadic Indo-European-speaking barbarians when they finally succeeded in broaching the city walls and the citadel where the remaining population had evidently taken refuge. The end may not have come as quickly as the scattered skeletons indicate, but one thing was clear: the new conquerors had no further use for the cities they had destroyed.

Except for the cities, perhaps the new invaders destroyed little of the Indus valley civilization. Under their rule, it is probable that village India was reincorporated and that the conquerors in time became the priests, warriors, nobles, scribes, and keepers of the records. In the beginning, as warriors they would doubtless have looked with contempt upon the traders and merchants; and it would be a long time before the latter resumed the trade that had been the lifeblood of the Indus valley cities. The villages and small towns were kept on, however, and the village religion preserved, though now overlain by the new gods and beliefs that the invaders brought with them. It is likely that the vast cultural influences expressed in the crafts, the knowledge, the beliefs, and even the writing (until it was changed later by the Aramaic alphabet from the west) continued in slightly modified form until the twentieth century in India.

The chief tragedy may not have been the destruction of the Indus valley cities by the invaders from the north as much as the earlier deterioration of urban civic consciousness when social mobility was closed off and birth rather than ability was the means whereby one became an administrator or a coordinator of the vast interdependent complex. Although the Indus valley civilization did not disappear and although its spirit lived on, its innovating period ended only a few hundred years after it had begun. The way of life might then have become traditional, conservative, and bound by precedent. The influence of administrators long dead may have weighed heavily on the minds of the living in the last centuries of its existence. The self-discipline that had prevailed in the early period could have ended in the tyranny of group discipline. Perhaps it was the group that insisted that not even the slightest change be permitted to interfere with what the past had ordained.

The villagers continued as they always had; but as the vast network of dikes, dams, irrigation canals, and reservoirs disintegrated through the indifference of the new conquerors, the peasants left their land for areas where rainfall was adequate. There they could rebuild their villages with land held in common and add their religious beliefs to those of their new neighbors.

A few of the native artists and craftsmen may have joined forces with the new Indo-European-speaking priests, who built temples, sculptures, and altars to their ancient deities as well as to the Indus gods they had taken over. The invaders inaugurated a caste system; and since they were lighter in pigmentation than the lower classes whom they had spared, color might have become one of the marks of caste differentiation. It is likely that the ancient inhabitants of Harappa and Mohenjo-Daro were a thoroughly mixed Caucasoid and Australoid population, the mixture being composed of ancient Sumerians, Iranians, Afghans, and the hill tribes of Kashmir plus the more darkly pigmented Australoid population coming in from Baluchistan and the Punjab (although these were already mixed with ancient Caucasoid stocks).

The Indus valley civilization ended in a bloody and drawn-out battle for the city of Mohenjo-Daro; but modern India, like the Phoenix, was born out of its ashes. Little was lost of its ancient knowledge as it became assimilated in the vast number of villages of northern India that the Indo-European-speaking invaders were to govern (and whose languages most of the natives would speak) for the next 2,700 years. Civilization would continue in northern India until the next great period, the birth of Gautama, or Buddha, around 500 B.C. The peasants would carry on their round of life almost unchanged from what it had been when they first came under the administration and supervision of the officials from the great urban centers of the Indus civilization. The oxcart would continue to move the grain from the villages to the small nearby administrative towns as they had done during the heyday of Harappa and Mohenjo-Daro. Buildings would be constructed in the same fashion, and life would continue to be regulated by the traditions of the past until the nineteenth and twentieth centuries when foreign innovators would attempt to introduce an industrial civilization, even then not affecting the peasant or his village very much.

Selected Bibliography

Basham, A. L., *The Wonder That Was India* (London, Sidgwick & Jackson, 1956).

Davidson, Marshall B., ed., *The Horizon Book of Lost Worlds* (New York, Doubleday, 1962).

Hawkes, J., and Woolley, L., *Prehistory and the Beginnings of Civilization* (New York, Harper & Row, 1963).

Mackay, E. J. H., *Early Indus Civilizations* (London, Luzac, 1948).

Piggott, Stuart, *Prehistoric India* (Baltimore, Penguin, 1950).

———, *The Dawn of Civilization* (New York, McGraw-Hill, 1961).

Powell-Price, J. C., *A History of India* (London, Nelson, 1955).

Wheeler, Sir Mortimer, *Early India and Pakistan* (New York, Praeger, 1959).

8

Crete and Its Influence

From the Indus valley we move westward to the Aegean Sea, which separates Turkey from Greece. Between these two are a series of islands that at one time were part of a mountainous landed area, including a land bridge where the Bosphorus is today. When the seas began to rise at the end of the last glacial period the islands became isolated. By the seventh millennium B.C., Mesolithic man was island-hopping with his bark and dug-out canoes from one side of the Aegean to the other. (The existence of Europe as a separate continent is due only to a late prejudice of the ancient Greeks from the mainland, who, in their ethnocentrism and provincialism, wanted to separate themselves from the peoples living on the other side of a sea that at its narrowest is less than forty miles between islands and at its widest is not even two hundred miles across.)

The largest and southernmost island in this chain is Crete, which is about two hundred miles long and less than forty miles wide. North of Crete lie the numerous islands of the Aegean. To the northwest lies the mainland of Greece, whose later Mycenaean civilization would be derived from Crete. To the northeast lies the mainland of Anatolia, the home of Neolithic pottery and early copper tools and a series of civilizations that began with the Trojans, a people as ancient as the Cretans.

The Early Settlement of Crete

Crete was first settled permanently after 5,000 B.C., when different groups of migrants (presumably from Anatolia, Syria, Palestine, and Lebanon, perhaps speaking a Semitic language but certainly a non-Greek one) arrived by boat, bringing with them agriculture, domesticated animals, a knowledge of mudbrick and woodworking, and a desire to carry on trade.

They also brought with them the cult of the earth goddess, whose male companion was either a lover or a son who was ritually sacrificed at the harvest and resurrected in the spring with the growth of new crops. This ancient earth goddess, who became identified with agriculture during the early Neolithic period, took on various names under different civilizations, such as Diana, Ishtar, Isis, and Astarte. She was both the mother of men and the producer of crops, but she needed to be made fertile. Thus the snake and the bull, both objects of male sexuality, were associated with her worship in Crete (as elsewhere in Eurasia). But it is she who is worshipped rather than her male consorts, who are considered relatively unimportant (a reflection of the family system in Neolithic times).

The early population was thus a mixed one, and it did not all arrive at the same time. As in the case of other civilizations, there was an infiltration by different peoples at various times, through intermarriage, the influencing of one by the other, and gradual interdependence. By 3,000 B.C. the Cretans began to build upon their different pasts; and by 2,500 B.C. (the beginning of the Bronze Age) they imported copper and tin from Anatolia and papyrus and sugarcane from Egypt. They built large wooden houses with porticoes supported by columns, a style evidently derived from tree trunks, which were originally cut and placed upside down so that they would not sprout roots. The Cretans also learned to make handsome pottery and stone vessels, some of which were put to use by the women for mixing their eye paint, rouge, and lipstick. The Cretans grew extensive crops, kept large herds of animals, and built sailing vessels in which they carried on trade with Egypt, Greece, and Anatolia. (At this time the inhabitants of Greece were evidently related to the inhabitants of Anatolia and apparently spoke the same non-Greek languages of unknown origin. Greek as a language did not come into this area until at least 1,000 years later.) The Cretans were influenced by all three regions, as well as by the more distant areas of Syria, Lebanon, and Palestine.

From the beginning the Cretans used an early form of writing that later became "Linear A," one of the two scripts they used. The second is called "Linear B," and its language has now been identified as very early Greek. There has been a good deal of controversy over the language of "Linear A." One source calls it early Phoenician or Canaanite, but no evidence so far indicates conclusively what it represented (although it is likely that it could have been early Semitic or Hamitic).

The early Cretans were influenced by all the areas around them and undoubtedly later affected others in turn. Increasingly after 2,200 B.C. Crete and Egypt were in close trading relations, the Cretans influencing Egyptian pottery forms and fashions and the Egyptians sending Crete their designs for jewels, furniture, and even textiles. (All of these were modified later on for Cretan use.)

MINOAN CIVILIZATION

Ionian Sea

Aegean Sea

EUBOEA

Orchomenus ■

Athens ■

Mycenae ■

■ Tiryns

CYCLADES

Delos

Naxos

Melos

Thera

Cythera

Troy ■

Asia Minor

Ialysus ■

RHODES

Carpathos

CRETE

Knossos ■   Mallia ■

Hagia

Phaistos

The Cretan Organization of Trade

The great palaces of Knossos, Phaistos, and Mallia were built after 2,000 B.C. for the benefit of the three rulers who presided over the various sections of Crete. Each palace had extensive labyrinths, drainpipes, corridors, airwells, tiled murals, alabaster throne rooms, and outside balconies. Knossos and Phaistos became the two great seaports with their supply of high-prowed sailing ships that carried on an extensive trade with Egypt, Lebanon, Palestine, Anatolia, mainland Greece, the Black Sea area, Spain, and perhaps with those people living along the northwest coast of Europe. In turn, the sailing ships of other peoples came to trade with the Cretans.

Crete spread the organizing spirit of early civilization far north. Competing with merchants from Troy, its ships and traders carried the evidences of a higher standard of living, of more efficient working methods, and of an improved bureaucratic organization to the unknown people of Europe.

The island of Crete may also have been the lost mythical continent of Atlantis to generations in Greece a thousand years later. Stories were told then of a great island civilization that suddenly perished during an earthquake followed by a tidal wave. The death of Crete would be a slow one however.

Cretan Religious Beliefs

Crete lies along an earth fault that produces frequent earthquakes and tidal waves. Those who have experienced earth tremors on the island report that they are accompanied by a rumbling noise that sounds like the roaring of a bull. The original migrants to Crete may well have come from regions where earthquakes were less frequent. As a result, the bull in the interior of the earth, possibly the consort of the earth goddess, became a figure of fear who had to be propitiated. The use of the bull as a theme in decoration and at religious festivals was widespread. (The Cretan civilization was known to the later Greeks as the Minoan, after the mythical Minos, king of Crete—son of Zeus and Europa—whose wife bore the legendary Minotaur, half bull and half man, who demanded sacrifices of young men and women brought to him in his labyrinthine depths.) Bulls were sacrificed to the earth goddess. Each year there were large festivals at which young men and women who were trained in bull-jumping turned somersaults over the bulls' backs by using the horns as a platform (evidently a dramatic rite indicating the conquest of the earth-bull). Afterwards the bull was sacrificed to the earth goddess, in whose honor this game was held.

The religious services of Crete were performed not in temples (at least none has been uncovered so far) but in palace courtyards, open enclosures, and mountain caves. The kings and queens were considered high priests and evidently directed the rites and ceremonies, with the people participating not only as spectators but as performers. Women appeared to play a role equal to that of the men in both religious and secular festivals.

The Technical Contributions of Cretan Civilization

Crete's great contributions to technical civilization lie primarily in the three great palaces. The chief one at Knossos had large stairways, central halls, corridors leading to private suites, and two levels built above and two below the central court. The royal suites in this palace had small bathrooms with earthenware bathtubs and apertures leading to a large drain for emptying not only the bathtub but perhaps other vessels as well. Each area of the palace at Knossos was served by a drainage system, which led into a main sewer that in turn led to a nearby river. Drains also ran from the roof through the walls to an underground passage leading to the sewers. Water was carried through terra-cotta pipes, slanted at certain sections to prevent the accumulation of sediment. Archaeologists have found that the Cretans had a knowledge of hydraulic engineering, as indicated by one example of an open channel that was built beside a steep stairway going from the central court to the river. The channel was constructed not at sharp right angles, as was the flight of stairs, but in parabolic curves to slow the flow of water so that it would not rush over its sides and make a waterfall of the stairway.

Cretan Shipping and Trade

The strength of Crete lay in its shipping, and perhaps especially in its warships, for no sign of fortifications appears on the island. From its rise as a civilization around 2,500 B.C. to its end after 1,500 B.C. Crete seems to have been spared from invasions. The three rulers, with the king of Knossos possibly the senior, evidently compromised their differences by dividing the island and the other areas of the Mediterranean into respective spheres of influence.

Knossos, for example, appears to have carried on an extensive trade with both Anatolia and mainland Greece; Phaistos seems to have been the center for trade with Egypt; and Mallia may have been the seaport for trade with the Levantine coast. But other towns have been found with wharves cut into their rocky coasts. It is possible that traders from these towns may also have scoured the western Mediterranean for copper and tin. They may even have sailed along the Cornish coast of England or further to the northwest searching for metals, minerals, and other trade objects. With the increasing importance of these metals, which even in the twentieth century are comparatively scarce, the trade for rare copper and even rarer tin, gold, silver, and nickel must have kept many merchants fully occupied seeking out new areas that possessed mineral resources.

The End of Cretan Civilization

Sometime after 1,400 B.C. an earthquake and tidal wave destroyed the city of Knossos and its great palace, but the civilization had been on the decline after 1,700 B.C. following its 300 years of greatness. Although the physical civilization of Crete deteriorated, the ideas and concepts that the Cretans had originally received from Anatolia, Egypt, and the Syro-Palestine coast now influenced the Mycenaeans, the archaic Greeks who entered the mainland of Greece after 1,900 B.C. and who may have ruled Crete during its declining centuries.

Perhaps the Cretans had decided around 1,700 B.C. to leave the risky jobs of sailing their ships and doing their fighting to the Mycenaeans, who also hired themselves out to the Egyptians as mercenaries. From 1,900 B.C. to 1,400 B.C. the relationship between these archaic Greeks (who may have come over from Anatolia) and the Cretans was extremely close. Perhaps, too, various Anatolians may have been hired as commission merchants to do the exploring and trading for the Cretan trading-princes.

As century after century of merchant-princes took over their inheritances, these individuals may have decided that they possessed all the luxuries they could want and that life was more enjoyable when one did not exert oneself too much. It is possible that their thinking may have run somewhat as follows: after all, why take the chance of losing one's life at sea when one can hire a foreigner to do the job just as well, paying him handsomely, of course, for his trouble. In the meantime one could remain at home to carry on various rites, to enjoy one's family and home, and to participate in the wonderful spectacles and performances that took place there. Life is too short to be risked, especially since there is no need to do so. One can always use one's wealth to hire others to do the work that one does not wish to do.

The Mycenaeans may have manned the large naval and trading vessels, while the Anatolians and other nearby people may have been sent out as salesmen to find customers for Cretan manufactured artifacts, olive oil, wine, bronze double axes, spears, fine linens, and cosmetics. Perhaps the Trojans and other Anatolians may also have served as middlemen in the sale of Cretan bronze weapons and may even have been given an exclusive franchise in the territory north of the Black Sea. (Within a few centuries, large migrations of warriors with double-headed battle-axes and bronze spears invaded Europe from the area north of the Black Sea, winning new lands with weapons that the technical civilization of Crete might well have supplied initially through their Anatolian salesmen.)

Again, we reach the end of a short chapter about an ancient people with the summary that once innovation ceases and opportunity no longer exists for the boy on the bottom to feel that he is as good as the rich boy on top, then other poor boys in nearby neighborhoods may take on the task of proving that they are better than the effete rulers of wealthier areas (whose military weakness cries out a challenge to strong men like themselves to come and take their possessions).

In Crete social mobility may have come to an early end at the time when innovation ceased to have value. Perhaps ascribed or inherited status may have become all-important, with peasants taking over the occupations of their fathers and learning to become content with their lot, thus leaving the problems of the universe to those more competent than they to handle or solve them. The latter may in turn have felt that these problems were best left in the hands of the earth goddess and her male consorts, who were after all more knowledgeable as to what needed to be done.

The Cretan rulers may have combined sacrifices with pleasant spectacles, thus enjoying what the earth goddess had given them. At the same time they doubtless permitted the Mycenaean mercenaries to become their military protectors and their neighbor Anatolians to serve as their bearers of profit. By 1,400 B.C., instead of giving the Cretan merchant princes a cut of their profits, both may well have decided to go into business for themselves. Evidently something of this sort may have happened, because at this time Crete as a powerful naval and trading power quickly went into a decline—although its civilization and level of comforts continued to motivate others. The ripples made upon the Aegean and Mediterranean world by the Cretan trading ships became wider and wider as the accumulated knowledge of technical and political civilization was taken on by new discontented peoples, who also wanted a chance to see what they could do to make themselves less dissatisfied. The attraction of early civilization became the power it conferred upon those who adopted its technology and its organization of men and resources.

Selected Bibliography

Childe, V. Gordon, *Dawn of European Civilization* (New York, Knopf, 1958).

Davidson, Marshall B., ed., *The Horizon Book of Lost Worlds* (New York, Doubleday, 1962), pp. 241–272.

Hawkes, J., and Woolley, L., *Prehistory and the Beginnings of Civilization* (New York, Harper & Row, 1963).

Hutchinson, R. W., *Prehistoric Crete* (Baltimore, Penguin, 1962).

Piggott, Stuart, *The Dawn of Civilization* (New York, McGraw-Hill, 1961), Chapter 7.

9

The Technical Civilization of Anatolia

The city-states and territorial units of Anatolia played the same subordinate role to the centers of civilization in Sumeria, Egypt, and Babylonia as Manchester and Birmingham do to London or as St. Louis and Cleveland do to New York and Washington. Although these minor contemporary cities have large populations, extensive residential areas, technical plants, and perhaps outstanding workmanship in certain technological fields, the centers of the business world are still located in government circles and in intellectual areas. In the past, it was the intellectual centers that gave us whatever we knew about various civilizations of the Ancient World. It was the scribe—whether he was a poet, government official, business-letter writer, philosopher, religious leader, early historian, or geographer—who wrote the records that remain imperishable and are translated, are read by others, and eventually become the standards of knowledge.

The ancient classical works of Greece and Rome survived because they were treasured not only by the educated men of their own civilization, but also by neighbors who were identified with them, who survived, and who continued many aspects of the Greek and Roman ways of life. The Indian and Chinese classics also survived because the civilizations during which they were written have continued until modern times, and great prestige was accorded those who knew their contents. Unfortunately, the thought of the Anatolian city-states did not survive, as that of Crete did in the remains of the Mycenaeans and in the myths of the later Greeks.

The Anatolian cities were destroyed at different times by conquerors who may have kept their technical achievements but who did not value their thought enough to codify it and did not value it as sacred or traditional. Because the Anatolian civilization had no direct heirs willing to honor their ancient family lore, they remained unknown until the end of the nineteenth century. Archaeological excavations have told us something of their achievements, but not enough work has been done so far to give us a coherent picture similar to those we have of the other civilizations. (We shall know more in the future; but for now we must be content with what we have, being thankful that we know more than we did fifty years ago, though not as much as we shall know fifty years hence.)

The City of Troy and its Trade

Troy, the legendary city of Helen and Paris, was perhaps the oldest city in Anatolia. By 2,400 B.C. it had arrived at a stage of development that produced great palaces, complex art, immense stone fortifications, and large houses. This Trojan period of greatness was only slightly behind the flowering of Crete; and it was still more than 1,200 years before the famous Trojan War, which may not have been fought over the abduction of Helen but rather over the control of trade routes through the Black Sea. Troy was evidently a great trading center for commerce with the Neolithic communities around the Black Sea. Isolated Trojan traders may even have penetrated up the great rivers of Russia, and perhaps up the Danube through Rumania, Bulgaria, Yugoslavia, Czechoslovakia, Austria, and possibly Germany. As a trading and manufacturing center, Troy may have been as important in the Black Sea area as Crete was in the western Mediterranean.

Troy and a great many settlements near it on the Marmara Sea were small, independent city-states, each ruled by a petty king, with a small elite of merchant-aristocrats controlling the labor of thousands of peasants in the surrounding area. The former carried on trade via those sea and land routes that they could control, using their own workshops, skilled workers, and supervisory artisans to fashion the bronze axes, daggers, spears, pottery, and finely woven cloth and carpets, which would bring fancy prices elsewhere in metals of all kinds, slaves, and uncut jewels.

Dorak

At the site of a city-state called Dorak not far from Troy, archaeologists in the 1950's uncovered graves, dating back to 2,500 B.C., that housed the bodies of two kings and a queen. With the skeletons were found scepters of pink veined marble encased in gilt with silver handles; fragments of a richly colored red carpet similar to those still being made in Turkey (ancient Anatolia) today; a dagger of silver; a sword with an iron blade (this is the earliest use of iron found thus far—1,500 years before the beginning of the Iron Age!); representations of sailing ships; and vases of gold and silver decorated with lapis lazuli and other semiprecious stones.

Alaja Huyuk

Underneath the Hittite city of Alaja Huyuk in central Anatolia at a pre-Hittite site dated certainly before 2,500 B.C., elaborate tombs have been found, which were even more richly furnished than those at Dorak. Thirteen graves were uncovered that contained excavations roofed over with logs, upon which were placed the heads of sacrificial oxen. The jewelry, metalwork, and weapons were on the same technical level as the Sumerian handiwork found in the large royal tombs of Ur. These excavations at Dorak and Alaja Huyuk brought to light the remains of small city-states that perhaps had formed close alliances with their neighbors, possibly exchanging gifts and royal daughters and even helping one another fight off distant and stronger neighbors.

Anatolian Influences

These city-states were very much affected by the Sumerian town-centers, by Egypt, and by the Syro-Lebanese settlements in between.

Crete also had its influences in Anatolia. In the southwestern part of Anatolia, a palace was excavated that was somewhat reminiscent of the one at Knossos, although it was constructed of mudbrick, stone rubble, and timber. The double horns of the Cretan symbol of worship were also used, indicating either Cretan influence or (less likely) the early home of some of the original migrants to Crete.

The Breakdown of Anatolian Isolation through Trade

Sumerian traders followed by Akkadian and Babylonian merchants may have scoured the highlands of Anatolia looking for metals. Egyptian, Levantine, and Cretan sailors sailed their boats into the coastal inlets seeking trade outlets. These traders evidently brought with them technical ideas, a knowledge of writing, political organization, religions, and literature to pass on to the various peoples who lived in isolated valleys, separated from one another by high mountains and difficult terrain.

The Hittites

Around 1,900 B.C. the Hittites, an Indo-European-speaking people, moved in from the northeast (as perhaps the Mycenaeans and Anatolians had done before them), bringing horses, iron, war chariots, and better ways of organizing military forces. From their mountain stronghold of Boghaz-koy, they periodically threatened Egypt; and for 500 years (from 1,700 to 1,200 B.C.) they ruled a large area stretching from northern Syria and Babylonia to the shores of the Aegean Sea.

Perhaps like the Mycenaeans, who at that time were their contemporaries living in mainland Greece, the Hittites were mountain people who dressed in long woolen robes and short upturned boots and lived on the crest of hills in citadels surrounded by strong walls and turreted towers for defense against invaders. Inside the citadels the ruling elites resided with their families and closest retainers; outside the gates the merchants and peasants lived behind the protection of a smaller wall. Although the Hittites conquered a large area, they seem to have had a rough humanity and a primitive sense of justice. As long as the conquered cities paid their tribute, they were left alone to govern themselves.

Like other Indo-European-speaking peoples at that time, the Hittites had a three-class system of nobles, peasants, and slaves. There were special privileges for the nobles but few rights for the peasant. Although the slaves were not treated harshly, they did not receive much from their masters to ease their servile lot. The king was also the high priest of the weather god, Teshub, the chief god of the Hittites and in many ways similar to Zeus of the Greeks; but other gods whose homes had originally been in Sumeria, Syria, and other nearby regions were also worshipped.

In some ways the ancient Hittites remind us of the early Norse with their rude, rough manners, their comradeship with those of their class, and their disdain for the peasants and slaves beneath them. They were forthright, apparently emotionally honest, and concerned with not doing evil to those who were dependent upon them. Kings discussed their problems in detail with their administrators and senior counselors. One gets the impression that the latter engaged in no formal protocol in reporting to the king but that the king was only the first among equals. Women were treated with a certain amount of consideration, and relationships were apparently close between a man and his sister's sons.

Hittite Religion

Apparently the Hittites had no unified religious beliefs, and no special priestly class held sway under the king. There were seemingly two contradictory religions (though perhaps this was not recognized to be the case by the Hittites). The worship of an earlier Anatolian earth goddess continued while the later worship of a sun god was added. The latter became more important than Teshub, the male weather god, who was now demoted to consort of the earth goddess.

Hittite Records

Detailed records were kept in Boghazkoy of the king's conversations, of his foreign affairs, of his business dealings, of circumstances of battle, and so on (written at first in cuneiform and later in hieroglyphics). All these writings contain little to indicate that the Hittites added much to the knowledge that they absorbed from the peoples to the southeast of them in Mesopotamia. Although they fashioned a few iron blades, they did not discover the techniques involved in smelting iron; these came from an unknown people to the northeast of them in the Caucasus mountains. (The Iron Age, which arrived later, is really a misnomer. Until fairly recent times it has been difficult to generate the high temperatures necessary to smelt iron ore properly.[1] In early times only small amounts of iron could be separated from the ore, and much work was required to separate the iron from its slag impurities. Iron was used in weapons and a few tools, but it was a metal never common enough to be used extensively before the rise of the industrial age.) Although the Hittites knew how to make some iron weapons, they still lived in the Bronze Age. In the thirteenth century B.C. they would be conquered by the Phrygians, a people coming from Thrace who had learned to use iron weapons more effectively than they.

The Hittites and many of the other people living in Anatolia and northern Syria spoke Indo-European languages. They did not differ physically from the people who live in these areas in the twentieth century. They were short and stocky, with sloping foreheads, beaked noses, and rounded heads. (The invaders from Greece drove many Hittites to the southeast into Syria and Palestine, but their intermarriage with the people there could not have changed the physical character of the population very much. Large, beaked noses were Sumerian and Egyptian as well as Armenian and Persian, French and English as well as Scottish.)

Selected Bibliography

Bibby, Geoffrey, *Four Thousand Years Ago* (New York, Knopf, 1961), Chapters 11 and 18.

Davidson, Marshall B., ed., *The Horizon Book of Lost Worlds* (New York, Doubleday, 1962), pp. 296–312.

Gurney, O. R., *The Hittites* (Baltimore, Penguin, 1954).

[1] Copper melts at 1084° centigrade; iron becomes liquid only at 1529° centigrade.

Hawkes, J., and Woolley, L., *Prehistory and the Beginnings of Civilization* (New York, Harper & Row, 1963).

Lloyd, Seton, *Early Anatolia* (Baltimore, Penguin, 1956).

Mongait, A. L., *Archaeology in the USSR* (Baltimore, Penguin, 1961).

Piggott, Stuart, ed., *The Dawn of Civilization* (New York, McGraw-Hill, 1961), Chapter 6.

10

The Trading Peoples of Syria, Lebanon, and Palestine

Although the oldest continuous town in the world was Jericho in Palestine, founded in the eighth millennium B.C., the areas of Syria, Lebanon, and Palestine were subsidiary to the more important centers of civilization that developed later in Sumeria and Egypt. Although agriculture and stock raising may have been practiced here earlier than in Egypt or in Sumeria (it was from this region that the early Neolithic period may well have spread to the peoples of Anatolia), we have as of yet no written records of its inhabitants until 2,700 B.C. At this time, Egyptian sources mentioned that forty shiploads of cedar logs had been imported from the Amorite seaport of Byblos in present-day Lebanon.

The Ancient Peasant Kingdoms of the Levant

The coastal strip of Syria, Lebanon, and Palestine was undoubtedly composed of small peasant kingdoms, each containing tiny fortresses and surrounding stone walls to keep away attacks from nomadic invaders coming by way of the desert. (The Hebrews were not the first of the pastoral desert peoples to believe that the land was relatively greener and the pastures richer in the coastal strip along the seaward side of the Lebanese mountains and Jordanian hills.) The area was never rich or extensive enough to be inviting to large groups: it was mainly a narrow plain surrounded by high mountains and arid wastes. Compared with the wealth brought to agriculture by the dike-held Tigris and Euphrates rivers, or the annually overflowing Nile, or even the rampaging Indus River, the Levantine area with its narrow streams was poor in soil and inadequately watered.

Only on the Mediterranean side did timbered slopes cover the Lebanese mountains and the Judean hills. Although agriculture was more efficiently practiced in Lebanon and Palestine 4,000 years ago than it was until recently, it was still a home only for small tribes, tiny peasant-states, and seminomadic peoples. (Its religious and trading importance to the later world would be much greater than the products of its scanty mineral, forest, and agricultural resources.)

The cultural contributions from the Levantine would be based not on architectural monuments nor on technical innovations for it made few of either, but rather on the ability of its peoples to synthesize what they received from nearby sources, living as they did on the crossroads of ancient technical Primary civilizations. Although they would strive to be independent of the great powers to the south and east of them, they would be defeated time and time again, partially acculturating themselves to those who conquered them. Only the Hebrews would carry on a losing struggle to be free of foreign rule and influence (in observance of a covenant that their ancestors had made with their God). The others bowed to their fate and assimilated themselves to their numerous conquerors in a greater or lesser degree.

The Amorites and the Canaanites

At the beginning of the third millennium B.C. there were two peoples living in the Syro-Palestinian area: the Amorites, some of whose descendants would become Babylonians, Assyrians, and Hebrews; and the Canaanites, later to become the Phoenicians and the founders of Carthage. Both peoples spoke the same Semitic language, but they were influenced by different cultural exposures.

The Amorites were strongly affected by the Sumerian city-states, which had begun their development some 500 years earlier. The Canaanites assimilated themselves to influences from Egypt, which had also become a civilization in its own right a few hundred years before. The Amorite towns included the ancient cities of Byblos (which lasted until Roman days), Tyre, and Sidon—later to become famous as Phoenician seaports—and Mari on the Euphrates, which carried on an extensive trade with the Sumerian cities to the south and the Neolithic settlements to the north. (Mari had originally been a Sumerian settlement and was taken over by the Amorites.)

The importance of Byblos as a trading port goes back past 3,300 B.C. By 2,000 B.C. its trading relations with Egypt had become extremely close, and its Semitic-speaking rulers (who were possibly vassals of Egypt at this time) adopted Egyptian court protocol as well as Hamitic names and terms.

Egyptian tomb paintings of 2,000 B.C. depict the Amorites as stocky and black-bearded with hooked noses. A tomb painting of 1,900 B.C.

shows them dressed in long multicolored tunics (such as might have been made by Jacob for his son Joseph) and wearing red boots. They are shown coming into Egypt with their wives and children, leading their donkeys laden with anvils (thus indicating that they were traveling artisans or metalsmiths). The men carried harps (perhaps they were also professional musicians) as well as bows and arrows.

The Canaanites settled along the coastal strip of Lebanon and Palestine; the Amorites lived in the hills to the west. It may have been from one of the Amorite hill tribes that Abraham's father came. (One of the tribes was also known as the Habiru, whose chief, one of the Hyksos invaders of Egypt in the eighteenth century B.C., was known as Jacobher.)

The Hyksos

Sometime in the eighteenth century B.C. a mixed group of Indo-European and Semitic peoples under the name of the Hyksos, or the Shepherd Kings, invaded Egypt. Just before this century, groups of invading Indo-European-speaking horsemen (who brought an advanced metallurgy as well as the horse and an improved chariot with them) had pushed the Amorites out of their northern territory. Pressure from the invaders upon the southern Semitic nomadic tribesmen may have caused the latter to invade lower Egypt—to be followed soon after by some of the Indo-European-speaking invaders, who then formed a temporary alliance with them. Together they ruled Egypt for 100 to 200 years until about 1,570 B.C., when the Egyptians finally crushed them. This invasion may well have formed the historical basis for the Biblical account that Jacob and Joseph found favor with the rulers of Egypt and occupied high administrative positions. Whether the later Hebrews were enslaved or were merely defeated tribute-paying vassals is a matter of speculation. The weight of scholarly research leans to the latter interpretation. (Even the story of the Exodus is partially legendary, for the numbers who left Egypt could not have been very large.)

The Mixture of Populations

Many languages were spoken in this area by 2,000 B.C., and the mixture of physical types was equally pronounced. The popular imagination tends to think of Semitic-speaking peoples as representing a specific physical form, but in fact their area has been a melting pot ever since the days of Neanderthal man. The Egyptian Pharaohs, ministers, and administrators, the Sumerians, the Babylonians, and even the Hittites all had the same mixture of physical features; and most of them, if living today, could fit with ease into the various populations of the Near East. (Even the Hebrews of the first century A.D. were varied—redheads and blondes mingled with darker Mediterranean types—as is indicated by the preserved bodies of their Zealot soldiers found in 1962 in caves near the Dead Sea.)

The Indo-European-speaking invaders remained in northern Syria as Hurrians, to be superseded later on by new migrants, who referred to themselves as Mitannians and who then became the overlords of the Hurrians. In the fifteenth century B.C. Canaanites and Hurrians evidently united in battle against Egyptian forces. The population in Palestine at that time indicated a new mixture in which Amorites, Hurrians, and Canaanites predominated, with the Hurrians ruling as professional warriors. References are found in Egyptian sources of this time indicating the existence of rich trading cities along the coast of northern Palestine and southern Lebanon that had been sacked by Egyptian forces.

For a few hundred years Egypt had a protectorate over Palestine and Syria. It might have been the withdrawal of Egyptian forces in the fourteenth century B.C. that encouraged the local Amorite tribes, called the Habiru, to take over the Canaanite towns weakened by Egyptian withdrawal. In their struggles the Habiru may have been joined by kindred tribesmen, who had either been nomadic vassals to the Egyptians or who had come up from the Sinai Peninsula, bringing with them the beliefs of a new volcanic god, under the leadership of a new high priest and prophet with the Egyptian name of Moses.

The Mitannians

Little is known of the Mitannians of northern Syria, whose armies the Egyptians attempted to defeat in the fifteenth century B.C. They evidently brought with them the Indo-European gods Viruna and Indra (also worshipped by the Indo-Europeans who invaded India from Afghanistan shortly before this time). Their princesses married Egyptian Pharaohs, and Egyptian cultural influences are shown in the use of the symbol of life on Mitannian seals (though the engravings and portraitures show non-Egyptian models).

The Phoenicians and the Mitannians

The Phoenicians had developed an extensive trade with the Egyptians by the seventeenth century B.C. At this time their purple dye (from the shell-fish murex) was used on both wool and linen. Egyptian tomb paintings indicate that their ships had high prows and sterns, a large steering paddle, and wickerwork sides. Cedar from the hills of Lebanon, jars of wine, textiles of various kinds, flasks of olive oil, and cattle formed the chief cargo of the ships coming from the Phoenician trading towns to the Egyptian delta region. Egyptian paintings show the Phoenicians in purple robes and the Mitannians in white robes. The women of both groups wore flounced white skirts, and their hair hung loose. From the fifteenth century B.C. on, Phoenicians and Syrians lived in colonies as merchants and traders in Egypt, acting as factors and commission merchants. They are depicted by the Egyptians as receiving ships bulging with goods from the Levantine.

Ugarit

Although Byblos continued to remain important until the Roman era, the new port of Ugarit (Ras Shamra) in the northwestern part of Syria soon outstripped Byblos in foreign trade. Between 1,800 and 1,400 B.C. a large Cretan trading colony, with its own residential and business sections, lived at this port. After 1,400 B.C. the Mycenaeans established business and residential quarters in the immediate harbor area and in the town itself. The pottery indicated that the sea routes between Rhodes, Mycenaean Greece, and Mycenaean Crete were well traveled. Nearby Cyprus with its extensive copper deposits was also under Ugarit's control. Cyprus and Ugarit used different scripts however, and the Aegean language that was used as a trade *lingua franca* has still not been properly identified.

Ugarit remained an important port city for over 600 years. It acted as the middleman for Aegean imports destined for Mesopotamia, and for Babylonian products going to the Aegean. At the same time it carried on an extensive trade of its own with Egypt and perhaps with areas as far as the western Mediterranean. Invaders from the Aegean Sea finally destroyed this port city around 1,200 B.C. (when the Hittite Empire was also overthrown by invaders from the west). These sea invaders may have been pushed out of Anatolia and Greece by the Phrygians and other large migrating groups from the Balkans. The sea peoples may perhaps have included the Mycenaeans and the ancestors of the Sardinians, the Sicilians, and the Etruscans.

The Philistines

The Philistines were one of these invading sea peoples. They gave the name of Palestine to the fertile coastal strip that they occupied between modern-day Haifa and Gaza. They were either Mycenaeans or a related people (the Bible gave their homeland as Crete). They brought their families, oxen, chariots, and carts with them in their high-prowed boats. Their stay in Palestine coincided with the Hebrew invasion of the hilly country behind the coastal strip. By the eleventh century B.C. the two groups were engaged in combat, but by the ninth century the Hebrews had evidently assimilated the Philistines.

The Philistines brought with them the beginnings of the Iron Age. They apparently enjoyed a monopoly of iron making in the Levant (their round shields and short swords were famous even in Egypt). They seemingly manufactured iron weapons in large quantities and shipped them from their port at Haifa. It was from the Philistines that the Hebrews learned how to smelt and forge iron.

The Importance of the Phoenicians

Despite the incursions of the sea peoples, the port cities of the Canaanites continued to trade their textiles, vases, and timber for food, metals, and slaves. After 1,200 B.C. Sidon and Tyre became important trading cities from which high-prowed, large-masted boats sailed in all directions to seek goods that were not produced in Canaan, and to give in return those goods that others could not make as skillfully themselves. The Phoenicians were originally Canaanites, although their name is of Mycenaean origin. After being defeated by the Hebrew invaders, they may have moved to their port cities of Tyre and Sidon, there to engage in manufactures and trade. Later they became famous as colonists in North Africa, Sicily, Spain, southern France, and Sardinia.

The Phoenicians as Colonizers

The Phoenicians as traders and craftsmen were second to none, and their colonization efforts were on only a slightly lesser scale than those of the mainland Greeks. The Phoenicians founded Carthage in the eighth century B.C., controlled Gibraltar by the sixth century B.C., and established trading posts along the North African coast and even sailed around Africa in the same century. (Carthaginian coins of the fifth century B.C. have been found in the Azores.) An extensive fishing industry was carried on in the Atlantic and the fish cured, salted, and dried for export in the North African ports. The British Cornish coast was known as a source of tin and other metals, as were the coasts of France, Spain, and even Scandinavia.

The Phoenicians (whose ports in Lebanon were destroyed by the Assyrian military invaders in the seventh century B.C.) used their small colonial population sparingly and efficiently. The colonies were composed of small groups of Phoenicians who usually settled among larger numbers of local residents, intermarried with them, assumed local leadership in matters of trade and industry, and soon influenced larger numbers than would have been possible if the settlements had been entirely Phoenician in origin. Even Carthage was more Berber than Phoenician, although its population would refer to themselves later as "Canaanites." Its oligarchic form of government was Berber in origin rather than Palestinian.

The Phoenician colonies were wealthy because their trade was based upon their extensive cottage industries. In certain fields the Phoenicians excelled all others, being improvers of the techniques that they had taken over from peoples more advanced than they. The Phoenician navy was large, as was Carthage's later, but the merchant-princes had little use for war. War only interfered with profits and produced liabilities. It was the small intermixed warrior class in Carthage that later brought about war with Rome: the Carthaginian merchants wanted only peace. Despite the expense of the Carthaginian mercenaries, the large navy, and the many forts, the merchants were able to pay their huge indemnity with little effort when Carthage was defeated by Rome. Unfortunately this was not enough to save them later from complete destruction at the hands of their Roman conquerors.

The Phoenicians were great diffusers of techniques. From the thirteenth century B.C. onward they spread the arts and crafts of Egypt and Mesopotamia to the western Mediterranean, and perhaps to the Atlantic coast of Europe. They were explorers and adventurers; but their greatest gift to later civilization lay not in their techniques or crafts but in the phonetic alphabet that they received from the other Canaanites, which had been derived from settlers along the Sinai peninsula where Egyptian hieroglyphic consonantal symbols were used sometime before the seventeenth century B.C.

The Alphabet

Writing goes back to the Sumerians, who first used pictographic symbols and who, by about 3,000 B.C., had changed the system into a phonetic syllabary. Egyptian hieroglyphics followed, with modifications into a script that allowed phonetic value to be given to initial consonants of words. The early Canaanites added new letters to those received from the Egyptians, but they now gave each consonant a separate symbolic value. The Phoenicians took over this phonetic alphabet by the twelfth century B.C. and diffused it to the early Greeks after the ninth century B.C. The Greeks took over the Semitic names for the symbols, modified them to fit the Greek system of sounds, and then referred to them as Alpha, Beta, Gamma, Delta, and so on. The Greek word "alphabet" then comes from the AB, or Aleph and Beth of Canaanite (which was similar in its spoken usage to the ancient Hebrew). The Aramaic, or later Semitic, alphabet spread eastward subsequently and influenced the growth of the various alphabets in India and southeastern Asia.

The Greeks passed their alphabet on to the Etruscans with new symbols for the vowels, which the Semitic writers (marking only consonants) did not use. The Etruscans in turn passed the alphabet on to the Romans, who modified the Greek letters. Western, or Roman, Christianity diffused it to western and northwestern Europe. Later on, the missionaries of Eastern, or Orthodox, Christianity, centered in Byzantium, would bring their modified Greek, or Cyrillic, alphabet to the Russians, Bulgarians, and Serbians.

The Influence of the Levant

The Levant occupies an important place in history. Many of the Greek philosophers came from the Syro-Lebanese area. The trading activities of the people were highly organized, and they influenced their neighbors as much as the latter influenced them. (For example, the Philistines aided the Hebrews in organizing their kingdom, while the Temple at Jerusalem was built by Phoenician architects and craftsmen. Even Solomon's trade with the western Mediterranean and the east coast of Africa from Elath was carried on with Phoenician help. The Phoenicians may well have used Hebrews as colonists in North Africa, Spain, and other areas, or may in later days have practiced Judaism in religion themselves.) They intermarried, assimilated, and influenced their neighbors: the term Phoenician was an all-inclusive one. To the Greeks and the peoples of Malta, Sicily, Sardinia, Spain, Morocco, and Tunisia, all peoples from the Levant or their descendants were referred to as Canaanites or Phoenicians.

But the Levantine civilization, like others we have already described, was not run for the benefit of the peasant or the poor. Rights and privileges went to those who could afford to purchase them. Class was based upon wealth and family. Slavery existed, although slaves were by law considered to be human beings as well as property and were often treated considerately. Male slaves were freed after seven years; female slaves could be kept for life, though children were freed if their mothers were kept as concubines.

Summary

Phoenician arts and crafts were influenced by Egypt and Mesopotamia. Unlike the Hebrews and the later Greeks, their literature and their philosophy would not affect other peoples, although perhaps both the Hebrews and the Greeks may have borrowed from the Canaanites. The

Hebrews were biased against the Canaanites, considering them an amoral people with their infant sacrifice, worship of gods and goddesses of fortune, and preoccupation with amassing property. The Phoenicians, however, survived as long as any of the other ancient peoples: their influential time span covered 1,000 years, from the thirteenth century to the second century B.C., when Carthage (now Berber) was completely destroyed by the Romans. For more than 500 years, however, Carthage was a great naval and colonial power in the Mediterranean, and its inhabitants were perhaps one of the wealthiest of the early merchant peoples. Only the Greek city-states were colonizers on a wider scale, but even they were no greater explorers or adventurers (and this takes into account the Macedonian invasion of Bactria, and the influences of Greek traders in India and southeastern Asia at an early date).

Selected Bibliography

Albright, W. F., *The Archaeology of Palestine* (Baltimore, Penguin, 1960).

Childe, V. Gordon, *New Light on the Most Ancient East* (New York, Praeger, 1953).

Coon, Carleton S., *Caravan: The Story of the Middle East* (New York, Holt, Rinehart and Winston, 1958).

Frankfort, Henri, *The Birth of Civilization in the Near East* (Garden City, N.Y., Doubleday, Anchor Books, 1956).

——, *Before Philosophy: The Intellectual Adventure of Ancient Man* (Baltimore, Penguin, 1959).

Harden, Donald, *The Phoenicians* (New York, Praeger, 1962).

Kenyon, K. M., *Archaeology in the Holy Land* (New York, Praeger, 1960).

Piggott, Stuart, ed., *The Dawn of Civilization* (New York, McGraw-Hill, 1961), Chapter 5.

11

New Ideas and Chinese Primary Civilization

Thousands of miles to the east of the Levant, in the great plain of northern China, along the loess-covered Yellow River valley, a Neolithic way of life with Mesopotamian origins came into existence after 4,000 B.C. Within a thousand years the entire Central Plain was occupied by a peasant people who lived in large villages, made serviceable black and painted pottery, worshipped ancestral spirits in small shrines, but still cultivated their lands primitively with stone and bone tools and wooden digging sticks. The peasants grew millet and barley and kept some sheep and cattle, although they preferred the pig. They augmented the diet provided by their skimpy crops with pork and with game and fish that they were able to find outside of their crowded villages. The villages were large and were dotted by small, rectangular or round thatched huts with walls of clay. (Later the houses would be shaped like beehives and made of mudbrick.)

Until the middle of the second millennium B.C. a visitor to the Central Plain would have seen a fairly simple peasant people living in largely undefended settlements and possessing a modest technology. By 1,000 B.C. moats would surround many of the villages, and the nearby land would be irrigated to grow wet rice. But further to the south, the Neolithic period continued until well into the Christian era. In the mountainous areas to the southwest the age would continue even to the twentieth century.

The invading peoples who brought agriculture and domesticated animals with them from central Asia must have been few. It was their ideas rather than their numbers that transformed the hunting and fishing population of the Yellow River valley from a Mesolithic to a Neolithic people. As in Europe agriculturists may have settled in the midst of hunting people. This is especially likely since the loess soil of the Yellow River was

exceptionally fertile. Over a period of centuries the agriculturists intermarried with the hunters and encouraged them to combine agriculture
and stock raising with their hunting and fishing. Millet, barley, sheep,
and cattle may have come with nomads from the west; rice and the pig
came from an area to the southeast.

Neolithic Family Life

The Chinese villages at this time were larger than those existing in Mesopotamia or Europe during their early Neolithic periods. The large size of
the villages may have resulted from a custom of keeping relatives together
and not allowing the young to start new satellite settlements. The avail-
ability of labor in these villages may have encouraged the cultivation of
rice, which requires a great deal of intensive labor both when grown on
dry soil and when raised in wet paddies. On the other hand, the growth
of population made irrigation and the planting of rice in wet fields a
necessity, since the quantity of food could thereby be greatly increased.

Family ties were close at this time, and the ancestral spirits must
have played an important role in the religious life of the villagers. The
dead were buried with pots of food and with stone tools that they had
used during their lives.

The Rise of the Shang Dynasty (1,700–1,100 B.C.)

At some time after 1,700 B.C. the first of the early Chinese peasant kingdoms arose in the Central Plain along the Yellow River. (Evidently the
concept of a kingdom also came from the West.) The peasant kings received the name of Shang, the first dynasty of kings to rule northern
China. The ruling class was composed of the king, a small number of
warrior-nobles living with him, a larger number of nobles living away
from the court (but holding a number of villages with peasants as compensation for the warriors they had supplied the king), and a small number of priests, who advised the king as soothsayers or as interpreters of the
will of the gods.

The influence of the Shang peasant kings was restricted to the villages in the immediate area of their fortified and walled-in seats of power.
The king was evidently considered the first among equals by his nobles,
who owed him the loyalty given by a warrior to his chieftain.

There was little change in the landscape of northern China as a result of the establishment of the king-warriors. A few artisans were employed at the court to supply goods and services for the king and his
nobles. The peasants tilled their lands as they did before the arrival of

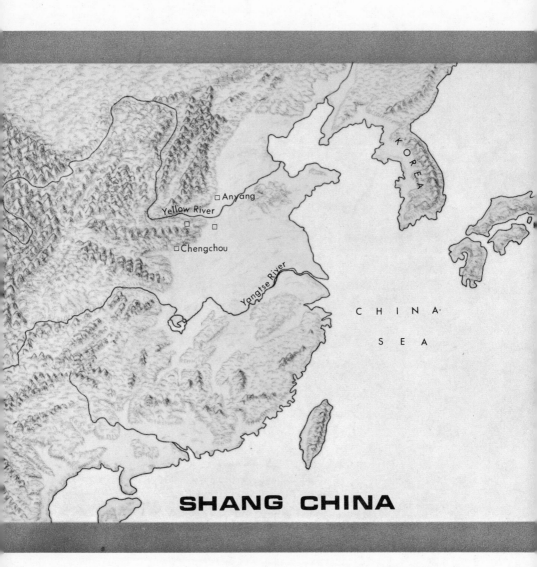

□ Anyang

Yellow River

□   □

□ Chengchou

Yangtse River

KOREA

CHINA

SEA

SHANG CHINA

the Shangs, but now they had to labor more intensively to supply the nobles and their officials with their share of crops, animals, and labor. The peasants were considered to be in the service of the nobles and king and had no rights that the latter needed to respect, although some sort of understanding existed at the court as to how far the officials of the king or the nobles could go in taxing the surplus products of the peasants. The peasants also had to supply conscripted soldiers and concubines for the nobles from among their extra sons and daughters. The artisans, entertainers, and priests also came out of the peasant ranks to supply the needs of the court and the regional nobles.

Whatever innovations came into China rebounded to the benefit of the king and his nobles. The peasants would use stone tools until well into the Christian era. Their lot would remain hard for thousands of years. They could turn only to the chief in their village for a sense of security. Although the kings would come and go, their demands would remain the same—sometimes increasing but never decreasing in number. The peasant would come under the rule of the king's officials, who would insist upon an ever-expanding share of his substance. Warfare, disease, hunger, and natural catastrophes would make his hard lot seem normal. He could only pray to his ancestral spirits that he would be permitted to work in peace, that he would be the father of sons who would carry on his name and make offerings to his spirit, and that he would take his place with his ancestors when he died. The peasant had to learn to be sly, to think only of himself and his descendants, and to place his faith in his own chief to help him when bad fortune struck. He learned to take his fate apathetically, but he remained suspicious of all who were not closely related to him. He assumed that all men, sometimes including his relatives, would take advantage of him if they could. The peasant in China was the low man on the totem pole, as he would be in Japan, India, and Europe until the twentieth century of the Christian era. Chinese civilization was for the benefit of those who controlled its political organization, not for the villager and his numerous progeny.

The Chinese Aspects of Shang Primary Civilization

The forms of Shang civilization were definitely Chinese in origin; but its ideas evidently came, within a time sequence of a few centuries, from Mesopotamia via the nomads of central Asia. Although the Chinese learned to make superb bronze castings only a short time after bronze castings came to them from the West, their workmanship and artistry soon surpassed those of the Mediterranean world at that period. The concept of pictographic writing soon developed into symbolic representation in the keeping of records. The horse and the chariot both came from the nomads of central Asia, but the Chinese chariot was lighter in weight than those used farther to the west. Like the Sumerians and the peasant kings of Anatolia, the Shang kings were buried with large numbers of slain prisoners of war, horses, and chariots so that all three could be at the service of the kings when they went hunting or warring in the spirit world. (Silk, a Chinese invention, was also known to the Shang kings.)

Government by Oracle

The administrative decisions (in fact all decisions, including whether or not the king should go hunting on a certain day) were in the hands of blind chance rather than in the realm of precedent or of past experience of the elders. All the king's decisions were based upon the size of cracks that appeared in the shoulder bones of animals when the bones were heated by the priestly soothsayers. The latter then translated the size of the cracks into "yes," "no," or "maybe" answers for the king. (The pseudo-certainty of astrology, numerology, and the oracles of Greece—as well as the chicken-liver readings of the Romans—were on as rational a level as the Chinese shoulder-bone rite. All these human strivings for certainty made the same wrong assumptions and had the same mistaken premises, using nonrelated causes for understanding seemingly causal effects.)

The Chou Dynasty (1,100–200 B.C.)

The Shang warrior-king dynasty was finally overthrown by the stronger Chou clan of warrior-kings around 1,100 B.C. Throughout most of man's political civilizations, the adage that the spoils and power belong to the man strong enough to take them remained a rule of conduct for the hunter-turned-warrior. The Chou followed this axiom, as would those who in their turn overthrew them. Early kings governed because they were trained not only as warriors but also as hunters of men and animals: hunting and fighting have been the twin pastimes of the king and noble all the way down to the twentieth century.

The Chou came from the neighboring areas of Shensi and Shansi (southwest of Peking). They learned much from the Shang kings; when they became powerful enough, they overthrew the last Shang king and assumed suzerainty over the Shang domain. To reward their military commanders, they gave each a fief of large tracts of land and dozens of villages. Each noble was also encouraged to build a fortified center on his land. The younger men were motivated to conquer the villages to the south and thus to receive their conquests as fiefs from the Chou kings. Feudalism was introduced to all of China, which now became the realm of the Chou kings.

Five classes of warrior-nobles were introduced. Obedience, loyalty, and tributary gift-giving moved upward from the bottom through the gradations of rank to the king on top. (All three factors would remain in the later Mandarin system of administration as the means for ingratiating oneself with one's immediate superior. The tribute moved upward while the plums of advancement were the rewards that moved downward to those who knew how to play this game.)

As more and more fiefs were created throughout China, the nobles stepped up their intrigues to cut down the power of the Chou kings. Some of the nobles even began to see themselves as possible rivals to the kings. To prevent the nobles from joining forces against the king, some of the most important among them were compelled to spend time at the king's court where their activities could be watched by the king's men and their families could be held as temporary hostages. There were too many nobles to watch, however; and soon feudalism divided the Chou kingdom into nine independent states, each headed by a feudal prince who considered himself absolute within his domain. From the eighth to the second century B.C. feudalism ruled supreme; but it was finally overthrown after the Chous and their successors, the Ch'ins, had disappeared from Chinese history with the arrival of a new dynasty, the Hans.

The Hierarchy of Privileges

Under Chinese feudalism the peasant represented only a type of property. He came with the land; and if the troops of a neighboring noble fought his overlord and won, he could be enslaved as part of the spoils and could thus be bought and sold like a domesticated animal. The artisans and merchants were ranked above the peasants but socially were considered little better than they. (Their lives and property were also subject to the momentary whims of their overlords.) Above these were the scribes, the administrators, the educated gentry, the lesser nobility (who were generally military assistants to the higher nobility), the chief nobles at the court, and the king and his immediate family. The merchant was not permitted to carry on trade freely, nor could the artisan go into business for himself. Trade, the making of salt, the manufacture of metal tools and weapons, the creation of bronze and jewel ornaments of all kinds, were monopolies belonging to the feudal princes and the king.

The prerogatives of the nobility and the administrators came directly from Heaven (a deity) through the medium of the king, who was the son of Heaven. He was the priestly intermediary between the mortal world of birth and death and the immortal world of deities and spirits. His mandate to rule came directly from Heaven; but if that deity was irritated with him or discontented with his rule, it could remove its protection and support. Thus, if the king was overthrown by his nobles, by conquering invaders, or by revolting peasants, this was a clear indication from Heaven that his mandate to rule had been revoked and that no subject owed him any further loyalty.

Filial Loyalty and the Status Structure

The king, as the son of Heaven, owed that deity complete obedience, filial piety, and loyalty. Similarly, all those beneath the king owed him the same filial obligations (unless his mandate to rule them had been revoked). Every official was thus in the position of a father to his inferiors. They in turn played the same role to those beneath them, all the way down to the peasants, who could expect the same filial obligations from their children. (The latter would have to wait until their parenthood for the same privileges.)

Society and the state were considered by the Chinese philosophers of the Chou period to be extensions of the family, which meant that fathers in an actual or a symbolic sense had to learn to be benign, considerate, and helpful to their children and to their subjects. The children and subjects repaid their obligations by obeying the rulings of the fathers, even dying for them if so ordered. The good son was the obedient one; the good father was the one who permitted his son to participate in those decisions that concerned him.

Family life entailed duties as well as privileges; and, in extension, social and governmental activities did also. One had obligations toward his kin, and the obligations were mutual. The Chinese philosophers accepted the hierarchy of statuses that existed in China during the Chou dynasty and reinforced them by creating new roles—in the form of expected behavior. It is not necessary to point out that these ethical codes became the basis for *expected* rather than *actual* behavior. Few Chinese mandarins (or scholar-administrators) behaved toward their subjects as the ancient Chinese moralists hoped they would.

Chinese Culture from the Fifth to the Second Century B.C.

Chinese technology became more complex toward the end of the Chou dynasty. By the fifth century B.C. tile roofing and iron had been brought from the West by Turkish and Mongol nomads. The Great Wall, extending 1,400 miles and including 2,500 towers (manned with a garrison of soldiers in each), stretched along the northwest border of the Chou kingdom and kept out the marauding Mongols, Huns, Turks, and Tartars, who sensed the treasures that could be theirs if they had the power to take them. (This Great Wall, as monumental in its way as the pyramids of Egypt or the roads, viaducts, and bridges of Rome, was built in the third century B.C.) Iron was cast, as it would not be in Europe until the fourteenth century A.D. A great invention, the crossbow with its triggering mechanism, gave the force of bullets to the metal points (first bronze and later iron) it fired. In warfare, the conscripted army was developed; and the noble with his retainers riding to battle in their wickerwork chariots came to an end. (The chariot was used only as transportation: it was not employed as the tank was in the twentieth century.)

In the meanwhile, art forms became more complex. Governmental workshops made lacquered objects of all kinds and created bronzeware and pottery for the use of the king, his retainers, family, and nobles. Until the third century B.C. agriculture and irrigation had gradually been spreading southward. At that time, the Chou dynasty was overthrown by the short-lived Ch'in, but by then agriculture had covered almost all of eastern and southern China. The Ch'in king was soon overthrown by the Han dynasty, which ruled China until the third century A.D. During the latter period, the complexity of technology was furthered by the work of craftsmen. For example, the piston bellow (evidently received from the south, where it was used to make fire) was improved to create a high enough temperature for the smelting of iron. Although the nobles until the third century B.C. had preferred bronze for their weapons, iron casting was reaching new heights during this entire period. Iron was used to line the peasant's tools and to make new weapons of war. The forging of iron came into use after the casting process had been discovered. (It was to be just the opposite in Europe where forging came into use first, to be followed almost 2,000 years later by casting.)

The End of Chinese Feudalism

As soon as the Han dynasty had stabilized its power, it set about destroying the institution of feudalism. To insure the loyalty of the peasants to the king and to destroy the economic power of the nobles, the lands were taken away from the feudal lords and sold to the peasants. New classes of administrators, owing loyalty only to the king, were instituted through a series of graduated examinations. These administrators dispensed justice and collected taxes, although the law they administered was the king's law and the taxes were used to multiply the administrators, warriors, and services for the king.

The new scholar-administrators could raise their own rank only by supplying their superiors with tributary gifts, which meant that as time went on the taxes became harsher and heavier. The need to squeeze those beneath in order to supply superiors with liberal favors meant that each administrative office came to be regarded as spoils. Honesty in such a bureaucratic setup was not rewarded but punished: the honest administrator remained at his lowly level for the rest of his working life, and his family suffered in consequence.

By the destruction of feudal rule the king gained loyalty, but his administration was neither more efficient nor more considerate of the lowly peasant and the artisan. Despite the teachings of Confucius, Mencius, and Lao Tze, the peasant was squeezed of what little he had—unless his family and he were strong enough to squeeze others less fortunate than they and thus be able to give the proper gifts to the district administrators for the privilege of being left alone. For special favors, one had to pay high tribute.

The Stability of Chinese Civilization

By the second century A.D. (toward the end of the Han dynasty), Chinese Primary civilization had become stabilized. The earlier pictographic writing had now become highly stylized and more abstract. Under the control of the Han kings, trade began to grow. Silk moved along the famous Silk Road to Persia and Rome, while Chinese ships began to trade with Korea, Japan, and southeastern Asia. Roman ships entered the various ports of southern China to trade for silks, spices, and rare jewels. Buddhism as a new religion had already come into China from India via southeastern Asia and Tibet. But it would be a different religion than that envisaged by its founder, who saw it as a nontheistic means of reforming Hinduism by ridding it of its castes and rituals. Buddhism, its founder having by now become deified, would change even more when it crossed into Japan. There it would become a religion concerned with guaranteeing a mortal a place in heaven after death.

The kings, their courtiers, and the mandarins would find their way of life comfortable. Learning and literacy would be for the benefit of the few, and calligraphy would be the mark of the leisured gentleman who dabbled in the arts and in literature. The villagers would remain, however, almost 100 percent illiterate.

Chinese Primary civilization was based upon having more than 90 percent of the population, who lived in crowded mud-brick villages, grow the food, perform the communal labor services, and supply the administrative and ruling groups with their surplus sons and daughters as servants, soldiers, and concubines. As long as this civilization maintained its basis for existence upon making life easier for those with wealth and power, it would not advance much further. The few on top were content with having the great majority of the population devote their lives to growing their food, making their silk, building their houses, and supplying them with the services that made possible their lives of leisure and comfort. Since the few had all they needed, they saw no reasons for change. Since there was enough labor available, there was no inducement to improve technology to make labor more efficient and productive. It was considered natural for famines to come and go, so there was no inspiration to introduce a more efficient system of dikes and dams to keep the raging floodwaters in check, nor to seek a more efficient system of transportation than the sampan, raft, or human back. It was a self-centered civilization for those who ran it; and they saw no need to concern themselves with improving the lot of the peasants, artisans, or servants. Since advancement was based upon traditional means of examinations and paying the proper tribute to those on top, there was no room for the social innovator. Nor would he have been welcomed by the mandarins, who would see him as one who would destroy their sense of security. Chinese civilization could only follow its past patterns. It could not change them, for there was no receptivity to change.

Until the nineteenth century, then, tradition would continue to be all-important: the sanctions of Chinese society would be used to keep dissent and dissenters at a minimum. Despite later conquests by the Mongols and the Manchus, the hierarchal way of Chinese life, which had become stabilized by the beginning of the Christian era, would crumble only 1,800 years later, when new and stronger nomads with a technologically superior civilization arrived from the West to batter down both the front and rear doors of China. And this time there would be no huge walls manned by competent soldiers to keep them out. Unlike the previous nomads, the new ones would bring revolutionary religions with them that in time would destroy the cultural supports of traditional Chinese society. A new system of education in Western values and technologies would make the Chinese trained in its ways even more receptive to a new type of organizing civilization, which would bring in its wake a more efficient political organization (totalitarian in its methods) and a more highly developed technology. Chinese Primary civilization on its deathbed would no longer be able to cope with these new and more effective agents of revolutionary change.

Selected Bibliography

Coon, Carleton S., *The Story of Man* (New York, Knopf, 1955), pp. 326–337.

Cottrell, Leonard, *The Tiger of Ch'in* (New York, Holt, Rinehart and Winston, 1962).

Fairbank, John K., ed., *Chinese Thought and Institutions* (Chicago, University of Chicago Press, 1957).

Granet, Marcel, *Chinese Civilization* (Cleveland, World Publishing, Meridian Books, 1958).

Goodrich, L. C., *A Short History of the Chinese People* (New York, Harper & Row, 1959).

Linton, Ralph, *The Tree of Culture* (New York, Knopf, 1955), Chapters 36, 37, and 38.

Needham, Joseph, *Science and Civilization in China* (London, Cambridge University Press, 1956).

Piggott, Stuart, ed., *The Dawn of Civilization* (New York, McGraw-Hill, 1961).

Reischauer, E. O., and Fairbank, John K., *East Asia: The Great Tradition* (Boston, Houghton Mifflin, 1960).

12

The Final Phases
of Primary Civilization

Hypothetical anthropological visitors from outer space ten thousand years ago would have reported that on Earth they had found only isolated groups of hunters living with their families in small bands, each having a roughly defined territory in which to roam. The decorative arts were highly developed in cave murals, in ivory carvings, and in various forms of clay and stone. Tools were made of chipped flint, obsidian, or stone. The simple bow and arrow, the spear, the harpoon, the flint knife, and many other tools were known.

If any metals were known at that time, they were used infrequently, for they had to be found in almost pure form in order to be utilized. No pottery was burnt, no bricks made, and no stone blocks cut. There was no agriculture, and fishing was still in an elementary stage. Men lived in tents made of skins or in underground thatch houses. (The log roof and house would depend on the future invention of the ax, although some trees could be cut slowly with the burin or the stone chisel.)

If our scientific visitors from outer space returned 2,000 years ago, they would have seen great changes. Cities now dotted the area around the Mediterranean, the Aegean, and the Black seas. Some of the cities, such as Alexandria and Rome, had as many as 500,000 inhabitants. Large municipal buildings and temples were made of stone. Streets were lined with two- and three-story houses (in Rome, slum tenements were as high as eight stories) and were paved with cobbles or flagstones. They led to large squares, on which monumental triumphal arches, temples, baths, or even palaces were located.

The Development of Trade to Northern Europe

About 4,000 years ago trade had been moving steadily from the Mediterranean through the English Channel to the shores of the North and Baltic

117

seas. Cretan, Mycenaean, and Phoenician traders in their small single-masted ships had been welcomed by the various coastal tribes. They brought with them ornaments of all kinds; leather boots lined in wool; smooth-textured dresses and skirts embroidered in bright blues, greens, and reds for the wives and daughters of the chieftains; fine woolen tunics that were warm in winter and more comfortable than leather or fur; purple linen cloaks for the chiefs; and jewelry, glassware, wines, oils, cosmetics, and other luxuries. They also provided directions on how to make objects that these tribes had never made or seen before.

Around 1,800 B.C. various unknown traders from the Mediterranean (Mycenaeans from Greece perhaps) might have taught the tribes in Britain and northern France how to build huge stone altars to the sun. They could have shown them where and how stone could be quarried, told them how the people of the eastern Mediterranean had transported their huge megaliths by boat, raft, sled, or even rollers, and perhaps shown them how to place these huge stones in a circle so that on the first day of summer, when the sun was at its height, one could sacrifice and pray to it. Both the sun and moon could be seen at various stages through the openings. Thus it was possible to ensure the continued goodwill of these sun-moon deities for the tribes who cooperated in this great work. (The remains of one monument to ancient human labor is Stonehenge in England.)

Traders and migrating peoples from Spain and the Balkans also brought the techniques of bronze casting to the tribes of France, Belgium, Holland, and Germany. One neighbor told another; and soon many different people were making bronze cups, bronze vessels, and other bronze containers. The smiths of these tribes might have learned their trade from their fathers, who perhaps had come from distant areas, married local women, and fathered sons to whom they taught these trades.

The goods of trade were intended almost entirely for the chiefs and their retinue. They were not for the peasants, whom the chieftains and warriors considered a different race of men, too weak and cowardly to become strong, brave fighters like themselves. Some of the peasants were free, and some were thralls who tilled the lands and herded the cattle, sheep, goats, and pigs for the chieftain and his warriors. Most of the European tribes were divided socially into the ranks of chiefs, warrior-nobles, serfs, and slaves captured on various hunting raids. (To the hunter there was little difference whether the quarry was a four-legged or a two-legged animal: he who could not defend himself deserved the fate of being hunted down.)

In earlier times traders had also gone through the Aegean into the Black Sea from Crete and other islands, and from Troy and the coastal areas of Anatolia. They carried with them bronze battle-axes, spears, arrow points, textiles, beads, jewelry, and other goods. Some of the traders went up the Danube by boat, perhaps encouraging the tribesmen living there to want the treasures that they brought. The tribesmen might have been afraid to molest the traders lest no more treasures come to them. So they did the next best thing: they followed the traders to their homelands and took over their treasures and skilled labor. This may have been the way in which the Phrygians (who moved into Anatolia after defeating the Hittites), the Dorians (who came into Greece, supplanting the Mycenaeans but retaining their language), and the Celts (who came into central Europe at about the same time) began their migrations.

Other Trojans, Cretans, and Mycenaeans moved into the Black Sea to trade with the tribes along the coast, who acted as middlemen for tribes further to the north. The trade consisted of bronze weapons, jars of wine for the chiefs, olive oil for anointing and cooking purposes, jewels, and fine textiles of linen and wool. Soon some of the artisan-traders remained permanently along the coast. Perhaps the chiefs had offered them wives and special privileges; or they might have settled on tribal land that had been given to them and brought their wives and children from their homelands.

Soon chieftains and their retinues from tribes living hundreds of miles to the north were perhaps fashioning large dugouts from tall trees with their bronze axes, putting their horses into the dugouts with them (the horse had only recently been introduced from tribes to the east), and riding the current of the rivers leading to the Black Sea. On the way, they might have stopped at various settlements of primitive peasants to demand tributes in grains, furs, and ores in order to have something to trade when they reached the mouths of the rivers, the home base of the traders.

At the trading center the chiefs and their warriors could have drunk a good deal of wine, perhaps boasting of their prowess and picking fights with their closest companions. (The trader and his retinue were undoubtedly "off-limits" since, if attacked, he might not welcome them again.) They then returned to their tribes with new weapons, woolens, cleverly fashioned crowns, diadems, and bronze drinking cups.

In such a manner the technology that had been molded by the earliest civilizations reached peripheries thousands of miles away. Barbaric Europe was becoming more receptive to the improved techniques, weapons, ornaments, and other goods that came from the traders. The chiefs and their leading men began to welcome civilization in its guise of better weapons, clothing, and luxuries. With the material goods, they would also import new ideas about warfare, political organization, and religion.

The Spread of Primary Civilization

In other parts of the world, civilization was spreading its thin veneer of fairly durable paint. The Babylonians would reign supreme in Mesopotamia until defeated by the Mittanians. The Assyrians would have a quick rise to fame and, in a bloodbath, organize a totalitarian empire. Their kings would boast that they had conquered the world and had found no equal in fighting ability. But they too would soon lose their fighting youth; and their empire would be taken over by the Medes and Persians, who built even larger empires of their own on the bodies of their dead warriors.

The Persians

The Persians would influence the great religions of the world with their belief that man was put on earth to follow either the god of light or the god of darkness (or the sun fighting its enemy, the night, to arise each morning anew). This belief in different guise would influence Judaism, Christianity, and Islam. The techniques of political and military organization and of new craftsmanship would influence the tribes to the north and east of the Persians and would bring even new migrations of nomads into Persia during the closing centuries of the pre-Christian era.

Further to the east, both India and China would spread their concepts of elementary civilization to southeastern Asia, Korea, Japan, and the Philippines.

The New World

Still further east, across the Pacific, two centers of civilization were beginning to appear. The first center was in the Petan region of Guatemala, where a great priestly civilization was in the process of forming (in which the yearly calendar would have a great ceremonial and religious importance). The zero, unknown in the classic world of the Mediterranean, would be invented here and perhaps brought back to India by way of the Atlantic or around Africa by Malayan, Indian, or Chinese sailors. (The zero may have been invented independently in India during the sixth century of the Christian era and brought into the Moslem countries during the tenth century, and later into Europe.)

The second center included two small civilizations further to the south, at the beginning of the Christian era. The Mochicas along the Peruvian coast advanced technology with their finely woven textiles of cotton, pottery painted with realistic faces, roads, stone buildings, and complex political and military organizations. (They had no writing.) The Paracas further to the south created an intricate class civilization.

These two New World civilizations would grow and be taken over by others; but their technology, art, and religious forms would spread thousands of miles to the north and south. Civilization in its early forms was almost indestructible in its ideas.

The Empires of the Mediterranean

If we had crossed the continent of the New World and the Atlantic 2,000 years ago, we would have passed beside the Azores, which had been known by various trading peoples for hundreds of years but which had no permanent settlements. (Some Phoenician traders even left some Carthaginian coins there a few hundred years before.) The great civilization of Carthage had been destroyed by the Romans 150 years earlier. By the second century B.C. the Romans had also destroyed the political power of the Greeks, who had defeated the Mycenaeans a thousand years before.

An Anatolian pirate people (to be known later as the Etruscans), who had been evicted from their homeland by invaders from the Balkans and had made a comfortable living raiding Mycenaean and Phoenician ships, settled during the ninth century B.C. among the peasants of middle Italy, whom they had conquered and made their serfs. The Etruscans absorbed much from the Greek colonies in southern Italy and Sicily, which had been founded after the eighth century B.C. (and which later became even richer than the Greek mother cities from which their first settlers had come). The Etruscans spoke a language that seemed to be unrelated to any other known speech, but their phonetic alphabet was adopted from Greek (which in turn, you will remember, was borrowed from the Phoenicians). The Etruscans learned to write epic poetry, to make complex sculptured forms, and to create tombs or houses for their dead. They developed a civilization that stretched from northern Italy to the Greek city-states in the south (these autonomous city-states were never united in a kingdom or empire) and built up a luxurious way of life for the few nobles and merchants.

The peasants in the Etruscan areas evidently had little to say about even those decisions that concerned them directly. It was as peasant-warrior vassals that the community of Rome got started under the protection of the nearby Etruscan kings. But it was as landlord-warriors that the Romans overthrew their Etruscan overlords in the fifth century B.C.

From 700 to 500 B.C. the Etruscans were masters of Italy, warriors of note, traders, craftsmen, and sailors. Even Rome was built into a city under the direction of the Etruscans. They were allies of the Phoenicians against the Greeks in southern Italy and later of the Carthaginians against the Romans. But over the centuries they lost out to the Romans, who were fewer in number but had greater support from their subject villages than the ruling Etruscans were able to command from theirs. From the eighth to the third century B.C. Etruscan influence upon Rome was enormous. It was from the Etruscans (as well as from the Greeks) that the Romans learned to become empire builders and political civilizers.

The Greeks and Romans

From the eighth century B.C. onward, the various small Greek city-states learned to survive in the Mediterranean world of trading and warring peoples. They had taken over the Phoenician alphabet and a world of gods and goddesses from the peoples who surrounded them. (Even the home of Zeus had originally been in Crete before it was moved by the Greeks to Mount Olympus.) Their architecture had been taken from the civilizations that preceded them, although they modified and improved much of what they took. (The column was to play as important a role in Greek as in Egyptian and Cretan architecture.) Even the tiles that they used to roof their important buildings had been invented more than a thousand years earlier. Their literature was indigenous, but they took much from other peoples' legends, myths, and stories. Their mathematics and elementary mechanical principles had come to them from Sumeria by way of Egypt and Babylonia.

The Greeks learned a great deal about urban planning from the Babylonians, who were especially talented as city planners. (The latter built their cities with sewage drains, paved roads, viaducts, and piped water.) Although Athens is considered to have been the center of Greek civilization, much of Greek philosophy, mathematics, political thought, drama, art, and literature came from the Greek cities in Asia Minor, southern Italy, and Sicily. By the third century B.C. cosmopolitan Alexandria in Egypt had become a great center of Greek learning; and contributions were made by Lydians, Phrygians, Egyptians, Syrians, and Hebrews as well as by Greeks.

In Athens, a few thousand citizens with wealth and leisure—out of a total of 42,000 Athenians—attended the academies at the various street corners or lolled around to talk, discuss, and argue. But they could have the leisure to do so only because over 300,000 slaves supported them with labor, goods, and services. Another 30,000 foreigners without citizenship were employed at making wine jars, textiles, metals, and other articles and trading them for the grain and imported foods that permitted Athens to exist. Although Athens talked of democracy, in practice it was an oligarchy in which only the few Athenians who were citizens were equal to one another. The foreigners and slaves, who were in the majority, had no rights of citizenship. Even at its height, during the Golden Age of the fifth and fourth centuries B.C., Athens and Greece were poor. Their existence depended on trade and the substance received from their daughter colonies. Most Athenians ate only one simple meal a day and perhaps had fish or meat no more than once a week. Wine was only for the few well-to-do, as were the crafted luxuries, the sculptures, the stuccoed homes with tile roofs, and the limited diversity of foods.

A good deal of xenophobia existed toward the other Greek cities (especially the wealthier ones in Asia Minor), toward the non-Greeks to the north, and toward the Persians further to the east. The Greeks built up a dichotomy between themselves, as "Europeans" (and therefore "Westerners"), and the Persians, as "despotic Orientals" (much as the Egyptians referred to the barrier that separated them from the "Asians"). While the Persians were certainly no protectors of the common man, neither were the Greeks.

On the other hand, in the field of ideas some Greeks were beginning to perceive that man was more his own master than he had previously supposed, and that often the deities who ruled men through oracles and priests were actually man's own projections of himself. The Greeks were the first to discuss ethics and morality, not in terms of divine revelation as had the Old Testament prophets, but speculatively and critically as men who were trying to understand the social world into which they had been born and which they felt they could still influence. (Even the Old Testament prophets believed, however, that men could make choices, although, unlike the philosophical Greeks, they were not very much concerned with uncovering the evidence for their premises.)

Despite their philosophical speculations, the Greeks accepted slavery, the subordination of women to men, the social evils that existed around them, and the inhumanity of man to man. (Complete equality of all men in society was not accepted in any of the ancient Primary civilizations.) They could speculate about poverty, slavery, and warfare; but they were not social reformers and were not interested in knowledge as a basis for improving techniques, for bettering interpersonal relationships, or for making life less of a risk for most people. Even Plato's conception of government was cast in a hierarchical and authoritarian mold. As long as slaves and oxen were plentiful to do the drudgery, the ruling groups were indifferent to such problems as improving the available supply of food, freeing the slave, building better housing for the lower classes, or increasing the amount of education so that more men could share in defining societal goals.

The rulers of the ancient civilizations of Greece and Rome were not interested in improving the lot of men but were concerned only with the advantages accruing to those who ruled or were men of wealth. These men learned to intrigue and organize politically to make certain that powers over others remained in their hands and that other would-be intriguers and political and military organizers were suppressed before becoming a danger to themselves.

Greece and Rome were peasant civilizations, and they continued the organizational patterns of complex society that had first developed in ancient Sumeria more than 3,000 years before. They were not Western civilizations in any modern technological or organizational sense, and they were not very different from the civilizations that preceded them. Even the Sumerians, Egyptians, Babylonians, Assyrians, Cretans, Phoenicians, and Hebrews were as Western as the Greeks and the Romans. If any of these were "Oriental" (using the term popularized by Greek ethnocentrism), then so were the Greeks, Etruscans, and Romans.

The Romans continued to a large extent the forms, spirit, and ideas of all the civilizations that had influenced them from the past. Rome at its height built roads, but so did other civilizations, including the Mexicans and Peruvians in the New World. Rome built viaducts, but so did the Babylonians. Rome built cities of marble-faced rubble buildings, but the Egyptians more than 2,000 years before had constructed huge limestone-faced stone monuments. Even the Roman use of bird and animal entrails for predicting the future (in decision-making situations) had come from China and southeastern Asia hundreds of years before.

These were all civilizations in which peasants and slaves played little part except as drudges. The luxuries, the leisure, the pride of human dignity, were intended only for men of wealth and power. Those who possessed wealth and power strove to make certain that they retained it, since its possession was the only guarantee of human rights. With wealth one could boast, as did Crassus, that he could feed a large army with ease and thus control an empire. Those who were defeated were expected to pay tribute; those who resisted (as did Carthage and Jerusalem) were destroyed—their sites symbolically plowed over and their furrows spread with salt, as signs of their future sterility. The defeated became slaves, a custom no different from the rules of warfare developed by civilizations long since dead. Although the Romans were shocked at the human sacrifices of the Druids in western Europe, they themselves had engaged in human sacrifice to propitiate the war and fertility gods and goddesses only a few centuries previously. Animal sacrifice was part of their temple worship (as it is even in the twentieth century among the Moslems who make the pilgrimage to Mecca).

The Romans were engineers, colonizers, empire builders, and organizers of men. Even the organization and spread of Christianity owes much more to the men of Rome than to the men of Judea. Latin as a means of communication spread throughout the Roman Empire, and though its use declined later in North Africa and ancient Britain, it was modified to become the popular language of Spain, Portugal, Italy, Rumania, France, and parts of Belgium and Switzerland. Latin vocabulary would influence the Germanic languages and even the Slavic ones. Finally, in a derived form, it would become part of a worldwide scientific language (along with a synthetic Greek never spoken by the Greeks).

The Roman civilization, which was derived from all the civilizations that preceded theirs and was fertilized by all the peoples they conquered, did not die out with the Romans. Its encyclopedic ideas (the ideas of civilization are complex, tenacious, and longlasting) continued in Europe, Asia Minor, and North Africa, and finally, though changed, came into the New World centuries after the Roman Empire had ceased to exist as a political force.

Roman civilization would influence the Celts, who had moved into Europe even before the village of Rome existed. It would be the basis for the later technological civilization in Europe that by the eighteenth century A.D. would create a new variant of Secondary civilization that would be as different from the Roman and the Greek, the Egyptian and the Sumerian, as all of them had been from the Neolithic.

Selected Bibliography

Barrow, R. H., *The Romans* (Baltimore, Penguin, 1951).

Bibby, Geoffrey, *Four Thousand Years Ago* (New York, Knopf, 1961).

Block, Raymond, *The Etruscans* (New York, Praeger, 1960).

De Burgh, W. G., *The Legacy of the Ancient World* (Baltimore, Penguin, 1953).

Cook, R. M., *The Greeks Until Alexander* (New York, Praeger, 1962).

Coon, Carleton S., *The Story of Man* (New York, Knopf, 1955).

Grant, Michael, *The World of Rome* (Cleveland, World Publishers, 1960).

Kitto, H. D. F., *The Greeks* (Baltimore, Penguin, 1951).

MacKendrick, P. L., *The Mute Stones Speak: The Story of Archaeology in Italy* (New York, St Martin's, 1960).

Mueller, Herbert J., *Freedom in the Ancient World* (New York, Harper & Row, 1961).

Who We Are

13

Primary Civilization Advances to the Beginnings of Secondary Civilization

As we have already seen, thousands of years may have passed before the Mesolithic culture merged completely into the Neolithic—when the hunters and food gatherers learned to become agriculturists and pastoralists. During the last phases of the Mesolithic and in the early stages of the Neolithic, both cultures may even have coexisted in the same geographic regions. In the beginning of the Neolithic there were very few agriculturists but a great many hunters; toward the end of this period hunters still existed, of course, but a great many had become peasants (though many characteristics of the hunters' beliefs survived in their newly settled way of life).

Several thousand years may have passed before the peasant's culture became stabilized enough to let him feel reassured that his way of life was right. The hunter wanted to be assured of a steady supply of animals to hunt; the agriculturist wanted to control and manipulate the forces of nature that affected the growth of crops and the breeding of domesticated animals.

Perhaps even more thousands of years were to elapse before informal controls of village organization became centralized governing bodies who kept city-states functioning as territorial units. Later these city-states would contain the first faint premonitions of the world to come: the spread of literacy, the awareness of technological forces that could be harnessed, the struggles of individual men to free themselves from social inequalities that doomed some of them to a sterile existence, and the scepticism with which a few men greeted the accepted wisdom of their day.

The growth of empires, of trade, and of organizations that answered the needs of large urban populations and growing professional armies brought into existence the first articulate ideas, which were to become (thousands of years later) the ancestors of a new type of urban civilization, a civilization that would offer as much hope and security to men as their magic rituals and their collection of gods and goddesses had given. Later men, like their predecessors, also attempted to identify themselves with the forces of nature so that they could manipulate, control, and utilize them.

Throughout the centuries most adult men found reassurance in trying to recapture the emotions of their childhoods, when they were dependent upon benevolent paternal and maternal figures whom they served and who in turn gave them the identification, security, and discipline they needed to make existence meaningful. As adults they continued to turn to these or to substitute paternal and maternal figures for guidance, for protection against the pains and tribulations of everyday living, and for assistance in meeting the grave crises of war, famine, and disease. Most men continued this earlier dependency when they themselves played the role of father figures for those who were younger. Men received knowledge not through their own reasoning, observations, or attempts to achieve a theoretical understanding that would make apparently unrelated facts fit into place coherently, but through carrying out the wishes and instructions of parents and substitute parents. Men knew what they had to do not by developing insights but by following the training given them by the family.

A few men began to look for other forms of knowledge. They were intellectually curious and took nothing for granted; they assumed that man learns only when he makes tentative explanations for the phenomena that puzzle him and then attempts to cross-check the validity of his assumptions. They were skeptical of all explanations that could not be verified by other men or that could not be understood in terms of their own observations, experiences, or insights. They were mistrustful of authority that brooked no opposition to its conventional teachings. They sensed that man had more control over his thought and actions than had previously been accepted and that man had within himself the resources for an understanding of the world about him. They even felt that man ought to stand before the deities with dignity rather than to crawl on hands and knees in the dust as he advanced toward them. These few wanted other men to emerge from their age-old dependency relationship with parental figures and to assume greater responsibility for the acquisition of adult knowledge.

In the Ancient World these men were few and far between. Some isolated examples have come down to us from the age of the Greek city-states and from the Alexandrian period. A few survived from the Roman period, from northern India, and from northern China. Perhaps a few isolated examples lived in other parts of the Ancient World; but because they wrote no books that survived or because they found no receptivity to their new ideas, they are unknown to us today.

Most men were content to live as their fathers and their fathers' fathers had done before them; to learn no more than they; and to emulate them well in the hope that their own children would view them also as models to follow. They were content to till the soil as others had done, to fashion crafts and art that copied works designed before their time, to govern as others had governed, to teach as others had taught, and to trade as others had traded. Men were thought to fulfill their goals by faithfully copying models of the past. Tradition was the final arbiter, and final guidance came from the old, who were keepers of the wisdom of the past. Men turned back to covenants made by their ancestors, to "Golden Ages" when daily problems and tribulations were fewer, and to the dependency worlds of their own childhoods.

For generation after countless generation, men left the world pretty much as it had been taught to them as children. The changes lay primarily in various catastrophes of nature, in cataclysms brought about by invading armies, and in the misrule of ineffective despots. Vast migrations of tribes took place; new religions spread and grew; and slight changes occurred in tools and ways of working. But in general one could say that previous generations would still have felt at home if they could have returned to live with their descendants. They would have had to adjust to new individuals, to new fashions, to a slightly transformed folklore, and to a language that might have taken on new meanings, new words, and changed pronunciation; but they would have been able to adjust fairly quickly to the way of life to be found hundreds of years later in most parts of the world.

The Migration of Peoples

Change of a sort took place as migrating and warring tribes crossed large areas of Eurasia and North America. The Bulgars, Huns, Avars, Vandals, Ostrogoths, Magyars, and Mongols traveled great distances to conquer or to settle. The Slavs moved cautiously into the vacuum left in central Europe by the retreating Celts. In North America the Aztecs moved in stages from the southwestern part of the United States into the Valley of Mexico, and the Sioux began their advance from the lower Mississippi River valley to the upper reaches of that river.

Pastoral and nomadic people became settled agriculturists. Some acculturated themselves to Primary civilization and became the new rulers of old empires. Out of the deserts of Arabia rode the conquerors of Alexandria and Persia as well as of Spain. A shaky empire was built on the ruins of the old Roman Empire by a mixed German-Celtic tribe of Franks. While Byzantium held on to its Roman and Greek heritage, the Mongols swept into China, the Middle East, and central Europe. (In the Middle

East the Mongols destroyed irrigation works; in China they debated whether to turn that agricultural country into a vast open pasture for their flocks.) In Europe the Scandinavian coastal peoples traveled far afield to win new lands, treasures, and homes for themselves. The Polynesians settled a string of islands stretching almost across the Pacific Ocean, while in the New World a whole series of peoples from the Mexican valley to the coast of Peru entered an elementary stage of Primary civilization roughly paralleling the stages of growth of agricultural and urban centers in the Eurasian world.

There was change everywhere, but the changes still seemed to be based upon ancient innovations. Despite the rise of new empires, the migrations of peoples, and the spread of popular religious movements, the vast majority of the people in the world still earned their livings in much the same ways as their ancestors. Land was still prepared for cultivation with simple tools that required much labor but did little to increase the yield. The Eurasian plow was no more than a large digging stick pulled by oxen, camels, or water buffaloes, and it only scratched the surface of the soil. In the New World a simple digging stick was also used, but there were no domestic animals to pull it.

The Innovators of the Classical World

The seeds of the coming Secondary civilization of industrial technology and science were planted many centuries earlier in the Ancient World, but even in hospitable soil they took a long time to grow into the entwining and interdependent roots that would support the modern technological age. Handfuls of innovating individuals existed in every age; and despite the indifference displayed by their contemporaries to their innovations, their numbers slowly increased during the later stages of Primary civilization. The men who had created the designs, organized the manpower, and made the tools to construct the first great pyramids, aqueducts, sewage systems, temples, and harbors were the direct ancestors of the later men who used their powers of observation and insightful thought to develop more efficient means of increasing the yields of nature by making both human and animal energies more productive. Although the initial improvements would be primarily in technology, some thought would also go into the observation of disease, with an isolated individual here and there being concerned with the physical phenomena of nature and the social complexities of man.

A few men also attempted to incorporate men into more efficient religions, which would be better organized than previous empires and whose influence would cover more territory than was encompassed by their contemporary secular governmental units. Even professional armies were being organized that would be far more complex, more efficient, and certainly more interdependent than their volunteer, part-time predecessors. Out of these new organizations would come the theoretical models for the complex urban and industrial societies of a later age.

In the Greek, Roman, and Alexandrian worlds, manual and artisan labors were performed by slaves and free workers who had little social standing. There was no shortage of human energy, for slaves were easily available through conquest, debt, or parental sale. Since human labor was cheap, there were no strong incentives for harnessing wind, water, or animal power to free man from the drudgery of his daily life.

The scholars of the Ancient World were more concerned with abstract philosophical knowledge than with the improvement of technical skills. Gentlemen debated seriously among themselves about the purpose of the world, about the organization and analyses of nature, and about the structure of the physical universe—but not about human poverty, slavery, or the inequalities of man's short span of life on earth (these were taken for granted). Men in the Ancient World did not dream that man's drudgery could be ended once and for all, that nature could be harnessed to do the laborious work that slaves were compelled to do, that men could be provided with the necessities of life so that their energies could be devoted to more important aims than those of mere animal existence.

Archimedes in Greek Sicily in the third century B.C. invented a complex winch, a spiral conveyor, and parabolic mirrors; but he preferred to be remembered for his mathematical theorems more than for his applied technology. Ctesbius, who also lived in the third century B.C., may well have been an early inventor of the windmill. Hero of Alexandria, who lived in perhaps the second or third centuries B.C., knew the force of expanding steam, which he harnessed for opening temple doors; he also was known to have experimented with compressed air and waterpower; but he had no interest in applying any of this knowledge to the development of machines that could save human labor. In India and China scholars were much more interested in the theoretical analysis of their mental worlds than they were in assisting peasants or artisans to lighten their labors. These scholars would have been deeply insulted if anyone had asked them to study the simple tools of the peasants or artisans to try to make them more efficient.

It was the isolated individual peasant and artisan in China, India, Persia, Syria, Egypt, Rome, Spain, and France who made the slight improvements and important technical innovations that made life a little more comfortable and efficient for their fellowmen. True, in Rome a few patrician landlords, who were encouraged by the ready market in wine, grain, and olives (due to the growth in numbers of the Roman legions and the increase in population in Rome and other cities of the Empire), began to experiment with increasing agricultural yields. They learned to cultivate the grape and olive more intensively and to increase their yields of grain by alternating the planting of peas and wheat. Although the production of grains was increased, the net effect added little to the standard of living of most inhabitants of the Roman Empire. One could truthfully say that in the 3,000 years from the beginning of Sumerian civilization to the height of the Roman Empire in the first century A.D., little had been added to improve the daily standard of living of more than nine-tenths of the Eurasian population. The Roman Empire with its professional legions, its administrative officials, its cities, and its engineering works was supported by the laborious drudgery of a huge peasant population, who scratched the soil with their wooden plows to supply a meager fare for the 10 to 15 percent of the population who were spared from agricultural work.

Although the Roman legions required large amounts of grain, armor, swords, clothing, leather, and tools, their suppliers had no incentive to increase production by utilizing machines that employed the energies of either water or wind power, both of which were known in theory by the first century. Huge fortunes were made by those who supplied the legions and the government; but the productive work was done by innumerable slaves, who were captured in a never-ending supply as the legions extended their conquests in Europe and the Middle East.

The crank was unknown to the Romans, but they were acquainted with the wheel, the axle, the lever, the pulley, the endless screw (which Archimedes had invented), the wedge, the cam, and the three forms of basic gearing (which were being used in very complex mechanisms by the beginning of the Christian era). These mechanisms were used in mining, in the construction of war machines, and in the building of aqueducts, bridges, roads, and large public buildings. There was no interest, however, in transferring any of the mechanical principles used in their construction to the production of goods in a factory system.

In their travels, the Roman legions had picked up a good many mechanical ideas that had been unknown to them previously. The waterwheel, for example, was discovered in the highlands of Anatolia, and the principle of this form of energy was brought back to Rome in the first century B.C. The Romans were thus able to change the primitive horizontal water turbine into a vertical overshot waterwheel, which produced six times more energy than the water turbine. Roman engineers wrote many manuscripts recommending that the new waterwheels be used to harness the energy of streams in grinding grain, in operating simple lathes, and in constructing more complex machines. The public authorities, however, saw no need to use public money to supplant fairly inexpensive slaves and donkeys. The military, however, did use some waterwheels to grind grain for their supply trains.

At this time grain was imported in large amounts from North Africa, but the grinding was done by slaves using primitive mills. The weaving of textiles was almost entirely a home industry. Patricians were proud of the linen and wool cloth woven by their wives and daughters; but as the Roman Empire became richer, spinning and weaving were gradually taken over by the slaves. Merchants bought the woven cloth and used slave labor to full (compress or tighten the cloth), dye, and finish it. Then they put the finished cloth on sale in their small shops. Glassblowing, which was probably invented in the Middle East in the first century B.C. (though glass as a commodity was known in Egypt almost 2,000 years before), had by the third century A.D. become an important industry in both Alexandria and Rome. Syrian and Jewish artisans dominated the production of bottles and window glass. (By 200 A.D. window glass, measuring as large as one by two feet, was also made in the small workshops around Rome.) Woodworking and the manufacture of glass, textiles, and iron were still performed in small workshops, as had been done in Sumeria, Mohenjo-Daro, Egypt, Crete, and Anatolia.

From Asia Minor, the water turbine and later the waterwheel spread to China via the Silk Road (it did not come to India until a few centuries later). Some evidence exists that a horizontal waterwheel driving a triphammer was used for milling rice in China in the first century A.D. The vertical waterwheel came in later centuries from the West. A waterwheel requires moving water to operate it; and in most parts of the Mediterranean region and in Asia, rivers are short and are dry for many months of the year. The Romans created an artificial water supply through expensively constructed aqueducts, but these made the total cost of running a waterwheel far more than the cost of labor of slaves or domestic animals. The waterwheel would not become economically feasible until it was taken north of the Alps centuries later to be used in swiftly flowing streams that contained as much water in summer as in winter.

Although some of the forces of nature were harnessed in late Roman days, these processes were still inconsequential; and manufacturing techniques and machines differed little from those that had been used in more ancient civilizations. In general, there was no feeling that human labor needed to be saved from drudgery or that men could achieve a higher standard of living by improving agricultural and industrial tools. At this time, little hope existed that man's life on earth could be bettered physically or that man could have other purposes on earth than laboring for his daily bread. Poverty was assumed to be fixed, eternal, and necessary.

The Technological Contribution of Europe During the Dark Ages

The Ancient World, however, did contribute some of the ideas that would be imaginatively applied in making changes in northern Italy and in Europe north of the Alps. Perhaps the first really important invention to come out of northern Europe was the heavy plow of the Saxons in the eighth century. This permitted the plowed soil to be turned over and furrowed rather than merely scratched. In ancient Rome it had been customary to plow a square plot of land first lengthwise and then crosswise. The light Roman plow had no coulter or mouldboard; it was in form and principle still the ancient digging stick pulled by oxen. The Romans in the first century A.D. in the northern part of the country constructed a heavier type of plow, added wheels, and pulled it with as many as eight oxen, but it still functioned as a larger digging stick rather than as a modern plow. In time, the heavier form of construction undoubtedly crossed the Alps, where some inventor or group of inventors along the North Sea added a coulter, a share, and a mouldboard, and by the eighth or ninth century A.D. had turned it into a modern plow. But even in this small area of Europe, it took hundreds of years for an invention such as the heavy plow to move hundreds of miles eastward or westward.

Population Changes in Europe

Europe north of the Alps went through a series of population changes from the fifth to the tenth centuries A.D. Invading tribes, influenced by the civilizations of the Mediterranean and Asia Minor (or driven out of the frontier regions of China), had been making their way into large parts of eastern and central Europe. Since the new immigrants or invaders settled in the midst of older settlers who had already preempted most of the good soils, there were almost insatiable demands for new land. These demands could only be met by draining marshes, cutting down forests, and filling bogs. The conquerors and the conquered interbred; and the resulting population explosion encouraged changes that would later lead to the gradual unfolding of a new form of urban civilization in northern Italy, France, the Low Countries, southern Germany, and England.

Between the eighth and thirteenth centuries, the heavy Saxon plow, which turned soil over in large furrows, enriched the land and thus made possible an increase in yields—the first time that there had been a proportional increase since the discovery of agriculture in the distant Mesolithic period. It was now no longer necessary to cross-plow the field as had been done in the past. The larger plow, pulled by as many as eight oxen, made possible the cultivation of heavier and richer soils in the drained marshes and river-bottom lands of Europe. Virgin land could now be opened to cultivation, thus increasing the food supply for both the old and the new settlers. The amount of energy required to cross-plow a field was lessened, thus permitting more land to be cultivated by fewer men. The new plowing of land in a straight line evolved into the medieval strip system. The large number of oxen and men required to drive and direct the heavy plows encouraged the peasants to settle close together in villages and to farm their lands collectively by pooling their resources.

The heavy plow permitted the extension of agriculture into eastern Europe as extensive woodlands were cleared to create more land for cultivation. Along the North Sea, marshes were drained and large forests cleared to make even more cultivated fields. In England, Scotland, and Wales, new cultivated lands cut into primeval forests to spread across hills, rivers, and marshes. By the thirteenth century, Europe had created enough land to permit its migrating populations to settle down peacefully.

The Horse Collar, Horseshoe, and Tandem Harness

The ox was a slow beast of burden, but the speedier horses could not be used as a substitute until two inventions had been made. In Europe, these had occurred by the beginning of the tenth century. One was the development of the collar, which permitted the horse to use its chest muscles to pull heavy loads freely. Heretofore the ancient yoke around its neck had cut off the circulation of blood and air if it attempted to move a heavy load. We do not know who invented the horse collar, but with its use a team of horses could pull a load five times heavier than with the ancient yoke. By the tenth century, it apparently existed along with horseshoes (which were invented only a short time before the horse collar) and the shaft. The shaft permitted horses to be harnessed in tandem and encouraged their use in preference to oxen for pulling heavy loads. Equipped with the horse collar, shaft, and ironclad shoes, a single horse could now pull almost triple the load that it previously could.

By the end of the eleventh century in England, a peasant using two horses equipped with collars, shafts, and iron horseshoes and pulling a wheeled plow (which cut the earth and turned it over) could cultivate thirty acres of land all by himself—an acreage far greater than in the past and much larger than most peasants in the underdeveloped areas of the world can cultivate today. By the eleventh century in large sections of northern Europe, men were growing more food in greater variety than ever before, even more than in Roman days. The grain-fed horse had displaced the hay-fed ox, but the greater speed of the horse permitted him to outperform and outpull the ox. Agriculture now led the way in the shift from the ancient Mediterranean world to a more advanced technology in the previously backward areas of northern and western Europe.

The Saxon heavy plow (which may have been known to the Germans along the Baltic Sea even before the sixth century) and the more efficiently harnessed horse changed agriculture again from the cooperatively organized village system (which had led to the feudal manorial system) to the more independent yeomen farms of England, France, and the Low Countries. One man could now cultivate more land, thus freeing more members of his family for other work, and could diversify his farming more than had been possible before. He and his family had more time for handicrafts, making other goods, and supplying food for the administrative officials, churchmen, and merchant-traders in the slowly growing urban centers. (Such items as butter and cheese were unknown to the Ancient World—just as milk was unknown to the Chinese—but sometime in the tenth or eleventh centuries they were introduced to the tables of the rich in Europe.)

The Agricultural Use of Iron

Iron was used in larger quantities in eleventh and twelfth century Europe than in the Mediterranean world. The plowshare was now made of iron, the horse-drawn harrow with iron teeth replaced the mattock and rake, and more diversified tools of iron were made for both cultivation and handicrafts. Although the Ancient World knew many of the tools that were used in the early Middle Ages, the northern European tools were more varied than those used by the Romans. The crank, for example, was unknown to the Romans, but it became known to the Europeans by the twelfth century, perhaps through Venetian traders. (Professor Lynn White, Jr., offers evidence that the crank was used by the Chinese in the first century of our era.) [1] The improvement of the crank as a windlass or carpenter's brace would not take place until the early part of the fifteenth century.

The Water Mill in the Feudal Economy

Although the water mill was known to the Romans by the second century A.D., its use spread mainly after the fall of the Empire in the fifth century. Roman soldiers spread its use wherever they were permanently encamped, but water mills as independent sources of energy began to multiply rapidly only after the ninth century. According to the Domesday Book, which was the first census taken in England, there were in 1086 over 5,600 water mills for the 3,000 communities then in existence. As early as the tenth century, the French and English lords of the manor insisted upon their right to grind all grain into flour, thus reinforcing the dependency relationship of the peasant village to the manor house. As feudal obligations developed in intensity during the next few centuries, the conflict between peasant and lord grew steadily more embittered: the

[1] Lynn White, Jr., *Medieval Technology and Social Change* (London, Oxford University Press, 1963), p. 104.

peasant attempted to preserve his village autonomy, while the lord insisted upon his economic rights over the village and its lands.

The Agricultural Crops

The Moslems, who were the middlemen between Europe, India, and China, introduced new crops such as buckwheat, rice, hops, sugarcane, and flax into Sicily and Spain and cotton into southern Italy and Sicily. Most livestock in northern Europe was still being killed in the autumn, since there was not enough feed grown to carry the animals through the winter. Only the plow team was spared, but even these horses were fed near-starvation rations of straw and hay. It was only at the end of the Middle Ages in the fifteenth and sixteenth centuries that the fallow lands were abandoned and root vegetables and legumes (peas and beans) grown as alternating crops to cereals. These new cultivating concepts, however, did not increase by very much the yield that the peasant was getting from his soil. During the late Middle Ages, for every two bushels of wheat sown per acre in England the yield remained at only ten bushels; for four bushels of oats sown the yield averaged from twelve to sixteen bushels. A definite increase in yield per acre would only come later during the agricultural revolution of the eighteenth century.[2]

But changes were taking place in European agriculture as a result of the pressures upon many monasteries to increase their yields and to diversify crops for the market. More attention was now paid on monastery lands to growing fruit and vegetables. By the end of the thirteenth century the Moslems had introduced into Italy and Spain the cultivation of mulberry trees and the raising of silkworms from the Far East. England, Spain, and Italy began to raise sheep for the export trade; by the thirteenth and fourteenth centuries Hungary, Poland, and Prussia replaced them as the chief growers of grain for the European market. The fishing industry of the North and Baltic seas was seeking new markets for its dried and salted fish, and by the fourteenth century the merchants in the Hanseatic port towns were packing and shipping in wooden barrels the herring caught in northern waters.

Elementary Manufacturing

A good many innovations in weaving took place in China, Persia, Egypt, and Byzantium from the sixth century A.D. onward: looms were improved, and special cloths and brocades were manufactured for the first time. By

[2] A. C. Crombie, *Medieval and Early Modern Science* (Garden City, N.Y., Doubleday, 1959), p. 192.

the eleventh century Italian and Spanish weavers had adopted these improvements.

By the first century A.D. glass had moved from Alexandria to Rome, and by the fourth century from Rome to Byzantium. The Moslem world and Byzantium remained the chief centers for glass manufacturing until Venice displaced both areas during the thirteenth century. Venice had traded with both Byzantium and the Moslem world from the ninth century on, and a good many of the innovations from Asia Minor and Byzantium (as well as from the areas further to the east) came to northern Europe only by way of Venice. By the early twelfth century Venice was making most of the stained glass windows for the cathedrals of Europe. (Glass would not be made on a large scale outside of Italy until after the sixteenth century.)

Moslem Spain was an important recipient of the technological learning of Asian Primary civilization; but Sicily under the Byzantines and Moslems (and later the Normans) and the great trading cities of Venice, Genoa, and Florence were the chief recipients of the innovations and the new learning of southern and eastern Asia, and of the repository of Greek and Alexandrian knowledge (which had gone from Alexandria to Byzantium, and thence to Baghdad, and from there back to the various centers of Moslem trade and learning in Egypt, Morocco, Spain, and Sicily). Linen paper, for example, moved from Spain into southern France in the twelfth century, after having taken centuries to move from China to Persia, and from Persia to Egypt and Spain. Textile manufacturing became an important industry in Florence at the end of the twelfth century as various improvements to the loom (including the treadle) were brought to that city from Egypt and the Near East.

The Hindu Numerals

Perhaps the greatest contribution to the growth of European knowledge after the tenth century was the introduction of the Hindu zero and numerals. Evidently the zero, which was unknown in the classical world (though present in Mayan calendrical events), was invented about the sixth century A.D. in India. With its simplified numerals and algebraic equations, the Hindu system was later picked up by the Moslems, who had conquered large parts of northwest India by the eighth and ninth centuries (the area formerly encompassed by the Indus valley civilization of 3,000 years before).

With the conquest of territory came the acquisition of Hindu mathematicians, who had worked on square roots, cube roots, trigonometry, and simple equations. This new mathematics was of great value to the Moslem traders, lawyers, builders, and administrators who now occupied the territory between the northwestern part of India and the Mediterranean area. The improved Hindu arithmetic, numerals, and simple algebra could now be used as tools in assessing legacies, settling lawsuits, handling complex matters of trade, building canals, laying out irrigation ditches, measuring land, and constructing monumental edifices.

The Trade in Manuscripts

Mathematical knowledge came to Italy and France from the Moslem world via the large trade in manuscripts that was carried on by the merchants of northern Italy. European monasteries were willing to pay handsome sums in gold and silver for manuscripts concerned with ancient Greek learning, Hindu knowledge, and what was known of technical matters (most of which came from the areas in Asia Minor that had been overrun by the Moslems after the eighth century). Certain individuals in Moslem Egypt (Alexandria), in Baghdad, and in Spain laboriously copied in Arabic all manuscripts of the Ancient World that came to their attention. These were then sold to middlemen who painstakingly translated them into Latin for the use of European men of learning, who at that time were almost entirely connected with the Church.

By the twelfth century, manuscripts written by Jews and Moslems in Spain were describing the water clock in great detail, the trigonometric tables for sine, the use of the zero and other Hindu numerals (which had already been modified by the Moslems in their own centers of learning), the technology and medicine of the Alexandrian period, and the surgery that had been established in the Moslem world. Even Aristotle's natural history, which was to play such an important part in determining educational directions in the later Middle Ages, first came to Christendom through manuscripts imported from the Moslems by the Italian traders. The do-it-yourself system of education through reading must have been in full force in non-Moslem Europe by the end of the twelfth century, and it may have greatly influenced the later acceptance and encouragement of both observation and applied technology.

The Technological Revolution of the Thirteenth Century

A technological revolution occurred in Europe in the thirteenth century whereby a whole series of inventions that were unknown to the Ancient World found a reception in the monasteries, manorial houses, and merchant homes of Europe. Like the first technological revolution, which developed out of the ancient Primary civilization, it benefited the man of education and wealth more than the peasant or the apprentice. (It would take the Industrial Revolution to distribute somewhat more equally the fruits of man's mental ingenuity.)

In Europe during the twelfth and thirteenth centuries, men's minds were struggling to solve practical problems. First of all, the water mill could be used only where there were swiftly flowing streams. If a dam were constructed in an area where the river ran slowly, it would cause dangerous flooding of low-lying lands, especially after heavy rainstorms. The answer in the Low Countries was an independent invention, the windmill, which used the energy of moving air rather than water to turn its vanes. The windmill was important in the flat lands bordering the North Sea, where it was used to grind grain and to pump water out of low-lying areas. The water mill came from Asia Minor to Europe; the windmill moved in the opposite direction, from Europe to the Moslem world and from there to China. Although the windmill was evidently first invented at the end of the twelfth century, it had already been accepted in China by the end of the thirteenth century.

The work that was being done on optics in England, Spain, Italy, Flanders, and France in the thirteenth century led to the invention of spectacles in Italy (perhaps in Florence around 1286) for correcting the farsightedness of the middle-aged and old. (Spectacles for the myopic, or the nearsighted, would not come until the sixteenth century.) No longer did the monastic scholar or the merchant require someone to read to him after he reached the age of 45; he could now continue his perusal of manuscripts and observation of minute forms almost until the day of death. This invention thus prolonged the usefulness of human beings and made old age less the handicap to scholarship than it had previously been. From Italy, spectacles diffused widely over the Eurasian continent. Their use was carried to China by the Venetian merchants (including Marco Polo in the thirteenth century).

In the thirteenth century Italy was the center of the technological revolution that brought in the rudiments of industry and the first signs of capitalism. Rome had been ruled by its patrician-farmers for hundreds of years, but it had left trade to the Etruscans to the north. Evidently trade and finance continued to be an important means of livelihood among the descendants of the Etruscans, even after the fall of the Roman Empire. By the twelfth century Florence had already become an important center for money-lending, trade, and handicraft manufacturing (thus competing with Venice, Genoa, Pisa, Naples, and Amalfi).

The Roman Catholic Church had far-flung dioceses that annually sent gold and silver to Rome. The Florentines became the first bankers of the Church in Rome. Someone had to handle these funds, changing them so that they could be used in Rome and elsewhere; and these bankers had to be Christians. (The myth has been perpetrated that the chief Medieval money changers and financiers were Jews: they were more likely to have been Italians.) Out of a need for someone to handle the finances of the Vatican, to invest its funds, and to make loans to other princes whenever necessary came the first bankers and financiers. And out of Florentine experience came credit and deposit banking—ideas that would later be taken to England, France, and the Low Countries by Lombard, Venetian, and Genoese bankers, who used their wealth to mortgage Crusaders as well as royalty of Medieval Europe. The Italian merchant-financiers were the first to develop double-entry bookkeeping and the first to use efficiently in their banking and trading records the higher arithmetic and Hindu numerals introduced by the Moslems.

During the twelfth and thirteenth centuries the merchants of Italy and the Moslem world were also carrying on a wide international trade (though it was small in modern terms), not only in cloth and other luxuries, but also in such metals as copper, tin, and even steel. Small amounts of steel had originally been imported from India by Moslem traders to their metal-fabricating centers in Damascus and Toledo; but by the thirteenth century the secret of making it had been uncovered, and these two cities then began to produce their own steel for export to Europe. By the fourteenth century, Moslem trade with India had almost ended as the Mongol invaders destroyed the intermediary trading and manufacturing centers in Asia Minor and Persia (which never regained their former importance as middlemen and artisans). The arrival of the Seljuk and Osmanli Turks later on almost completely destroyed the importance of southwestern Asia.

By the beginning of the fourteenth century in Europe, the Italian merchants had influenced the growth of other merchant-traders in England, Flanders, France, and Germany. The commerce in fine textiles, spices, armor, and weapons had created a good deal of wealth in northern European merchant hands; and it now became common for both bishops and lords (as well as kings) to borrow money from these urban merchant-traders whenever they needed funds to carry on limited warfare. (The confiscation of merchant wealth by absolute kings did not take place until the seventeenth and eighteenth centuries.)

The reaction of the Medieval Church against merchants who charged interest on their loans to bishops and kings encouraged the establishment of credit banking, whereby the interest became a fixed charge for overhead as well as profit. Although there was also a reaction against the charging of interest, money could be borrowed in the Middle Ages in no other way. Eight to ten percent interest was considered very little for the Italian bankers to charge, considering the risks they ran in lending money to poverty-stricken kings who had few assets to call their own.

The Importance of the Thirteenth Century

It is difficult to mention all the important changes in the thirteenth century that permitted Europe to surpass the Ancient World. In that century Rouen and Ypres became important manufacturing centers; Florence combined handicrafts with finance capitalism, a combination that would remain unequaled until the sixteenth century; and Venice, Genoa, and Lübeck became important merchant centers.

Trade had already changed the small, urban cathedral towns of Europe from a barter to a money economy, based on abstract units such as gold and silver coinage (which went back to the sixth century B.C., as we have already seen), letters of credit, and bills of exchange (Italian inventions that were unknown in the ancient Roman world, in India, and in China). The new commerce encouraged mathematicians to compile tables to cover interest, discount, and exchange. And this in turn encouraged a growth in mathematical thinking for use in navigation, astronomy, and mechanics. For example, by 1290 the latitude of Paris was discovered by measuring the angle of the sun overhead at noon on March 21 to be 48° 50′, a figure still accepted as basically correct.

Until the thirteenth century, spinning had been performed slowly with the distaff held in one hand while the wool was twisted with the other, but the invention of the spinning wheel with its belt transmission of power helped to develop a cottage textile industry in Florence, Flanders, and England. Perhaps the two greatest inventions of this century, however, were the mechanical clock and gunpowder—and here the monastery must be considered to have played the leading role.

In the ancient Greek and Roman worlds, philosophers were not concerned with applied technological knowledge. Whatever innovations took place technologically came from the rule-of-thumb speculations of artisans and military engineers, who rarely wrote down their observations. In Europe the demand for technical knowledge came from educated monks, who had taken vows of poverty and practiced religious humility by working laboriously with their hands. These were the individuals who encouraged scribes in the Moslem world to ferret out ancient manuscripts dealing with technological innovations and to pass on technical information in the fields of agriculture, horticulture, medicine, time measurement, handicrafts, and construction. The monks of a religious sect that was moving to Florence from Alexandria in the thirteenth century first used the spinning wheel, the treadle on a loom, and the various innovations developed in Persia, China, and India from the sixth century on for the production of brocades and other expensive textiles. The monasteries used workshops, engaged in agriculture, and attempted to cure the sick. At the same time, they had to protect themselves from being taken over by neighboring feudal lords who envied their wealth.

The Mechanical Clock

The mechanical clock could only have been invented in a monastery. In the thirteenth century there were thousands of monasteries throughout Europe. In the monasteries time was regulated: there was a time for prayer, a time for work, a time for meals, and a time for meditation. The day was divided into hours, and all activities had to be carried out with discipline and order. Only a mechanical clock could work with precision, automatically striking the hours of the day and night. The sundial could not be used when it was cloudy or dark, and the water clock could not operate automatically. As Lewis Mumford [3] suggested in *Technics and Civilization,* the mechanical clock was an automatic machine that served as a model for later machines. Without the clock there could have been no Industrial Revolution with its discovery of how to use power from outer sources to manufacture a product. "Smiths could have hammered thousands of suits of armor or thousands of iron cannon, wheelwrights could have shaped thousands of great water-wheels or crude gears, without inventing any of the special types of movement developed in clock work, and without any of the accuracy of measurement and fineness of articulation that finally produced the accurate eighteenth century chronometer."

Although the mechanical clock was a thirteenth century invention, it was not until the fourteenth century that a minute hand and a dial were added. After 1350 the division of the hour into sixty minutes and of the minute into sixty seconds became common. In 1370 Charles V of France ordered all churches in Paris to ring the hours and quarters. By 1400 the mechanical clock in a city-hall tower, containing complicated mechanisms of knights, archangels, angels, and devils all performing when the clock was struck, had become an important status symbol for all towns proud of their growth and wealth.

Although the clock became extremely important to Europe after the thirteenth century (even though the pocket watch was not invented by the Nuremberg Germans until more than two centuries later), it played no role in the Moslem world, in India, or in China. Prime Minister Nehru, in *The Discovery of India,* wondered why the Mogul emperors of India who received gifts of clock pieces and watches from the Dutch and the Portuguese in the seventeenth century had no interest in having them

[3] Lewis Mumford, *Technics and Civilization* (New York, Harcourt and Brace, 1934), pp. 15–16.

copied and made in their workshops.[4] The answer lay in the fact that time meant little to them or to the Hindus. Time was meaningful only if one accepted an abstract concept of time as a regulator of one's daily life: for religious men with prayers, for merchants with appointments to keep, for those who had to produce certain products within a given period of time. But time was not meaningful if one assumed, as the Moslems and Hindus did, that time on earth was relatively unimportant and that it could best be measured in the long units of childhood, adulthood, and old age, which were observable without the aid of a mechanical object that ticked off the minutes of one's life relentlessly and inevitably. To appreciate time one must have the European concept of "Time is money," along with a life that is directed, managed, and governed by the passing of time intervals.

The mechanical clock was a harbinger of a future that would be governed by time, a way of life that would measure each hour and day as if they were products being parceled out by nature, of a time span that encompassed man's life from birth to the grave, ticking off each second through pulse and heartbeats. The clock was the first mechanism that could be used to simulate human energy. In this, it was the first great mechanical creation of an automated life. It was as if man were paralleling the original mystery of the creation of life by creating a mechanical one. This deed in itself may have given late Medieval man enough self-confidence in his abilities to encourage him to try to improve upon nature, to seek out the mysteries of the world through scientific observation, to believe that he had been endowed with enough intelligence to stand on his own feet, to be a creator in his own right, and to break his childlike dependency upon supernatural father figures who told him little and kept important secrets from him by making all of life a mystery that could only be revealed to him in bits. Even the Deists in the late seventeenth and eighteenth centuries could think of no more flattering title to refer to the Deity than as a creator who had made the world the way a clockmaker made the clock. He had wound the world up, and it was up to man to understand this clocklike world by studying the mechanical laws of nature. Perhaps the creation of the complex mechanical clock engendered in man an overweening confidence in himself that later made possible our scientific and industrial civilization. Perhaps in the case of Moslem man, a lack of confidence in the ability to regulate life made the Mogul emperors indifferent to the workings and need of the clock. The clock gave man optimism, and perhaps the optimistic conviction that he possessed the ability to change the world led man slowly to create the technology and science that would in time transform his universe.

[4] Nehru, J., *The Discovery of India* (Garden City, N.Y., Doubleday, 1960), pp. 164–165.

The Invention of Gunpowder

The invention of gunpowder also had momentous repercussions in the life of European man: with it he was able to substitute energy for brute strength. In his various attempts to increase the power of the genie that he had called to life, he turned to the careful measurement and examination of the natural world. But instead of starting off with an axiomatic theory, he began by examining his own assumptions through observation and attempts to make the theory fit the facts, rather than vice versa.

Gunpowder is composed of 75 percent potassium nitrate, 15 percent sulphur, and 10 percent carbon, though in its earlier years the proportions may not have been as exact as these. Gunpowder for use in firecrackers was known to the Chinese a century before it was used in Europe. And it is quite possible that the secret of making gunpowder may have come to the Chinese during the ninth and tenth centuries from Moslem traders, since a primitive form of gunpowder had been one of the ingredients in Byzantine "Greek Fire," first invented by a Syrian toward the end of the seventh century.

The transmission of the knowledge of gunpowder to Europe may have been by way of Venetian merchants who accompanied the Mongol invasion into Europe. (These merchants were used for intelligence purposes by the Mongol Khans, which explains why Marco Polo had no problems in traveling through Mongol territory to the court of the Kublai Khan.) At any rate, gunpowder was quickly put to use after its ingredients became known. The monk Roger Bacon toward the end of the thirteenth century described its explosive power when enclosed in a solid container. Although the cannon was a European invention, first used in 1319 in England, the original idea for it came from the Byzantine copper tube that contained the explosive Greek Fire. The first European cannon were long wooden tubes with iron rings that shot solid stone balls. Wrought iron was first used in the early part of the fifteenth century, along with lead shot. From then on the pressing need of princes to secure better cannon led to more efficient smelting and casting methods, as well as improved machine tools for boring iron and bronze cannon.

Merchants became wealthy seeking out metal deposits and erecting small furnaces and workshops near them for manufacturing cannon and firearms. The growing demand for metal soon made mining increasingly expensive, as deeper seams had to be worked. This meant that practical measures had to be taken to pump water out of deep mines, to ventilate the long shafts, and to haul the ore through intricate tunnels to the outside furnaces. The demand for metal for cannon also led to the training of mining engineers to cope with the problems besetting mining. Soon only those merchants with a good deal of capital were able to finance the complex mining ventures and the smelting and casting of ore.

The Lombards, the Florentines, and the merchant families of Augsburg and Nuremberg were the only people wealthy enough to finance most of the mines of continental Europe. The Fuggers, a wealthy Roman Catholic merchant family of Augsburg, obtained their initial capital by serving as bankers for the German bishops and princes. They had started as merchant mine-owners in the fourteenth century, but by the sixteenth century they had amassed so much capital from their mining ventures in Styria and Tyrol in Austria and in northern Spain that they were able to finance both the acquisition of heavy cannon and the hiring of mercenary troops by the Holy Roman Emperor, Charles V. In fact, the Fuggers even supplied the dowry for the Emperor's daughter.

The Fourteenth Century and Its Innovations

Other rivulets also led into the stream that would later become the scientific and industrial civilization. In the fourteenth century, these were the growth of trade and industry in Italy and the Low Countries, the improvements in navigation brought about by this increased trade, the development of encyclopedic treatises on technology, and the compilation of more exact studies on the physical world. These studies are exemplified by astronomy, which was initially studied for practical purposes, such as determining the date of Easter, measuring latitudes, and defining true north for navigational purposes; chemistry, which was initially explored to develop new colors and pigments for the textile industry, but was later used for advising on better distillation processes and improved manufacture of gunpowder; mechanics; and optics.

Few of us today realize how important certain small towns in the fourteenth century had become as manufacturing centers. At this time, however, cities were few and far between, and their populations were fairly small compared with our modern metropolitan centers. Milan, for example, employed some 60,000 workers in its handicraft woolen industry (most of them were undoubtedly part-time peasants). Florence, in 1306, possessed 300 workshops, which employed 30,000 workers (an average of about 100 workers each) and produced 100,000 pieces of cloth. In the Low Countries both Bruges and Antwerp were important weaving centers; and Ghent employed more than 3,000 weavers. By the thirteenth century the Flemish, who had learned the art of making fine woolens from Spain and Italy, had begun to migrate in numbers to England, settling with their looms in the countryside around London and southeastern England.

The art of fine weaving had been diffused from Byzantium to the

Moslems of the Middle East, and from there to Italy and Catalonia. From Italy and Spain, it moved to northwestern France, Flanders, and England. By the end of the thirteenth century, Basel, Strasburg, Cologne, Regensburg, Passau, Augsburg, and Magdeburg were competing with Italy and Flanders for the growing markets for cloth among the feudal lords and their retinues, the churchmen, the burghers, and the small but steadily increasing class of independent artisans and craftsmen.

The increased wealth of the fourteenth century had little effect upon the peasants. Despite an increase in food production resulting from earlier agricultural improvements, the fourteenth century wars that broke out between neighboring barons, princes, and kings so devastated large areas of farmland and standing crops that almost no surplus was able to accumulate for the benefit of the peasants. The rise of the fortified cathedral towns encouraged the growth of a merchant-artisan class, who learned to defend themselves with arms against the onslaughts of their feudal neighbors. The security of the new towns stimulated an increased migration to them by the younger peasants, who sought to free themselves from ever-mounting obligations to their lords.

Florence in the Fourteenth Century

Florence in the fourteenth century reflected the changes that were taking place as the local merchant-financier became the prototype of the London, Flemish, Hanseatic, and Dutch burghers of later centuries. As the Florentine merchants became wealthy through their trade and moneylending activities, they hired mercenaries to fight their battles against neighboring towns and feudal lords. As the rural estates around Florence were taken over by the merchants through conquest and as neighboring towns became occupied by the merchants' soldiers, the surplus serfs were ordered to Florence, where they became a labor force for the growing textile industry. When this did not solve the shortage of labor, a "putting-out" system of spinning was organized, which was to last until the eve of the Industrial Revolution, when workers and machines would be placed under one roof with the strict supervision and military discipline of foremen and supervisors. Under this putting-out, or cottage, system traveling agents of the merchants brought raw materials to the peasant villages where the spinning wheels and looms were located, paid the workers (mostly women) for their labor, and brought the semifinished goods back to Florence for fulling and dyeing.

As the fourteenth century drew to a close, Florence was shifting over from handicraft methods of production to large-scale water-driven and hand-operated transmission belts connecting many spinning wheels, looms, or lathes. By 1300, Florence had already been making and selling fairly good imitations of Chinese silk brocades to churchmen, princes, and men of wealth. Raw silk was obtained from China, wool from Spain and England, and chemicals for dyeing from Byzantium, Anatolia, Syria, Persia, and India. (The Mongol invasion of Persia in the fourteenth century stopped this importation of dyes and compelled Italy—and handicraft Europe in general—to seek new substitutes.)

Wealthy merchants and financiers managed and financed the production and distribution of Florentine goods and textiles. (Florence at this time also manufactured the armor, swords, spears, and other paraphenalia needed for war between feudal lords or between towns.) Though the value of the textiles sold to other parts of Europe was small in contrast to present-day trade, the total was much larger than any previously known. Florence until the sixteenth century was truly one of the great manufacturing areas of Europe. Only trade, industry, and finance could have paid for the churches, palaces, and works of art that adorned Florence in profusion at that time. By 1338 the value of Florentine textiles came to the equivalent of some 14 million dollars. By 1410 it had doubled, and the manufacturing of textiles had now become so specialized that their manufacture from raw materials to finished goods required more than thirty separate operations, each performed by a separate individual.

The factory system was already in existence in embryo. Florence had a floating population of landless laborers (many drawn from other countries of Europe, including quite a number from Flanders and southern Germany), large workshops in which the workers were closely supervised, and numerous salesmen who traveled all over Europe seeking orders for Florentine goods.

Fifteenth and Sixteenth Century Developments in Technology and Industry

The infant industrial age of the thirteenth and fourteenth centuries soon became a mature way of life for many small cities and industrial towns in Italy, Germany, Flanders, France, and England after the sixteenth century. The growing expense of war contributed to this industrial development, as cannon and firearms became more efficient and thus more deadly. Granulated gunpowder, invented by the end of the fifteenth century, exploded with more violence than the earlier poorly made dust. The demand for ore now became insatiable. Between three to four tons of bronze were required to make a large cannon (copper and tin have never been common metals); and an iron cannonball in the sixteenth century weighed more than 100 pounds, some as much as 150. Another two tons of metal were required to make the heavy iron bolts on the gun carriage, the long chain, and the iron hook. Even the axles and wheels had more iron in them than ever before, and the metallic tires encasing the wheels were now made of wrought iron.

The production of finished iron doubled, tripled, and quadrupled between 1460 and 1550 in Germany, Bohemia, Hungary, and Austria. By 1550 central Europe alone was producing more than 100,000 tons of iron and steel per year, which, though little compared to our present-day annual world production of more than 300 million tons, was more than ten times the total annual world production of that metal at the height of the Roman Empire. Iron was scarce in the Ancient World; it became much more plentiful in sixteenth century Europe as new mines were opened and more efficient methods of smelting ore came into operation. At the same time the annual average copper production in the sixteenth century was over 15,000 tons, as compared to more than 1,000,000 tons per year in the United States in the middle of the twentieth century. But copper is a rarer metal than iron, and it took a good deal of ingenuity for Europe to produce its 15,000 tons per year with its primitive mining and smelting techniques.

Smelting iron requires a much higher heat than smelting copper.[5] Until the Middle Ages iron was a difficult metal to smelt because it was impossible to obtain temperatures high enough. Iron was always in a half-molten state in primitive furnaces, and the bits of iron that had been wrested from the iron ore by the low heat had to be separated from the rest of the ore by intensive hammering. In the early Middle Ages a water-run bellows had been invented to increase the heat of the charcoal fire; but it was not until the sixteenth century that a blast furnace was invented, into which a steady current of air was forced by large bellows, thus increasing the heat and permitting more complete smelting. Iron came of age in the sixteenth century when it could be heated to a completely molten stage, poured as a liquid, and cast in sand molds. This decreased the time involved in making pig iron and created a stronger iron, not by hammering as wrought iron had been fashioned previously, but by melting the iron completely and then casting it in molds as was done with copper, brass, and bronze. (As we have seen, in the period before the Christian era the Chinese cast their iron by using piston bellows to obtain a much higher degree of heat than their European and Asian contemporaries did at that time.) Iron thus became a more common metal and was used in a wide array of tools, cannon, weapons, and even household utensils. But it would not be until the eighteenth century that a better grade of iron was made by substituting coke for coal or charcoal (whose impurities combined with the iron to make it brittle), and it would not be until the nineteenth century that the invention of the Bessemer blast furnace enabled mankind to enter the iron and steel age.

[5] Copper melts at 1084° C.; iron at 1529° C.

The Industrial Age Moves to England

By 1560 the town of Namur in Wallonia (present-day Belgium) had more than 35 blast furnaces. Within a century, however, England had displaced both Wallonia and western Germany as an iron-making center. In 1650 there were over 150 blast furnaces in England alone. France also made great strides in its iron-making industries, as a result of the official support given to manufacturing by Colbert, the First Minister to Louis XIV. Sweden also became an important iron-making country, as a result of Dutch efforts to exploit Swedish mines.

By the beginning of the seventeenth century, however, England had been slowly pushed into the role of industrial and scientific leader of the Eurasian world. There were many reasons for this, but perhaps the long period of peace enjoyed by England from the fourteenth century onward was the most important. This brought about the immigration of Italians, Flemings, Germans, Frenchmen, and other European skilled artisans and merchants who wanted to escape the continuous and depressing wars of Europe, which destroyed capital, farms, towns, workshops, and mines. Although England was certainly a backward country until the sixteenth century (overshadowed by the northern Italian cities, by southwestern Germany, and by Flanders in total production of entrepreneurs, businessmen, and inventors), within a hundred years she had taken a commanding lead over the other European countries—a lead she would not lose until the end of the nineteenth century when she would be passed by both the United States and Germany.

The growing textile trade of England (she was permitted to manufacture textiles in peace for a Europe devastated by war) and her expanding trade in metals, ships, and household goods contributed to the accumulation of capital. She also carried on an extensive trade with Europe in fish, sugar, and timber, which she obtained from the New World. The piracy of her merchants (supported by the throne during the sixteenth and seventeenth centuries) also contributed to the accumulation of a large supply of gold and silver with which she could attract competent technicians, enterprising merchants, and applied engineers from continental Europe. Increased trade also meant better communications between Englishmen of education and the growing number of individuals who were stimulated by the new learning and science in Italy, France, Germany, Flanders, and Belgium in the sixteenth and seventeenth centuries.

The quickened growth of knowledge that transformed the seventeenth century into the new Industrial and Scientific Age was brought about by the first assembly line for mass production in Europe, the printing press. In its various components the printing press was old.

Presses were already known by the fifteenth century in the manufacture of wine and the printing of cloth. The type itself was based upon old techniques of wood carving, engraving, and the casting of metals—a process that went back to the Sumerian period. Even the principle of printing with fixed and movable blocks had been known previously to the Chinese and the Koreans, and it was these ideas that Italian merchant-travelers brought back to Europe. Yet the printing press as a production line was new; as an industry for which Europe and Asia were ready and waiting, it was new; and as a means of bringing together individuals whose ideas would never have met, it was new.

The invention of the printing press was necessary by the middle of the fifteenth century. The need for its products was growing as a result of the multiplication of schools and the great increase in learning. After the tenth century the important monasteries and cathedrals opened schools to train laymen as well as priests. Although the number of literate individuals increased slowly and imperceptibly, by the fifteenth century at least 5 percent of the Western population knew the mysteries of the written word. The well-to-do merchants educated their children in the great Latin schools of the day; the lesser administrative officials of the lords, princes, and kings also looked favorably upon the acquisition of literacy; and the increase in numbers of accountants, lawyers, notaries, and clerks made possible an industry that, by cheapening costs through mass production, opened up to the ordinary literate man in the growing towns and cities what had previously been a luxury trade. The new universities that had been established after the eleventh and twelfth centuries in the cities of Italy, Germany, France, Bohemia, Poland, and England added to the growth of an insatiable consumer demand for the simple printing presses of the fifteenth, sixteenth, and seventeenth centuries. The growth of Protestantism, with its emphasis upon the authority of the Bible, encouraged simple artisans, lesser merchants, and even workers and peasants to laboriously follow the letters with their fingers so that they could read the word of God for themselves. Even before Lutheranism, the Hussites of Bohemia and the Waldensians of southern France encouraged literacy among their followers so that each man could reach a decision for himself about his beliefs, based upon the authority of the Bible, a book that had previously been out of reach.

Printing thus raised the quality of living of the lower classes by giving them more confidence in themselves. They now believed optimistically that literacy could enrich and improve their lives and thus make them more nearly the intellectual equals of the upper classes. Printing and literacy would make possible the growth and spread of both scientific and political knowledge. Even the charges and countercharges involved in the growth of the Reformation and the Counter-Reformation were issued through the media of tens of thousands of books and pamphlets.

The new society to be inaugurated after the nineteenth century would require a mountainous production of infinite variety in the printed word, both to fulfill the teaching needs of the proliferating schools, technical colleges, and universities and to supply means of communication to the growing industries, businesses, research laboratories, and government administrative offices. The world was entering a new era in which the production of ideas would be as important as the production of industrial goods.

The Egalitarian Movements

Along with this opening of new horizons to the human mind came a strong desire for equality, which swept from one part of Europe to the other. We know little of man's past dreams or demands for self-esteem, self-confidence, and independence of spirit, which until then had been the virtual monopoly of the wealthy, the titled, and the powerful. In the Ancient World there had been revolts against injustice and tyrannical conquerors. In the first century B.C. slaves had risen under Spartacus and terrorized southern Italy for almost two years. Voices against man's inhumanity to man had been raised in Palestine, India, and China. Even in the classical world of Alexandria and Rome, there were many who did not accept the extreme inequalities of social status that existed between master and slave. In caste-directed India individual holy men had preached against the injustices of caste. Jesus had insisted that the poor would inherit the kingdom of Heaven and that it would be difficult for the rich and powerful to receive any rewards there. The authoritarian concept that whatever exists does so because it is right was never quite accepted by those who were influenced by other scattered ideas that moved from one part of the Eurasian world to the other.

In Europe from the twelfth century on, resistance to the blind acceptance of authority had been inadvertently supported by the reaction of the Church against the infallibility of such classic authorities on the natural world as Pliny and Aristotle. The Moslems had found Aristotle more congenial than the Christians had. Aristotle had postulated a fixed universe, operating by natural laws that even God could not change; the Moslems accepted the idea that a fixed universe determined man's fate and that it could not be changed. This was anathema, however, to the churchmen in Paris and England, who believed that God could create a void, make worlds, and change the laws of the universe. A changing universe was more amenable to scientific hypotheses than one that was inscrutable, mysterious, and immutable. In an effort to prove Aristotle wrong, many churchmen encouraged commentaries that led to speculation about an infinite universe and the possibility of empty space, to observations about falling bodies, and to the substitution of mathematical for philosophical thinking.

Science grows by attempting to refute all traditional hypotheses, by observing and theorizing until a coherent understanding of the phenomena under study is accepted by most individuals working in the field concerned. Where there can be no confrontation and refutation of traditional knowledge, either because the subject is considered too sacred or because no way can be devised of obtaining evidence against tradition, it is difficult if not impossible for scientific thinking to grow.

Although early scientific thinking was mixed with magical and occult forms of thought (in which cause and effect were not interrelated), enough skepticism had been generated against traditional ways of thinking and doing things to encourage experimentation that would lead to important discoveries. Even the alchemists, with their use of nonrelated causes and effects and their preoccupation with the mythology of words, inadvertently brought about an advance in knowledge of distillation, dyes, chemicals, and pharmaceuticals, which would lead in a few centuries to a more rational understanding of chemical phenomena that had been observed.

Scientific thinking requires that men possess an optimistic self-confidence if they are to make an effort to understand the world about them, to explain its mysteries, and to expose its myths, dogmas, and taboos. Scientific thinking implies a respect for man's intellectual capacity to pierce the dark forests of ignorance and to seek unknown ways to a new enjoyment of life. It posits a role in which man rejects gods who keep their knowledge from him, and denies that man is a puny, humiliated, craven being who should spend his days masochistically bemoaning his sinfulness, faults, and vices and voicing his self-hatred. Scientific thought assumes an optimistic belief in man, not as one who has fallen, but as one who is rising—a being who has tremendous capacities for learning, discovering, and understanding.

Medieval asceticism, with its professed hatred of the qualities that make man the human, thinking, and problem-solving being he is, could lead only to a paralysis of the thinking function. Seventeenth century science, on the other hand, required the go-ahead signals of intellectual freedom, of liberty of conscience, and of the right of every individual to examine critically all phases of his social and physical life, to speculate about the universe in nontraditional terms, and to accept no authority blindly. An authoritarian civilization that was indifferent to this sense of human optimism and contained individuals reared to believe that nothing can be done to change what already exists could not have created the scientific spirit that was to find its home in western Europe during the seventeenth century.

This scientific spirit went hand in hand with the belief that man could also change his social world. The Church had already stressed the importance of man's deciding for himself whether to follow good or evil, although it had punished him severely when his "free will" led him away from the sacrosanct teachings of the Church. Various movements in the later Middle Ages attempted to combine this free volition of man to choose good with the right of all individuals to be pleasing in the sight of God. Father John Ball, an English priest who had participated in a peasants' revolt in 1381, had intoned, "When Adam delved, and Eve span, who, then, was the gentleman?" (In other words, there were no classes in the Garden of Eden.) The fourteenth century in England had also seen the spread of an egalitarian priestly movement whose members, called Lollards, wished to reform the Church by doing away with its social inequalities. The Lollards were later to influence the equally egalitarian movement of peasants called the Hussites in Bohemia. Even before the Lollards, the Waldensians in southern France had insisted upon the right of the lowly individual to follow his own conscience rather than authoritarian tradition in finding his way to God. All these dissenting movements were part of a minority reaction throughout Europe against the absolutist restrictions then placed upon the human mind.

The new Scientific and Industrial Age also required a receptivity toward its concepts of freedom of thought from those who were the secular and religious authorities at that time. Part of this receptivity was found among some high churchmen in France, Germany, and England, who were themselves mental dissenters against higher Papal authority. Part was found among an educated segment of the public in a growing spirit of optimism, in a feeling of expansiveness, and in a belief that mankind was capable of making itself wealthier than ever before. And part was found among those mercantilist kings and ministers who saw opportunities in science and industrialization to make their realms and themselves richer and more powerful than ever before.

The rising merchant classes in Europe, who had amassed wealth in trade and cottage industries, were also receptive to these new waves of mental self-confidence that seemed to promise so much in increasing the wealth and power of the age. The increase in literacy created by the spread of schools and universities and by the use of the printing press to bring learning to the middle classes encouraged many to believe that the new knowledge could make man free of his traditional fears. It could do away with human drudgery, it could create tolerance between the different parts of the known world, and it could bring a peace in which men could build the good life without fear that war would destroy what intelligence and thrift had accumulated.

In no previous age had men been so attracted to the pursuit of technical and scientific knowledge as in the countries of western Europe at the beginning of the seventeenth century. Men were taking their first steps away from authoritarian mental controls. Dissenting opinions against the traditional Aristotelian thought of the thirteenth and fourteenth centuries at Paris and Cambridge were continued in the seventeenth century, when Galileo at the University of Padua attempted to find evidence disproving the Aristotelian concept of the fixed order of the universe, a concept then accepted by many churchmen in positions of authority in Rome.

In many ways the growth of the scientific spirit of the seventeenth century was as much a means of hitting back at the authority of the Church, both Roman Catholic and Protestant, as it was a means of rebelling against the traditional ways and wisdom of the past. Whereas men in previous ages had been afraid of being considered heretics if they criticized traditional opinions on the functioning of the physical universe, certain individuals in the seventeenth century were no longer afraid, despite the fact that in many parts of Europe the Counter-Reformation discouraged any expression of anti-authority sentiments.

A mental climate had been created during the previous four centuries that encouraged a few men in authority to give their protection not only to those engaged in studying the universe objectively, but also to those engaged in criticizing the traditional knowledge of the past. Some of those in authority who accepted the new ways of thinking, observing, and understanding the universe were to be found in Venice, the Low Countries, the free Hanseatic cities, France, and England. Although for many centuries the rest of the Eurasian world resisted these ideas, this new way of viewing man and his universe would spread from a mere handful of individuals to hundreds, and then to thousands. And these thousands would transform the traditional assumptions of man's mental world during the coming eighteenth and nineteenth centuries.

On the other hand, the overwhelming majority of individuals in Europe at this time were still unaware of the new trends in thinking. They lived as their fathers before them had lived. They were illiterate, and they accepted unquestioningly the prevailing authority over their minds. They would remain passive spectators to the coming Scientific and Industrial Age, which would employ them though they had little identification with the mental spirit that produced it. Even the Protestant reformers of the sixteenth century had little sympathy for this new age, for they had no use for a point of view that did not consider man a fallen, craven creature. In encouraging free will and criticism of the Aristotelian concepts of nature, the Church had opened a Pandora's box, whose effects it would feel in the coming centuries. In permitting the scientific intellectual to probe the workings of human nature as well as of physical nature, the secular authorities were in effect weakening the strong ties of allegiance that the educated mind would feel toward them.

By the seventeenth century, a good deal of old and new knowledge had been printed (some of it going back to the Ancient World); a large number of individuals had been trained in the technical processes that had been slowly accumulating through the centuries; merchants had widened their horizons by importing and exporting more and more goods from all parts of the world; ships had become larger, faster, and safer; mines that utilized new processes of mining had been opened; iron and steel were made in larger quantities; incentives existed for young men not only to learn new callings but to experiment in broadening older ones; administrators were more sophisticated in their understanding of the governments and industries they managed; and the well-to-do everywhere were increasing their expectations of what the good life should hold for them. All this constituted capital: the knowledge of how to exploit the resources of both nature and men; the knowledge of how to fashion raw materials into goods that could be sold; the knowledge of how to hire those who had special skills, training, and talents to apply to practical problems; and the knowledge of how to encourage imaginative innovators to develop new ideas and processes that could create even more wealth (as the blast furnace had increased the production of iron with less labor and at smaller cost, or as the heavy plow and tandem horses had contributed to the greater production of crops), thereby freeing men for other productive purposes.

Over the centuries, the mere accumulation of gold and silver without correlative increases in agricultural production, without increases in skilled men who could utilize the techniques of the past to fashion new processes, and without increases in technical thought over the years, would have meant that England in particular could not have been ready for the Industrial and Scientific Age. Capital has little meaning except in terms of resources—resources that include trained manpower able to transform various processes that did not exist a few centuries earlier into goods and services.

It would have been impossible for even the wealthiest king to have brought about a Scientific and Industrial Age in a country composed entirely of illiterate peasants. Wealth was in knowledge rather than in an accumulation of gold and silver, which had exchange value only because they were symbols for the "x" number of raw materials, goods, and services that could be produced by skilled men who had learned to be more efficient through insightful thought.

For Selected Bibliography, see end of Chapter 18.

14

The Industrial Age Begins

A series of fortunate circumstances helped England to become the first modern industrial nation of the world. As an island, she had escaped the repeated land invasions that had destroyed the workshops of Antwerp and northern Italy. She had enjoyed a period of peace that enabled her to benefit from the skills that had been developed in other parts of Europe and were brought to her shores by refugees from Italy, Flanders, France, and Germany. The refugees were attracted by her natural isolation from the destructive acts of war then raging in Europe. The Thirty Years' War, for example, had destroyed large parts of central Europe. The persecution of the Huguenots by Louis XIV had sent tens of thousands of craftsmen, small industrialists, and merchants into England with their accumulated knowledge and techniques.

Skilled men from Italy and the German states also flocked to England in order to be free to carry on their trades and handicrafts without pressure from the existing guilds. They brought their wealth, which was not so much in gold and silver as in tools, training, and ideas. These skills plus abundant natural resources, good harbors for coastal and foreign shipping, highly skilled shipbuilders, merchants who were able to fulfill an increasing demand for goods in both domestic and foreign markets, and a surplus of food supplies that could be used for purchasing raw materials from abroad all helped to encourage the spread of the new seventeenth century "know-how" that would lead to even greater wealth for England.

From the sixteenth to the seventeenth centuries, England had benefited enormously from a growth in trade and an accumulation of technical knowledge from Flanders, the Low Countries, Italy, and France. By 1650 her colonies in the New World contained greater skills, more capital, and more merchandising talents per capita than the colonies of either the Spaniards or the French. Only the Dutch would surpass the merchants of England at commercial skill in opening new markets, although in the New World the French and the Spaniards would become the explorers par excellence.

In 1540 London had fewer than 50,000 persons; it had grown slowly from the thirteenth century when it had 30,000. By 1640 London was bursting at the seams with more than 300,000 inhabitants. In 1540 London depended upon the surrounding countryside for its food, firewood, manufactures, and labor. By 1640 London was using coal brought by barge from the Newcastle region, and its food came from all parts of England and Ireland. In London alone, the market for coal, grain, fish, meat, vegetables, timber, bricks, household utensils, and clothing far exceeded the market for food, clothing, and weapons demanded by the great armies then devastating Germany in the Thirty Years' War. The demands of a population that grew faster than that of any European city created a need for wholesalers, jobbers, retail merchants, suppliers of all kinds, transportation media, and craftsmen who could make new, better, and cheaper commodities for the growing world market.

By 1640 England was the leading manufacturing country in Europe. The Dutch Republic was its only competitor, but Dutch merchants were more merchant intermediaries than manufacturers (although at this time they did make the best ships on the continent and had invented the "Dutch frame" for making ribbons and other narrow textiles). Flanders had been devastated by more than sixty years of war, and its best craftsmen and merchants had already left Antwerp and Bruges for Amsterdam and London.

The Italian cities had contributed enormously to the scientific sum of knowledge of the day and were at the height of their economic powers. Soon, however, commercial and industrial competition from England and Holland and the invading armies from Austria and France would put an end to the manufacturing and commercial lead of Venice, Florence, and Genoa. In the seventeenth century, Venice was a large and wealthy city of 190,000 inhabitants, with a thousand merchant-patrician families in its ruling oligarchy. It was the largest glass-manufacturing center in Europe. The city was the chief outlet for Florentine textiles and metal goods. Venice had a state arsenal that was a model of efficiency. It employed thousands of men and built ships, cannon, and small arms efficiently, speedily, and profitably.

Increasing competition and the inability to obtain enough raw materials from a continent almost continuously at war handicapped the industrial expansion of Venice during the seventeenth century. By the end of the eighteenth century the Italian cities had ended their long period of great commercial importance, which had begun with the decline of the Byzantine Empire in the tenth century and had ended when greater land powers occupied the capital city and hinterland.

As we have already seen, a confluence of circumstances left England to lead the way to a new civilization that would be based upon a large urban industrial population, a diminishing rural population, and a growing number of individuals and entrepreneurs whose task it was to invent, to organize production, and to build up markets for their plants to supply. For all their imaginative pioneering in creating the rudiments of the Industrial Age, Venice, Genoa, and Florence were still living in the midst of Primary civilization, in which agriculture employed a majority of individuals and handicrafts occupied only a small minority.

The Venetians and the Florentines had been intermediaries between the Ancient Worlds of Alexandria and Constantinople and the new Secondary civilization that was to arise in Europe. They had helped transfer to the new Europe skills in manufacturing luxury goods and rudiments of capitalistic finance that had existed in Alexandria and Constantinople long after the Roman Empire in the west had ended. From Constantinople, Venetians had learned to make fine glass; from Alexandria, Florentines had learned finance and skill in making fine embroidered cloth. Despite the contributions they made to world civilization, however, Venice, Genoa, and Florence remained minor cities with populations of less than 200,000. They were too isolated from their hinterlands, whose way of life was still agricultural and whose peasants had no incentives to change themselves into more efficient farmers or skilled craftsmen manufacturing for the urban markets.

No matter how many skills were present in Italy, her population could still not have played the role that England did in the seventeenth and eighteenth centuries. She lacked a large internal market, she had no important raw materials nearby (Venice was dependent upon Austria for her iron ore and other metals), she was not strong enough militarily to protect the lines of communication with her sources of raw materials, and she did not have markets large enough to take an increasing supply of goods from her. Competition from England meant that Venice would have had to learn to cut the costs of production to meet the lower prices of English goods. This required an era of peace and a willingness to learn new techniques of production; but these the oligarchs of Venice did not have.

Italy possessed the scientists, engineers, skilled workers, efficient merchants, and financiers; but she lacked manufacturers who could learn from others, who could cooperate, and who could exchange knowledge through licensing patents. This cooperation might have increased industrialization; but the geographic handicap of being in the line of march of French, Austrian, and Spanish armies during the seventeenth and eighteenth centuries perhaps prevented the cities of Venice and Florence from putting their energies completely to work to solve their growing problems in the changing world of those times.

England in the seventeenth century was in the fortunate position of having little competition from France, Italy, or the German cities. English artisans and craftsmen were becoming more efficient than the French and had become more practical in learning from experience. France was not interested in a large internal market for her goods. Her manufacturing was done for the king, his courtiers, the landed aristocrats, and the very wealthy burghers of the cities, all of whom preferred to have their goods handmade by skilled and painstaking artisans. (Unlike the English and the Dutch merchants, French interest in the New World extended only to securing furs and sugarcane.)

From the Italians and the Flemish, the English early learned the advantages of concentrating workers under one roof so that their output could be supervised and guided. In the first half of the sixteenth century, John Winchcombe built a woolen factory employing 200 weavers, 200 apprentices, 100 female carders, 200 girl spinners, and 150 boy sorters of the raw wool—a force of over 850, excluding the supervisors and the clerks! Winchcombe was not the only large employer of labor, for there were several others like him in the sixteenth century.

The fields of agriculture and industry were becoming more related and interdependent than ever before. During the sixteenth and seventeenth centuries, the putting-out system of cottage handicrafts had expanded enormously. (The Florentines had developed this system from the fourteenth century onward. From Italy this method of using cottage industry spread to Flanders and from Flanders to southeastern England.) In one village in southeastern England, an observer in the late seventeenth century reported that fewer than six farmers out of sixty derived their entire income from their lands; the rest supplemented their incomes by working at home with their wives, daughters, and sons as spinners and weavers. Although agricultural production was increasing, the smaller farmers tried to increase their standard of living by doing extra work at home. In the seventeenth century the population was growing and there was a need for more consumer goods as well as food.

England during the seventeenth century forged ahead industrially not because of any special abilities that resided in the English people, but because her merchants took advantage of a European continent at war. For example, by the end of the sixteenth century London had begun to displace Antwerp as a center for sugar refining. Spanish and French troops fighting one another had so destroyed the refineries of Antwerp that many sugar merchants and their skilled workers fled to London or Amsterdam seeking a peaceful location in which to start again. Even the cloth makers could not survive the sacking of their towns and workshops by the invading troops, and a good many of the masters and merchants moved to Hamburg, Amsterdam, London, and Rouen.

In the middle of the sixteenth century, the Spanish Netherlands had been the leading manufacturing area of Europe; but by the beginning of the seventeenth century, a good part of Flemish industrial capital and large-scale industry had moved across the channel to England. England thus gained from the secrets and experience of the large numbers of skilled craftsmen and merchants from all over western Europe who came to England seeking sanctuary. Only Holland offered equal facilities; and the seventeenth century was also an era of great prosperity for the ship-builders, merchants, traders, and artisans of the Dutch Netherlands.

Industry in Europe in the seventeenth century developed not as a result of scientific speculation, but out of the rule-of-thumb experiences and pragmatic judgments of its highly skilled workers. Few cities in Europe at that time had more than 100,000 inhabitants. These included such urban centers as London, Paris, Antwerp, Amsterdam, Genoa, Venice, Florence, Rome, and Naples. Most of Europe was still peasant-centered, with a scattering of small towns.

We must not exaggerate the changes that took place in Europe during the sixteenth and seventeenth centuries. They were still minor and mainly in detail rather than in overall structure. Handicrafts had changed little over the centuries. Farming would not change drastically for almost another hundred years. Roads were still full of potholes, harbors were primitive, and canals would not be built until after the middle of the eighteenth century.

At this time, most European populations were still strongly authoritarian and looked upon any change in their lives as a threat to their personal security. Few individuals were free enough from anxiety to be able to see the profitable opportunities for expansion that lay before them. A few optimistic spirits desired change because they believed that their own status would be enhanced as a result. It was consequently they who moved forward in science, technology, trade, and even agriculture.

But these innovators were still only a tiny number, although their numbers were perhaps three to four times as great in the seventeenth century as in the fifteenth. These individuals had a need to prove themselves superior to the traditionalists; they needed to feel that the world was their "oyster." But they would have to grow more numerous and optimistic before their influence would be felt among the elites in the populations.

The Need of the English to Be "Equal"

In the seventeenth century, England also underwent a profound cultural change. The egalitarian movements that had grown during the fourteenth century culminated in a middle-class revolution by the seventeenth. The lower gentry, the yeomen farmers, the town merchants, and the artisans combined to defeat the aristocracy, the king, and the churchmen, culminating in a religious republic under the guidance of Sir Oliver Cromwell. This need of the middle classes to assert their equality to the aristocrats who had treated them with contempt would lead to an increasing status for them. The English middle classes wanted to prove themselves the equals both of the large number of foreigners who had come to England with their queens and churchmen, and of their own aristocracy and churchmen, who were also considered "foreign" to middle-class behavior and aspirations.[1]

England had been invaded and conquered by Celts, Romans, Angles and Saxons, Danes and Norwegians, Normans, a large number of foreign prelates who had come with the Roman Catholic Church, and non-English-speaking courtiers attached to the Spanish and French princesses who married English kings. The middle classes of England wished to have the same status as these foreigners rather than to occupy a position of inferiority to them. They wanted to be as skilled as the refugee Flemings, Italians, and Huguenots who had come in large numbers during the past two centuries, and as wealthy as the landed aristocrats who disdained them. In the seventeenth century, it was not the poor peasantry who opposed the king, the established church, and the aristocracy (as they had under Wat Tyler and John Ball in 1381), but the more prosperous yeomen, the lesser gentry, the merchants, and the artisans. Out of these groups the future industrialists and innovators of England would come in the next century. These groups believed that their status should be commensurate with their own images of themselves. They were optimistic enough to believe that with proper governmental direction life could be made better not only for themselves but also for the rest of the population. This striving for an increased sense of importance motivated their sons and grandsons to seek a greater respect from others through scientific, managerial, and technical innovations. The descendants of these groups and other dissenters like them would become the leaders of England in the eighteenth and nineteenth centuries.

If these ambitious men with a need for achievement had been denied the opportunities to show what they could do, the Scientific and Industrial Age would never have come into being in England. The country would have continued to be a backward, poor, traditional country of villages and small towns, with a population content to work and live as their ancestors had, tilling their lands, making a small variety of poor-quality goods, and living only for the day.

These few innovators refused to live as their ancestors had because they wanted higher status and greater respect from the elites. They were

---

[1] Despite the increased privileges of the middle classes, the lower classes were hardly much better off than they had been in previous centuries. Their need for equality would not be translated into action until the nineteenth and twentieth centuries.

confident that they could win recognition of their mental abilities from those who had previously disdained them.

Wealth had become an important goal in itself for these potential innovators from the lower middle classes. They had seen that the aristocrats of the seventeenth and eighteenth centuries in both France and England had accorded a grudging respect to those who had won wealth as a form of power. Until the eighteenth century, the largest palaces in Europe had been owned not by the nobility but by the wealthy merchants of the German Hanseatic cities, Amsterdam, Italy, France, and England. It was the eighteenth century aristocrats who found it necessary to amass wealth in conspicuous display in order to compete with the wealthy middle classes.

Respectability Comes to Science

The seventeenth century witnessed the development of science as well as the growth of merchant wealth. With the end of Oliver Cromwell's puritan oligarchic republic in 1660, a Royal Society for the encouragement of scientific thought (as opposed to puritan ideology) was established under royal protection. The Royal Society attracted its membership from the educated aristocracy, the wealthy, educated merchant class, the intellectual gentry, and various university people, rather than from the lower middle classes, who would produce the innovators, the businessmen, and the practical engineers. The Society was the prototype of all the later scientific societies on the continent of Europe and in the colonies of North America. It gave elite approval, or status, to the scientific intellectual and provided him with an audience and a sounding board for his theories and speculations.

Scientific thought had now become eminently respectable both in England and on the continent. Science and scientific thought were given an intellectual prestige that encouraged many inquiring minds to become fascinated by the nonconformist and nontraditional ideas that are part and parcel of scientific knowledge. A freedom of thought unheard of in the authoritarian past enabled dozens of nontraditional minds to seek out satisfying intellectual explanations for the workings of the universe, of the human body, and even of society.

Technology Becomes More Efficient

Other nontraditional individuals, dissatisfied with the inefficiency of seventeenth century technical processes, sought more efficient machines, which could be directed to do everything that skilled hands could do and do it faster and with more regularity. The Neolithic tool had been an extension of the human hand; the seventeenth and eighteenth century machine was a substitute for the human hand that could operate semi-automatically, doing the same work over and over again without fatigue, boredom, or moodiness. The machine required less guidance than the hand tool, and in time it would require even less supervision, as men put their minds to work to uncover more practical means for improving the crude machines of that century. Efficiency in work output now became an important goal for the merchant, the small manufacturer, and the skilled mechanic. Inefficiency and waste became obstacles to the procurement of more wealth. But to obtain this greater efficiency, non-traditional merchants, or proto-businessmen, were needed who would encourage the mechanical innovator with financing. England in the late seventeenth and early eighteenth centuries had these men, though not in the numbers that would be found there in the next hundred years. In these two centuries, most individuals would remain authoritarian traditionalists who saw every innovation introduced by others as aggression directed against their way of life (an assessment that in many cases would be correct).

The Growth of Science

The seventeenth century was a great period for the growth of scientific thought throughout western Europe (with the exceptions of Spain, Portugal, and southern Italy, which were still not mentally prepared to become part of this new civilization). Great mathematicians appeared in France, England, Italy, Germany, and Poland. The universities of northern Italy produced a large number of pioneers in the fields of mechanics, optics, and engineering. In England, Harvey made his contributions to the knowledge of the human heart and circulation of the blood; Newton assessed the laws of falling bodies and of light; Boyle made his observations on the behavior of gases; and Locke made his contributions on man and his government. These men were not ascetic puritans trying to assure a place for themselves in the next world, but optimistic men using free thought to guide them to a more efficient, secure human world. They sought not spiritual absolutes but the reality of the world as it was.

The Transformation of Agriculture

To support the increasingly large number of individuals who earned their livelihood through trade, industry, and science, England had to transform her agriculture in order to supply extra food. This revolution took place from the end of the seventeenth to the middle of the eighteenth century under the stimulation of profits that were made through more efficient husbandry, tillage, and breeding. Part of the stimulus also came from the Royal Society's scientific interest in soils, fertility, and botany. Most of the work was done by the gentry and lesser nobility, who sometimes became almost cranks in their missionary attempts to change past agricultural practices.

To illustrate the changes brought about by selective breeding, we should point out that at the beginning of the eighteenth century the average weight of oxen sold in the English country markets was about 370 pounds; by the end of the century it increased to over 800 pounds. The average weight of calves sold in the markets was about 50 pounds in 1700; it became more than 150 pounds a century later. In 1710 the weight of sheep sold by farmers was less than 38 pounds; at the century's end it was over 80 pounds. Nothing describes more dramatically the revolution in stock breeding that took place in England in the eighteenth century than these contrasting figures.

The agricultural revolution was pushed through by a small but extremely influential group of educated upper-class landowners, who almost singlehandedly changed English agriculture from the traditional way of life of illiterate peasants, who farmed much as their ancestors had, to an experimental, highly technical business enterprise employing educated farmers who learned their techniques from books and lectures. The revolution on the land was a revolt against wasteful traditionalism, nonempirical conventional wisdom, and the inefficient peasantry. The revolution could not have been carried out by the poor, but only by the wealthy: it took a good deal of capital to carry on many of the unprofitable early experiments designed to increase the fertility of the soil or the weight of domestic animals. Profit incentives encouraged the wealthy landowners to experiment in new techniques. Food prices increased as the market attempted to supply the growing population, and the man who produced more earned more.

From 1700 onward, various educated landowners were enthusiastically writing to their country friends about the advantages of deep plowing, crop rotation, and continuous cultivation. The farmers of England had been using manure as fertilizer for centuries, but the concept of using plants to enrich the soil was definitely new to most well-to-do landowners.

The changes in agriculture that took place during the eighteenth century followed the gradual transformation of the aristocrat from a feudal military lord into a managerial landowner who had more in common with the merchants in the towns than with his ancestors of a few centuries before. Turnips and clover became slogans for many of these new managerial landlords, who now discovered that wealth could be obtained through greater fertility of the soil and that profitable cattle and sheep could be obtained through more selective breeding. Because improved agricultural techniques and husbandry required closer supervision of the entire farming and stock-raising processes, the wealthy managerial landlords sought sanction through parliamentary legislation to do away with the formerly communal open fields and grazing areas, and to enclose them within their managed lands. Although these special enclosure laws of the eighteenth century forced many of the smaller yeomen, tenants, and laborers to leave the land that had been tilled by their ancestors for centuries, the law was on the landlord's side. The common land had never been free, but had always been subject to the rights of the lord of the manor. Legally the land belonged to the large landowners whose lands adjoined the common land. The tenant farmer, the landless laborer, and the small yeomen, who had used the land on the assumption that it was communal, soon discovered that, although feudalism in the past had permitted the free use of unused lands, it had never surrendered its ownership rights over them.

Government Management Comes Into the Picture: The Rise of Mercantilism

By 1700, men were beginning to think of the advantages of farming more profitably, of governing more effectively, and of producing more efficiently. Government was looked upon as the chief means of helping the realm amass more wealth through the encouragement of better agricultural techniques and more efficient industrial processes and through assistance to the merchants in finding new markets for their products. Mercantilism thus became the philosophy of the government of that day. It was claimed that the state could become wealthy only through amassing gold and silver and that these precious metals could be obtained only by having a greater amount of exports than imports. The state thus used its power to protect the merchants and industrialists from outside foreign competition by spurring its citizens to produce for external markets but at the same time to become self-sufficient in supplying internal markets. Even the colonies were looked upon as a means of increasing the industries and agriculture of the mother country. They were not to compete with the merchants of the mother country by trading with other countries directly, but to use the mother country as an intermediary.

The amassing of wealth became an important goal not only for the aristocrats and merchants but also for the state. The patterns for the later Secondary civilization of industry and science were sketched in the increased preoccupation of the wealthy and educated parts of the population with more efficient organizational techniques. By 1700 some English authors were pointing out that production would greatly increase if work processes were made more specialized, with each worker doing only one task. In 1701 one English author was convinced that pocket watches could be mass-produced by analyzing the watch into its smallest component parts and training only one worker to make each part.

Even before the growth of the factory system, many managerial thinkers were convinced that the more efficient the organization of work, the less the cost in labor, time, and overall production. For the first time since the Ancient World, men were experimentally putting their ideas to work and were organizing men and their labor more efficiently so that greater wealth could be created. In the beginning of the eighteenth century, men were no longer content to follow or imitate nature: they now wanted to improve upon it.

Although many thinkers in France at this time were convinced that men could do no better than by learning from nature and following her, others in England optimistically believed that man could work to change nature for the better. In eighteenth century England and France, men were gaining confidence in their abilities to create the increased wealth that could come from experimental thought.

By 1776 Adam Smith, a professor of philosophy in Glasgow, could use as an example of the efficient organization of production a pin factory in which twenty specialized men produced 48,000 pins per day. If one man had had to do all the work by himself, he would not have been able to make more than twenty pins per day. Twenty men working side by side, each making an entire pin, could produce only 400 pins per day. But by breaking down the manufacture of the pin into its simplest component parts, the same twenty men, each doing only one task, produced more than 100 times as many pins daily. Here, almost twenty-five years before Eli Whitney's efforts in the manufacture of interchangeable parts in musket-making and over 130 years before Henry Ford's production of his famous Model T automobile, was the principle of mass manufacturing. But the owner of the pin factory had accomplished nothing really new even for those times. For decades men's ideas about the organization of work had been changing. Others in Europe had also been thinking of using mass-production methods in the manufacture of muskets as well as of watches. (Thomas Jefferson, as Minister to Paris, had described in a letter to Congress the attempts of a French gunsmith by the name of Louis Blanc to mass-produce muskets.)

Throughout the eighteenth century, one industrial event meshed into another, creating an acceptable cultural climate that would make England into the first great modern industrial nation. Although capital was then being amassed through slavery,[2] this capital had little to do with

2 At the middle of the eighteenth century, out of a world total of 97,000 slaves transported annually from West Africa, English merchants carried more than 60,000 in their slave ships. The Dutch and the Portuguese carried most of the remainder.

creating the eighteenth century Industrial Revolution (though the capital would be used later on to finance partnerships and to buy shares in new and growing industries).

The new Industrial Age, it must be repeated, came out of the increased technological learning and the application of new mechanical ideas, which developed during most of the seventeenth and eighteenth centuries. Labor per se was not solely responsible for the increased productivity in mining of iron ore and coal, but this increase was rather the result of the new managerial concepts that utilized the increased technological knowledge of the times. The eighteenth century blast furnace using coke as fuel produced more iron than could have been hammered out by hand a few centuries previously. Not harder physical labor but more efficient ways of smelting iron ore made this increase of pig iron possible; in other words, it was possible because of clearer ideas based upon a realistic understanding of how the chemistry of ore smelting took place.[3]

Efficiency was thus the keynote of the eighteenth century, even though at this time the drive toward attaining it was carried on by only a few individuals in England and continental Europe. Yet despite the existence at the beginning of this period of the century-old use of the horse and iron plow, most farming in England was still done by illiterate peasants using oxen, the wooden plow, and ancient, traditional means of cultivation. This drive toward more efficient utilization of existing techniques came later in the century when a few well-to-do landowners saw in the greater utilization of scientific farming not only an opportunity to earn more wealth, but also a challenge to make farming more efficient than it had been. This compulsion toward efficiency was also found in the development of the steam engine from the end of the seventeenth century to the end of the eighteenth (though the factory system was associated in its first years more with the use of waterpower than with steam energy).

The Coming of the Steam Engine

At the end of the seventeenth century, as mines became deeper with the ever-increasing demand for ore and coal, a need arose for more efficient pumps to remove the water from the deep shafts. Various experiments

[3] Whether we are dealing with the first tools, with the invention of the bow and arrow, with the complex discovery of gunpowder, with the building of the Great Pyramid, or with the construction of the first Gothic cathedral in France, we must see the importance of these attempts to gain insights into the way the physical world operates in order to find solutions to technical, chemical, and architectural problems. The same intellectual curiosity about man's biological and social worlds would change man's cultural outlook as much as his technological innovations; for technology cannot exist apart from the men who develop, organize, and use it.

with different kinds of hand-operated pumps in the seventeenth century had created a pressing demand for a mechanical pump.[4]

In 1698 Thomas Savery met this need by inventing a pump that used steam to create a vacuum within a cylinder, thus utilizing atmospheric pressure to raise water as much as a hundred feet. This steam pump, crude though it was by later standards, raised fifty-two gallons per minute, which was more than could have been pumped by hand. In 1705 a partner of Savery, Thomas Newcomen, improved the steam pump and in 1720 improved it still further by making the steam's entrance into the cylinder a more automatic process. Soon the steam engine spread to various parts of England and to the continent of Europe. The improved steam engine of 1720 developed the energy equivalent of fifty horsepower, and by 1765 almost seventy such engines were functioning even in so restricted an area as the coal mines of Newcastle.

The Savery-Newcomen engine was very inefficient, since the cylinder had to be doused with cold water to condense the steam and thus create the necessary atmospheric pressure to operate the pump. The engine was primarily a pump that was not constructed to transfer power (though it could have been if its beam had been connected to a crankshaft to transmit force).

The Watt Steam Engine

Not until the 1760's was the Savery-Newcomen engine improved further. One of the engines had been sent to James Watt, a skilled Glasgow mechanic, for repair. He immediately sensed its inefficient use of fuel, since the cylinder had to be cooled with each stroke in order to create a vacuum. In 1764 he changed the Savery-Newcomen engine from one using atmospheric pressure to one using steam pressure. He did this by developing a cylinder in which the steam could be condensed without dousing the cylinder with cold water. The principle was a simple one. The steam leaving the boiler entered one side of a cylinder, where it was condensed. Its force then pushed a slide-valve to the other end of the cylinder, thus permitting the steam to escape into the atmosphere after it had done its work. Steam from the boiler immediately entered the other end of the cylinder and pushed the slide-valve back to its original position. By alternating the entrance of steam into the cylinder, an automatic means was created to utilize the tremendous amount of pressure exerted by expanding steam. With the slide-valve connected to a crankshaft mechanism, the steam engine could now become a driving force, transmitting energy to

[4] The pump was a sixteenth century invention. Without its existence, it is doubtful whether Harvey would have been able to understand the workings of another pump—the heart.

transmission belts or wheels. As a pump the steam engine would have played little role in stimulating the Industrial Age. As a source of motive power, it displaced the waterwheel, the horse, and even man.

The Growth of the Iron Industry

The steam engine could not have been manufactured in quantity earlier than the latter part of the eighteenth century. The new industry required strong, cheap iron; and without an improved blast furnace, it would have been very difficult to give the steam boiler the strength it required. Abraham Darby's discovery of coke as a substitute for coal made possible a less brittle iron. In the 1760's the introduction of pumps worked by a waterwheel increased the stream of continuous air going through the furnace, thus raising the heat even higher. A blast furnace that had previously produced only ten to twelve tons of iron per week now produced more than forty.

The invention of rolling mills and metal-working machines in the 1760's and 1770's helped standardize iron-manufacturing operations, thus reducing both the amount of time spent in making an engine and the labor costs. By the 1780's the method of puddling, or better mixing of the molten iron, was discovered, a step that again increased the production of iron. English ironmasters had learned to make steel in small sealed crucibles as early as 1750, and had thus increased the supply of that material for use in machines and tools requiring harder cutting or grinding surfaces.

The Development of Iron Machines

From Sumerian times until this period, most machines had been made of wood. Even the geared wheels of the later Middle Ages were wooden. The first machine tools, such as the lathe and the milling machine, had been developed for working with wood; the tools themselves were mostly wood with only the cutting edge made of thin metal. The development of a more efficient iron industry in the eighteenth century made possible for the first time in human history the common use of iron for machines and wheels.

The Machine Age

The Industrial Age was initially a mechanical rather than a scientific period. Only in the latter part of the eighteenth century did science come into its own, when studies were initiated to utilize the abstractions of observations about the physical world. The first machines were not steam driven, but used the energy transmitted by the waterwheel. It was not until the middle of the nineteenth century that steam as a means of transmitting energy displaced water power.

Most early mills were located near running streams in order that the waterwheel (which goes back at least to the first century) could be used to drive the machines. Water as a source of energy was cheaper than steam and in many ways more efficient. Unfortunately it was rather limiting in the amount of power it could transmit (until the age of electricity), and in the location of sites that could be used for factories. There were not enough rapidly flowing streams near the eighteenth century sources of labor or cheap transportation that could be employed for the erection of textile factories. And it was the textile factory in England that inaugurated the opening of the Industrial Age.

For Selected Bibliography, see end of Chapter 18.

15

The Factory System Is Born

During the first half of the eighteenth century, the increase in handwoven textiles created a demand for thread that could not be met by the usual means. At that time, six spinners were required to provide one weaver with sufficient thread. Spinning, however, was not a full-time but only a part-time job. The spinners spent most of their day working at farm chores and consequently had little time left for spinning thread. Thus thread became increasingly scarce, and it became necessary to overcome this shortage. The small merchant-manufacturers in the textile regions of England began to put pressure upon mechanics to try to find ways to increase the production of wool thread.

Hargreaves' invention in 1764 of the spinning jenny, which permitted one operator to take care of the equivalent of at least ten spinning wheels, and Arkwright's invention in 1768 of the water frame, whereby a spinning machine more complex than the spinning jenny could be operated by water power, were direct answers to the prayers of the merchant-manufacturers.

Although it is doubtful that Arkwright invented the water frame (it appears more likely that he stole the idea), his genius as a businessman was proven by his setting up the first modern factory, supervising its production, and improvising from day to day improvements of all the steps of manufacture, from the raw materials to the selling of the finished thread. Many competitors sprang up who emulated Arkwright, but few were able to manage both the men and the production of thread as efficiently as he. He was not the first of the new species of merchant-manufacturers; he was, however, one of the first of the modern businessmen, or entrepreneurs.

By 1768 there were no engineers to help Arkwright design better spinning machines, and the scientists of that day were certainly not interested in their construction. Arkwright himself had been a barber with no experience in building or repairing machines. In 1771, however, taking the ideas of a great many around him, Arkwright hired millwrights and blacksmiths to build his machines, the concepts for which may have come from others. He then installed the machines in a large shed, taught land-less and poverty-stricken men and women to operate them, and then selected and trained his supervisors.

He could not delegate any of his authority to his underlings since no managerial learning existed at that time. Arkwright had to function as the entire government within his plant; he had to be the general who trained his staff and recruited his men. It was Arkwright who sought out markets, secured financing, and dealt with greater sums of money than any of the previous merchant-manufacturers for purchasing large amounts of raw materials.

Arkwright had to locate his markets, which meant that when he was not supervising production, he was out selling its products. As his firm grew larger and as others learned from him and also built factories nearby, he and men like him continued to improvise new forms of fac-tory management to run them. The factory was a state within a larger state. It was highly centralized and extremely authoritarian, with the workers who labored there hardly better off than slaves, although they were free to leave and starve elsewhere. On the job, they had to be strictly disciplined to become as much like the machines as possible; to work for as little as was necessary to hire them; to start work when the factory bell rang at a definite time; to work steadily from dawn to noon; to attend the needs of the machine; to eat rapidly; and to work again until late at night, working by dim artificial light in the long English winters when the sun set at three o'clock in the afternoon.

The workers earned somewhat more than laborers in agriculture at that time, but their expenses were greater in the growing factory towns around Manchester. They lived in cheaply constructed rental housing and received fringe benefits such as extra food and wood. The harsh discipline was similar to that of the army; and in the eighteenth century, men did not become soldiers if they had any other alternative. As in the case of soldiers, those who were old or ill were cast off, to fend for them-selves as best they could. Since few adult men could accept this type of discipline without rebelling, the new factory managers sought out docile women and children, who were more amenable to the harsh regulations, to tend the machines. The eighteenth century employment policy of the new merchant-manufacturers demanded that the workers be submissive and blindly obedient. They were looked upon mainly as adjuncts to the machines, possessing no rights of their own but willing to work long hours for a bare minimum standard of living, subject continuously to the harassment of their supervisors.

Later economic theory would rationalize this harshness and minimum standard of living as being part of nature's "iron laws." Its well-to-do originators stated flatly that only a small part of the gross income of the factory could go into wages, so if some workers were paid more, others would be paid less. As in the case of the peasants in the beginnings of Primary civilization, industrial civilization in its earliest stages had little interest in the well-being of the workers. (In the twentieth century the Communist countries also industrialized by putting the workers under a disciplined paramilitary system. By receiving the bare minimum in wages and by working as long hours as possible, the workers thus amassed products, which were then sold to create additional capital for further industrialization.) Despite the hardships of the early factories at the end of the eighteenth century (and working conditions would get worse in the first quarter of the nineteenth century before they would slowly become better), there is little doubt that the unemployed, landless workers who were being pushed off the land in the eighteenth century by the new enclosure acts were even worse off than those working in the new factories and mines.

England needed a landless, poverty-stricken, illiterate, mobile laboring class for industrialization to develop. (Other countries in Europe and Asia would also require reservoirs of cheap and docile labor in the nineteenth and twentieth centuries.) A self-respecting peasantry would not take employment in factories, any more than the sons of the Yankee small farmer would work in factories when they were first built in New England in the early nineteenth century: they preferred to go West in search of cheap land. Consequently it was the landless immigrants from the poverty-stricken peasantry of Europe who were invited to tend the machines of the New World.

The Role of the Market

The early manufacturer quickly became aware that he could not take all his goods for sale to the nearest town, for the local market was too small to absorb his increased production. In the last quarter of the eighteenth century, the entire home market of England was too limited to purchase the ever-growing supply of manufactured textiles, both woolen and cotton. Owners traveled to other countries to find middlemen who could take their goods and sell them to the growing number of retailers in the New World, France, Germany, Spain, Italy, and Russia. Even India became an important market for English textiles when the English cottons undersold Indian ones; poor Indians bought the cheaper English cloth in preference to the more expensive but finer quality Indian cloth.

The First Modern Manufacturer

Matthew Boulton could be called the first modern manufacturer in England, to distinguish him from his predecessors, who were merchants and traders rather than manufacturers. Between 1759 and 1764, he built a small, modern metal-fabricating plant near Birmingham. His partner, Fothergill, spent most of his time traveling in Europe, seeking new outlets for the metal buttons, watch chains, and steel buckles that the plant manufactured in ever-larger numbers.

Boulton carefully supervised the quality of his products, trained his workers personally, and attempted continuously to improve his machines and production techniques. Fothergill knew the tastes of his customers in the various European countries and constantly traveled about seeking orders, new products to manufacture, and patterns to imitate. Boulton and Fothergill's markets grew more extensive, and the firm soon acquired an international reputation. In 1765 Sweden made a tempting offer to Boulton to settle in that country, but he refused. Boulton was a wealthy man and well-educated for his period. His father had been a wealthy manufacturer of toys; his wife was a well-to-do heiress. He could easily have retired and lived in comfort, but he was attracted by the pioneering opportunities of the early factory and fascinated by the growing technology.

The Steam Engine Industry

Boulton spread the uses of the steam engine even further than Newcomen had done. In 1774 he offered a partnership to James Watt so that his improved steam engine could be built using all the resources of a modern factory. Boulton and Watt then supplied steam engines to the mine owners of Cornwall, to the ironmasters of Wales, to the cotton spinners in the Manchester, Glasgow, and Derby areas, and to the growing potteries of Staffordshire. (Josiah Wedgwood was as much a modern manufacturer as Boulton. In his pottery works he supervised the making of all pottery, improved the quality of his products, lowered his prices, and scoured the world for markets as well as ideas.) For the first twelve years, Boulton made no profit in manufacturing steam engines, suffering a steady loss until he could make production more efficient. In 1775 a Boulton and Watt steam engine could pump water three times faster than a Newcomen engine, and at less cost. In 1776, as a result of Boulton's salesmanship, a steam engine operated an air blower for Wilkinson's Iron Works and thus raised the heat for the smelting process higher than before.

In 1779 a Boulton and Watt steam engine was exported to France, and in 1785 another was sent to Germany. In the meanwhile, Watt and others were improving the steam engine. In 1781 Watt developed the transmission of rotary motion, which turned the steam engine into a greater source of motive power. The steam engine began to turn the machines of the new factory system. In 1784 Murdock, a foreman trained by Boulton and Watt, made a model locomotive that traveled more than eight miles an hour on a circular track. By the 1780's the steam engine was being used for power in a few flour and malt mills, sugar refineries, potteries, and ironworks. The first steam spinning mill was opened in 1785, and by 1794 many woolen mills were operating their spinning and weaving machines with steam power.

There had been no precedent for making steam engines on a mass basis; Boulton had to create a new industry from scratch. Workmen had to be trained to be exacting in their work. Machine tools had to be invented for manufacturing the various component parts of the engine. Unlike the textile mills, the new steam engine factories required not women and children, but men with good work habits, great muscular strength, mechanical intelligence, and steadiness of hand. The locksmiths, tinsmiths, and millwrights of former days were now replaced by boilermakers, foundry workers, and skilled smiths. Cylinders of the most painstaking geometrical accuracy, pistons that fitted exactly, gears that were as accurately milled as those of a watch, and boiler pipes of standardized diameters had to replace the former crude and often ill-assembled parts that were generally the cause for failure of past steam engines. Unlike artisan production, the new factory had to standardize the parts of its products in order to make certain that all the components of a steam engine fitted exactly.

Within a few years, the factory system would lead to the manufacture of interchangeable parts, whereby all the parts could be easily fitted together—even to parts made months or years before. The English workman of the seventeenth century was not yet skilled enough to standardize his products through careful measurements, although the watchmakers of Nuremberg and France had learned to standardize watch parts before the end of that century. The new factory required a special type of professional engineer, who could help invent the machines and train the men to work them. The machine transformed workers as well as work habits.

With the advent of the steam engine, science made its first appearance as a junior partner of industry. In previous decades inventions were not brought about by the abstract speculations of men in isolated university laboratories, but were the result of practical needs empirically determined. By 1785 the rule-of-thumb period of the Industrial Age ended because it was not exact enough, and the Scientific Age with its more careful measurements arrived. This did not mean, however, that industrial empiricism would not continue to precede theoretical science well into the end of the nineteenth and even into the twentieth centuries in the establishment of new industries, in improved means of communication, and in the area of transportation.

The Weaving Industry Becomes Mechanized

Although spinning had become mechanized by 1790, weaving was still being done on handlooms. About forty years elapsed between the introduction of Arkwright's frame and Jacquard's invention of the mechanized loom in Lyons, France. In the forty years between 1764 and 1804, a close interrelationship had existed between machines for spinning and machines for weaving. The improved machines that increased production in one stimulated improvements in the other. The first mechanical weaving machine had been invented by an Englishman, Edmund Cartwright, in 1784; but it was not efficient enough because its number of designs was limited. Jacquard's invention in 1804 made weaving even more automatic than spinning and permitted the introduction of innumerable designs. (In 1779, Crompton perfected the spinning mule, which was an improved combination of Hargreave's spinny jenny and Arkwright's water frame, plus a device that permitted even more spindles to be handled by one operator.)

With the invention of the completely automatic weaving loom, the textile industry came of age as a modern factory system. The Jacquard loom was improved upon, as were the various spinning machines; but the basic principles of mechanization remained unchanged. A good weaver working on a handloom at the end of the eighteenth century could make 172,000 moves per week. With the introduction of the automatic weaving loom, one worker could look after two mechanical looms doing 900,000 weaving moves per week. Within fifty years, one worker could operate four mechanical looms with over 2,000,000 moves per week. This is a dramatic example of the great savings in production time and in labor costs brought about by the machine.

The Spread of Industrialization

During the second half of the eighteenth century, industrialization as a new urbanized way of life spread rapidly from England to the continent, though England continued to keep her commanding lead until the 1880's when the United States passed her. By 1788, over 125,000 workers were employed in the mechanized textile industry in Prussia, which exported more than half of its production to underdeveloped countries of the world. Industrialization in Prussia increased coal production in the Ruhr from 52,000 tons in 1764 to 231,000 tons in 1791. New iron mines were opened in Upper Silesia, and the production of iron ore doubled, tripled, and quadrupled from year to year.

During this same period, France had also industrialized rapidly. Her iron furnaces in Lorraine produced more than 136,000 tons of pig iron annually at the eve of the French Revolution. (The iron production in England, Scotland, and Wales at this time was less than 68,000 tons per year.) Scores of factories in France employed 100 workers or more, and several gave work to more than 1,000.

The two manufacturing systems—the handicraft system and the centralized factory system—existed side by side in France and Prussia, as in England, until the middle of the nineteenth century. But each year more artisans saw their small home markets decreasing while industrial production rose.

As in England, the ancient artisan guilds in France reacted strongly against the deadly competition of the factory system. In England, unemployed artisans destroyed machines under the call to action of the imaginary King Ludd; in France, similar attempts were made to wipe out the monster that doomed the artisan to unemployment. But the workshop could not meet the lower costs of the factory; its days were numbered in producing for the mass market, although in diminished numbers it would continue to make handmade goods for the wealthy. Industrialization would not make goods more plentiful for the rich, but it would slowly raise the standard of living for the poor. The rich would continue to have their clothing, shoes, furniture, carpets, and carriages made by hand. Even in the later days of the automobile, the rich would buy not the mass-produced car but the expensive custom-made one.

Industrialization Comes to the United States

In the United States of 1800, more than 95 percent of the population lived on small, self-sufficient farms, where they grew food for themselves but not for the market. The urban areas were small, and workers were skilled artisans rather than unskilled factory workers. In 1791, a small textile mill was established in Providence, Rhode Island, but industrialization would not move rapidly until after 1815.

The colonies in the eighteenth century contained many scientists, including such outstanding men as Benjamin Franklin, Thomas Jefferson, and David Rittenhouse; but the concept of science was quite separate from that of industrialization. (Eighteenth century science left a heritage of empiricism and skepticism and a strong desire to fathom the workings of the mechanical world.) On the other hand, there were many practical, inventive Americans who were ahead of their times. In 1784 John Fitch made a practical steamboat but could get no financing for it. Oliver Evans built an unusual steam engine dredge in 1803 and a completely automatic flour mill in 1806. Eli Whitney invented a simple cotton engine, or gin, in 1793, which, by combing out the seeds of the cotton pod, enabled growers to produce more cotton with less labor for the English textile mills. In 1797 Whitney started the manufacture of interchangeable parts in a small factory near New Haven, Connecticut, producing muskets for the War Department. He was followed by gunmakers and clockmakers who used his techniques of breaking down the product into its various work components and standardizing the tasks so that any unskilled worker could be trained to do the job easily and quickly through the help of jigs and other mechanical guides attached to the lathes, milling machines, and bushing machines.

Instead of waiting until competent workers could be trained, the American system emphasized skilled management, industrial and production engineers, and semiautomatic machinery, with the result that in the early part of the nineteenth century even untutored immigrants could start work in a factory and learn any of the semiskilled tasks in a few weeks or months. Long apprenticeships were no longer necessary for learning a skill. The demand was for imagination in improving existing machinery and for the managerial talents necessary in organizing tasks and men.

The merchants of New England and Philadelphia and the wealthy planters of Virginia laid the groundwork for the acceptance of the Industrial and Scientific Age by stressing the importance of knowledge. Respect was given to those who were identified with science and technological learning. In fact, in upper-class circles of the few cities of the eighteenth century colonies, there was more approval given to nontraditional attitudes and nonconventional wisdom than would be given in the same cities 100 years later. In the eighteenth century (before the religious revivals of the early nineteenth century and the growing political and social influences of the traditionalist frontier settlements), approval was given to the optimistic point of view about man that assumed that he could employ his intelligence for the recognition as well as the solution of his problems. A few enlightened individuals attempted to break out of the mental authoritarianism that had surrounded human beings for tens of thousands of years, and a basis was laid for the recognition of dissent as an important ingredient in the freedom of man.

The Diffusion of the New Civilization

The modern age was thus in its infancy during the seventeenth and eighteenth centuries, although we have seen that its conception took place in a more distant past. A new urban civilization was slowly coming into existence, in which more and more individuals worked in towns and cities and fewer in agriculture and other primary pursuits. In this sense, there was a complete break with the ancient classic Primary civilization, which had been peasant-based and tradition-oriented.

The new Secondary civilization would be urbanized, factory-organized, market-oriented, literate (using schools rather than family life to spread the new culture), and opposed to provincialism and regionalism. Its spheres of influence would be wider, and the peasant would have little or no place in this civilization. In 1800, 95 percent of America's 5 million people were still living on farms. In 1860, a little more than half the population lived on farms. In 1965, less than 7 percent of America's population was involved in farming.

As we have seen, the new industrial civilization, which started in England, spread rapidly to the United States, France, Belgium, and Germany. Its scientific counterpart developed independently in Italy, Holland, France, Germany, Sweden, England, and the United States. By the middle of the nineteenth century, however, both streams joined to form a new torrent, the scientific and industrial civilization, whose onrushing tide would sweep through the entire world within a century.

Secondary civilization spread further in less time than the old Primary civilization of the ancient city-states; it had transformed the old cultures more quickly than the Primary civilization had changed the Neolithic cultures that preceded it. But this new civilization would itself become transformed into Tertiary civilization within a matter of a century, with even newer drives and professions. In the Tertiary civilization, the factory worker would go the way of the peasant; and the aristocrat-warrior, who had become the merchant-manufacturer, would be transformed into a new professional manager. By the beginning of the twenty-first century, the latter may well change into an even newer group of professional problem-solvers.

The Secondary civilization spread slowly in the midst of the older civilization that nourished it. In the thirty years between 1770 and 1800, the cotton industry grew some fifteen times, displacing the old putting-out system and destroying the Indian cotton handicrafts. English production of iron went from 68,000 tons in 1788 to more than 250,000 tons in 1806, only eighteen years later. Between 1790 and 1810, hundreds of cloth merchants with access to capital and with acquaintance with the new manufacturing techniques opened mills for the mechanical production of textiles. The new manufacturers had no problem finding labor, for England had tripled her population during the eighteenth century. From 1800 to 1900, her population would increase four times again as a result of better sanitation, improved medical care, and more food coming from increased productivity abroad and from large farms in England owned by wealthy landowners.

Still, England was not transformed overnight. Industrialization was a slow process in which changes took more than fifty years to be noticed. Although the factory system started in 1771, it was not until 1850 that it spread to the entire textile industry; and it would be 1900 and later before most consumer goods would be made in factories rather than by artisans in their small workshops. Even in the middle of the twentieth century, the construction industry is a mixture of handicrafts, and most houses are still built by hand.

In the beginning, even the important inventions took years, sometimes decades, to spread from town to town and from factory to factory. One could say that there was a lapse of at least twenty-five years, even at the beginning of the nineteenth century, before the average small factory adopted a new invention. (In the eighteenth century it had taken over seventy years for the fly shuttle, invented in 1733, to reach isolated country districts; and Neolithic tools may well have taken even more time to spread.) Once new machines had been installed, owners hesitated to change them, even when more efficient machines became available. Although competition from large factories was increasing in the middle of the nineteenth century in England, a good deal of woolen cloth was still woven by hand without the use of mechanized looms. In the twentieth century, Harris tweed is still being woven by hand in the islands off Scotland.

Slowly at first, and then in ever-widening circles, the factory system spread—introducing wage labor on a large scale and a technology that changed both agriculture and the landscape around the burgeoning industrial towns. As the forerunner of cultural change, it showed its effects in political as well as social shifts. By 1815 England had felt the initial impetus of industrialization, which moved fairly quickly across the channel into Belgium, northern France, Germany, and by the end of the nineteenth century into Austria, Hungary, Poland, and finally into Russia. At the end of the eighteenth and during the early nineteenth century, the industrial epoch crossed the Atlantic, carried by immigrants on sailing ships. Although all skilled mechanics had been forbidden to leave England and to take their knowledge with them, they managed to evade the English customs men. Within sixty years, the factory system and its cultural changes transformed the United States from an almost completely agricultural country into one that was more than half under the influences of the new civilization. By the middle of the nineteenth century, the new ideas had crossed the Pacific with travelers on slow steamships and had secured a firm foothold in Japan. By the last third of the twentieth century, the new civilization would spread its seeds of change everywhere—in China, India, South America, and Africa.

Secondary civilization was at first carried by a small number of individuals, who were its faithful followers and who slowly transformed the old Primary civilization into an intrinsic part of the new. For a long period of time, however, the two civilizations dwelt side by side, much as the hunters and the first agriculturists must have done for hundreds if not thousands of years. Although most individuals today have moved partially into the mental climate of the Secondary civilization, many vestiges of the Primary still remain in the conventional thoughts of most men about themselves, about their relationships with others, and about the world they live in. It is necessary to see the Scientific and Industrial Age not as a revolution, which it was not, but as a slow process of mental growth. A few individuals gradually educated a few others in the new concepts of efficiency, of optimism in man's intrinsic organizing abilities, and of confidence that deprivation, like famine and disease, can be conquered. We can now understand its impact as it spread slowly from one country to another.

The Political Changes

The technical changes that took place were only part of the picture, for technological innovations brought political and social changes in their wake. The new industrialists and their followers began to play an important part both in the British Parliament and in the American Congress. In England, the industrialists insisted upon their "natural" right to have their interests protected by the Government. To sell cheaply abroad, they needed to have labor costs lowered at home. Anything that cut daily expenses for the worker was all to the good for the manufacturer, for it enabled him to cut the workers' wages so that the total cost of the product could be lowered sufficiently to enter new markets competitively.

Food was the most important item purchased by the early industrial workers: almost 75 percent of their wages was spent on minimum necessities. The manufacturers, therefore, exerted pressure for a long period of time on the middle-class members of Parliament to repeal the protection of home-grown grain and thus permit foreign cereals to enter England duty free. The manufacturers could afford to be the defenders of free trade since, until the second half of the nineteenth century, they had little industrial competition from any other country. Although free trade would force the aristocratic landowners to become more efficient in their farming in order to meet the cheaper prices of foreign grain, the mid-country manufacturers and their urban allies had little sympathy for them; in fact, they looked upon the landowners as their economic and political competitors.

The enmity between these two important elite groups prompted both the investigation and the reform of factory conditions by the landowners sitting in Parliament, who suddenly developed an identification with the impoverished factory workers in order to hit back at the industrialists. As in the case of the slave owners in the southern part of the United States, who felt sorry for the exploited factory workers in the North in reaction to northern abolitionist attempts to free their slaves, in England the movement to extend the vote to skilled workers, to cut down the hours of child labor, and to supervise the undoubtedly bad working conditions in the factories at that time certainly stemmed out of the defensive predicament of the landed gentry, who saw their political influence being whittled down by the expanding industrial and commercial middle classes.

Social Reaction to the New Industrial Age

At the same time, a reaction against the new industrialists and financiers developed among those who were identified with the religious egalitarian movements, which had continued from the past. These forces were given a new lease on life by the various enlightenment movements in the eighteenth century and by the rationale concerning the importance of man that lay behind the encouragement of theoretical scientific thought in the seventeenth and eighteenth centuries.

To most of those in the dissenting groups, industrialization seemed to bring contradictory results. Instead of moving men toward equality and brotherhood, the new Industrial Age seemed to create even greater social and economic inequalities. The wealthy manufacturers were now viewed as latter-day feudal lords. Their power over their workers when the latter were in the factories was in many ways as absolute as the rights of the lord of the manor over his serfs. The lord of the manor, however, had been obligated to protect his serfs against outside force; and the feudal serf could not leave him without permission. The chief weapon of the industrial employer was that he could cut the worker's dependency upon him by discharging him if his behavior was unsatisfactory.

With few exceptions, manufacturers insisted upon their right to discipline those working under them. They felt no obligation to protect their workers and insisted that it was part of natural law to pay the lowest wages possible. The employers exerted continuous pressure upon Parliament and the courts to prevent the workers from "conspiring" to raise their wages by combining into syndicalist, or union, organizations. Labor unions were looked upon as criminal attempts to prevent workers from freely offering their labor at the market price. The concept of natural law made any attempt to restrict the supply of labor through strikes a conspiracy against the state, which was thus made the protector of the market and its "laws."

Although science in its inception was considered beneficial because it offered mankind the opportunity to free itself from past ignorance and superstitions, many of the educated individuals of that period considered industrialism anti-libertarian. For example, Thomas Jefferson saw the industrial workers and the factory system as inimical to the functioning of a free democratic society and postulated a country of small agricultural freeholders, each owning his own land and dependent upon no man for his living. The Industrial Age was thus considered antithetical to the growing scientific spirit and as ending the eighteenth century democratic dream that mankind could be raised from its poverty-stricken, unequal depths through a new brotherhood of man based upon reason and enlightenment.

The adherents of eighteenth century deism and scientific enlightenment thus reacted strongly against any attempt to create a body of economic knowledge on the basis of the existing status quo. Such a series of descriptions, they felt, would only continue the past pessimistic outlook about mankind and its future. If one had to rely upon a market conception of economic society, then one had to assume that very few would do well and most would fall by the wayside. Although this market conception of economics could have been accepted in an age that postulated that most people were born to be unfortunate and only a few to be members of "God's elect," this somewhat fatalistic point of view was difficult to accept in a century that had been influenced by the beliefs that man could make his own destiny and that no "natural" conditions existed that mankind could not change.

Enlightened social opinion considered it a backward step to accept contemporary economic axioms that postulated that the higher the wages paid to workers, the more the workers would be encouraged to marry early and have many children. The children, upon growing up, would then flood the labor market and thus depress wages. On the other hand, low wages would force workers to delay marriage, which would again create a scarcity of labor, and in time wages would go up again.

In contrast to the optimistic tone of the eighteenth century, the nineteenth century opened with the baleful warning that mankind had been increasing faster than agricultural production and that instead of industrialization being a blessing, it could only continue economic inequalities, poverty, and low standards of living for most citizens. Economists spoke of the "iron law" of wages, which postulated a wage fund fixed in proportion to the amount of capital invested in the plant. If wages were raised for a few, therefore, they would then have to be reduced for the many. Few of the economists of that day were optimistic enough to believe that if productivity or output per work hour were increased by innovations and greater efficiency, it would then be possible to use some of the savings to raise wages. Such an optimistic point of view, which assumes that wealth can be created through the application of human thought, would come only in the middle of the next century. In the early nineteenth century, the hardheaded men of economics thought that the world was becoming too overpopulated, was outrunning its sources of food and raw materials, and was being filled with individuals who did not understand that wishes and dreams had nothing to do with the workings of the market. Facts were facts, and though they were not pretty to look at, one could not go against "nature."

But eighteenth century egalitarian thought was still strong enough to react against the new ideas and inequalities that industrialism brought in the nineteenth century. If this was what industrialization was doing to cherished dreams of mankind, they said, then it was born of the Devil, and a new series of goals had to be developed to bring mankind back to the past visions of egalitarianism, brotherhood, and an optimistic belief in the human spirit. In the first half of the nineteenth century in England, France, and Germany, men dreamed of a new respect that would be given to the man who worked with his hands or with his brains; and they hoped that opportunities could be provided to enable men to escape their dreary, amoral worlds by creating a new moral society in which to live.

In the second half of the nineteenth century, men reacted to dreams of a new morality, which they now considered impractical, by turning to political organization as an agent of social change. Under governmental decrees, they felt, men could be educated to carry on further industrialization and greater scientific endeavors through the incentives of working for mankind rather than for oneself. Some men even assumed that the lowly semiliterate worker could be taught to see that the economic system did not function in his behalf and that he could train himself eventually to supplant the manufacturers, as the latter had displaced the feudal aristocrats.[1]

Out of these protests came the various socialist and anarcho-syndicalist movements of Europe, South America, North America, and Asia. Socialism saw the free ballot for the worker as ushering in a new democratic system in which society would run the large-scale industries for its own benefit. Anarcho-syndicalism, on the other hand, had little use for the organized political party; workers, it insisted, must topple the government, which was their enemy, through a paralyzing general strike and

[1] The new industrialist was actually a descendant of the trader-merchant, who in his search for raw materials had brought the ideas of the Neolithic and of early Primary civilization to outlying peoples of the Ancient World.

displace the industrialists and their state by workshops cooperating to produce the goods for a new society. In the early part of the twentieth century, an authoritarian combination of both views would take power under the label of Communism and would inaugurate a military control over both the individual and the workshop. Although it would do this in the name of the workers and peasants, it would actually govern through the new bureaucratic and technologically educated middle classes.

For Selected Bibliography, see end of Chapter 18.

16

The Scientific and Industrial Age Reaches Maturity

The scientific and industrial civilization came of age after the middle of the nineteenth century. England had been the pacesetter between 1770 and 1860. After that date she fell behind the United States, although she continued to share the role of industrial leader with France and Germany. The rate of industrialization in England had not been as fast as among those who followed her in the second half of the nineteenth century, nor as rapid as among those who would take advantage of the industrial and technical skills of others in the first half of the twentieth century. Between 1800 and 1860, England increased her industrial output by almost 300 percent, or by an average of some 3½ percent per year. But since her population was also growing at the rate of almost 3 percent per year, the net increase in per capita wealth was still slight. In this period, England was exporting people as well as textiles, machines, and ideas.

Only in the second half of the nineteenth century did the promise of industrialization seem to be partially fulfilled. In the first half of that century, industrialism had expanded by coordinating more and more factories and building up markets for their ever-increasing products. Science was still working in isolation, with some of the great scientific inventions and contributions being made by single individuals operating in isolated laboratories. Colleges and universities still stressed traditional knowledge, and more lawyers and ministers were being trained than scientists or physicians.

In the first half of the nineteenth century, the industrialists had been men who could quickly see the practical value of inventions and use them for their profit. In the second half of the nineteenth century, a new trend began in which the industrialists were slowly displaced by the corporation, by the paid manager, and by the directorate. The research scientist was now supported by the industrial corporation, although fifty years would elapse before he became an established part of the industrial staff. The state assumed the role of banker for the industrialist, and in many ways paid for the social overhead costs of supporting an industrial system. The state did not, however, plan the growth of industry, as France had done under Colbert in the first half of the seventeenth century; but this would come in the twentieth century when the Communist states would play the roles of both entrepreneur and banker.

Industrialization Begins to Increase the Worker's Standard of Living

The first half of the nineteenth century had been a dismal period for the factory worker; but by the end of the second half of that century, his living conditions improved to the point where he had a higher standard of living than his counterpart on the small peasant farm. In fact, the chief attraction of the European cities and the New World for the sons of the European peasants was that they could save enough money working in industry to buy themselves small plots of land to which they could retire as small farmers.

As they migrated to the United States, millions of peasants dreamt of opportunities to buy land cheap or to receive it almost free. Although most immigrants remained in the burgeoning industrial cities, enough were able to purchase some of the marginal farms in America to make them feel that their dreams of independence had been realized. The richest lands in the United States had been preempted by the older American stock, who purchased their lands from land companies or from the state before the mass immigration from Europe started in the late 1840's. By 1862, when the Homestead Act was passed, only the land in the drier parts of the country was available.

The industrial civilization could not bestow its blessings until it had taken over much of the production of the economy and had displaced both the small, self-sufficient farmer and the handicrafts of the cottage industries. This would not take place until after the first part of the twentieth century.

The nineteenth century was a period of rapid growth to maturity. The eighteenth century in England had provided a background of freedom for the merchant and the manufacturer, an acceptance of efficiency as a measurement in both agriculture and the production of goods, and tacit identification with a spirit of enterprise and innovation. It had also seen the Industrial Age take form, and as the first generation it had set the stage for the training of individuals in new patterns of thought. The second and third generations carried the Industrial Age still further, much as relay runners take the torch from previous runners. But it was the fourth generation that would lay the basis for the cultural and legal complex of interrelationships and interdependencies for those who would live in the midst of the industrialized twentieth century.

The New Transport

Before industry could absorb the energies of more than a quarter of the population in England, the industrial areas, which were widely scattered in the latter eighteenth and early nineteenth centuries, had to be tied to the new markets by cheaper and faster transportation. Men began to think of ways to reduce the high costs of transporting goods and raw materials to and from those settlements that were distant from seaports. The construction of canals had occurred almost simultaneously with the establishment of factories in the Midlands area of England, that is, from the middle of the eighteenth century to the first part of the nineteenth. Roads were also improved for the first time since the Roman period. The techniques for building modern roads were laid down by such builders as Metcalfe and McAdam. (The macadamized road is a memorial to McAdam's construction techniques, though the use of the asphalt binder would not come until the first part of the nineteenth century.)

Experiments were made in the 1780's in the use of steam motive power for boats and for wagons on roads. Miller, Taylor, and Symington built a workable steamboat in 1788. John Fitch had built a steamboat that was in regular service between Philadelphia and Wilmington. Rumsey also built a practical steamboat. In Paris in 1803 Robert Fulton operated a steamboat on the Seine River; in 1807 his *Clermont* sailed under its own power from Albany to New York, a distance of 145 miles. Soon afterwards, steamboats were used in coastal traffic and on navigable rivers. In 1819 the *Savannah* crossed the Atlantic Ocean under its own sails, assisted only partially by steam. By the 1840's steamers were going back and forth across the oceans of the world under their own power.

Canals were built in the United States from the 1820's onward, the states guaranteeing their costs. Canals connected Albany with Buffalo and the Great Lakes, Philadelphia with Pittsburgh, Cleveland with the Ohio River, Chicago with the Illinois River and thence with the Mississippi River, and so on.

The Birth of Railroads

After the 1780's, when the wooden rails that had been used to transport coal cars out of mines were given an iron-strip covering, experimentation with railroads began. Many individuals experimented with the construction of a steam engine that could run on rails and pull a heavy load. The first successful inventor of a workable steam engine was Richard Trevithick, who in 1801 constructed one that pulled a heavy load on a circular track.

By 1825 the first commercial railroad was operating in England, and in 1829 this new form of transportation was introduced to the United States. In the 1830's the new system was introduced to France, Belgium, and Germany; and in the 1840's into Austria-Hungary, Italy, and Russia. By the 1850's railroads were introduced into India, and in that same decade New York was linked to Chicago by an iron belt. By the 1860's the railroads stretched from New York to the Missouri River, and in 1869 the first transcontinental line tied Oakland, California, to Omaha, Chicago, New York, and Boston. By the 1870's the railroad was introduced to Japan, and the first line ran from the new capital of Tokyo to the harbor at Yokohama, eighteen miles away.

In the 1880's there was a boom in railroad building all over the world, with three more transcontinental railroads built in the United States between Chicago and California. In 1840 the United States led the world with over 3,000 miles of track. Sixty years later, over 200,000 miles of railroad track crisscrossed every state in the Union, transporting grain, meat, timber, and coal to the growing cities and returning with huge piles of raw materials, manufactured goods, steam threshers, steel plows, harvesting machines, and other efficient tools for the farms and small towns of America. Chicago's population and wealth expanded as thin bands of iron rails tied state after state of the West and South to that city's grain mills, slaughter houses, and factories.

The New Iron Industry

The railroad industry required an adequate supply of iron for rails, locomotives, freight, and passenger cars. To satisfy this almost insatiable demand from the middle of the eighteenth century on, the iron furnaces of England and America had to improve their processes continuously in order to support the railroad industry, as well as numerous other industries and mechanized farming. From that time on, furnaces became larger, the blasts of air became more powerful, and furnace heat was raised high enough to smelt iron ore completely and in larger quantities. New slitting and rolling mills could produce large quantities of pipe for boilers and of rails for railroad track.

As early as 1779, for the first time in man's technological history, a cast-iron bridge was built in England, with an arch having a 100-foot span and a height of over 45 feet—an almost impossible feat even 100 years earlier and a technological task virtually out of the realm of possibility for the Romans. By 1787 this builder of iron bridges, John Wilkinson, had manufactured iron boats of twenty tons displacement weight. In 1788 he made forty miles of cast-iron pipes for the water supply of Paris. In the same year he erected mills to make solid cast-iron wheels, fly wheels, pinions, and shafts. Under ironmasters such as John Wilkinson, wooden machines, with their irregular motion and rapid wear, quickly became obsolete. Steam engines, iron spinning-machines, and looms required accurate machining, metal-cutting tools, and standardized parts that fitted perfectly. By the 1780's the new iron industry of England was equipped to supply these quality tools and shapes.

The rapid growth of industrialization in the United States demanded more iron than the furnaces could supply at their locations in the northeastern part of the country. New villages were built around the furnaces, which made pig iron from bog iron, low-grade iron ore, and coking coal. Limestone was now added to the mixture of coke and iron ore in the furnace to unite with the impurities in the ore.

Steel, however, remained in short supply, for it was still made as it had been made in the eighteenth century—in small quantities, in crucibles, and with a good many impurities. The entire gamut of alloys still lay decades away, although in Europe individual metallurgists were experimenting with various new metals and with alloying these metals with steel. In England, the United States, France, and the Ruhr, iron making improved little in the fifty years between 1800 and 1850. The early nineteenth century was an iron age, as the Ancient World had never been; but it was still not an age of steel. In 1847 an American named William Kelly invented the converter method of making steel in large amounts, a process independently invented in 1856 by Henry Bessemer in England. The Kelly and Bessemer methods, which were very similar, made steel from cast, or pig, iron. Oxygen was blown through the molten iron, thus oxidizing the impurities and at the same time raising the heat of the molten iron. The Bessemer process required higher grade ores than had previously been used. This necessitated a shift in the steel industry from small isolated villages to important river and railroad junctions near coal mines, iron ore supplies, and limestone. At first the steel industry in the United States moved westward to the Harrisburg area, but within a few years Pittsburgh and Cleveland became the important steel centers they are today. Steel became a post-Civil War development, when the first practical Bessemer steel mill was erected in 1867 at Steelton, Pennsylvania, south of Harrisburg. (The first pilot plant was built at Wyandotte, Michigan, in 1864.) By 1870 the small steel industry was turning out less than 100,000 tons of steel per year. By 1960 steel production was over 100 million tons annually in the United States and over 250 million in the entire world. The Bessemer process in the 1870's was made more efficient by the Siemens-Martin open-hearth process and by various other techniques that steadily improved the making of steel and steel alloys. Innovation was now the lifeblood of industry, and the plant that did not adapt itself immediately to new techniques and productive methods was asking for competition to put it out of business.

The United States Takes the Lead

The United States early took a lead in absorbing the new industrial civilization and extending it further. The capital that had been built up during the eighteenth century in slaving and trading throughout the world was now put to work employing technicians and engineers to build turnpikes, canals, factories, and railroads. By the late 1840's American railroad engineers were in Russia, building the first railroad line, the St. Petersburg-Moscow run. By 1850 American railroading had developed new techniques, which sharply differentiated it from English or French railway construction. In the United States more track had to be built and laid quickly with sharper curves over a greater area and at less cost. The result was that by 1850 American railroad builders and engineers had developed new forms of track, locomotives, and passenger and freight cars to fit American conditions.

The wealth that could be made in building railroads with government assistance encouraged a great many financiers and businessmen with political friends and acquaintances to organize companies to construct railroad lines after the Civil War. For example, the promoters of the first transcontinental railroad line could get little private capital to buy their construction bonds since most capital was entering the more profitable manufacturing industries at this time. But, by getting Congress to distribute free lands equal to the size of the state of Texas and then permitting the promoters to use them as a first mortgage for the issuance of bonds, the new companies were able to make more profit than they could possibly have received from the construction of the road alone. The town, city, and state governments along the proposed route were coerced into buying most of the bonds by threats that the route would be changed if they did not. One Congressional investigation of the building of the first transcontinental railroad line indicated that the construction companies organized by the initial promoters had made over 100 percent profit on their construction costs even before the railroad line had been finished. And yet, without this climate of easy money for those "in the know," the transcontinental railroads might not have been built until decades later, and then perhaps only one or two might have been constructed.

The New Class of Managerial Entrepreneurs

During the nineteenth century, probably more industrial fortunes were made in the United States than in any other industrial country. They were made by a new class of men who, if they had lived in the past, might have left a mark upon history as military conquerors, builders of great public projects, or entrepreneurs of religions. In the period after the Civil War, these men preferred to organize new industries by consolidating a great many small ones that had been created earlier. They had a series of perceptive talents: (1) without being inventors themselves, they could grasp important factors in new innovations and ways to utilize them; (2) they knew how to tap available sources of capital for financing; (3) they could recognize technical talents and supervisory skills in others, and knew how to encourage those possessing them to utilize their abilities to organize new industries or to improve old ones; (4) they were acquainted with the marketing possibilities of whatever they were producing or selling; (5) they were knowledgeable about production techniques and how to mass-produce whatever they had decided to make; (6) they knew how to get market outlets for their products through new techniques of selling and distribution; and (7) they knew how to organize the energies of the large number of specialized employees and to use them to train and manage the rest of the labor force.

The New Manager

Managerial skills were not inborn but had to be learned from others, either through an apprenticeship or by hiring a highly trained staff. Hundreds of years of previous merchant and banking experience went into the preparation of the nineteenth century entrepreneur in merchandising, marketing, and financing. In the eighteenth century, for example, a New England merchant had to be familiar with the names of the agents in every known port in the world where his ship's captain could sell and buy, receive credit, and be kept informed on the state of the market. The Fuggers in sixteenth century Europe had their own sources of information in all important centers of western Europe, which kept them informed as to who needed loans, who had discovered new sources of metal, and who was about to carry on a war or a campaign. The chief competitive advantage of the Rothschilds in the early part of the nineteenth century lay in their possessing their own network of intelligence agents. No entrepreneur worth his salt could ignore the importance of having such a personal network in the second half of the nineteenth century. A successful entrepreneur had to keep ahead of his competitors by knowing more than they did.

The businessman shared a good many skills with the warrior, but there was one difference: the businessman was competing with a great many others like himself and, unlike the military man, he discovered that it was more often to his advantage to combine with his competitors than to fight them. The price wars in the United States in the second half of the nineteenth century, for example, were often attempts to force a combination; if the latter was not possible, then the competitors had to be pushed out of business.

The entrepreneur's advantages lay in having knowledge that none of his competitors possessed and in being closer to the sources of financial and political power than they. In rural America the promoter-businessman was often looked upon as an enemy, although he was also envied and admired for his self-confidence, his abilities, and his ease in amassing wealth. It was here that the businessman had to take advantage of the political opportunities that came his way in order to offset the suspicion of him that existed in rural circles. The need between 1861 and 1865 to provision one million Union soldiers with clothing, food, supplies, and guns enabled the entrepreneurial businessman with the proper political acquaintances to expand his plants and take advantage of a ready and well-paying government market. The growth of railroads, which were encouraged by land grants after 1865, enabled men with a wide circle of political friends and access to ready financing, as well as railroad buyers, to enter the rapidly expanding steel business. Until the arrival of the automobile, the railroads represented the most important market for steel.

A new role was thus being created for the entrepreneurial businessman both in the United States and in Europe. But, at the same time, he needed an overall view of his particular part of the industrial world in order to determine his place in it. He needed technological and financial knowledge, which would enable him to make perceptive judgments as to which innovations would be important and which would not. Although he talked of risk-taking, he could not afford to take very many risks. He needed to know as accurately as possible, which meant that he had to learn to rely upon the expert knowledge of others. He had to know where to get in touch with such experts and how to command their loyalty. He needed people to advise him, assist him, and help him to plan. He could be successful only as long as he had others who were as well-trained as he to manage the myriad details of everyday production, financing, and marketing.

Precedent based on authority became extremely important for his underlings; too many management innovations would have made it impossible for the plant to be managed efficiently and smoothly. On the other hand, although precedent was very important for the plant bureau-cracy that was created, enough leeway had to be permitted to allow innova-tions to be incorporated in the productive processes of the plant, in the techniques of marketing, and in financing lest the plant become mori-bund and noncompetitive. This meant that certain officials had to be given the freedom or the delegated authority to make decisions about changes of product, processes, and management without being restricted by precedents or the authority of their superiors. The stick that would keep them from making too many errors would be severe punishment for failure, and the carrot would consist of great rewards for success. Minor risks could be taken by the beginning entrepreneur who was convinced that he had a sure thing; but once the organization had been built up, decisions had to be based on the most precise knowledge possible, and this created a market for the consultant, or adviser.

The Education of the Entrepreneur

A good deal of knowledge, then, went into the education and training of the nineteenth century entrepreneur. Unless one had access to other individuals with this particular type of learning, it would have been vir-tually impossible to organize or become an innovator in a new industry. The first entrepreneurs in New England, for example, were well-to-do merchants, their relatives, or their assistants. Most of the early inventors were from Massachusetts or Connecticut, where access to knowledge of contemporary technology, marketing, and financing was greatest.

Social respect, or status, was accorded those who became wealthy by building up specialized knowledge of how to produce or sell to the market. Many men in the northeastern part of the United States during the early years of the nineteenth century started their careers as peddlers, opened up stores, became interested in producing a new product, and knew how to finance the services of others to help them manufacture, market, and improve the item.

Bankers became industrialists because of their access to ready financ-ing, and inventors beat a path to their doors asking for assistance. The bankers had to be knowledgeable about the marketing possibilities of new patents, and this meant that they had to rely upon the judgment of the expert or else become experts themselves. The temper of the times was such that few entrepreneurs needed to be gamblers; few men would risk their finances on an unsure thing when there were so many oppor-tunities for sure things. A new industry had to be one that could be easily visualized.

By 1900 the industrial culture had produced a new type of manager, who had few roots in the past. Most of the entrepreneurs in the early nineteenth century had been sons of merchants or farm boys with special access to urban sources of technological information. At the end of the century the entrepreneurs who promoted and financed new businesses were more often urban-bred. Some of the more spectacular new industrialists, however, such as Carnegie, Rockefeller, and Ford, were farmers' sons who had adapted quickly to the new culture of the industrial cities. A large number of entrepreneurs were sons of urban businessmen, with ready access to new sources of industrial information.

Most of their numbers in the United States were born in the Northeast. Young men in the Midwest and the South did not generally have as much access to the cultural stream of the industrial civilization as did the sons of professionals and businessmen growing up in northeastern urban centers. In these urban centers one could know entrepreneurs personally or could be continuously instructed, as part of family socialization, in technical and business knowledge, as well as in the personality characteristics that were necessary for becoming an entrepreneur. A young man raised in a family where father, relatives, or close friends of the family acted as professional teachers occupied a more advantageous position than the culturally-deprived son of an illiterate backwoods farmer in Tennessee or the son of an immigrant factory worker.

Expert knowledge by itself, however, was not enough. One had to belong to the new world of industrial and financial ideas or to be of value to those of economic importance. As in the case of the military or the church, one had to start off as a second lieutenant or as a priest before one could become a general or a bishop. As a rank outsider, one could not hope to jump over these steps.

The British Entrepreneur

In Great Britain in the nineteenth century, entrepreneurs came from roughly the same backgrounds as their counterparts in the United States. The man from Glasgow, with his knowledgeable access to technology, with his specialized learning about production, financing, and marketing, and with his close relationships to those with capital to invest, stood a far better chance of becoming the innovator and organizer of a new business than a friendless lad from the country districts around Aberdeen. The boy who grew up in a merchant-manufacturing family in Manchester stood a better chance of becoming an independent entrepreneur in the textile industry than the son of a poverty-stricken mill-worker.

The eighteenth century innovator was often a religious dissenter, since only those of respectable social and religious backgrounds could hope to advance in the government, in the military, in the Church, or in the restricted official financial circles of London. The dissenter, being somewhat socially deprived, had a strong need to achieve, to become as wealthy and important as those who looked down upon him. If he were held in too great contempt, however, his chances for possessing enough self-confidence to compete might be damaged. If dissenters had been totally unacceptable to those in authority, their opportunities to enter new businesses freely might have been almost nonexistent. There must have been some approval for dissenters, otherwise they would have ceased to exist, as in seventeenth century Spain. In eighteenth century England, they were numerous enough to have left their influences upon the country.

The Transformation of the Entrepreneur into the Professional Manager

In the eighteenth and nineteenth centuries, the entrepreneur was also a managerial executive. By the twentieth century a new managerial class had come into existence, not only in the private enterprise countries, but also in the Communist ones.

In the past the owner and the manager had often been one person; in the twentieth century the owner and the manager were often separate individuals. In the eighteenth and nineteenth centuries, the individual entrepreneur financed his factory with one or two partners, each of whom had separate spheres of operation. In the twentieth century, the corporation came into existence, as an artificial legal personality, with its hired managers and closed self-perpetuating board of directors; ownership received part of the profits but had little to do with either the direction or innovation in the plant. By the middle of the twentieth century, it had become difficult to say who owned what. Insurance companies, banks, pension funds, and investment trusts owned a large share of American industry, but it is doubtful that they had much to do with actually running it.

The Rise of a New Industrial Elite

As an example of the way the learned behavior of the new industrial culture was developed in New England, let us take the case of the first modern textile factory in the United States, started in 1814 by the savings of fifteen merchant families known to history as the Boston Associates. By hiring individuals with technical skills, they were soon able to branch out from their first textile mill into other manufacturing activities connected with the cotton textile industry. Their annual profits averaged almost 20 percent for the first ten years. With their surplus profits they bought into new and more diversified industries, each family supplying the new executives from within its own ranks. By 1850 the descendants of the original fifteen families controlled more than one third of the cotton spindles of New England and had an important managing voice in all of the New England railroads, most of the Boston banks, and most of the New England insurance companies, including the wealthy ones in Hartford. By 1860 these families were supplying capital for building railroads westward, so that Boston could become a depository for western timber, coal, and grain and in return supply manufactured goods to the West.

The first three to four generations were executives and managers; the fourth and fifth generations more often became dividend clippers, although they had much control over who represented them in their widespread and diversified interests. The knowledge they had picked up of the industrial and financial worlds would not be lost to their children. Even though they would not manage directly, their thoughts and actions were born out of the behavior, ideas, and accepted goals that had been handed on through family education for more than 150 years.

The descendants of the first industrialists would attempt to become the new managers in politics, in education, and in the everyday task of setting goals and aspirations for the rest of the population. They would be well-represented in the policy-making boards of trustees of the major private universities and liberal arts colleges and of most of the important foundations, banks, insurance companies, and publishing firms.

Many of the grandchildren of nineteenth century entrepreneurs became governors of states, senators, and even candidates for the presidency. They would share power with other groups, but they would articulate even more than their grandfathers the dreams, hopes, and aspirations of the less articulate parts of the population. When compared with the aristocrats of the past, the new elite of the wealthy possessed the advantage of being psychologically and culturally ready for the decision-making opportunities that would come their way.

The wealthy have the great advantage of being independent of other men's favors, of being able to do what they want to do because they have the financial freedom to do so. This independence is also the goal to which the rest of the American population aspires for the future. Financial independence and its concomitant self-confidence would remain the chief dream of those who hoped for a better future for mankind.

For Selected Bibliography, see end of Chapter 18.

17

The Twentieth Century as a Transitional Stage

The structure of industrial society would change even more in the twentieth century than in the preceding one. The corporation through its hierarchy of decision-making managers would control the details of the working lives of tens of millions of individuals in a setting similar to that of the military in its hierarchical arrangements of welfare-state care for its employees.

The early nineteenth century owner had been interested primarily in production. Although he was a one-man office, he tried to spend at least one or two hours in the plant everyday. Within a matter of fifty years, from 1830 to 1880, the United States had become the most important manufacturing country in the world, largely because of the personal attention the owner-manager gave to the most minute details of manufacturing.

Fifty years later, in 1930, the owner-manager had been replaced by the hired manager in the corporation, which had become as specialized in its managerial skills as the factory itself. Men were hired for the separate tasks of managing, producing, marketing, and financing, and for such new skills as public relations (to give the corporation with its legal personality a new cultural personality, or "image"), labor relations, personnel, and research.

The Behavior of the Corporation

The corporation, no longer the paternalistic family domain of the nineteenth century entrepreneur, in which the workers and employees were considered as hired hands and servants, had become a new, closed, self-perpetuating, oligarchic form of government, similar to that of Medieval Venice or Genoa. Although somewhat hampered by its size, laws, and precedents, it was compelled to keep some decision-making posts free from the restricting bonds of traditional behavior lest the organization become fossilized and unable to adjust to changing conditions.

The corporation as a new entity of societal government had to remain continuously aware of its own behavior. In the second half of the twentieth century, it was spending part of its profits for computers and programming machines that would enable it to know at a glance how it was feeling, living, and adjusting. It required more and more expert advice from the outside to help its leaders see alternatives and make decisions, to know where future markets would be located, and to decide what products it must manufacture in the next ten to twenty years.

The corporation would not make only one product, but would diversify. Freight car companies would go into packaging food or building household appliances; gasoline companies would go into insurance and such enterprises as restaurants and department stores. The corporation, no matter how big, could still be put out of business by new competition, by a new product, or by new mechanization utilizing vast amounts of capital for automated machinery. Even a large, competitive automobile corporation with great supplies of capital could theoretically still be put out of business by one of the other two giants automating at a faster rate.

More and more the medium-sized industries of the United States became swallowed up by even larger companies. A few hundred large corporations turn out more than three quarters of the country's production, and only the fear of government antitrust laws keeps their expansion within reasonable bounds. As corporations became wealthier and larger, they tended to try to control most of the industry's production; and competition tended to be more between giants than between Davids challenging staid Goliaths.

The new corporation would be compelled to transform its semiautomatic machinery into automatic operations in order to cut down costs and make production more efficient. As industry becomes transformed into a more mechanized means of production, doing away with the human hands that tend its semiautomatic machinery and becoming a self-sufficient and self-perpetuating substitute for routine human tasks and skills, society, as an organization of individuals sharing common goals, changes even more dramatically than when a large part of the peasantry became unskilled and semiskilled industrial workers.

The know-how of the skilled workers and technicians is being upgraded to that of today's engineers, who will tomorrow become the industrial planners, programmers, and machine tenders of the future. Both in agriculture and industry slow change is moving Secondary civilization into Tertiary civilization; the peasant and the factory worker are gradually becoming obsolete as minimum skills are being transformed into maximum ones.

Social Aspects of Secondary Civilization

The slow shifts from the Mesolithic period to that of our own Secondary civilization have led mankind into greater interdependency, more specialization, more organization, and more extensive knowledge, understanding, and action. Within a matter of thousands of years, political organizations have grown from small bands of fifty or more individuals to great superpowers and regional blocs of nations embracing hundreds of millions of individuals. Within the same span of time, mankind has steadily become more interdependent in satisfying its basic requirements for food, clothing, and shelter. Whereas one man could become a jack-of-all-trades in the Neolithic period, he could no longer do so during the flowering of Primary civilization. One man such as Arkwright or Wilkinson could manage all the details of production during the eighteenth and even nineteenth centuries (or in the transitional stage between Primary and Secondary civilizations), but this has become virtually impossible in the mid-twentieth century.

In the seventeenth century, Europe had only thirteen cities of more than 100,000; in the mid-twentieth century the world is filled with metropolitan areas with populations of one to fifteen million and with thousands of cities containing more than 50,000 inhabitants. The United States alone in 1960 had more than 130 cities with over 100,000 people and such metropolitan areas as New York with 15 million people, Los Angeles with 7 million, Chicago with 6 million, and Philadelphia with 4 million. The United States Census Bureau would speak of megalopolis and of strip cities containing tens of millions of people, living in solid urban and suburban areas stretching from Boston to Washington, Chicago to St. Louis, or San Francisco to Los Angeles. Over fifty cities in the world would have more than 1.5 million people, and the number would increase each year.

Education Under Secondary Civilization

In the simple Neolithic societies, education took place within the family, where parents and relatives taught children all they needed to know to become functioning members of the group. The arrival of Primary civilization, however, made knowledge more specialized; and few parents were equipped to cover the ground of the specialists of the day. But as yet, education was not too particularized and a boy could in a matter of five or six years acquire enough fundamentals of knowledge to serve him in most governmental and religious roles. Artisans could still learn from parents or by becoming apprentices to masters.

By the late fifteenth and sixteenth centuries, the growing complexity of life required a more formal kind of education. Merchants, civil servants, and churchmen came to be educated in schools, where they absorbed the fundamentals necessary to let them assume their respective clerical and priestly roles. In the sixteenth century, education also became an important symbol of social class, and even the well-to-do guildsmen and traders sent their sons to school at least for one or two years to learn the basic requirements of literacy.

Protestantism in the sixteenth and seventeenth centuries encouraged the growth of schools by insisting that each individual had to be able to read the Bible, the source of Protestant religious authority. In the seventeenth and eighteenth centuries the compulsory school for both sexes became increasingly important in New England. In the United States, the Northwest Ordinance of 1787 pioneered in education by stipulating that certain lands in new territories and states be set aside for the support of free public schools.

As the nineteenth century passed its sixth decade, public support for elementary and secondary schools became increasingly common. In the United States especially, federal and state aid went to colleges specializing in the teaching of agricultural, engineering, and scientific subjects. Most liberal arts colleges of the nineteenth century were still affiliated with religious denominations, because religions were more interested in training future ministers, school teachers, and professionals than they were in developing new generations of agronomists, engineers, or applied scientists.

Not until after the middle of the nineteenth century did the larger private universities offer courses in the sciences or establish scientific schools for the training of theoretical scientists and engineers. Education was still for the professional or for the scientifically minded engineer. Business had little need for formal training for its executives until around the end of the nineteenth century, when schools of business administration were organized within the larger universities in the United States and as separate institutions in Europe.

By the twentieth century forms of higher education had become formalized and traditional, teaching the generalized and specialized courses that were expected to educate the students not for the future but for the day. A few professors were looking forward to the future and trying to assess the kinds of information that they felt future leaders and educated laymen might need. But in general the universities grew more to resemble the business corporations than their earlier predecessors, the Medieval universities, where both teachers and students were free to change the subject and content of the lectures, depending upon what they considered their intellectual needs to be at the time.

The culture of the Scientific and Industrial Age is in large part transmitted by the schools. Because technical and professional training becomes increasingly a prerequisite for membership in the new managerial elite, the furtherance of education is an important activity in the countries undergoing industrialization. The training of generalists as well as specialists is in response to a demand for more and more teachers, lawyers, technicians, scientists, and managerial talent to take over the specialized tasks of the complicated management of schools, industries, businesses, and governmental units.

In the beginning the schools reinforced the family in the education of their sons and daughters, with the family giving the children their basic attitudes toward the Industrial and Scientific Age and the schools carrying them forward during its years of training. Increasingly, however, the schools began to take over the development of even basic attitudes among the young. There was talk that the schools could offer a better setting than the family in providing desirable attitudes for the future. This was especially true among the culturally deprived, where the obsolete attitudes, lack of interest, and absence of confidence on the part of the family handicapped the child in forming any identification with the new culture of the Scientific and Industrial Age.

In the United States the schools helped the rural and immigrant child acculturate to the world of the educated urban middle classes. In the totalitarian countries of the twentieth century, the state insisted that schools teach its own special interpretation of the urbanized scientific and industrial culture. In the underdeveloped areas, both the mission and the state schools acted as instructors to introduce the children of peasant agriculturists (still living technically and mentally in the late stages of the Neolithic or the early stages of Primary civilization) to the urbanized way of life of Western Europe and the United States.

Just as the Roman soldier and teacher had brought Roman culture and the Latin language into all corners of the Roman Empire, so too the nineteenth century European conqueror initiated a heritage embracing certain aspects of the new Secondary civilization and a widespread usage of both the French and English languages.

After the middle of the twentieth century, as Secondary civilization was slowly giving way to Tertiary, education would become one of the truly great enterprises of the Scientific and Industrial Age, not because of the number of teachers employed (which would be in the millions throughout the world), but because of the importance of training individuals for the future field of research. The continuing necessity of problem solving would generate innovations, inventions, wealth, and ever more problems. Mankind, by aspiring to more and more varied goals, creates chains of problems that multiply endlessly, necessitating ever more research in quest of solutions.

The Increase in the Standard of Living

The twentieth century witnessed the growth of the Industrial and Scientific Age to new heights of achievement. The standard of living doubled every twenty to thirty years as a result of increasing production in both agriculture and industry and decreasing costs in supplying individuals with their basic needs. In the twentieth century men living in the industrial nations would consume more varied food and possess more luxuries than royalty in the seventeenth and eighteenth centuries had ever had.

The railroad, the automobile, and the airplane brought all parts of the world within easy reach; travel time became shorter, and by the middle of the twentieth century no part of the globe was more than one day away by plane from any other. Although the isolation of peoples had been considered normal 500 years ago, this was no longer so as the twentieth century moved toward its end. Most people, through schools, books, films, television, and newspapers, knew of the existence of countless others and had an interest and identification with them as fellow human beings. Men knew more about themselves and their physical world than ever before, and they were becoming increasingly aware that many of their human problems had been created by themselves. Yet, most men were still living in the past rather than in the future. They were educating their children to live only in the present, ignoring the fact that more of the child's life will be lived in the future than in the present.

The Technological Age failed to bring freedom from anxiety, though it did provide satisfaction of basic needs for the middle classes of the industrial nations. It also failed to fulfill its initial promise of providing mankind with the confidence to create a world where individuals could realize their varied potentialities to the full.

Mankind would continue to be traditional and would look upon the past as having created both wisdom and security. Man would hesitate to look too far ahead into the future lest it appear too different from the accustomed present and past. Man would talk about change, but he would still fear it as an impersonal blind force that could not be kept within the bounds of technology alone. Men will gladly accept the physical aspects of technological change, but they tend to shy away from those forces of technological change that may upset their societal and mental lives. Man gave up a pseudo-independence when he changed his self-sufficient Neolithic peasant life (though he made his own decisions, he was completely unaware of the tremendous range of choices that were theoretically open to him), and he has not been able to regain even this semblance of independence in the transitional civilizations through which he has since passed. Man has always sought security, but he learned early in his development that he could achieve it only by going back to a childlike dependency upon others.

In the modern world man makes few decisions for himself; most of his decisions are made by others, whether by the corporation that employs him, the government that regulates his activities, or the peer group that articulates his goals and aspirations. As he begins to take an even longer stride into a changing future, man still needs to win his mental independence as a human being.

For Selected Bibliography, see end of Chapter 18.

18

The Scientific Age Catches up to the Industrial Age

Until now, we have been concerned primarily with the technological aspects of our Industrial Age. Although science today plays a leading role in directing our lives and has become an important component of industrialization, it is nevertheless true that it had relatively little influence upon the growth of industry and transportation during the eighteenth and early nineteenth centuries.

The paths of industrialization and science were not even developing parallel to one another in their early stages, although they began to converge somewhat after the beginning of the nineteenth century. During the eighteenth and early nineteenth centuries, most of the innovations that resulted in the textile industry, the new ironworks, and the factory system in general were created by mechanics and technicians rather than by scientists. Science at this time was abstract and mathematical and not at all concerned with the production of goods.

The British, French, and Italian academies of science were established during the middle of the seventeenth century, and their founders hoped that the encouragement of scientific thought would result in beneficial inventions for mankind. This noble aim was restricted, however, by the seventeenth century axiom that a gentleman scholar ought not be concerned with the practical, which could be safely left to the less educated mechanic. Seventeenth and eighteenth century scholars were more interested in receiving applause from their peer groups than respect in the abstract from mankind.

The mechanics and the proto-engineers of the eighteenth century were unconcerned with the abstruse theories and complex mathematical formulas of their scientifically oriented brethren; and so they went their own way, experimenting with forms and designs, learning their laws crudely through experience and observation.[1] As a result, the early

[1] Even in the United States, eighteenth century scientific speculation was the work of gentlemen. Although a Rittenhouse was applauded for his complex astronomical

engineers and mechanics made a good many erroneous observations and conclusions, which were not corrected until the scientist joined hands with the engineer for the solution of common problems in mechanics and building. Later on, each learned from the other, the engineer using his instruments and measurements to develop insights about mechanical problems and the scientist theorizing on what the problems were and how they happened.

The Engineer and the Scientist Cooperate

In the early nineteenth century, practical attempts to build better steam engines, more powerful machines, and stronger bridges were handicapped by a lack of proper understanding of the theoretical problems involved. A superior steam engine, for example, required a new theory of heat. French and German engineers became aware of experimental and theoretical work pertinent to their problems which was then being done by isolated individuals at university laboratories. New textbooks on the applied aspects of mechanics began to disseminate the mathematical thinking of the scientists, whose ideas were now spreading beyond the meetings of the various academies of science. In the industrial cities of the United States, various mechanics' libraries were opened to acquaint ambitious, self-educated mechanics with the work being carried on by this new combination of engineer and scientist.

The Training of the New Carriers of the Technological Age

Both in Europe and in the United States, there was no shortage of skilled workers who could be trained in elementary engineering knowledge. Boulton and Watt, for example, had many mechanics in their machine shop who were later able to develop innovations of their own. (One was a foreman named Murdock, who developed a practical locomotive and discovered a method of extracting gas from coal for illumination purposes. By 1798 the Boulton and Watt machine shop was actually lit by gas.)

In the early part of the nineteenth century the textile plant in Lowell, Massachusetts, trained many skilled mechanics and supervisors; and the Lowell Machine Shop raised an entire generation of practical, self-taught engineers and production superintendents. With the introduction of railroads in 1830 the Lowell Machine Shop pioneered in building locomotives that could take sharp curves and poorly ballasted roadbeds. Many of the early locomotive drivers, or engineers, were recruited from

---

clocks, a John Fitch was given almost no encouragement in developing an early steamboat that ran.

the young mechanics associated with the shop; a good number became the master mechanics and the practical superintendents of transportation in the new railroads that were expanding southward and westward.

The superintendents of the new textile mills were expected to spend a good part of their time improving the mechanical defects of the machines, thus making them more efficient. The more successful among the superintendents were later able to obtain financing to start factories of their own.

Sons of owners started off as mechanics and were expected to go into business for themselves when they had become highly efficient in their fathers' plants. Few had any theoretical training or theoretical knowledge of the mechanical principles that they were attempting to utilize, although a good many tried to keep themselves informed of theoretical developments.

In 1824 a young Massachusetts physician established the first chemical laboratory for the study of industrial problems. In 1826 he accepted an appointment as chemist to a large textile plant nearby to devote his entire time to research on improving the printing and bleaching of cotton. Another young man, brought to Massachusetts from England in the 1820's, became a self-educated expert on hydraulics.

Bright young men of merchant families were even sent to Europe during the first half of the nineteenth century to study in French and German technical schools. (The wealthier families of Boston at that time preferred abstract or pure science to applied engineering. They associated the latter field with the less educated manufacturing families.) These returning students subsequently planned many of the new railroads, industries, waterworks, and gasworks of the growing American communities. Some of them even found time to carry on theoretical research in their respective fields and to influence the establishment of scientific schools and courses at the eastern universities of their day. In 1844 a young draftsman from Connecticut named Corliss turned his inventive abilities to the improvement of steam engines. He succeeded in making the most important improvements since the days of Watt and within four years had received enough financing to organize his own company to build his new steam engines, which used less fuel per pound of steam than locomotives.

The Differences Between American and European Engineering Practices

At this time American engineering was less science-oriented than French or British applied mechanics. The emphasis in the United States was upon labor-saving machinery, ease and rapidity of construction, and mass production of consumer goods. The Europeans stressed greater efficiency of design and savings in materials and fuel. But they considered the practical applications of science from different points of view. The Americans later placed great emphasis upon the application of scientific ideas; in fact, many European scientific ideas were first applied not in Europe but in the United States. The Europeans, especially the British, viewed such application of their scientific discoveries as being too "practical," more fitting for factory mechanics than for educated men.

Although the United States produced few first-rate scientists during the nineteenth century, it stood first in the world in finding practical application for the scientific ideas that came out of European university laboratories. Although Great Britain had a wealth of first-rate scientific talent throughout the nineteenth century, her manufacturers were slow to utilize scientific ideas to increase industrial productivity. After 1870 British industries lost both their monopolies and their competitive edge in textiles, ship construction, machine building, and steel production. Few industrialists were interested in copying American mass-production techniques or diversification of production until after the middle of the twentieth century.

By the end of the nineteenth century, industry in Great Britain and France had become traditionalized, with the plant priding itself on old-fashioned precedent, skilled workmanship, and traditional models. On the other hand, at the end of the nineteenth century, Germany had already combined pure science with industrialization to outdistance the other industrialized countries in the quality of her steel, chemical dyes, drugs, and optical wares of all kinds. Throughout the fairly long industrial history of the United States, no other country except Germany attempted to compete with her for world markets. American industries before World War I moved from mass production of clocks and sewing machines to automobiles and small electrical appliances, satisfying internal demands far beyond the capacities of European industries at that time.

Although science became respectable by the middle of the eighteenth century, it was not until the nineteenth that it came of age. In that century important work in electricity led to the invention of the electric telegraph, the telephone, and electric power industries. Chemistry was born and came of age in the nineteenth. Biology, genetics, and bacteriology among others were nineteenth century sciences, as were geology and seismology. The new social sciences of anthropology, sociology, psychology, and social psychology began in the nineteenth century. Economics was eighteenth century in origin, but most of its development took place in the nineteenth.

The Role of Science in Industrial Research

As the twentieth century passed through its earliest years, science moved closer to industrialization and was put to work doing the thinking for both management and production. In Germany, after 1870, an efficient chemical industry emphasizing scientific-industrial research and new-product innovation had been built up by organized teamwork. Industrial research, the Germans discovered, could keep their plants beyond competition and in a position to dominate world markets with their products.

Industrial research came much later to the United States, though earlier than to Great Britain. The first scientific-industrial research laboratory in the United States was established in 1902 by the DuPont Company. The General Electric Company organized a laboratory to carry on research in 1904, and the American Telephone and Telegraph Company started one in 1907. World War I forced American industry to go into large-scale research, building extensive laboratories and training large numbers of scientific personnel. World War II and postwar government funds made scientific research a large-scale industry devoted to invention, innovation, improvements, and cost-cutting. Scientific research in the twentieth century has made possible a greater production of food with fewer farmers, and a larger output of goods with fewer workers. Although it has solved many productive and competitive technical problems, it is creating newer, even more complex social ones, which will need to be solved if mankind is to benefit from the great outpouring of goods that the Scientific and Industrial Age has made possible. Foremost among the social problems to be solved is an increasing population of unskilled and semiskilled workers and farmers whom modern technology and science have made almost obsolete.

Science Develops a Culture of Its Own

Although technology made life more pleasant for those who were recipients of its largesse, science went further to change men's understanding. One could say that the fruits of the technological progress that had taken place from the sixteenth century onward were emotional in enjoyment, but that the benefits of science were intellectual. Science opened up new vistas for man and provided him with a clearer picture of the physical world and growth of life than he had ever had before. No longer was it necessary for him to stand awestricken before the cataclysms of nature. He could now understand them and even attempt to control their destructive forces. Science enabled man to become more important than he had ever been, to have greater confidence in his ability to control his own destiny, to understand why and how he behaved as he did, and to know what forces his mind could unleash. Science enabled man to see his role in the world about him and to fulfill his destiny as a human being by utilizing creative thought to understand, control, and even master areas of life in which he had previously been an insignificant bystander. Instead of adjusting to a world he did not make, he could now create new worlds of his own by making the outside physical world adjust to his growing needs. Through science he could fight a delaying campaign against disease and old age, and win a whole series of skirmishes against the infirmities resulting from malnutrition, poverty, and neglect.

Science enabled man to see himself more clearly and to recognize his part in the development of life. Scientific observation enabled him to look at the heavens and see the majesty of the solar system, and to pay greater respect to the awe-inspiring distances of the galaxies than he had previously done. No longer were the stars looked upon as candles, as insignificant openings in the sky, or as misunderstood forces that controlled his life from birth to death. They now became majestic suns, blazing with the forces of atomic energy trillions of miles away. Man could see in the heavens huge untapped sources of energy, which his mind could translate into innovations that would increase his power and that would help him change from a formerly weak and insignificant animal to a creator of solar energy and a harnesser of gravitational forces. As man looks into the heavens and sees the galaxies stretching away endlessly, billions of light years away, he can see the tasks of discovery that still lie before him.

Nineteenth century science, beginning with Darwin, helped man see himself clearly as part of the chain of life. He now knew that he had developed over a period of billions of years from a half-inorganic, half-organic, form of simple life to a very complex creature able to take a microscopic look at himself and able to make a strong and healthy existence out of his former weakness. From being dependent upon the vagaries of fate and his own ignorance, man grew to be independent and no longer afraid of the unknown. He no longer needed to bow in humbleness and self-deprecation, but could stand up straight, study the unknown, and discover to his great satisfaction that knowledge erased fear. He could look back at the path he had traveled and feel a certain amount of pride that he had successfully come so far. At the same time, he could also hope that his descendants would move even further ahead.

Freud and his followers did not shame man by pointing out what he had always feared to recognize: that his intelligence was emotional as well as intellectual and that his childhood conditioning and his personality spoke a definite language of their own, insisting upon the right not to be humiliated or demeaned, or to bear the inhuman suffering of non-recognition or lack of esteem. It was man's revolt against being demeaned that gave him dignity, that made him take the path to independence.

His angry refusal to feel unimportant in his relationships with the supernatural world and with other men made him struggle to master both himself and his animal fate. Man became human when he took the apple of the tree of knowledge and used it to break away from an existence that was idyllic only to those who never had to suffer it. By putting an end to a perpetual childhood in which he was not master of his senses, he cut his dependency on his animal past and took the first step toward becoming an intellectually curious human being.

All these scientific advances, then, enhanced man's confidence in himself and gave him an ability to see the world as it actually was. More than that, it gave him new directions at which to aim. As he created new goals for himself, he also had to find the means to achieve them.

In early Paleolithic times, man's goals were simple: to enjoy the company of his fellowmen and to have enough to eat. As he entered the Neolithic age and his food supply became more plentiful, he began to find pleasure in using his intellectual capacities. He felt stimulated by his ability to master, though largely in his imagination, all kinds of frightful threats existing in the world around him, by his belief that he could find meaning in a world that sometimes treated him unkindly, by his faith that he could find believable theories to explain what was happening to him, and by his conviction that he could decipher the disorderly world and make it more orderly for himself.

As man moved along the path of civilization, he experienced the creative pleasures of constructing immense buildings that did not exist in nature, of writing down his thoughts and being able to read the thoughts of others, and of cultivating and changing the face of the earth through vineyards, orchards, roads, viaducts, palaces, and sprawling cities. His creative drives encouraged him to seek new technological means to make his life easier and more emotionally satisfying. Unfortunately, a long time would pass before he learned to identify himself completely with others or to imagine how he would feel if he were placed in their shoes. Although he learned to voice these concepts of empathy quite early, he had not learned to translate these values into strong action or behavior patterns—even by the last third of the twentieth century.

In the beginning, science dealt with things rather than with people. During the nineteenth century, science advanced by achieving insights into the functioning of life and heredity, into the growth of the stars, and into the structure of the physical world; but it developed few insights into the traditional relationships of man to man. In France in the first half of the nineteenth century, Comte had argued that scientific thought was more advanced and therefore more positive than the mystical and metaphysical, but men could still not agree on what scientific thought was and whether it was preferable to other ways of thinking. In the nineteenth century, men did not feel any strong needs to build a body of knowledge that would offer them alternative insights into their interpersonal worlds.

The social sciences came into existence at the end of the nineteenth and in the early twentieth centuries, but no unanimous agreement existed among them (as among the physical and life sciences) as to what their initial assumptions should be and what subject matter needed to be studied. Although the social sciences were not harassed unduly (except in the authoritarian political regimes of the nineteenth and twentieth centuries), neither were they given much academic or financial support.

The social sciences began to receive encouragement when they helped make decisions that gave the business and governmental worlds more confidence in themselves. Men would be hired, promoted, and even fired with the aid of consulting psychologists. Sociologists would be used to promote better prison surveillance, although they would not be used to shape a more efficient human society. Political scientists would be used by the government to prove what was already known or suspected, although they would not be used to help create a more efficient or democratic government.

After World War II the physical and biological scientists were trained and employed in huge numbers to create better and more deadly weapons systems, to experiment in harnessing solar energy for future workaday tasks, and to send men into space. The biological scientists had increasing opportunities to study the problems of life; and while being pressed to discover the cures for diseases, they learned far more about the structure of life than had been known previously.

From a handful of individuals in the sixteenth century, to a slightly larger number in the eighteenth, the innovational scientists by the middle of the twentieth century began to multiply into hundreds of thousands. This rapid expansion occurred as both the developed and the underdeveloped countries recognized the value of the scientist in articulating problems and using his specialized knowledge to solve them. The nineteenth and twentieth century executives could make decisions only when presented with alternatives; but their training did not encourage them to develop within themselves the qualities of mental discipline necessary to understand the possible alternatives available in their decision making.

The scientists were gradually taking over the former roles of the king's first ministers, who devised and implemented the decisions the monarch had to make. In the modern world scientists were becoming decision makers as well as leaders of public opinion. They were becoming the new interpreters of the modern world, supplanting the priests who had held sway from the early days of Sumeria. In the twentieth century, most individuals in the developed and the developing areas of the world were becoming convinced that science would become the single most important force in making the world prosperous, interesting, and healthy.

The scientists, the technological innovators, and the intellectually oriented executives and engineers are still a tiny minority in the total world population, yet their influence has changed the course of history. Without the development of the technological and industrial civilization after 1500, the world would not have been able to house, feed, or clothe a population that grew from about 500 million to seven times that number by 1965 (and will become more than twelve times as great by the end of the twentieth century). Without the benefits derived from science, most men today would not be able to live past the age of thirty. Technology and the industrial system have shrunk the world and have enabled men to learn faster from one another than ever before. Although men have thus far failed to suppress their quarrels and aggressions, history has compelled them to become at least conscious of their hostilities.

In the sense that man has become aware of his actions and is gradually assuming responsibility for many of them, he is freer today than he has ever been before. He is now conscious of his behavior and the limitations that he and others put upon it. In the future he will attain greater freedom, when he learns to master himself and becomes aware of his potentialities for creating greatness in himself and in his fellowmen. In terms of time, it is difficult for man to sense his own powers, for he has had only a few hundred years in which to become conscious of only a few of them. If he can keep his hostilities submerged long enough to learn how to adjust peacefully to his fellow human beings in different parts of the world, then he may continue the promise of millions of years of future human development. If he can learn to bring to the perusal of national and international questions the dispassionate and critical analysis of problems as it is theoretically practiced in the laboratory or in the scholar's study, then he may continue to build upon the achievements of the present and the past, and he may pass on to his children the possibility of some day fulfilling their creative potentialities.

Within a few centuries, it is possible that 15 percent of the population will be trained as innovators to spend their time solving the problems of the other 85 percent. And who knows, perhaps thousands of years from now, over 90 percent of the population may be trained to spend their lives identifying, describing, exploring, and solving ever new problems. We are still so close to the animallike goals of securing sufficient food, clothing, and shelter that we take it for granted that leisure from work means more time for entertainment. We forget that new goals thousands of years from now may keep individuals engrossed in their daily work even though their basic needs are automatically taken care of.

Science and technology, then, require a mental climate that permits growth and gives approval and sanction both to thought and to the scientist. If the world had been composed, say, of groups such as the Amish, there would have been no development of science or technology; the few embryonic scientists would have been shunned even before they could have begun to progress. The growth of science and technology in the Western world came about because of encouragement from those in the power structure who appreciated and wanted its benefits. Technology and science in themselves did not change the world so much as men's changing attitudes toward their goals in life and their awareness of themselves.

Those who were pessimistic about man's ability to master his destiny attacked the scientific thought of the day as heresies, and some were even aggressively hostile toward the new technology. From the thirteenth to the twentieth century, masochistic asceticism has always provided an alternate spirit to the age (including those phases in the United States when legislatures reflected popular opinion by attempting to forbid the teachings of scientific theories that contradicted folk knowledge). Still, this negative emotionalism never seemed to offer as much satisfaction to those in positions of power as the pleasures involved in producing more material goods and in achieving greater independence through intellectual maturity. Educated men have often believed that life needed to hold more than merely the satisfaction of their physiological urges. Their goals have become more complex as they have sought the intellectual enjoyment to be received from rising above their past levels of achievement.

The Technological and Scientific Age has thus represented a continuum in man's development. Once man took his first steps, he had to take the others. Once he understood the advantages of obtaining his food more efficiently, he began to seek equal efficiency in other aspects of his workaday world. Once he set goals for himself, he felt uncomfortable until he achieved them. He also felt a great sense of satisfaction when he had achieved what had once appeared to be impossible. Man was testing himself and discovering that he could take longer steps, dream larger dreams, think more clearly, and aspire to greater heights than he had ever before thought possible. Although the self-confident and self-reliant were few in the beginning (the others gave up before they even started because they insisted that man was puny, insignificant, and too dependent upon father figures to undertake anything by himself), they still influenced others and created situations in which increasing numbers of individuals were given the opportunity to show what they could do. Perhaps in some dim future, after man has become accustomed to his intellectual affluence, the self-confident and the self-reliant will form the majority of the population.

A civilization possesses a momentum that is carried by those inhabitants who are able to perpetuate its ideas and add to its strength through innovation. Although Florence and Venice were handicapped by their isolation in a sea of peasants and feudal lords, their ways of life became almost immortal as their banks, handicraft industries, trades, and skills spread and became part of the economic and cultural strength of other cities. The Florentines and Venetians were secretive about their skills and prohibited publication of their special knowledge (as England also did at the end of the eighteenth century in the hope of keeping her textile and mechanical secrets from spreading to other countries), but in time everything they knew became common knowledge to even their bitterest competitors.

The Florentines punished by death the theft or dissemination of knowledge of their seventeenth century silk-throwing machine, but it was not long before English mechanics knew how it was made. The same impossibility of secrecy occurred when the English learned the secret of Chinese porcelain in the eighteenth century and when the Americans learned the secrets of making English textile machinery, English and French steel processing, and German pharmaceutical and chemical formulas. European businessmen were more secretive than European scientists; they wrote little down concerning how they reached decisions or how they learned their management skills. Despite this, most of their knowledge was passed on and enough spilled over to enable competitors and individuals in other countries to learn from them. The special skills of the artisans of India and China passed to craftsmen in Europe through the intermediaries of Persians, Mongols, and Venetians. Secrets have not been kept very long in the development of world technology and science. What was discovered in China in the first century A.D. came to Europe by the twelfth. Conversely, what was discovered by the Europeans in the thirteenth century was adopted by the Chinese in the fifteenth and the Japanese in the sixteenth. Little scientific or technological knowledge has ever been lost. Rather, the losses to mankind have lain in the inability of human beings to utilize their talents completely.

For tens of thousands of years, mankind has been building up its wealth. As men become skilled in seeking greater efficiency and in improvising new ways of making life easier for themselves and generations to follow, wealth diffuses to cover a more widespread area. If we project into the future the directions that man has thus far taken, it is clear that even greater wealth will be created in coming generations when more men are given the opportunities to utilize their imaginations in articulating, planning, projecting, and visualizing improvements and innovations. Only man can push himself ahead by means of the goals he sets for himself. The concept of "progress" originated in the latter part of the eighteenth century; and its acceptance as an important value for mankind has been pushed in each century by a few daring, imaginative men who wanted to make a more efficient tool, develop more accurate observations and measurements, or articulate a more coherent and understandable theory.

The Scientific and Industrial Age has just begun, and the effects of its unfinished work will change humanity and the face of the earth more than they have been changed thus far. Man may be mortal, but mankind has the hope of being immortal. As more and more men carry the way of life, the behavior, and the ideas of Secondary civilization (and few countries will be able to escape its effects during the next century), a new variant of this civilization will be born from the minds of its intellectuals, decision makers, and scientific and technical personnel. And as one civilization over a long period of time slowly replaces the last one, mankind may well reach the point when most human beings will for the first time carry their intellectual weight—and thus make the earth an even more interesting place to live in than it has been before.

Selected Bibliography

Barbour, Violet, *Capitalism in Amsterdam in the Seventeenth Century* (Ann Arbor, University of Michigan Press, Ann Arbor Paperbacks, 1963).

Beard, Miriam, *A History of Business,* 2 Vols. (Ann Arbor, University of Michigan Press, Ann Arbor Paperbacks, 1962–63).

Butterfield, Herbert, *The Origins of Modern Science, 1300–1800* (New York, Collier, 1962).

Cochran, Thomas C., *The Age of Enterprise* (New York, Harper & Row, Harper Torchbooks, 1961).

Crombie, A. C., *Medieval and Early Modern Science,* 2 Vols. (Garden City, N.Y., Doubleday, Anchor Books, 1959).

Eco, Umberto, and Zorzoli, G. B., *The Picture History of Inventions* (New York, Macmillan, 1963).

Feuer, Lewis S., *The Scientific Intellectual* (New York, Basic Books, 1963).

Forbes, R. J., and Dijksterhuis, E. J., *A History of Science and Technology,* 2 Vols. (Baltimore, Penguin, 1963).

Hagen, Everett E., *On the Theory of Social Change* (Homewood, Ill., Dorsey, 1962).

Johnson, E. A. J., and Krooss, H. E., *The American Economy* (Englewood Cliffs, N.J., Prentice-Hall, 1960).

Lewis, Roy, and Steward, Rosemary, *The Managers* (New York, New American Library, Mentor Books, 1961).

Mantoux, Paul, *The Industrial Revolution in the Eighteenth Century* (New York, Harper & Row, Harper Torchbooks, 1961).

Metraux, Guy S., and Crouzet, Francois, eds., *The Evolution of Science* (New York, New American Library, Mentor Books, 1963).

————, *The Nineteenth Century World* (New York, New American Library, Mentor Books, 1963).

Rostow, W. W., *The Stages of Economic Growth* (New York, Cambridge University Press, 1960).

Sarton, George, *Ancient and Medieval Science During the Renaissance* (New York, Barnes, Perpetua Books, 1961).

Struik, Dirk J., *Yankee Science in the Making* (Boston, Little, Brown, 1948).

Thrupp, Sylvia L., *The Merchant Class of Medieval London* (Ann Arbor, University of Michigan Press, Ann Arbor Paperbacks, 1962).

Weber, Max, *General Economic History* (New York, Collier, 1961).

White, Lynn, Jr., *Medieval Technology and Social Change* (London, Oxford University Press, 1963).

19

Culture, Civilization, and the Peasant

Thus far, we have been concerned with the trends of civilization as various people and countries took up the accumulation of knowledge and advanced it further. We have seen that civilization is a way of life and that its diffusion is not based upon word of mouth alone, but also upon the written word. Civilization is urbanization combined with literacy. It is not necessarily passed on from father to son but is learned formally in schools. Receptivity to its varied ideas may be greater in some families than in others, but no individual can learn to be a carrier of civilization through the family alone.

Civilization is the specialization of labor, first simple and then increasingly complex, as urbanization becomes the norm for most people and few are able to supply their needs through their own efforts. Civilization requires interdependency of peoples—not reliance upon relatives but dependency upon complete strangers, who supply food, make implements and clothes, carry on scientific research, manage, innovate, heal, and teach.

In civilization some will be leaders, others will be diffident guides, but most will be passive followers living from day to day with a faith in their leaders to provide for them and in their guides to show them what to do and where to go. As civilization becomes more complex and as more and more people are drawn into its vortex, previous ways of life will still be represented among those who are the recipients of its bounty but still remain passively insulated along its outer fringes.

The Secondary civilization of industrialization and science is more than a mere enumeration of railroads, factories, utility plants, office buildings, government bureaus, schools, and universities. It is a complex way of life that is learned by living in it, by being formally trained to understand its forms, and by being initiated into its particular ways of thinking. Although peasants and illiterate workers can live within Sec-

221

ondary civilization and can even learn to operate its cars, machinery, and some of its tools, they belong mentally in the previous Primary civilization, in which the peasant could live peripherally to the urban civilization but remain unaffected by its thinking or its ways of looking at the universe. The carriers of the new Secondary civilization are the thinkers and innovators who improve it, manage it, and make its important decisions; but these carriers may also retain in their minds the ideas of past ages and scientifically obsolete ways of looking upon themselves, their fellowmen, and the universe.

There is no problem involved in having peasants or farm laborers work in factories; most can learn the discipline and the habits of work, as well as deference to hierarchal authority, in a fairly short period of time. A difficulty arises, however, if the peasant is encouraged to become a plant executive, production engineer, or research chemist. These professionals are the mental adherents of Secondary civilization. It takes years of training, plus the complex development of a confident, achieving, goal-centered human personality before we have an individual capable of participating in this behavioral and learning climate of Secondary civilization.

Although the roles of those who are the physicians, the parents, and the tutors of Secondary civilization are indeed complex, and are becoming more so each year, the evolving roles of the progenitors and guardians of the coming Tertiary civilization may become even more complex. As we look forward to the distant future with its successions of even more complex and interdependent civilizations, we can see that despite our technology, our science, and our management skills (of which we are rightly proud) we are still in our infancy in the area of human development. Few of us can visualize the forms our technological civilization will take during the next several hundred years, and even fewer can try to imagine the sort of mentality that will go with it. Since man continuously recreates himself culturally through his thoughts, the possibilities for man's future as he becomes more aware of his talented potentialities stagger our imaginations.

The Definition of Culture

Man's way of life is not inborn but learned; and it is learned because man, being human, is able to symbolize his experiences and his thoughts through words. Without language we would be unable to innovate, manage, or participate in our respective cultures. And the simplest explanation of culture is that it represents all the shared thoughts, ways of doing things, ways of behaving, and ways of imagining that the individual learns from infancy through his parents, his peer group, his formal and informal teachers, and his own socialized perceptions as to what he expects of others and what others expect of him. The keynote of culture is its relativity. It changes as men's thoughts evolve into action, as values become transformed, as daily behavior becomes affected by new goals or shaped by the reconsideration of intellectual and moral viewpoints. Man's culture is taught by socialization, which he undergoes throughout his life and which makes him a bearable and cooperative member of his group and community, and also by unwritten as well as written laws that define the responsibilities, obligations, and rights of the individual living within a societal setting. (Culture reflects all the intricate ideas, thoughts, perceptions, habits (motor as well as experiential), and moral and religious systems that determine the individual's outlook upon himself, his relationships and behavior toward others, and his expectations of himself and others.

Culture represents all the learned ideas, concepts, and behavior (including inhibitions) that make an individual at home in a particular society. What would be one person's cultural meat in one geographic area, however, might be another person's poison in another. Culture is taught. The particular cultural behavior displayed by an upper social class has nothing to do with "breeding" or biological inheritance, but is the result of years of training and punishing the young so that the taught behavior will appear to be natural in the adult who has been thus indoctrinated.

Culture, then, represents the learning that is part of man's human nature, the words that are father to the thought, the mental processes that lead to action, and the emotional reactions and impulses that are unvoiced thoughts about self-esteem and past personality needs that have developed with the individual. Even such emotional concepts as honor, masculinity, femininity, adulthood, loyalty, love, and so on, are inarticulated symbols concerning the individual's own concepts about himself and his relationships with others. Men can talk about such symbols and receive some sort of understanding as to what they imply. Man becomes more human as he learns to express his feelings through words. With his power of speech comes his remarkable talent of thought, or his ability to abstract such complexities as human actions, machine designs, and physical laws of the universe and such concepts as illness and death.)

Cultural Change

Because culture represents man's thinking about the reality of the universe he lives in (including his own world of family, friends, and neighbors), it can never be absolute in limits or unchanging in values. It is a compilation of all the concepts, verbalized as well as unverbalized, indicated by the individuals who live within a common society. Society represents the interactions of individuals sharing the goals of a common culture; or, put another way, culture represents thought, behavior, and society—and the forms that express them. Because the ideas of men in our contemporary civilization are in a state of flux, cultural change is also continuous (the results of thoughts initiated by the decision makers). As new concepts of family life are expressed by psychiatrists, sociologists, theologians, peer groups, and so on, the expectations, responsibilities, rights of husbands and wives, and methods of rearing children also change.

If we have been reared to believe that our culture is absolute and not subject to change, that its concepts are not the effect of men's thoughts but eternal in our heritage, then we will resist new ideas or cultural change with strong emotional distaste and consider them threats to our stable estimate of ourselves and our parents. One has to be taught to live with cultural change; but change can be threatening if it does not help the individual achieve his goals, if it is directed against him, or if it is harmful to his sense of well-being.

A worker displaced by automation does not have an appreciation for the progress of science in increasing the factory's productivity, but views it as the loss of his job, his self-esteem, and his opportunity to earn the income that his family and he have expected. A peasant in a developing country does not see the tractors, the machinery, the improved seed, and the chemical fertilizer as production aids but as agents bringing new stresses into his life by making it impossible for him to anticipate his future in terms of the past that he knows. A locomotive fireman does not see the introduction of the diesel engine as cutting costs and increasing efficiency in transportation; to him it means the loss of his job.

In most instances, cultural change does affect a great many individuals adversely, although they may have faith that in time their children will benefit. Since cultural change has become a normal aspect of our American society, we need to provide cushioning effects against its initially adverse reactions and to rear individuals to anticipate its shocks. In addition, our educational system should be training young people to live in the future, since they will spend most of their lives doing so, rather than teaching them to adjust to thought patterns of the past, which most of them will know only secondhand.

Cultural change can be frightening if the individual has been reared to feel that the habitual should be the norm and that the reward for having learned one's lessons well is absense of threat. The individual cannot count upon the realization of his goals if cultural change inhibits or prevents him from progressing toward them. If one cannot anticipate the innovating thoughts of unknown thousands of decision makers in one's society, it becomes doubly difficult to plan one's life according to parental precepts and conventional school training. Cultural change is not a phenomenon of nature, but a result of the decisions of tens of thousands of individuals in varying positions of authority.

If we see cultural change as brought about by important individuals whose decisions affect our health, technology, employment, taxation, interpersonal relations, and personal stress, we will then understand the strains experienced by those seeking personal security in a world where their lives are regulated and directed by others and not by themselves. In a world containing millions of strangers, few of whom ever become personally involved with us, it is difficult for most people to feel any assurance that decisions made by others will not adversely affect their personal lives. In a Neolithic village society, a good many decisions affecting the group could be made within the group. In our complex Secondary civilization, now evolving into a Tertiary one, few decisions affecting the welfare of the many can be made by those involved. And as the world becomes more specialized, even the daily routine decisions will be made by professional teams of experts working with complex computers and research tools.

The Peasant in the Midst of Secondary Civilization

Although the material benefits of the Industrial Age can readily be grasped by most of the people of the world, the Scientific Age still remains outside their ken. The large industrial city with its factories and service industries attracts the landless peasants of South America and Asia, and this urban conglomeration introduces their children to the dreams of a technological world rather than a scientific one. In the rural areas, the values of the past still survive in interpersonal obligations and in the ascribed social identities of all members of the village. In the city, new relationships are formed and new goals set to help compensate for the deprivations of the past. For most migrants from the rural districts, the traditional and the innovational meet in the city. Here a money economy flourishes, and acquiring money becomes an important goal because of the security and independence in making decisions that it gives.

In the past, hundreds of millions of peasants changed their traditional ways of behaving by their migration to the growing cities of England, Germany, France, the United States, Russia, India, China, and Japan. It was in the cities that their traditional peasant values of security were joined with the new middle-class values of financial success. In the cities of the nineteenth century, the varied and complex culture of the middle classes was taught to the children in public schools, although it was in the factories that the peasants' children learned to adjust themselves to a world of strangers—a world that stressed work, discipline, and anxiety.

On the land the peasants had generally experienced cataclysms in the form of droughts and floods. In the city workshops, the perennial disasters for their children were man-made: economic depressions with their resulting unemployment, technological changes that shifted employment from one medium to another, and mergers that abolished a certain number of jobs. For most first and second generation workers in the cities, the risks involved in keeping employment were as great as the adverse factors that had affected the agricultural production of their parents on the land. In the cities of Europe, Asia, and the Americas during the nineteenth and twentieth centuries, most workers learned to become as resigned, suspicious, and apathetic as their parents had been in the villages.

The Industrial Age impinges upon the peasant and the unskilled and semiskilled workers both at work and in recreation, but neither the peasant nor the worker is a true participant of the age. They are passive spectators and recipients, able to manipulate the machinery and to adjust fairly quickly to a world of television, radio, automobiles, electricity, and supermarkets. Their labor is used similarly to that of the ancient peasants who built the great works of Primary civilization and returned to their village homes where their traditional ways of life began again for them. Although workers and peasants can work within the Industrial Age and even live in its depressed urban areas, they are not participants in its thinking, values, or leadership. They are the followers of the Industrial Age, the soldiers but not the officers (though a good many become its noncommissioned officers). Only a small percentage of their children will leave their traditional cultures and become innovational and creative personalities within the industrial and scientific civilization; most of them will receive only enough training in literacy to qualify for the semiskilled work that will be taken over by the automatic machinery of the future.

There are few isolated places in the world today that are unaware of the forces of the Industrial Age. Even the small stack of goods at the village store in Africa or in India has made the peasant aware that there is a production of great variety in the outside world. This material plenty has even impinged upon the consciousness of the marginal peasant in the nonliterate areas of the world. To them planes, automobiles, radios, and canned goods are only the obvious symbols of the new Industrial Age. The miracle drugs and vaccines have been spread by government and mission doctors far beyond the borders of the industrialized and urbanized countries. Diffusion of the mountains of products of the new Industrial Age moves much faster and over wider segments of the earth's surface than the slow spread of agricultural techniques thousands of years ago. This century may be the last in which marginal peoples are isolated from the mainstreams of the innovational Technological and Scientific

Age. Certainly during the next two or three centuries, few areas will not contribute their intellectual share to the ever-mounting accumulation of innovations and insights into the new domains of scientific knowledge.

In the meanwhile, although an awareness of the Industrial and Scientific Age has entered the folk knowledge of many people living on the subsistence level of the Neolithic peasant, there are still large segments of the world's population that will remain passive spectators of the new age for decades to come. In the past, diffusion of technological knowledge was on a simple level; and the use of new tools or forms of cultivation and manufacture could easily be taught over a period of years to a few individuals, who in turn became the teachers of the new forms. The diffusion of pottery, toolmaking, agricultural techniques, boatbuilding, and so on were concepts that could be easily grasped by those living in a peasant culture. But how is it possible to diffuse to a peasant people the understanding of an oxygen blast furnace, or a physicochemical laboratory, or a computer, or a pharmaceutical factory? How can peasant villages be motivated to cooperate in building roads and railroads in the way that irrigation canals and reservoirs were once cooperatively constructed? How is it possible to diffuse the complex managerial and entrepreneurial skills demanded by the specialized and evolving Scientific and Industrial Age without changing the entire fabric and spirit of peasant society?

The peasant and his village are in many ways anachronisms, and the great problem that will plague future decision makers will be what is to become of them. They will not be able to provide their share of the nation's production without being transformed into technically trained farmers, who can transmute large amounts of chemicals and machines into enormous supplies of food. As peasants they cannot feed or clothe themselves adequately, or supply the services their children will need if they are to lead lives less deprived than those of their parents. The new civilization will not be able to utilize the labor of inefficient peasants as the old one did; machines are a superior substitute, which, though initially more expensive, are cheaper and more productive in the long run.

Governmental Problems in the Secondary Civilization

The industrial culture bringing more and more peasants into the vortex of modern urban civilization was initially brought about through the efforts of perhaps hundreds of men in the eighteenth century and thousands in the nineteenth century. In the twentieth century hundreds of thousands of creative and innovational personalities are required to keep this civilization going; in the twenty-first century the number will be in the millions, and by the end of that century perhaps in the hundreds of millions. These men with their training in problem solving are changing the physical face of the earth faster than nations are able to adjust their political thinking to the results.

The implications of further inevitable technical and scientific change to the lives of present populations have not been explored in depth by most governments, which are wholly unprepared for the political shocks created by burgeoning cities, population explosions, and mounting unemployment. Untold numbers of surplus peasants in South America, Africa, and Asia will leave their villages over the next few decades and move into growing governmental and industrial centers, seeking to satisfy their new expectations. The increased social costs of supplying schools to provide for the future out of the paltry savings of the past and of developing a minimum of good public health care, lest the poor sanitary conditions of the new slums sweep the urban populations with epidemics and diseases, can overburden most governments in the developing areas. Secondary civilization requires a far greater investment in educated minds and social services (roads, railways, schools, communications, public health, police, and welfare) than most of the developing countries of the world are able to supply out of their meager resources. Most peasants in the developing nations are too poor to tax for funds to build a new industrial and scientific civilization, which requires greater resources of educated minds and raw materials than were necessary for the creation of the Mogul Empire in India or the Industrial Age in England.

Secondary civilization requires an initial investment of great wealth, even for the promise of greater wealth to come. This wealth is to be found only in the developed industrial and scientific nations; and their meager surpluses in the form of technical assistance, foreign aid, or even long-term financial credits are not enough for the creation of new centers of Secondary civilization among two-thirds of the populations of the world whose per capita income is less than three hundred dollars per year. Poorly developed countries that double their populations every twenty to twenty-five years cannot be changed overnight from economies based upon peasant civilizations to economies based upon industry, technical schools, universities, research laboratories, and manned space flights.

The Industrial Revolution in England grew slowly during the eighteenth and nineteenth centuries, but the underdeveloped areas of the world today cannot emulate England's slow industrial evolvement. By the time these areas would be able to bridge the gap between the eighteenth and twentieth centuries, their populations would have become too unwieldy. Those populations being educated by the cultures of the developed countries might become highly impatient and might try to quicken the birth and growth of the new industrial civilization by armed political insurrection, which would lead to disciplined totalitarian governmental action.

Since the sixteenth century, the world's population has multiplied seven times as a direct result of better living conditions, improved food supplies, and medical care in the industrial nations. The developing areas have gained from the eradication of nationwide epidemics and plagues through the work of the scientists of the wealthier countries, and have achieved lower mortality rates through improved sanitation and better instruction in infant care. In most of the developing countries, where the peasants are concentrated today, the average food intake may be no more than 2,000 calories per person per day, as compared with over 3,000 for the developed nations; and the average protein intake is less than 20 grams per capita per day, as compared with a minimum daily need of about 75 grams. Children in the developing countries are often reared with low-grade malnutrition and vitamin deficiencies, and thus suffer a lowered body resistance to infections.

Secondary civilization with its emphasis upon efficiency in production has made the inhabitants of the developed industrial nations healthier and better fed, clothed, and housed today than at any other time in human history. Certainly there is no comparison between the living conditions of an unskilled factory worker in Western Europe or the United States and the living conditions of a peasant in the villages of Iran, Pakistan, India, or China. Even the industrial workers of the Midlands in England in the latter part of the eighteenth century, poverty-stricken though they may have been, were still relatively better off in food and shelter than their displaced rural parents and grandparents. There have been no famines in the industrial regions of Western Europe or the United States as there were in seventeenth century France, eighteenth century Russia, or nineteenth century Ireland, or as there have been in twentieth century India, Russia, and China.

The End of Universal Poverty

Under Primary civilization, poverty in the villages and towns was assumed to be the norm in men's lives. The majority of the population was poor in a way that not even the unemployed American or English worker of the 1930's could visualize. Housing was simple, if not crude; food was limited and consisted mostly of carbohydrates. Clothing was handwoven, or if purchased was worn until little of it could be redarned or patched. Necessities were few and on a minimum level. With the peasants living on the borders of subsistence for most of the year, it was natural that religious holidays, weddings, births, and even deaths should provide a means for the peasant to forget his drab poverty in feasting for a few days as if he were wealthy. Even the village rich (in relative terms) did not engage in conspicuous consumption; they possessed only a larger hut, or their wives and daughters wore more jewelry. Their wealth was perhaps in land. They ate more carbohydrates (they were the only ones who could afford to be stout) but in general their lives differed little in quality from those of the peasants. Not until the fifteenth and sixteenth centuries in Renaissance Italy would the wealthy merchant begin to consume a good part of his riches by building a large palace, acquiring elaborate furniture, eating more varied foods, entertaining at banquets, and purchasing fine works of art. This would also become the way of life for the wealthy of Western Europe in the eighteenth and nineteenth centuries. In the Ancient World, luxurious living was rare and became prevalent in a small segment of the population only with the growth of empires. Today there are individuals in the upper middle class living on a more luxurious scale than even the wealthiest emperors of the Ancient World enjoyed.

It was our recent Industrial Age, then, that permitted men to see that poverty was no longer a necessary prerequisite of human existence. The abject poor of the fifteenth and sixteenth centuries in Western Europe had largely disappeared by the end of the nineteenth century, and they disappeared completely in the twentieth. (Men would regress at times to this previous poverty but only during wartime sieges or military occupation.) Individuals no longer starved to death because crops failed; enough surplus existed in other parts of the world to be easily transported to the famine areas. Although men died in the Russian Volga famine of 1921 and in India and in China at numerous times in the early half of the twentieth century, these tragic events were the last gasps of a dying age. During the past twenty-five years, no famines in which millions of people died have occurred, as they did in the previous twenty-five years. The greatest decimations have come with the new human scourge of industrialized warfare, in which tens of millions have died on the battlefield, in concentration camps, and at the hands of authoritarian police states, and where hundreds of thousands have died indirectly from starvation or disease while under siege, as in the Soviet Union and China during World War II.

By the last third of the twentieth century, poverty and disease as previous ages knew them had become rare in the developed countries. And both were slowly being eliminated from the developing nations, as the new technical and medical skills from the outside were learned and adapted. Pockets of poverty still existed in certain areas of the developed countries; but these were caused by poor resources, low levels of education, and an absence of entrepreneurial skills. In the United States the rapid spread of industrialization and industrial skills had bypassed certain groups such as the Indians on reservations, rural dwellers in the South, unskilled Negroes, and the unskilled and semiskilled labor in the Appalachian highlands. In Italy the peasant farmers of the South had been unable to adjust to twentieth century demands. The North of Britain formed another pocket of poverty. In France the sizable number of small landholders were unable to compete with the larger and more mechanized farms. In Germany the small peasants, though subsidized by the state, were unable to achieve the standard of living enjoyed by even the unskilled workers in the cities.

In the developing nations one sees the difference in standard of living between those peasants who still adhere to Primary civilization and those growing middle classes who are participants in Secondary civilization. The city is the home of the increasing, technologically trained middle classes, for Secondary civilization has brought into being large numbers of individuals who are trained to serve the needs of both industrialization and government. The rural area is the home of the peasants, working inefficiently with little scientific assistance to raise the single crop that pays for the tools and machines imported by the urban upper classes, who often own the land the peasant works.

Brazil as an Example of Development

In Brazil the cities have become part of the Industrial Age; and a good many technicians, professionals, and managers have been trained. In the rural northeastern part of the country, almost half of the population is still illiterate, malnourished, and subsisting on the cash equivalents of $30 to $50 per month. Although such a standard of living would have been considered above normal in fifteenth century Europe, it is abnormal in the twentieth century world when compared with the way the middle classes now live in the larger Brazilian coastal cities. The rural per capita income of $150 per year is low when compared with that of more than $2,500 in the United States, or the $1,900 in Sweden, although it is higher than the rural incomes in Bolivia, Paraguay, or Haiti.

In 1940 Brazil had 40 million people, and more than 80 million twenty-five years later. By the year 2000 she may have more than 250 million inhabitants, the vast majority of whom may still be untrained, semiliterate, and poor. Although Secondary civilization is growing in Brazil, with large industrial plants dotting her great cities and universities turning out tens of thousands of trained technological middle-class individuals, the contrast between the two civilizations creates enormous political stresses.

More than 30 million illiterate, landless, and untrained peasants remain in the vast backlands and fertile maritime belt. Their per capita income averages less than $150 per year while in the cities it amounts to more than $600 per year. It takes decades, however, to transform the children of the agricultural peasantry into urban middle classes containing trained individuals capable of planning, managing, and innovating. Brazil has too many peasants and too few technical and professional managers.

Factories are only part of an industrial system. A new culture must also be developed, with individuals who are trained to think, behave, and operate within an interrelated society. Peasants cannot adapt themselves to this new culture without making basic changes in their way of life; but even more than change is required. What is needed is a complete transformation, which cannot take place without (1) long years of formal technical training and (2) the amount of time necessary to learn the facets of technological and industrial behavior within the plant itself.

The peasant can supply some of the labor needed to operate the industrial plant without changing his own thinking very much, but he cannot become a functioning part of the industrial system without ceasing to be a peasant. There is a fundamental disparity between the two cultures. The technological culture can be sustained only by a trained middle class of technicians, professionals, and managers to whom the world of industries, production, marketing, and innovation are accepted as normal facets of behavior. This trained middle class knows where to get the knowledge it lacks; and its members are convinced that if this knowledge does not exist, it must be developed through research and consultation.

The Peasant Culture

The peasant lacks confidence in his ability to achieve anything more than his parents did. He fears being placed in situations that he cannot understand and that reinforce his feelings of inadequacy. He projects his fears to the elites above him, who then appear to behave toward him as he expects them to. He can predict what will happen in his own village, but he finds the city unpredictable because to him its population operates from whim and fancy rather than from any patterned behavior that he can fully understand.

In the European past, the peasant suffered at the hands of landlords, who had little interest in him as a person but were interested only in the services and money that he made possible for them. In Asia, both west and east, he was looked upon primarily as a source of rents. Living on the subsistence level with the prices he receives for his food lower than the cost of outside goods he needs to buy, he has learned to react with suspicion, if not downright hostility, to traders, shopkeepers, police, and government officials. Government is "they," and "they" have traditionally treated the peasant as someone to exploit. And so the peasant reacts with suspicion, hostility, and hidden anger. He has little identification with government, schools, or the other controls that come from the city, which he suspects are trying to destroy his traditional and accepted way of life.

In all countries undergoing change, the peasant has been considered as an enemy of the state if he is aggressive in defending his way of life, and as someone to guide like a child if he is submissive. In the Soviet Union from the early 1930's onward, the middle peasant was looked upon as an enemy of the state, or as one needing to be shorn of the little bit of security that he possessed in his land, in order that he might become the new worker in the agricultural factories. The medium-sized landholder, or kulak, was considered a potential counterrevolutionary, and in the 1930's hundreds of thousands of them were driven into slave labor camps so that they could not interfere with the urban drive for the collectivization of land. Only the poor, passive, resigned peasants and landless laborers were considered sufficiently friendly to the state to be trained to do its will. In China the small landowner also became the target of Communist enmity, a situation that only confirmed the peasants' centuries-old suspicion of the role of government.

The peasant in Europe and Asia has accepted the city for a long period of time, but he has looked upon it as having values contradictory to his own. His values are based upon the family, upon the possession of land, upon the traditional forms of his society, and upon his ability to provide his children and grandchildren with as much security and land as possible. He sees wealth as a by-product not of innovation but of luck and good fortune. However, a conspiracy of various outside forces has always appeared to him to prevent his obtaining even a modicum of security. The three wishes of the genie in fairy tales, who offers untold wealth to its possessor, reflect the dreams of the peasants, who generally believed that wealth acquired through hard work would always be taken away from them by outside forces and that only miracles and fate could improve their drab, humdrum lives.

Because the peasant felt that bad fortune was awaiting him from the outside, he was suspicious of those coming into his village either to sell or to buy. He never considered that centralized government was working in his best interests. For centuries, war and invading armies meant the destruction of his fields and the confiscation of his small surplus, if not the loss of one or more of his children. He bitterly envied those who received the good fortune that he desired, and often he looked upon them as having stolen his good fortune away. From his point of view, there was only so much good fortune to be had; and if others got it first, little would be left for him. Wealth, like land, was fixed; and if some had more than their share, others would get less. If, therefore, some peasant family became well-to-do, it meant that it had taken its wealth by doubtful means from the rest.

Thus, cooperation within and between villages became difficult, since each villager saw himself and his family as pitted against other families and even other villages. Each man was on his own, and his rise or fall depended upon no one but himself. He had to be self-sufficient and self-reliant; if he fell, only the members of his family could help him and if they were weak, then no one would give him a helping hand. If he became well-off, he knew that others would envy him and take everything from him if they were given the chance to do so. The well-off peasant, then, had to assure his protection and security through the extended family. It became important for him to form marriage alliances with other well-to-do families in order to protect the security of his person and his property.

The poor peasant could count only upon his small family for protection. Sons became extremely important to him for they represented his old-age security. Marriage meant children, who in turn meant insurance during sickness and the trials of old age. By marrying within the village, he was able to increase his ties with another family, yet retaining identification with his own. If he married outside the village, he acquired another family he could turn to in case of some calamity to his village.

Religion was more important to the peasant than to the gentry. The peasant considered that his good luck or fortune came from the myriad forces that surrounded every phase of his life, which he had to appeal to and placate. Religion inserted a note of certainty into a life that was fairly uncertain, with death, disease, famine, and devastation appearing often within a single generation. A peasant woman might give birth to ten or twelve children, but only one or two would survive to adulthood. Livestock continually died of hunger, and crops often failed.

The peasant's values were connected to his sons, his land, and his animals. He asked nothing more than that they multiply and that his sons and grandsons continue to live as he had. He wished to be nothing other than a peasant. If he lost his farm or did not inherit any land and had to seek work in the city, he dreamed of the day when he could return with money to buy land and be a peasant again.

This dream motivated a good many peasant sons who came by the tens of millions to the New World during the nineteenth century and the first part of the twentieth. And it was this dream that brought middle-aged European workers back to the villages to buy a small plot of land, a goat, or a cow. In western Norway, for example, it has long been the practice for landless peasants to work in coastal industry while paying for a plot of glaciated land, which, during their free weekends and evenings, they clear of its myriad boulders and gravel. When they retire from their work, they take up the role of small peasants. The possession of land has long made the peasant feel secure in a very insecure world; with it he could feel independent of the whims and desires of other men. Although few peasants have ever achieved this dream, still it has kept most of them content to till the land until the day they can no longer do so.

Where the Peasants Live

In the last third of the twentieth century, the peasant is still found in Central and South America; in eastern, central, and southern Europe; in the Middle East; in southern and eastern Asia; and in northern, western, and eastern Africa. The peasant does not raise food for a large market, but primarily for his family and himself. He uses no machines, but has only his own and his family's labor and perhaps one draft animal. In many parts of the world, the peasant owns no large draft animal but only small stock such as sheep, goats, and pigs. His way of life and his means of working have changed little over the centuries, even though he is surrounded today by the apparent results of the Industrial and Scientific Age (just as the peasants of China, India, and Egypt remained largely unaffected living on the peripheries of urban civilization). The peasant's goals, way of life, and thoughts are shaped much more by his early formative years than by anything that comes out of the universities, research laboratories, or business offices.

In eastern and southern Europe, the peasant lives in villages populated by individuals very much like himself. If the village is a large one, there are a few artisans, a number of landless laborers, a priest or two, a few shopkeepers, and one or two individuals who represent the government. The well-to-do peasant has a house with a living room, which may be open only for weddings, funerals, or other important occasions; a large kitchen, where the family generally does most of its entertaining and where some members of the family sleep; and three or four rooms that can be and often are used for the storage of grain, hay, or vegetables.

Magic and the Peasant

In the peasant world, magic is everywhere: witches abound; the Evil Eye can be found even in unsuspecting individuals; and men attempt to control others through wax images, pictures, clothes, and parts of their bodies (as Paleolithic men attempted to control the animals that they painted). In Africa, death for young men seldom happens normally but is often considered a result of magical manipulation by others. In southern and central Europe, one fears the Evil Eye and the potions and philters made by those who want to entrap the unsuspecting. There are no cause-and-effect relationships in nature; anything can happen, miracles as well as catastrophes, magical events as well as unforeseen ones. The peasant accepts on faith whatever occurs because nothing surprises him. He has lost whatever questioning or curiosity he had when he was small. In the peasant areas of Europe, the Devil still marks time; one goes to church as much to ward off the machinations and evil ways of the Devil as to insure one's soul after death. Outside of magic and religion, the peasant considers that there is little that men can do to fight their fate. One leaves to a tomorrow that will never come the problems that beset one today. The peasant's feelings of inferiority and his lack of confidence make him feel unable to solve his problems or change his life. He enjoys the material benefits of industrial civilization and sees no contradiction between his material aspirations and his social and mental resistance to change, but he also has no incentive to become a part of this civilization.

The Village Gentry

There is little difference in the villages between the way the gentry live and the way the peasants live. The former generally have larger families, and a good deal of their power comes from their family connections. In India, China, and Iran, gentry families are extensive and may include brothers and sisters and their children, as well as close cousins and grandparents. It is the gentry who possess whatever literacy exists in the village. Whatever is earned by any of the members of the family is used for the common good of the family: for dowries for the girls, for support of the family, or for higher education for those sons who have been selected to receive it. Although a gap in social status exists between the gentry and the peasants, both groups share similar thoughts about the world and together are outside of the boundaries of the intellectual stimuli that came from seventeenth century Italy and eighteenth century England. The village gentry are often as unable to change as are the village poor.

Summary

The peasant and the gentry in the Middle East and in southern and eastern Europe take pleasure from their masochistic asceticism, in which they grumble about their plight and boast of their sufferings; but they are unable to do anything to relieve themselves of these discomforts. They are similar to the Orthodox Jew in the ghettos of Eastern Europe in the nineteenth century who gloried in his neurotic self-hate; to the American Plains Indian who has lost all semblance of self-respect in his dependency upon government welfare; to the Negro in black ghettos who waits apathetically for something to be done for him by the outside world, which he is sure looks upon him with contempt; of the white in

Appalachia who does not know what initiative he could take to offset his lifelong poverty.

The peasant in the Middle East, Europe, India, Pakistan, Indonesia, or China represents the agriculturist of the Neolithic age who became subservient to the hierarchy of Primary civilization, who learned to live with his fate by cursing it, but who remained passively resigned and obedient toward those who put themselves above him in status and authority. He tends to be authoritarian in his loyalties and prefers to stay where he is because change is upsetting and because he is accustomed to a life that is easily predictable. He has been trained to lean upon authority rather than to depend upon himself, and he lacks both the confidence to visualize himself in another role and the optimism to believe that he could improve his lot even if he wanted to.

The traditional peasant is also found in all industrial countries among the unskilled and semiskilled workers, who have also been reared to live for the day and to depend upon others for their satisfactions. In most industrial countries, they tend to be passively resigned to their subservient social position; and they also lack confidence in their ability to manage their lives and are equally suspicious of those outside their group. Like the peasant, who is strongly affected by what his fellow villagers think of him, workers are more concerned with their reputations among their co-workers than among others outside their group. The peasant's regard for himself as a man and as a member of his rural group is as important to him as life itself. As long as this is left untouched, he can take a good deal of humiliation from the outside. Like the adolescent peasant who may become a brigand, the young among the industrial workers may also rebel or attempt to find shortcuts to higher status through delinquency or even criminality.

As long as the village keeps its social system intact, the peasant will adjust himself to his trials and tribulations and will receive his satisfaction in complaining bitterly about his lot in a milieu he cannot change unless he adapts himself to a new culture. And this no peasant can initiate by himself. The new culture of industrialization and scientific agriculture requires an entirely new setting for its missionary activities; it demands formal schools, agents, government pressures, and informal acceptance of the new age among the elite of the villages. The two most important ingredients for the acceptance and self-perpetuation of the new civilization are man's optimistic belief in his ability to change the world and sufficient confidence that he can do it if he wants to.

The peasant is thus limited by his lack of knowledge of what he can do with his land, his family, and himself. He lacks the confidence to venture into an unknown world seeking answers to the problems that trouble him. He can operate with some confidence in the traditional work that he knows best, just as the small businessman does in the world of larger and more administratively complex corporations and governments. Neither one can venture very far afield from his traditional ways of doing things, although the small businessman will accept change somewhat more readily than the peasant. Perhaps in Tertiary civilization, which will come into existence by the end of the twentieth century, men may have acquired enough self-confidence through formal education to feel capable of meeting and solving most of the problems that affect them.

The peasant is thus a man of Primary civilization, although there remains a good deal of the peasant in most workers, most businessmen, and even most teachers and professionals. Like the lungfish who were not quite fish or amphibians, most of us are still products of two contradictory civilizations. Few of us are yet completely members of the new Scientific Age; even the great entrepreneurs of the eighteenth, nineteenth, and twentieth centuries were men who were quite conventional in their thought and felt more at home in Primary civilization than they would have in the scientific one of today.

The peasant in Primary civilization could easily have felt at home within Neolithic culture; similarly, most of the world's population today still feels somewhat uncomfortable in the evolving civilization wrought by the Industrial and Scientific Age. Most people would prefer to combine the mental comfort of the traditional way of doing things with the advantages to be obtained from the technological innovations of contemporary industry. The two are still evolving at different rates.

Selected Bibliography

Arensberg, C. M., *The Irish Countryman* (Gloucester, Mass., Peter Smith Publisher, 1959).

Coon, Carleton S., *Caravan: The Story of the Middle East* (New York, Holt, Rinehart and Winston, 1961).

Foster, George M., *Traditional Cultures and the Impact of Technological Change* (New York, Harper & Row, 1962).

Hagen, Everett E., *On the Theory of Social Change* (Homewood, Ill., Dorsey, 1962).

Halpern, J. M., *A Serbian Village* (New York, Columbia University Press, 1959).

Halpern, Manfred, *The Politics of Social Change in the Middle East and North Africa* (Princeton, Princeton University Press, 1963).

Kroeber, A. L., and Kluckhohn, Clyde, *Culture: A Critical Review of Concepts and Definitions* (New York, Random House, Vintage Books, 1963).

Levi, Carlo, *Christ Stopped at Eboli* (New York, Farrar, Straus, 1947).

Lewis, Oscar, *Five Families: Mexican Case Studies in the Culture of Poverty* (New York, Basic Books, 1962).

Murphy, Gardner, *In the Minds of Men* (New York, Basic Books, 1953).

Redfield, Robert, *Peasant Society and Culture* (Chicago, University of Chicago Press, 1955).

Sinai, I. R., *The Challenge of Modernization* (London, Chatto & Windus, 1964).

Turney-High, H. H., *Chateau-Gerard: The Life and Times of a Walloon Village* (Columbia, University of South Carolina Press, 1953).

Wagley, Charles, *An Introduction to Brazil* (New York, Columbia University Press, 1963).

————, *Race and Class in Rural Brazil* (New York, Columbia University Press, 1963).

Wiser, William, and Wiser, Charlotte, *Behind Mud Walls, 1930–1960* (Berkeley, University of California Press, 1963).

Wylie, Laurence William, *Village in the Vaucluse* (Cambridge, Harvard University Press, 1957).

20

Africa:
A Continent in Transition

The continent of Africa has had a long association with the history of man, although much of it was unwritten (like that of man elsewhere) until recently. East Africa was the home of the early Australopithecines, including the tool-making Zinjanthropus (or *Australopithecus robustus*), the slightly more advanced *Homo habilis,* and other ancient hominoids. From millions of years ago to the present, Africa has continuously been the home of men, both hominoids and *Homo sapiens.* Although the origins of the Negro are somewhat uncertain, it is assumed by most scholars that his ancestral home was in West Africa.[1] We do not know what the genetic relationships are between the Negro and the Pygmy, or whether the two are physically related, although there does appear to be a common origin. Scholarly opinion believes that the Bushman and the Hottentot have a different classification than the Negro.

Asia influenced Africa in many ways. Although agriculture originated in southwestern Asia, it is possible that some form of garden horticulture may have developed independently (perhaps through diffused ideas) along the Niger River in western Sudan more than six thousand years ago, just as cotton may have been grown first in the Sudan before it was diffused to the Indus River valley.

East African cattle, for example, are chiefly of East Indian origin, and the complex of cattle raising as such evidently came with migrants from southwestern Asia to the Nile valley thousands of years ago. The diffusion of cattle to East Africa came with the Sudanic-speaking Negro tribes. Pottery making could have had an independent development in the Sudan, but evidence is strong that its probable point of origin was in Anatolia. Another example of southwestern Asian diffusion is iron making, which came to Negro Africa from Egypt and the Sudan in ancient historic times. It is of interest that East Africa seems to share a good many

[1] Negroids are ancient in southeastern Asia and in the string of islands from New Guinea to Fiji and the Philippines. What the connection is between the Negroids of Asia and those of Africa is not well understood at present.

of the ancient cultural characteristics of southwestern Asia, although time has given these patternings an African flavor.

It also appears quite likely that thousands of years ago East Africa and much of the Sahara Desert area were occupied by Bushman-like hunters. They were subsequently driven out of these areas by nomadic peoples (perhaps early cattle tribes) coming down from North Africa, who were of mixed Negroid-Caucasoid-Bushman background. A mixture of three peoples may well have occurred over a period of thousands of years. About one to two thousand years ago, West African Bantu-speaking Negroes may have pushed out of their forested homeland, moved eastward and southward, and mixed with the Negro populations already there, thus laying the basis for the Bantu-speaking populations who today occupy central Africa from the Congo to Kenya and southward to the Republic of South Africa. The remnants of the ancient Bushman stocks were perhaps pushed into the desert regions of southwestern Africa, where they remain to this day. The population of East Africa is thus more hybrid than that of West Africa, although the latter is also mixed to some degree.

Although little is known of the time sequence in which the Negro developed in West Africa, one can safely say that the Negro as a *Homo sapiens* is as old and as highly developed as the other races of man and that together all variants form only one species of man. Despite the population mixture of Negro East Africa with its Arab and Ethiopic influences, complex cultures, including large tribal towns and kingdoms, were chiefly found in West Africa. Both East and West Africa, however, have been influenced by cultural currents crossing the wide Sahara, in ancient prehistoric days as well as in historic times. After the seventh century of our era, Islam made its influence felt in the regions of Africa north of the tenth parallel. From the fourth century on, there were several Negro kingdoms, such as ancient Ghana and Mali in the northern part of West Africa. (Present-day Ghana is more than a thousand miles to the south; parts of today's Mali are contiguous to the ancient Mali kingdom.)

Africa south of the Sahara is not open to influences from the sea for the coastal regions are poorly indented and natural harbors are rare. Most ships need to anchor away from the shore and unload their cargo in small boats that can brave the surf and shallow coastal waters. The new harbors of West Africa tend to be artificial ones. A narrow coastal plain exists along the East and the West, with the ground a few miles behind rising abruptly to high plateaus. Only after one has reached higher ground are the rivers navigable for short distances; rapids on their lower reaches make them virtually impassable for boats from the sea. As a result, the vast interior of Africa in the past has been almost inaccessible from the outside. To the north another sea, composed of sand, isolates Negro Africa from Berber and Arab North Africa.

Yet, despite these geographic barriers, people moved southward and northward across the Sahara in prehistoric times. From the fourth century on, countless caravans traveled southward to the historic Negro urban centers. Among the trading termini for caravans after the twelfth century was the town of Timbuktu. Sailors from Malaya, Iran, Iraq, India, Saudi Arabia, and Yemen must have traded with the coastal regions of East Africa for thousands of years. Christianity and Judaism came early to present-day Ethiopia from Egypt and southern Arabia. Arab influences left their mark on small urban centers along the southern coast of East Africa, some of them going back to the seventh and eighth centuries of our era. An ancient, ruined stone settlement, Zimbabwe, in Rhodesia, was a gold-mining center that carried on most of its trade with Persia and India. Its ruins have been dated to the seventh century and show strong Arab, Cushitic, Ethiopic, and Indian influences. Malayans from the area southeast of India settled in Madagascar (then almost empty) during the first centuries of the Christian era; Arabs brought Negro slaves to the northern part of that island after the eleventh century.

Moslem invaders from Morocco destroyed the Ghana kingdom at the end of the eleventh century (after that kingdom had been in existence for almost 800 years). The Moslem Mali kingdom reached its peak during the fourteenth and fifteenth centuries; the Songhai Moslem kingdom, with Timbuktu as its capital, lasted through the fifteenth and sixteenth centuries. (Timbuktu had previously been in the possession of the Malis, who had conquered it. Invading Moroccans sacked it in the sixteenth century.) Bornu, a kingdom that stretched from Lake Chad to the Niger, lasted from the thirteenth to the nineteenth centuries. After 1800 another Negro Moslem warrior tribe from the north, the Fulani, settled in the north of present-day Nigeria and Cameroun.

The Sahara was thus no barrier to the invading Berbers, or to the slaving and trading Arab caravans, which linked the Negro areas of West Africa with the Mediterranean regions to the north. In East Africa intensive trading for raw materials and slaves was carried on along the coast by Phoenicians, Arabs, Persians, Indians, and Malayans from prehistoric times onward. Although the main interior was fairly unknown to outsiders, it appeared to be well traversed by conquering Bantu-speaking agriculturists, moving eastward from the seventh century on, and by Sudanese-speaking cattle tribes, moving southward from the Sudan after the tenth century.

The Europeans Come to Africa

The Portuguese were the first Europeans to see both the west and the east coasts of Africa. In the fifteenth century, they explored the coastal regions and established trading posts on both coasts. In the beginning,

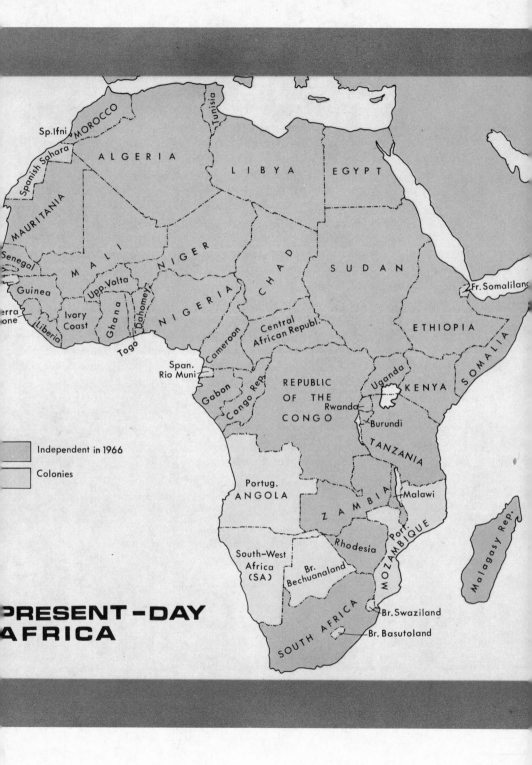

Sp. Ifni
MOROCCO
Tunisia
Spanish Sahara
ALGERIA
LIBYA
EGYPT
MAURITANIA
Senegal
M A L I
NIGER
CHAD
S U D A N
Fr. Somaliland
Guinea
Upp. Volta
NIGERIA
erra
one
Liberia
Ivory
Coast
Ghana
Dahomey
Togo
Cameroon
Central
African Republ.
ETHIOPIA
SOMALIA
Span.
Rio Muni
Gabon
Congo Rep.
REPUBLIC
OF THE
CONGO
Uganda
KENYA
Rwanda
Burundi
TANZANIA
Portug.
ANGOLA
Z A M B I A
Malawi
Port.
MOZAMBIQUE
Rhodesia
South-West
Africa
(SA)
Br.
Bechuanaland
Malagasy Rep.

Independent in 1966
Colonies

PRESENT-DAY
AFRICA

SOUTH AFRICA
Br. Swaziland
Br. Basutoland

the Portuguese seemed to be more interested in trade with India; Africa was considered primarily as a way station. The Spanish, Dutch, and British soon followed the Portuguese. Africa was initially important to them only as a source of not very plentiful raw materials. It became more important, however, in the seventeenth century, when the expanding plantation system in the New World made profitable the provision of African slave labor for its fields. During the seventeenth and eighteenth centuries, various European trading nations (including Denmark) established small forts along both the west and the east coasts of Africa, although the forbidding interior kept them out of inland areas until the end of the nineteenth century. These forts were established through the cooperation of the more powerful chiefs of the coastal tribes, who acted as procurers of slaves in this profitable trade.

Slavery

In the past, slavery had been as accepted an institution in Africa as it had been in the Mediterranean world. Christianity in its early centuries of power had gradually eradicated the heritage of slavery that had existed throughout most of the European continent. (In the Moslem world, slavery continued in, for example, Saudi Arabia even past the middle of the twentieth century.)

In Africa, slavery became very profitable for the more powerful Negro tribes and kingdoms; men, women, and children from enemy villages were captured and sold to the European traders at their coastal forts for trinkets, guns, powder, textiles, and implements. From the seventeenth to the nineteenth century, millions of Africans were torn from their homes by enemy raiding parties. Those brought to the west coast were sent to the New World on slave ships, which could make only two or three voyages before they were destroyed because of the odor created by packing slaves almost like sardines into poorly constructed ships that were intended to make a large profit even after only one voyage. More than half the slaves died before they reached their destinations in the Americas. Along the east coast through the middle of the nineteenth century from their home ports of Mombassa and Zanzibar, Arab slavers ranged hundreds of miles inland as far as the lake regions of Uganda and Tanganyika to purchase slaves for Saudi Arabia, Yemen, and Iraq.

Africa Before European Colonization

Until 1875, almost all of Negro Africa was politically self-governing; thousands of tribes and dozens of small kingdoms ruled their villages with traditional codes of law and inherited councils of elders. Paramount chiefs and petty kings enjoyed high status, but even they could not operate by whim. Their actions had to follow traditional precedents and tribal customs.

Though no European masters ruled the occupants of the vast area south of the Sahara to the Transvaal of the Boers, the life of the average African was by no means idyllic. Hunger and disease were rampant, and witchcraft and danger at the hand of enemies lurked everywhere. Only those who could run with the pack could escape being the pursued. In the east of Africa, there were sharp conflicts between the descendants of the Sudanic warrior-cattle castes and the agricultural Bantus in the settled peasant villages; the former looked with contempt upon those they ruled, who tilled the soil (as the ancient Hebrew sheepherders treated with disdain the Canaanite agriculturists whom they had conquered).[2]

Everywhere in Africa south of the Sahara, there were laws, traditions, tribal courts, definite religious beliefs, polygamy, communal land ownership, respect for the elders (who would soon become venerated ancestral spirits), and belief in the efficacy of magic. Traditions were oral; the only area with written traditions was the isolated Christian Coptic but Hamito-Semitic-speaking region of Ethiopia. Social position tended to be inherited, with castes of both aristocrats and royal families; and there was little interest in anyone outside one's immediate village, although tribal links when confronted by enemy groups were strong and enduring.

The Afro-Americans and Anglo-Africans

In the early part of the nineteenth century, colonies of ex-slaves from the United States, England, and the West Indies were resettled along the west coast of Africa by various Protestant missionary societies (with the blessings of their home governments). The new colonists brought with them the American and English attitudes with which they had been reared, and their behavior toward the Africans both of the coast and the interior was roughly similar to that of the white Europeans. The Afro-Americans in Liberia and the Afro-Anglicans from England and the West Indies in Sierra Leone soon became the ruling elites in their areas of settlement. Both groups stressed middle-class standards, literacy, and education for their children. They welcomed missionary activities among neighboring pagan tribes as a means of making them more like themselves. Although these ex-slaves had been returned to West Africa to regain their ancestral identity, their identification in fact was with the Western variant of Primary civilization, to which most of them had be-

---

2 In Rwanda in 1963 the peasants overthrew the cattle-raising aristocracy and drove tens of thousands of them into neighboring Burundi.

come acculturated as a result of two hundred years of living away from Africa.

Until 1875 European settlements were entirely along the immediate coasts of West and East Africa. Most of these settlements were trading posts and military forts, and missionary activities were restricted almost entirely to the coastal tribes. Only the Arabs from the east coast traveled into the interior of the continent. They carried with them a coastal Bantu language, Swahili, which they had long used in their slave trading and which subsequently became a *lingua franca* in East Africa.

The descendants of the Dutch and French farmers, who had settled along the Cape of Good Hope in the early part of the seventeenth century, moved northward during the first half of the nineteenth century toward the relatively uninhabited territory of the later Orange Free State and Transvaal. They wished to escape British rule and the British banning of slavery. With their rifles, Bibles, and slaves, the Boers made their long trek, like a Chosen People directed by the hand of God to a new Promised Land. The creation of the Orange Free State and the Transvaal brought them into prolonged conflict with the Bantu-speaking Zulu and Basuto tribes.

In 1830 France moved into North Africa and began a series of conquests of the various principalities of Berbers and Arabs, which she united into a colony called Algeria. Until the 1870's the interests of France, like those of Great Britain and Germany, were in Europe rather than Africa. Until 1865 she even had a strong interest in Mexico and, with the support of her soldiers, placed a Hapsburg archduke temporarily on the throne of that country. With the end of slavery in Europe in the first half of the nineteenth century, few European powers saw any advantage in taking over territory in the vast, unexplored continent of Africa.

The European Scramble for Africa

The scramble for territory in Africa began after 1871, when explorations of the interior by Livingstone, an English missionary, and other explorers such as Stanley, Speke, and Baker had indicated the vast extent of the interior and the ease with which one could enter the territory of the various tribes living there. Germany had initially encouraged France to turn her attentions to Africa so that France would feel compensated for her loss of Alsace-Lorraine to Prussia in 1871. The rapid industrialization of Europe after 1870 had revived the mercantilist idea that a nation would become wealthy if she possessed colonies that could purchase her manufactured goods. King Leopold of Belgium had been the first to carve a private domain out of the Congo basin, and his territory was recognized by the other European powers in 1885. The exploitation and inhuman cruelty toward the Africans by the private company that had been set up by Leopold led to the annulment of its charter by the Belgian Parliament in 1908; the territory was then made into a paternalistic colony of Belgium. After 1880 France took the territory to the north of the Congo and moved quickly into the land gaps left by Portugal, Spain, and England.

Between 1885 and 1890 unoccupied Africa was rapidly parceled out among Britain, France, Germany, Portugal, Italy, and Belgium. British trading companies began the exploration of Nigeria in the 1890's, and in 1900 the British Government took over that vast territory as a colony. The Ivory and Gold Coasts were quickly taken over by the French and British. The Portuguese pushed into the interior from their coastal positions in Angola and Mozambique, and their new possessions were also legitimized by the other European powers. Explorations of the sources of the Nile by Lord Lugard of Great Britain in the 1890's resulted in the territories of the kingdom of Baganda and its vassal satellites being taken over as a protectorate in 1902 under the administrative name of Uganda. The colony of Kenya was a by-product of British attempts to link Uganda to the coast by railway. Between 1885 and 1900 Germany took over Tanganyika and Southwest Africa along with small beachheads in West Africa such as Togo and the Cameroons, which had been overlooked by the French and British in their scramble for territory. As a result of Germany's defeat in 1918, Tanganyika was put under a League of Nations mandate, although for administrative purposes the colony was actually divided between Great Britain and Belgium. The Togo and the Cameroons were shared by France and Great Britain, although the territory remained technically under the control of the League of Nations; and Southwest Africa was placed under British trusteeship. Italy acquired the territories of Eritrea and Somaliland in the 1890's and gave them up in 1945. In 1935 Italy conquered Ethiopia, which she held until 1941, when her troops there were defeated by British forces.

The New European Influences Upon Africa

All these artificially constructed colonies, whose borders followed no tribal, linguistic, or even geographic rhyme or reason, helped in creating local nationalisms whose identifications were with the territories and the administrative cultures set up by the Europeans. Since there were not enough Europeans to govern every village, the African was permitted to govern himself within the limits set by the occupying powers. Chiefs and kings could govern as they always had, although they were subject as vassals to the laws and orders of the colonial administrators. Native administrators were used to recruit labor for the mines, the plantations, and the cities. They were the tax collectors, the policemen, and the employment agents for the controlling authorities; and it was their responsibility to see that no harm came to the missionaries or the Europeans who settled in their midst. They were requested to treat them as if they were the unofficial representatives of the colonial authorities.

Colonization with its differences between rulers and ruled in ways of life and technical knowledge developed marked caste lines between the Negroes and the Europeans. The vast majority of Africans were still living in the post-Neolithic period when European colonization began.[3] Many towns had been founded hundreds of years before the nineteenth century, but most of them were trading and agricultural villages rather than administrative and temple towns and functioned similarly to the villages that had existed in the Primary civilization of the Ancient World. The Europeans in Africa, whether they were Roman Catholic or Protestant missionaries, traders, businessmen, planters, or administrators, were self-consciously aware of the differences in technical knowledge that existed between themselves and the Africans. They consequently considered themselves primarily as teachers. Although the African had been self-governing for millennia, the European equated the African with a child who must be guided, nurtured, and led by hand. The African was viewed as a backward and primitive human specimen, not quite as biologically advanced as the European but with the potentiality of eventually becoming like him. Every semiliterate European, who owed his social position in Africa to the fact that his country had carved out large portions of that continent in its frantic race with other European countries to see who could acquire the most land, believed that it was his mission to teach Africans to become counterparts of the Europeans. This ethnocentrism, which went with the mission schools and government administration, was accepted even by the Africans, who saw themselves as apt pupils eventually becoming like their teachers.

The African Before European Colonization

It is difficult to characterize the ways of life of the Africans before 1875. African societies ran the gamut from the small hunting bands of the Bushmen in Southwest Africa with their few dozen people to organized kingdoms like the Buganda in Uganda and the Ashanti in Ghana with their millions. Most African tribes consisted of a hundred thousand or more members, although a dozen or so were in the million category. The tribe considered itself descended from a definite ancestor; it included villages

[3] Despite the use of iron among most Africans at this time, African culture in general came closer to the pre-Bronze Age villages of Mesopotamia than to the Iron Age villages of Eurasia.

and subtribes, each subdivided into clans, and was headed by a paramount chief. The chief had a series of village chiefs under him who owed him loyalty. If the tribe had become part of a kingdom, the paramount chief owed his allegiance to the king. In most parts of Africa, both kings and chiefs inherited their positions. Each village that had a chief also had a council of elders. The paramount chiefs and the kings also had councils to advise them—as well as queen mothers, sisters, and other relatives who were empowered by tradition to give their advice. Chiefs and kings were judges in addition to rulers, and appeals could be made from the lower village court, composed of neighbors, all the way to the judgments of the courts of the paramount chiefs or kings.

Although the Bushmen, the Pygmies, and a few of the Negro tribes lived by hunting and gathering seeds and roots, the vast majority of the West Africans were self-sufficient peasants who owned some domesticated animals. Separate cattle or agricultural tribes lived in the eastern and southern parts of the continent.

African agricultural crops were of the grain and root types, the grains growing in the grasslands and cleared forest areas, and the roots being indigenous to the tropical rain forests (though most of the African agriculturists south of the Sahara gradually began to grow both). The tools used in cultivation were the digging stick and the hoe. Many of the villages carried on the "slash and burn" technique of cultivation, moving when the soil in one area became exhausted to a new area where the vegetation could be cut and burned. Land was permitted to lie fallow to restore fertility, since the use of fertilizers was unknown; and some crop rotation was practiced. In the cultural area of East Africa, cattle herding was extremely important; and among the cattle tribes cattle represented both individual and family wealth. Milking was known in East Africa, but cattle were rarely slaughtered for food. Among the Masai of Tanganyika cattle were bled as well as milked, and the blood was drunk by the owner and his kin. Cattle were used as a form of currency for marriage; and the bride price, which was not a form of purchase but merely the means whereby the bridegroom compensated the bride's family for losing a valuable worker and bearer of children, was usually in cows. Because of the tsetse fly, cattle raising is today restricted to a few areas in East and South Africa; but before 1870 the range was much wider. Sheep and goats were used by most tribesmen in Africa.

Most of the Negro tribes in both East and West, though not the Pygmies or Bushmen, were acquainted with iron making, which evidently spread from Egypt before the Christian era. Relatively few Africans used copper or its alloys, brass and bronze. These metals were evidently introduced into West Africa by the North African Moslems after the eighth century. By the fifteenth century, western Nigeria was producing a high quality brasswork. Wood and ivory carving were known in West Africa, where the working of both became a complex art. After the fifteenth century in the western Sudan, guilds of artisans began to develop when cultural influences from the Moslem and Mediterranean north were brought in with the desert caravans. Although the craftsmanship was indigenous, the areas affected by the termini of the caravan routes at the large trading centers in West Africa contained the largest number of artisans and the most complex art forms. During this period, however, most Africans were too close to the subsistence level for many artisans to be employed full-time in the market towns. The native crafts had to await development until the arrival of colonization and the growth of urban locations as commercial and administrative centers.

The Educational Heritage

African children in the past had been reared and taught in an informal family surrounding; formal schools as such were found only in the northern areas, which had been influenced by Islam after the eighth century, and in the Roman Catholic and Protestant missions, which were established after the middle of the nineteenth century. In the French colonies secularization of schools began during the early part of the twentieth century; the British followed with the development of government schools for training clerical and technical help. In the Moslem areas of Africa the schools were established to teach religious precepts. In the Christian areas the missionaries taught the cultures of Western Europe and the United States as much as they did Christianity.

The Christian schools were originally intended to train future African ministers; the government schools were to educate clerical assistants to help in the administration of government. No African colony had universal free elementary education. The schools were mainly intended to train elites. They were attended by the sons of chiefs, village elders, traders, and artisans (in that order) whose parents saw education as a means of benefiting from the obviously superior technology of the Europeans. Within a matter of a few decades, however, elementary and secondary education, whether in the mission or in the government schools, became a highly desirable attainment for the sons of clerks, artisans, peasants, and even laborers. Education became the magic that enabled one to have as high a standard of living as the European, as well as to enjoy superior social status.

The Rise of African Nationalism

Today's African nationalism was born in the schools established by the Europeans. It was nurtured there and received its final approval from the teachers, who taught the African to think as a European but to retain his awareness that the Europeans would never permit him to actually become one of them. The African wanted the superior status of the European, and although he was educated to become as much like the European as possible, he also learned that he would never be granted the same status. He would always be the African, someone to be tutored but never someone to be allowed to teach.

The African knew that the European looked upon him as a "boy" with all the connotations of immaturity that this term implied, but he still preferred to compete with the European for status in the prestigious fields of education and technology than to try to escape the humiliation of being African by withdrawing to his tribe. In British schools the African student learned to see the world through British eyes; to play cricket, tennis, and soccer; to have afternoon tea; and to develop interests in those intellectual subjects that were approved by the missionaries and the administrators. In French schools, with their policy of assimilating the African to French culture, he tried to feel French and even wrote on examination sheets about "our ancestors, the Gauls." In Portuguese elementary and secondary schools, the few Africans who were able to gain admission were taught that they were Portuguese rather than African and that the attainment of Portuguese culture and citizenship should be their life goals. In the former Belgian Congo, African children were educated to become clerks, tradesmen, mechanics, locomotive drivers, and factory workers, but not to become professionals, government administrators, managers, or scientists. Despite all this the Africans who sent their children to mission and government elementary and trade schools hoped that even an elementary instruction in French would help them later to make their way in the world of the European.

Within fifty years after Africa was divided by the Europeans, the urbanized Africans, who had become aware of the importance of education in the European technological world, had become insistent that their children learn from the Europeans. For the urban African who was trying to find an identity for himself, education offered his children a chance to forget the humiliation of being under European control through identification with their rulers. Education opened the pathway to an urban world of apartment houses, automobiles, electricity, and all the other appurtenances of a European middle-class standard of living.

In the schools the curricula were patterned after those in Europe and had little pertinence to African conditions. Literacy was not viewed as a means to knowledge that could be of practical benefit to the Africans, but as an attainable symbol of the white man's status.

The educational revolution in Africa has been a fairly recent one. Schools, whether under the Christian missions or the government, have been open only during the past sixty years. The first generation of secondary school graduates to attend European and American universities were educated only after World War I; most of them began their higher studies in the late 1920's or early 1930's. In the main, the elder nationalist leaders of present-day Africa were part of the first generation to receive their educations abroad. These include men such as Azikiwe of Nigeria, Nkrumah of Ghana, and Kenyatta of Kenya, all of whom received their university educations in the 1930's.

Not until after World War II were institutions of higher learning established in Negro Africa. The first university was Makerere in Uganda, established in 1946. This was followed by the opening of one in Ghana and another in Nigeria in 1948. The French opened their first institution of higher learning in Africa at Dakar in the Senegal in 1950. By the middle 1960's, Nigeria had nine institutions of higher learning and planned to open more. Ghana had three schools of university status, and other new nations of Africa were planning new colleges of their own.

As an example of the changes that have taken place in Africa during the past few years, we can take Nigeria, a nation of between 40 and 55 million inhabitants. (Despite a census taken in 1963, no one really knows how many people live in Nigeria.) In 1950 almost 90 percent of the Nigerian population was illiterate. In 1965 attendance at elementary schools was expected to be almost universal in southern Nigeria. No country spent as much of its tax budget on education (43 percent) during the initial years of independence after 1960 as Nigeria, but the country was producing too many lawyers for its needs and not enough physicians and scientific professionals. (This was because British administrators, who were generally trained in the law, served as models for the Nigerians.) By 1964 over a third of a million Nigerians left schools each year, hoping that the government would provide good jobs for them. Thousands of Nigerians were supported by parents and relatives as they went through the higher schools, in the expectation that their education would bring financial returns to the families. In the first development plan, which extends from 1962 to 1968, some 10 percent of the estimated expenditures are being devoted to education—or the equivalent of some $200,000,000. Of this, over $15,000,000 have been allotted for university scholarships alone.

As pupils from the villages attended secondary and higher schools, their desire to return to their places of birth receded. As is true elsewhere, few employment openings, except in teaching and government administration, existed in towns of less than 10,000 for those with university education. In Nigeria, Ghana, Kenya, and Uganda, for example, employment possibilities are best in the large government and commerical centers. When the expenditures for education increase, as they will, urban populations will undoubtedly expand as rapidly as they have in other parts of the world.

The Growth of the City

Trading towns existed for hundreds of years in West Africa, although few of them could have been termed cities even in the early classical or Medieval European sense.[4] Their past populations have been estimated from about 12,000 to 50,000. They were larger than the tribal villages and provided a more extensive area within which small traders could display their wares; their architecture, however, was similar to the thatched-roofed mud or clay-daubed housing of the villages. The sanitary facilities in these trading towns were no different from those of the villages, and their administrative political organization was in fact only a trifle more complex and similar in form to that of the small village.

The export of raw materials and the import of European manufactured goods and the concomitant administrative and transportation functions led to a rapid increase in the growth of commercial centers along the coast during the first half of the twentieth century. The construction of railroads from the coast to the interior meant that roundhouses and shops for the maintenance of locomotives and rolling stock had to be erected at the termini. Both the British and the French at great expense crisscrossed their colonies with railroads (although the goods and passengers carried annually would not return the initial costs of construction for decades to come). Electric plants, telephone and communication equipment, street paving in the commercial and administrative areas, local public transportation, commercial and governmental buildings, schools, stores, hotels, and movie theaters turned the coastal forts and trading posts into bustling cities, which doubled, tripled, and even quadrupled in population each decade. After 1920 hundreds of thousands of young Africans voluntarily left their villages for the cities to earn money for taxes, for bride prices for themselves or other relatives, or for purchasing commercial goods, the proliferation of which had increased enormously as the direct result of the twentieth century consumer revolution in both Western Europe and the United States. The old African cities of Kumasi in Ghana, Kano in Nigeria, and Segou in Mali continued to increase their populations; and a whole series of new cities arose elsewhere as administrative, commercial, and industrial centers. The old African towns were often left relatively undisturbed as European commercial and administrative districts were built adjacent to them. The architecture in the new cities changed somewhat; the more prosperous African middle classes and the rising groups of artisans and skilled workers adapted European and African housing details to allow for the hot

[4] No West African town had the level of technology, architecture, or learning that existed in the Medieval European or Asian trading towns.

African climate but at the same time to retain the conveniences of modern European living.

The town of Lunsar in Sierra Leone had a population of less than thirty persons in 1929; by 1963, it had more than 25,000. The district capital of Enegu in eastern Nigeria was only established in 1909, but by 1963 it had more than 85,000 people. Accra in Ghana had a little over 17,000 inhabitants in 1901; in 1960 its population had grown to almost 400,000. Dakar in Senegal grew from less than 30,000 in 1930 to more than 235,000 in 1960. In Nigeria, Ibadan had become the largest Negro city in Africa with a population of over 800,000 in 1963. Lagos had grown to 675,000, while two other Nigerian cities had more than 150,000 inhabitants each. Nairobi, the capital of Kenya, was founded as an administrative center a little over fifty years ago; by the time independence came to Kenya in 1963, it had more than 200,000 citizens. Leopoldville, the capital of the Republic of Congo, had more than 450,000 Africans; and Brazzaville, the capital of the Congo Republic across the Congo River, contained 100,000 Africans within its city limits. Douala in Cameroun had more than 125,000 people, as did Conakry in Guinea. As the new nations entered the last third of the twentieth century, the cities in Africa had begun to expand and proliferate.

The Rise of the Independence Movements

Nationalism in Africa is a post-World War I phenomenon, for the new nation-states of that continent are contained in the artificial borders of the former European colonies. As a result of over fifty years of European administration and education, however, the former narrow loyalty to the tribe and to the small kingdom has been replaced by allegiance to the leaders of the new nation-states. These nation-states are a recent development arising from mass political parties and were organized by European- or American-educated Africans, who hoped thereby to supplant the European colonial administrators.

Nationalism in Africa has undergone three stages thus far. The first step took place after World War I, when the Pan-Africanism of West Indian and American Negroes, which had begun as a protest movement against white discrimination after 1900, gave a new identity to some African students then studying in American and English universities. The West Indian and American Negroes wanted more social justice, which would permit the Negroes to become part of the educated leadership without having to overcome the insuperable obstacles placed before them by white prejudices. The second step took place after World War I, when Pan-Africanism became part of the African scene and encouraged the demand for more self-government, rather than independence. The European teachers of the various secondary mission schools had indirectly encouraged a protest movement among their African pupils by stressing concepts of social justice as part of the European egalitarian tradition. Many of the missionaries were in competition with the European trader and settler, and their reactions to both were passed on to their pupils. It was no accident that the first protests of African egalitarian nationalism developed among the pupils of the mission schools in Nyasaland (now Malawi) after 1910, led by John Chilembwe, who had been educated in the United States, where he had been influenced by the Pan-African sentiments of W. E. B. Dubois. (Dr. Dubois, who died in Accra, Ghana, at the age of 95 in 1963, was a former professor of sociology at Atlanta University, who had organized the second Pan-African conference in London in 1912.) Dr. Hastings Banda, who was also educated at a mission school in Nyasaland, left home for Europe in 1915, the same year in which Chilembwe led an unsuccessful tribal revolt against British rule. Banda became a physician and practiced in London until his return to Nyasaland in the late 1950's when he resumed leadership of the local nationalist party.

During the 1920's, various "Back to Africa" movements among American and West Indian Negroes influenced African students studying outside Africa and made them conscious of their inability to become socially equal to Americans and Europeans, whose exclusiveness encouraged many of them to organize anti-colonial egalitarian-nationalist movements in their home territories.

During the 1930's the Communists saw African nationalism as a first stage in the road to an eventual Communist assumption of power in Africa. Many of the present-day egalitarian-nationalist leaders of Africa were given hope for an ultimate independence from European colonialism by the moral and material support they received from European Communists, Laborites, Social Democrats, Christian Socialists, and American and West Indian Negro egalitarian-nationalists. George Padmore, a West Indian who had been a Communist during the 1920's before he became disillusioned with Communism as it was practiced in the Soviet Union under Stalin, organized a West African Students' Union in the 1930's to struggle against European colonialism in Africa. As a result of his efforts, the Fifth Pan-African Congress held in London in 1945 was controlled by Africans for the first time since the initial organization of the Pan-African movement. (The previous Pan-African Congresses held in England and in New York had been run almost exclusively by West Indian and American Negroes.) Kwame Nkrumah, first President of Ghana, Jomo Kenyatta, first Prime Minister of Kenya, and various other West Africans, East Africans, and South Africans had been *rapporteurs* and delegates at the 1945 conference. Out of this Student Union developed the leadership for many of the later African nationalist parties.

The third stage in African nationalism took place when the ethno-centric nationalism born out of an alienated and snubbed tribalism merged with the egalitarian nationalism born out of international stu-dent experiences to develop an elite leadership. From these initiators came the single mass party (with the hero or messiah-leader) campaigning for independence. The mass party, which attempted to include all ele-ments of the region, was based upon European totalitarian organizing experiences. The African mass party differed from the Communists in that national independence rather than the class struggle was its chief goal. There is little doubt that Kwame Nkrumah of Ghana and Sekou Touré of Guinea, for example, learned much from the mass organization of the Communist party in the construction of their own totalitarian parties. Both men organized the national mass parties tightly around themselves and built a strong machine organization, which was loyal to them and which controlled various segments of the urban populations through planned national emotional appeals. Loyalty to the national and African cause was tied to personal loyalty to the leader. The differ-ence from Communism lay in the immediate goal. To Nkrumah, Touré, and Kenyatta, independence for all of Africa, moving toward an African socialist society rather than toward a universal Communist society, rep-resented the first goal to be achieved.

This Pan-Africanism, with its possible ultimate continent-wide al-legiance to a United States of Africa, which would lead eventually to a new African political organization, represents the still unfulfilled goal of African nationalism. So far, there has been an extremely loose federation of Ghana, Guinea, and Mali, and unfocused talk about an East African Federation, combining Kenya, Tanganyika, and Uganda with perhaps Rwandi and Burundi. But not all of the new states are willing to follow the African leadership of Ghana, Guinea, or Mali, which are small states when viewed beside the much larger Nigeria, Republic of Congo, or the former French colonies. These latter include the Congo Republic, Da-homey, Chad, the Ivory Coast, Gabon, Senegal, Niger, the Upper Volta, and the Mauritanian Republics and all of them now have a loose eco-nomic federation with France. Although these new nations have earned political independence, they are still economically dependent upon France for development funds and for access to the European Common Market for capital and markets. In many ways, the new French-speaking republics are more dependent economically upon France than the Eng-lish-speaking nations are upon Great Britain.

African nationalism is double-edged in its protest forms. It is a re-action against the Europeans for their refusal to accept the African elites as social and intellectual equals, but it is also an acculturated Western indictment against the Africans who are still part of a tribal past. The new nationalisms have been born out of past social humiliations at the hands of the British and the French administrators, as well as the Belgians and the Portuguese. These educated the elites of the new nationalisms in their values but refused to permit them to assimilate when it became clear that because of their education they had little in common with their illiterate tribal villagers. Perhaps if the elites had been given opportunities to become participants in the British or French communities, they might have accommodated themselves eventually to becoming Britons or Frenchmen. The various differences in European colonialist attitudes toward African assimilation made the nationalism of the former French colonies less anti-French than the anti-European reaction of the former British colonies, who feel compelled to prove themselves the equals of the English in everything they do.

The nationalism of Ghana, Guinea, Kenya, and Tanzania is also as much a reaction of the elites to the humiliations of their tribal past as a partial protest against the refusal of the European colonial upper classes to accept them as equals. The new African socialism is thus an attempt to bring the subcontinent south of the Sahara into the path of Secondary civilization without following too closely the models of the outside world. The new leaders feel compelled to create an original technical civilization during the next century without using the examples of the non-African superpowers. The new technical and scientific civilization, they are convinced, must be African in its emotional identity with the other Negro Africans, and indirectly with the snubbed Negroes in the New World. "Negritude" is the term used by the French-speaking Negroes of the West Indies and Africa to express their feelings of being psychologically outside the white community; that for better or for worse, the Negroes will rise or fall in future status as Negroes rather than as Nigerians, Ghanaians, or Kenyans. This sense of being compelled to seek understanding and a feeling of kinship with other Negroes because of their physical bond provides some of the motivating force toward Pan-Africanism among many of the university-educated Africans. Their sense of competition toward the European will undoubtedly increase during the next century as the gap between the developed European and American continents and the developing African countries becomes steadily wider, with the African leaders encountering more and more difficulties in bridging the gap.

The new elites are thus supersensitive and somewhat ashamed about their African past, but they are trying to make their peace with it. They feel the need to build up an African identity, although they would prefer that the past did not intrude so blatantly at the present time. Reporters have been expelled from West African countries for reporting that female circumcision was still practiced in the hinterlands. Well-meaning Englishmen with a peculiar sense of humor were expelled from Uganda for holding a party in which they satirized by song the end of the "white man's burden in Africa." Not only has the European become a scapegoat for all the frustrations involved in making the new nations economically as well as politically viable, but competing with him has made the African in power project his own inadequacies upon the European to the point where he feels convinced that the latter has little faith that the African will be able to overtake him. Because the new African elites have an overwhelming need to prove themselves and their peoples, one can expect a good deal of political instability in Africa during the next few decades.

The new African states will also feel the need to win the approval of Western Europe and the United States, even though they may at times flirt with the Communist powers. The United States must assume that Africans cannot take over Communist institutions without admitting to themselves the superiority of the outside world. The new governing elites can find themselves only by proving that they can create their own guidelines for the future. The European administrators, businessmen, and settlers were the symbols of the bourgeoisie; but now that most of them are gone, the African elites see no need to stir up a reaction on the part of the peasants and urban workers against themselves as representatives of the new middle class in power. The African is not competing against his own wealthy, who make him aware of his inadequacies and failures, but against the industrial nations, including the Soviet Union. It is quite possible, however, that the next generation of African university graduates may feel the need to prove themselves even better than the Europeans.

The Communists in the Soviet Union and in China are convinced that the African elites are creating an unlikely hybrid, bourgeois socialism, by emphasizing egalitarian nationalism rather than the total reorganization of African society on Communist lines. Both the Soviet Union and China, and their satellites, will certainly make efforts to influence the future elites of the various African nations, although it is questionable whether the African leadership will be willing to undergo the humiliation of guidance by non-Africans again. One can expect a good deal of experimentation with the term "African socialism" with emphases upon communal land ownership, government planning and capitalization, and crash programs to increase technical and higher education.

The Inner Conflicts

The one-party governments in several African nations have banned all overt political opposition, insisting that dissent belongs within the party so that it can be controlled rather than on the outside. However, a good deal of latent emotional opposition to the governments still exists, most of it undefined and uncoordinated. The underground opposition will continue to be a refuge for all those who find no gratification in being molded against their will. In Guinea the cultural differences between the more urbanized South and the more tribal North make the unity of the country more of a hope than an actuality at the present time. In Ghana a good deal of opposition exists among tribal chieftains from the North and among those removed from the governing elite. The Federation of Nigeria, with its 45 million[5] people and more than 300 tribes, is also split into two large divisions, North and South, with the latter divided again into East, Midwest, and West. The South is more literate and richer, but smaller in population than the North. The North is almost entirely Moslem; more than half of Nigeria is Moslem in religion, one-fifth is Protestant and Catholic; the rest follow African beliefs.

Northern Nigeria is closer to the Primary past than is the more enterprising South. The Emirs in the North ruled with an iron hand; and until Nigeria's independence, the courts dispensed only Islamic law. From the city of Kano in the North, special flights took Nigerian Moslems to Jiddah in Saudi Arabia for their holy pilgrimages to Mecca and Medina. The first Prime Minister of Nigeria, the late Alhaji Sir Abubakar Tafawa Bakewa, a son of a Hausa butcher, made the pilgrimage to Mecca, and was thus permitted to use the title Alhaji (or one who has taken the pilgrimage) before his name.

The previous government of Nigeria began as a federation of the Northern People's Congress party, which had more than half the seats in Parliament, of the Action Group of Western Nigeria, and of the National Council of Eastern Nigeria. (A new region called the Midwest was carved out of the West in 1963.) East and West Nigeria are again dominated by the Ibo and the Yoruba, the two leading tribes in those regions; the People's Congress party was influenced by the Moslem Emirs and the chiefs of the Fulani and the Hausa tribes. All four regions thus differ markedly between themselves in culture, outlook, and goals; and their present Federation, though fraught with weaknesses, is an amazing memorial to the British, who united these distinct and warring tribes in a matter of fifty years.

Nigeria still retains a tenuous identification with Britain and the West; and all four governing groups in the Federation's government are insistent that Nigeria, the largest nation in population in Africa, must play an independent role commensurate with her power in building a new African Bloc. Although the other African countries may talk of

[5] A good deal of doubt exists as to the accuracy of the November, 1963, census, which indicated a population of 55 million. Most experts seem to believe this figure is considerably exaggerated. In 1952 the British found 31 million living in present-day Nigeria. It is quite possible that the total population may be no more than 45 million. The census of 1963 was evidently exaggerated for political purposes.

"African socialism," Nigeria under military rule at the moment has no brand of socialism of her own but is concentrating upon increasing her national economy by a rate of at least 4 percent per year with whatever means are available. The Nigerian elites want to compete with the Europeans, and they feel confident that they can.

Kenya has her conflicts with the local Somalis, who insist upon their right to rejoin their brothers in neighboring Somali. The Congo is going through the growing pains of trying to make a nation-state of differing tribes and regions. Uganda has the problem of the Baganda, who make up one-fifth of the population, uniting a government with dissident tribes who form the remaining four-fifths.

The External Conflicts

The Brazzaville (or French) group of African nations has found little in common so far with the unstable federation of Ghana, Guinea, and Mali, with Nigeria, or with the other English-speaking states. Nigeria and the former Belgian Congo are more concerned with keeping Moslem North Africa and the Pan-Africanist Organization of African States at bay. In the Portuguese territories, where the goal has been assimilating the African "child" to the Portuguese family system, the opportunities for education are so meager compared to those of the former British and French colonies that only a few Africans have been able to identify themselves with the Portuguese ruling groups. As a result, the Portuguese territories are faced with external conflicts; and the other African nations view the Portuguese colonies as a continuous reminder of their past dominance by the European powers.

The Africans, Arabs, Asians, and Lebanese

Another conflict exists in East Africa between the Africans and the so-called Asians, or Pakistani and Hindus, who number some 300,000. Many of the Indians are descendants of the laborers imported into Africa by the British to build the railroad from the coastal port of Mombassa in Kenya to Lake Victoria on the eastern border of Uganda. Today the Indians are the chief storekeepers in the larger villages of East Africa, as the Lebanese and Syrians are in West Africa.

As the Africans compete for middle-class status, the Indians and the Lebanese will find it necessary to achieve even greater wealth and status than before in order not to be left behind. But the Indians and the Lebanese will continue to be outsiders, for they are excluded by race from the concepts of Pan-Africanism and African socialism. They will continuously remind the Africans of their lack of unification within Africa, and their existence as minority groups could easily lead to conflicts between themselves and the Africans. The conflicts between the whites in the Republic of South Africa and the African majority may also remain sharp for decades to come, as they will between the Republic and the other African nations. As long as any Africans are being humiliated by whites in Africa, the other African nations will forget their differences long enough to express an identification with them.

The Balance Sheet of Colonialism

The greatest defect of European colonialism was its social humiliation of the African elites whom it created and governed, but its existence was not all unadulterated evil. Without colonialism as a catalytic agent, sub-Saharan Africa would not be as close to entering Secondary civilization as it is today. The education of the African elites took place under colonialism, and even the values dealing with the importance and equality of Africans, which made possible the organization of political parties to strive for independence, came to them from the mission and government schools, which were built with the blessings of colonialism.

During the first half of the twentieth century, African mining and agricultural exports were not great enough to pay for the initial construction of railroads, harbors, roads, administrative centers, utilities, hospitals, and schools and for the continuing costs of maintaining them —plus the expenditures of the government. Sub-Saharan Africa as a peasant and tribal continent was far too poor to pay for its own development. Most of the capital, as well as the skills, had to be supplied by the colonial powers. Although huge profits did come to the commercial companies that invested in Africa, the profits were not taken from the poverty of Africa, but derived largely from the ideas of Secondary civilization which these companies brought with them.

If colonialism had never existed and if the Africans had continued to live in self-governing units, there would have been no cities, railroads, schools, industries, hydroelectric plants, and research bureaus in the Africa of today. One needs only to compare the Liberia and Ethiopia of 1950 with the progress of Ghana, Nigeria, or Uganda at that time under British rule.

There is, of course, colonialism and colonialism. West Africa was fortunate to have had wealthy Britain and France rather than poverty-stricken Portugal or Spain as colonial rulers. The latter are still too poor in skills and industries to pay for the social overhead that is necessary before a colony can be developed. Copper, iron, gold, and diamond mines require railroads, harbors, housing, and plants even before the sources of their wealth can be removed. Colonialism ceased to exist in the second half of the twentieth century because it became too expensive to retain as a national status symbol. Great Britain, for example, is today better off economically now that her empire is gone, because the expense involved in upholding law and order, administering government, paying for an armed force, creating better sanitation and public health, and opening schools, roads, and communication facilities amounted to far more than the British received in taxes from their colonies.

Underdeveloped colonies in today's world are not profitable, despite myths to the contrary. They require too great an initial investment if they are to be made profitable. Only the very wealthiest of nations can afford to be colonial powers. Colonies may make a nation feel that it has arrived on the international scene when it can see its far-flung possessions on the map, but no modern power owes its economic wealth to the possession of colonies. Portugal, despite its colonies in Africa, is still an underdeveloped country with an annual per capita income of $250—only a little above that of Ghana and less than twice that of Nigeria.

This is not to imply that individual companies or individuals did not find colonies profitable after their home governments invested enough money to make commercial investment profitable for them. But in general one can say that the overall social costs spent by the colonial powers in Africa were far greater than the taxes they received from the commercial houses, the settlers, or the Africans. Industrialization is expensive when it is first being introduced; and few industrial concerns are willing to make the initial investment in plants, managerial skills, and trained manpower unless large profits are sure and they are promised relief from taxes for a sufficient number of years to pay for their costs. Until the recent independence of the African nations, the colonial powers had to subsidize industrial and commercial investments with taxes from the citizenry of their homelands.

Great Britain introduced the planting of cocoa and coffee in both Ghana and Nigeria, which led to the development of a fairly well-to-do peasantry in both countries. Great Britain also introduced the cultivation of cotton in Uganda to the Baganda and their neighbors, and this commercial crop made peasants out of the agricultural tribesmen. On the other hand, Great Britain refused to permit the poverty-stricken Kikuyus of Kenya to grow coffee lest their poor-grade coffee trees spread blight to the nearby coffee plantations of the white settlers in the Kenya highlands. There was, then, both good and bad in the long-range administration of France and Great Britain in Africa; but in general one can say that their overall effect in giving new cultural incentives to the Africans was good.

It is possible to attack British colonialism on ethical grounds, especially in terms of what it did to humiliate Africans; but it would be difficult to criticize it on economic scores. Even in Kenya, the former presence of white settlers had much to do with encouraging the Africans to become acculturated to the technical civilization that the settlers brought. At the same time, educated Africans were able to appeal on ethical and moral grounds to educated British and French public opinion for social justice. They could not reach the educated in South Africa, Portugal, or even Belgium as readily. If the colonial powers of France and Great Britain had been as authoritarian and strongly opposed to dissent as some of the new African nations are, no political parties could have arisen to take over power from them.

The Economic Problems of Africa

The problems of the new nations of Africa are as much economic as political: more than 80 percent of the sub-Saharan populations still live in villages, tilling their land primitively on a subsistence level. Although horticulture has taken on a farming connotation among the cocoa and coffee growers of Africa's west coast and although the new nations are extending their efforts to increase the productivity of the soil, most African peasants till their lands roughly in the same way as their ancestors did hundreds of years ago. The plow has only recently been introduced; mechanized equipment is used mainly by the large commercial plantations growing specialized crops for the world market.

In most of Africa, cattle were raised for purposes of wealth and prestige rather than for food. The tsetse fly restricted their range to parts of East and South Africa. In West Africa, chickens, goats, and sheep were used for food; but most of them were scrub breeds, scrawny, sickly, and ill-fed. In Africa, good agricultural land is spottily located; two-fifths of the continent is desert, two-fifths is semiarid grassland, and only one-fifth is tropical or forested. Most of East Africa is dry grassland. On the west coast, rain forests cover a good part of the coastal regions; but their soil is leached and poor. In the northern parts of Ghana, Nigeria, Mali, the Upper Volta, and the Central African and Chad Republics, the rainfall is low and the soil has poor grass cover. In all the various French-speaking republics (an area two-thirds the size of the continental United States with a population a little over 25 million), there is a shortage of good land resources.

In soils, resources, and population, Negro Africa is relatively poor. Most of her population is illiterate, unskilled, and malnourished. It is only in the more fortunate areas of southern Nigeria, Ghana, and Uganda that the inhabitants have enough to eat. And, when compared with Europe or the United States, Africa is poor in both agricultural soils and natural resources. The continent needs far more technology than it has at present to compensate for its liabilities. As sanitation and infant care

are improved, the people of Africa will increase at rates that may mean a doubling of the population in about twenty-five years. This means that agricultural productivity must triple every twenty years to take care of the increase in population and at the same time satisfy the rising standards of consumption. In fact, to eradicate malnutrition and to end the shortages of proteins and carbohydrates, food production must increase at least 400 percent during the next twenty years. Countries such as Nigeria and Ghana are attempting to increase agricultural and industrial yields by at least 5 percent per year to take care of the increases in both population and the levels of living. At present, sub-Saharan Africa has a population of 200 million. This will easily be doubled by 1990 as more physicians, nurses, and public health workers are educated.

The Agricultural Problems

The wealth of West Africa has been due somewhat to the cocoa and coffee crops that were grown there for export. For example, the $700,000,-000 which Kwame Nkrumah spent in the seven years from 1957 to 1964 to build a new industrial welfare state came from the dollar earnings of Ghana's greatest export, cocoa, whose production represents slightly over one-third of the world's total. Cocoa trees are grown on 300,000 individual peasant farms of less than six acres each, whose owners learned from the British how to work for the world market. Altogether about one-fifth of the total population is dependent upon the growing of cocoa for its livelihood. More than twenty extension stations have been established in Ghana to grow superior cocoa seedlings for the farmers, and to improve methods of cultivation. The export tax on cocoa during the first seven years after independence in 1957 enabled the government to finance new electric plants (including the Volta Dam), housing, and its share of new industrial enterprises. The government of Ghana also established a Community Development Program to encourage greater agricultural productivity through cooperative farming.

Despite the relative wealth that Ghana has derived from selling cocoa on the world market, most of the Ghanaians still have a poor diet. The northern region, which contains one-third of the country's population, has widespread malnutrition because the soil is exhausted. A study made by the Harvard School of Public Health in 1959 pointed out that the average daily caloric intake "swung from a summer high of 1,600 calories to 1,100 in February. Among some large groups of people the range was even more dramatic, from 2,065 calories a day in summer to a winter low of 675. The recommended dietary allowance for the United States, as formulated by the National Research Council, is 2,600 calories." [6]

6 *The New York Times,* November 2, 1959.

The Ghanaian Government in 1962 signed a three-year contract with the United Nations Special Fund to direct a program that would triple the agricultural yield for the 2 million inhabitants of northern Ghana. As late as 1965, agricultural techniques were still primitive and modern tools were lacking. Advanced systems of cultivation were still years in the future. The most pressing problem facing the Community Development Program of Ghana was the lack of agricultural technicians in numbers sufficient to make a dent upon the mentality of the peasants, who still used the "slash and burn" technique of clearing the soil and then cultivated it with a primitive hoe. The program envisaged by the United Nations included plans for training a group of skilled Ghanaian agricultural professionals and technicians by 1966 to act as future Extension Agents and instructors of agricultural change. The Ghanaian Government had put aside a large part of its budget to spend on increasing educational opportunities in the north and in the south, hoping that the products of the new schools would become agents of change within the families and villages of both regions.

What has been said of Ghana holds equally true of all the other African nations, both east and west. Most areas have not grown enough food to feed their populations adequately on a balanced diet. Agricultural techniques everywhere have been poor and the soils exhausted. Almost no fertilizers have been used, and plows came into use only in the areas adjacent to former European settlements. To feed a population that is growing rapidly, Africa can no longer use her traditional, inefficient methods of farming. The 80 percent of the population still remaining on the land must be taught to grow enough food to feed the one-fifth of the continent living in the cities.

Resources

Africa is potentially rich in natural resources. Iron ore and bauxite are found in large quantities along the west coast; oil in quantity in Nigeria; manganese in Ghana; cobalt, uranium, and copper in the Republic of Congo (though little coal and few minerals have been uncovered thus far in East Africa). Because of her broken topography, Africa contains more than 40 percent of the world's potential hydroelectric power, which, as in the case of the Volta Dam in Ghana, can eventually be used for industrial purposes.

On the other hand, Africa is poor in managerial, professional, and scientific skills; and the number of students at technical and higher schools is still too few to carry on the industrialization that the continent must have to satisfy its immediate aspirations. Africa will make great technical strides during the next twenty-five to fifty years, but it will be a long time before she can take her place with the nations that have already entered Secondary civilization. Most of Africa's population is still in the beginning stages of Primary civilization. Although she exports large quantities of cocoa, palm oil, sisal, sesame seeds, and peanuts, most of her agricultural population is still engaged in subsistence farming. Her cities are still few and far between, and the spotty local industrialization does not even supply her elementary needs.

Problems in Africa

Independence came to Africa largely because the colonies were becoming too expensive for Britain, France, and Belgium to subsidize. Even including technical assistance, the amounts Great Britain and France today give to their former colonies do not equal the sums that were once required to maintain them. Africa must now supply her own economic needs, and although she has trained thousands of administrators and technicians to take the places of the Europeans who were displaced, her needs require that she train millions rather than thousands.

The African nations will remain underdeveloped for at least sixty years or more because their problems are greater than those of the industrialized nations of Western Europe or the United States. Africa is beginning her industrialization with a large population, at a time when many of her people are aware of the benefits to be derived from the new techniques. They are anxious to enjoy these benefits during their lifetimes rather than to receive vicarious satisfaction from hoping that their grandchildren will be better off than they.

With the exception of Nigeria, none of the new African states has a large enough population for a mass market. Transportation problems are immense. And because of the unusual handicaps of topography, rainfall, and poorly distributed resources, Africa needs even more technological innovators than the industrialized nations of Europe or the United States. She requires a good deal of help if she is to find compensation for her deficiencies in soil, resources, and markets. If she is to become an industrialized continent not in 1965 but in 2025 when the problems of a developing worldwide Technological and Scientific Age will be even more complex than they are today, then she needs continuing assistance. Proportionately, Africa will need even more technologists, managers, and scientists to become industrialized than Western Europe or the United States required in the nineteenth century.

With large populations still living culturally in previous epochs, the leaders of the new African nations face enormous problems in trying to catapult mostly illiterate populations into a scientific and technological civilization within the time period of a generation or so. Most of the leaders are strongly motivated to effect enormous changes in their countries within their lifetimes, and they hope to bring about their revolutions with as little opposition as possible. These leaders in a hurry have too little time to spend in erecting democratic foundations for their decision-making policies or to act as teachers for the rest of the population.

Kwame Nkrumah, the first President of Ghana, was the man in the greatest hurry. He had a compulsion to make Ghana a model for the rest of Africa. Since Nkrumah could not conceive of an Africa in which he did not play an important, if not a leading, part, he felt the need to be a continuous source for the new concepts of Pan-Africanism and its socialism. Unlike the other apostles of African socialism, who see its economic and political bases in the clan and the tribal village, Nkrumah saw socialism from angles somewhat similar to those of the European left-wing socialists and the Communists, that is, in industrializing and completely remaking the structure of the country so that it would be adaptable to the new scientific ages of the future. Nkrumah had little patience with any organization, any social system, or any age group that he, as the "Osagyefo" (Redeemer) of the nation, could not use to lead the people to new technical and social levels.[7] Opposition was crushed, a police state was put into being, and the Convention People's Party turned into a personal vehicle to carry out Nkrumah's plans for Ghana's future.

Sekou Touré of Guinea, who was educated by French trade unionists, anarcho-syndicalists, and Communists, is another of the new authoritarian leaders who are attempting to turn Africans into adherents of the new Scientific and Technological Age in as short a period of time as possible. Like Nkrumah and most of the leaders of the new Africa, Touré is more a part of Western culture than he is of the tribalism that he has been fighting in Guinea. In 1959 at the Royal Institute of International Affairs in London, he said: "Education brought us into contact with other cultures. A certain number of us adopted the civilization of other countries, and the result has been the cultural dichotomy of Africa. May I quote a personal example? I feel more at home in the company of French friends than of my older brother, who has never been to school. Colonization meant a chance of advancement for a small African elite, but at the cost of a deep gulf between us." [8]

Touré has been attempting to narrow this gulf by increasing the numbers of those who are being educated to become the new technical and scientific elites. To do this, he must destroy the power of the tribal chieftains in more than 4,000 villages of Guinea, supplanting them with his own political instrument, the *Parti Democratique de Guinée* (The

[7] Until he himself was overthrown by the military in early 1966.
[8] Quoted by Fritz Shatten, "Guinea's Sekou Touré," *The New Leader*, October 15, 1962, p. 12.

Democratic Party of Guinea), one of the best organized mass political parties in a continent of mass political parties, whose local leaders are loyal only to him. Besides the party units in the country, Sekou Touré controls the towns through a federation of trade unions holding Pan-African ambitions, the *Union Genéral des Travailleurs d'Afrique Noire* (The Workers' Union of Negro Africa). The young are organized by the League of Young Pioneers with himself as leader.

Like Nkrumah of Ghana, Touré is wedded to a Pan-African Union of Nations, which will solve its economic problems through a state-centralized socialism, similar in form to the socialism of Communism, though entirely different in content. None of the new nations of Africa can permit outsiders to dictate either their socialist ideologies or their plans of action in industrializing and educating large masses of their populations.

African Socialism

Although some of the new nations may appear to be moving closer on the ideological level to the various Communist powers, the combination of egalitarian nationalism with local authoritarian economic controls may make alliances between them quite unlikely. Touré, for example, has little desire to replace French controls with Russian or Chinese ones. And to the Africans, the Russians and the Chinese are only lesser varieties of Europeans.

The new African nations will take aid wherever they can, from whatever bloc is willing to offer it. They will turn to a centralized state socialism because most of the commercial houses, trading complexes, mining ventures, and even small industries in their countries are in the hands of Europeans or non-Africans. The Africans feel that they cannot compete with the Europeans, Asians, or Levantines on their terms and levels, for they do not have the confidence or the connections that the latter possess. They would prefer that the government with its capital be used to develop competitive enterprises in which the African elites would be trained to compete with confidence on their own terms and levels, that is, within an administrative or scholarly framework.

The west coast nations have large numbers of native women traders, some of whom have been able to become small wholesalers and retailers. Although many of them have become wealthy, few of them so far have been able to compete with the large establishments of the British and Levantine companies. In time, it is likely that new female industrialists and entrepreneurs could come from their ranks, if private enterprise is permitted to play a role in supplying the needs of the future. A mixed economy will perhaps arise in many of the new nations, but in others authoritarian economic controls or cooperative organizations may become the means whereby Africans will take over the supplying of their own needs from the hands of Europeans, Asians, and Levantines. The fact that the latter are non-Africans will make it easier to displace them with government or cooperative organizations. While Ghana and Guinea may be apostles of government control for both industry and trade, East Africa may well be the seat of the new cooperative, autonomous trade and industry associations.

Julius Nyerere of Tanzania conceived of African socialism as being based upon communal organizations, which implies that some form of cooperative farming and industrialization will be tried with the village as the base. Jomo Kenyatta of Kenya believed that government could participate by owning certain parts of industry or by creating the infrastructure that would guide the country into certain areas of development or simply by working out an economic plan within which any development can be fitted. Thus, in Kenya, the government would engage in producing power, providing education and health facilities, building roads, and establishing markets. Mining would be nationalized, and land would be cultivated on a cooperative basis, with government supplying the instruction, capital, and plans. East African socialism may change and become more like the West African varieties; but at the present time, as in India, "socialism" to the African elites has become a "beautiful word," and they would rather talk and plan for socialism than for political democracy. Only Nigeria is planning for a welfare state without too many socialist overtones.

The Future of Africa

In the meanwhile, the cities may continue as the areas where the future African civilization will be designed, argued over, and carried into action. The new classes will consist of the educated elites of government officials, managers, technicians, and supporting professionals. Changes will continue to be made as the elites envisage and develop their ideas of a continent competing with Europe in all phases of Secondary civilization.

Africa will incur a good deal of future cultural change as her peasants become transformed into halfhearted carriers of a new civilization, sometimes with their blessing but most often against their wishes. Education in the Technological and Scientific Age will become more important as the new nations devote more of their revenues to the task of creating wealth for their future. The outside observer will find it fascinating to watch the various forms that the new variants of African civilization will take, although there will be many growing pains, many blunders, and a good deal of cruelty and inefficiency as governments and single mass parties attempt to translate paper goals into living realities.

Whether Africa will be able to unite her large number of nations into viable regional federations will depend upon the Africans themselves; most of the new nations are too small and weak to be able to enter Secondary civilization by themselves. Some of them may combine into larger economic units that will be able to stay alive, and some may be taken over by more powerful neighbors. Perhaps the stronger ones, such as Nigeria, Ghana, Guinea, Kenya, and Uganda, may attract their poorer neighbors to join with them peacefully. It is difficult at this point, however, for anyone to visualize what forms the future Africa will take politically, socially, and economically.

Selected Bibliography

Baulin, Jacques, *The Arab Role in Africa* (Baltimore, Penguin, 1962).

Bohannan, Paul, *Africa and Africans* (Garden City, N.Y., Doubleday, 1964).

Boyd, Andrew, and van Rensburg, Patrick, *An Atlas of African Affairs* (New York, Praeger, 1962).

Friedland, W. H., and Rosberg, Carl G., *African Socialism* (Stanford, Stanford University Press, 1964).

Geiger, T., and Armstrong, W., *The Development of African Private Enterprise* (Washington, D.C., National Planning Association, 1964).

Gould, Peter R., *Africa, Continent of Change* (Belmont, Calif., Wadsworth, 1961).

Herskovits, Melville J., *The Human Factor in Changing Africa* (New York, Knopf, 1962).

Judd, Peter, ed., *African Independence* (New York, Dell, 1963).

Kimble, George H. T., *Tropical Africa*, 2 Vols. (Garden City, N.Y., Doubleday, 1963).

Labouret, Henri, *Africa Before the White Man* (New York, Walker, 1962).

Mair, Lucy, *Primitive Government* (Baltimore, Penguin, 1962).

Murdock, George P., *Africa: Its Peoples and Their Cultural History* (New York, McGraw-Hill, 1959).

Nkrumah, Kwame, *I Speak of Freedom* (New York, Praeger, 1961).

Oliver, Roland, and Page, J. D., *A Short History of Africa* (Baltimore, Penguin, 1962).

Oliver, Roland, *The Dawn of African History* (London, Oxford University Press, 1961).

Ottenberg, Simon, and Ottenberg, Phoebe, *Cultures and Societies of Africa* (New York, Random House, 1961).

Post, Ken, *New States of West Africa* (Baltimore, Penguin, 1964).

Segan, Ronald, *African Profiles* (Baltimore, Penguin, 1962).

Wallerstein, Immanuel, *Africa: The Politics of Independence* (New York, Random House, Vintage Books, 1961).

Wills, A. J., *An Introduction to the History of Central Africa* (London, Oxford University Press, 1964).

21

Asia in Transition to the Secondary Civilization

More than half of the world's population lives on the continent of Asia. By the time the twentieth century ends, its population will have doubled to equal the entire world's population as it was in 1965. In the 500 years from 1465 to 1965, the population of the world increased about seven times. If present population trends continue, it may increase at least ten times the 1965 figure during the next 100 years, giving the world a population of at least 35 to 40 billion, of which more than half would be located in Asia.

Asia is more of a figure of speech than an actual continent or culture. It is extremely difficult to lump Soviet Siberia, Turkey, Israel, Iran, Saudi Arabia, Pakistan, India, Indonesia, China, and Japan together as being "Asian." Their cultures and their physical types are as varied as their landscapes. Israel on one end is atypical because she is in the midst of Secondary civilization, as is Japan on the other side of the vast expanse of Asia. And Soviet Siberia belongs culturally to the European part of the Union of Soviet Socialist Republics.

Most of the populations of Asia live close to the sea. In the past, cultural innovations came by boat, for although land travel is comparatively easy in the north, it is very difficult in the south. Mountainous deserts separate Syria from Iran, and the latter from Pakistan and India. A traveler by plane feels that he is flying over the wastelands of the moon when he goes from Teheran to New Delhi. Moving eastward, one finds dense jungle and almost impassable mountains separating India from Burma. To the north, the tall Himalayas act as physical obstacles to the movement of people and goods between India and China. In the past the cultural contacts between these two nations came by sea rather than by land.

Asia is a conglomeration of isolated people, subdivided into clans, castes, and villages whose members are reared to have little interest in or knowledge of any people not within the immediate neighborhood. To be interested in people thousands of miles away is a characteristic of modern Secondary civilization. To identify oneself with others is a moral concept to be found in those cultures where many years of formal schooling are available.

Asia is also the home of such metropolitan cities as Tokyo, Peking, Hong Kong, Manila, Singapore, Calcutta, and Bombay, where Secondary civilization brushes elbows with Primary and where educated industrialists, engineers, physicists, and surgeons live in a world separated by only a few miles from the world of illiterate landless laborers and peasants.

India, China, and Japan represent the three great cultures of Asia that have influenced one another in the past; yet today they are as different from one another as the United States is from Vietnam, or the Philippines is from Great Britain. India and China represent roughly two-thirds of the population of Asia; and, within the next thirty to thirty-five years, they may contain a population greater than that of the entire world in 1940.

China and Japan borrowed their Buddhism from India, where it had initially been a religion of personal denial and asceticism. But in China and Japan it became a religion that offered its followers a definite assurance of heaven after death. Although Buddhism developed in India as a reaction to the caste system, it had little importance in China or Japan as a social movement of protest.

Of the three, India has been longest in touch with the Mediterranean and European worlds. Greek learning, art, and architecture came with the invasion of Alexander the Great in the fourth century B.C. Islam came in the eighth century A.D. and spread over northern India by the fifteenth. The Portuguese, Dutch, and French came to the coastal areas of India in the sixteenth and seventeenth centuries, and the British followed in the eighteenth.

From the first to the fourth century, China carried on some trade with the Romans both over the land-based Silk Route and by sea from southern China. An extensive trade in luxury goods also existed between southern Chinese ports and Indonesia, India, and the Philippines from the seventh century on, and between North China, Korea, and Japan from the fourth century on.

During the thirteenth and fourteenth centuries, the Venetians acted both as traders and as intelligence agents for the Mongols. It was during this period that Western influences reached China through the Mongols. China in turn had been the teacher for both Korea and Japan from the fourth century on, and for southeastern Asia after the tenth century.

Japan was influenced both by Korea and China after the second century, with Chinese influences becoming most important after the sixth century when Japanese young men were sent to the courts and urban centers in China to learn the patternings of Chinese civilization.

INDIA

India is a subcontinent possessing at least seven important language sub-families and a caste system embracing over 3,000 castes and subcastes, in which individuals follow the occupations or trades of their forefathers, marry only those whose fathers are in the same work and caste, and eat and worship only with their fellow caste members. India is also divided culturally into a fourfold division of North, South, East, and West. The North contained a high percentage of Moslems (by the seventeenth century, the rulers were Moslems as were over 25 percent of the population), while the civilization in the South was more Hindu in form. In both North and South, the Hindus were divided by four separate theological systems and by numerous sects following different deities. Some of the Indian peasants were high caste *Brahmins;* others ranged through the entire gamut of the castes. There were also tens of millions of Untouchables (or *Harijans*—Children of God—Gandhi's term for them), who were outside the Hindu caste system but who graded themselves into varying subcastes based upon occupation.

Caste in India is called *Varna,* and the four chief historic castes have been (1) the *Brahmins,* or priests; (2) the *Kshatriyas,* or warriors; (3) the *Vaishyas,* or traders and merchants; and (4) the *Sudras,* or peasants, artisans, and laborers. Originally, in Vedic times (around 1,000 B.C.), *Varna* meant color; and it differentiated the light-skinned Indo-European-speaking invaders from Afghanistan and central Asia from the rest of the population. The indigenous peasants tended to shade in color from brown to almost black—the result of the ancient strata of Australoid and Negroid people who at one time had lived in various parts of the Indian subcontinent. It is possible that the caste system may have been taken over by the Indo-European invaders from previous conquerors, who might have inaugurated this system of classifying the population thousands of years before. Even today, most *Brahmins* (except for those in the South) tend to be lighter in skin color than the *Vaishyas* or *Sudras.*

The caste system was evidently introduced comparatively recently to southern India because the same number of castes, such as the *Kshatriyas* or the *Vaishyas* in the North, are not found here. The Untouchables, however, tend to be southern in origin. The South also has a higher percentage of non-Hindus, such as the hill tribes, Christians, Moslems, and Jains, who are all outside the Hindu caste system.

Each of the castes is subdivided into hundreds of subcastes. For example, not all *Brahmins* today are priests; they are divided into a large number of subcastes, each with its own distinctive name, geographic area, and language. Many are cooks, mechanics, factory workers, clerks, and school teachers. The six million Sikhs, who broke away from Hinduism in the early sixteenth century to develop a monotheistic religion that was opposed both to priesthood and to the caste system, are completely outside the caste system, though they feel more closely identified emotionally with Hinduism than with Islam, which persecuted them in the seventeenth and eighteenth centuries. Today the Sikhs follow in varying degrees some of the caste and religious practices of the Hindus. The 50 million Moslems in present-day India, plus the 10 million Christians, are also outside the caste system, although they too have adopted Hindu castelike social gradations. The Parsis, who are the descendants of the Zoroastrians (who fled from Persia in the seventh century when that country was conquered by Islam) have almost become a caste of their own, as have the Coorgs of South India, the Jains (who developed in the sixth century B.C. as a reaction to Hinduism), and even the few Buddhists who still live in India today.

With the exception of the two main castes, it is extremely difficult to rank the others in terms of their social superiority or inferiority to one another. Subcastes change as new religious restrictions are adopted or as the members become more pious in their rituals. All the other castes are agreed that the Untouchables are on the bottom of the social heap: their occupations tend to be the least skilled, their members are the most illiterate, and they possess the least confidence in their ability to rise socially. Until half a century ago, an Untouchable could pollute a member of the higher three castes by having his shadow fall on him or on the food he was about to eat.

There are many subcastes who insist that they have a higher social standing than others are willing to give them. The *Kayasthas* of Bengal, who rank themselves as *Kshatriyas,* insist that they were originally warriors; they became scribes under the Moslem Mogul emperors and government clerks under the British. The *Kshatriyas,* on the other hand, insist that the *Kayasthas* were actually Untouchables who by an act of good fortune became indispensable to the Moguls, thus raising their caste and hence their social positions. Today the other castes rank them slightly beneath the *Brahmins.*[1]

[1] Neither China nor Japan had anything like the caste system. China was organized on the basis of clans—as Japan was initially—in which individuals within the clan felt a sense of kinship with others bearing the name of an original common ancestor. In China the clans were divided into subgroups, which were roughly similar to large extended families. In the Chinese clan, membership was inherited through the father; one's ancestors were paternal, and there was a sense of relationship with all those who were related to the father. The wife lost her identity with her own family upon marriage for she became a member of her husband's clan.

The Japanese were organized into clans and classes fairly early, although one caste does exist today in Japan—the *Eta.* These may have been ostracized by the Buddhist monks when Buddhism first came into Japan during the sixth and seventh centuries.

Acculturation Begins for India, China, and Japan

Although formal British control of India took place only after 1857, British cultural and political influences had become quite strong by the middle of the eighteenth century. By that time, they had eclipsed the Portuguese, the Dutch, and the French in trade and military prowess. Hinduism, as an organized mass of religious beliefs, spread rather early to all corners of the Indian subcontinent; but political unity proved more difficult to attain than religious unity. The history of India is a story of clans feuding and weakening one another while outside conquerors (beginning even before Alexander the Great) attempted to carve personal domains for themselves out of the North. Persians, Afghans, Moguls (who were the central Asian Moslem descendants of the Mongols), Marathas (from the present Bombay region), and others conquered large areas of North India but were unable to found a stable political state. The Moguls ruled for 300 years, during most of which time the Portuguese, the Dutch, the French, and the British carved small trading empires out of the coastal regions, fortifying them and demanding tribute from the neighboring rulers. North and South India were traditionally separate and were only united by the British in the nineteenth century.

The British established trading posts at the sites of the modern cities of Madras and Calcutta (both cities are thus lineal descendants of these seventeenth century ports), and by the middle of the eighteenth century had extended their influence for hundreds of miles around. As a result of the Seven Years' War, the French were virtually eliminated from India and after 1763 held only a few coastal towns for trading purposes (which they continued to hold until the 1950's, when they ceded them to the new Indian Government). The British East India Company had originally expanded its territory in order to protect its trading ports. By siding in local disputes with the weaker antagonist and by offering its British-trained Indian troops as mercenaries to help various local rulers, the

---

The *Eta* at that time were leather workers, scavengers, and butchers. Although the Japanese were not vegetarians, as the Buddhist monks were, the Buddhist disapproval of those who took animal life may have carried over into Japanese culture to make the *Eta* into Untouchables. The Indian Untouchables were also leather workers, butchers, or those who handled the carcasses of dead animals.

Like feudal Europe, Japan by the twelfth century was organized into classes consisting of lords, or Daimyo; knights, or Samurai; peasants; artisans and merchants; and the caste of *Eta*. The merchants were ranked below the peasant and the artisan, although many merchants became quite well-to-do by the seventeenth century and many of their daughters married Samurai. A peasant could become a warrior, and a warrior could sink to the peasant level. Even descendants of Daimyo could become peasants over the centuries. Above this four-class system were the court nobles, whose positions were hereditary, and the Emperor, who had no temporal role but was considered as the fount of all secular power. He was a sacred chief, the high priest of the nation, greatly respected and revered, but eclipsed by the secular chief, or military Shogun.

Company was able by the end of the eighteenth century to create a trading empire out of the chaotic political conditions then prevailing.

The trading ports of Madras and Calcutta plus Bombay (which came as a wedding dowry from Portugal to Charles II in 1662) attracted Indian merchants, scribes, and artisans. With the British there were employment possibilities, chances to sell one's goods, and opportunities for learning. For hundreds of years, the educated elites of North India had been influenced by the Persian culture that the Moslem rulers had brought with them. From the seventeenth century on, however, British culture took on the role of teacher to the Indians.

In the seventeenth and eighteenth centuries, the bright young Englishmen who had been brought to India by the East India Company had been more influenced by Indian culture than they had been able to influence the thoughts of the few educated individuals with whom they were able to associate, but this was no longer true a century later. By the middle of the nineteenth century, the Parsis of Bombay and the merchant castes of Bombay and Bengal had learned to manufacture the goods that the British wanted. In Bombay, Calcutta, and South India, ships were made to British specifications (though on the artisan level, for the Industrial Age did not come to India until the early twentieth century). As the British extended their political and economic power, many young Indians of the upper castes learned to adjust themselves to it in order to gain economically. And finally, through the British and British-organized colleges and universities to which many young Indians were sent, the technology and science of Secondary civilization came to India during the latter part of the nineteenth and the early twentieth centuries.

Although the British created many jobs for the Indians, British manufactures proved to be very stiff competition for the output of the local Indian artisans. As a result of laws in force during most of the nineteenth century which discriminated in favor of British imports, Indian artisans found themselves pushed to the wall by the rising tide of textile and metal imports, which were sold at cheaper prices than the goods they made locally.

British efforts at sanitation, medical care, and new sources of food, however, increased the Indian population enormously between the eighteenth and the twentieth centuries. Despite famines that arrived almost every twenty years and killed millions, the population increased more than 400 percent between the eighteenth and the twentieth centuries. Since India had always had a large population, even when compared with preindustrial Europe, the increase in numbers without a concomitant increase in agricultural production led the landless and the poor to flood the administrative centers that the British had founded in search of employment and food. The British added to this problem by organizing a new class of landlords in the villages to collect the taxes and by turning the previously communally owned land over to them. These landlords, or *Zamindars,* increased rents but did not increase the production of food.

Despite its highly developed Primary civilization, India had been predominantly a subcontinent of peasant villages with few large trading centers or temple cities. When the British first came to India in the middle of the seventeenth century, at least 95 percent of the population had been self-sufficient peasants, tilling their lands under communal rule or lease and growing only enough food for their needs. (Despite the expanding industrialization of modern India, more than 80 percent of the population are still peasants who grow food for themselves rather than for a market. India still finds it difficult to increase food production sufficiently to feed her population, which jumps by almost 10 million each year.)

Cultural Worlds in India

As in the case of other populations, both the Hindus and the Moslems of India are reared in the cultural worlds of their parents; and there most of them remain for the rest of their lives. A small percentage breaks away by going to the formal elementary schools originally established by the British and other Europeans, where they meet entirely different views of cultural concepts and values. As they progress through secondary school and the university, the compartmentalization of their separate worlds becomes more difficult; at certain cues they must mentally leave one world and enter another. Each of their separate worlds has its own concepts and values, and some of these may be contradictory. A *Brahmin,* for example, may study physics and chemistry at the university and become proficient in thinking of the physical world in terms of its cause-and-effect relationships, with each effect requiring convincing and detailed evidence; but at the same time he may eat only with those belonging to his subcaste, marry only a girl selected by his parents from certain families, consult an astrologer or a *guru* (holy man) for advice and counsel in his personal life, and in general behave traditionally in carrying out the cultural values given him in his childhood by his parents and close relatives. They are the ones he wants to please as long as he lives within the extended family. In India, most well-to-do upper caste individuals are born and live within an extended family, which includes uncles, aunts, and grandparents, as well as mother and father. It is headed by a male, who plays the role of patriarch, although relationships are closer between mothers and sons than between fathers and sons, as they are in Japan though not in China.

The Relative Unimportance of Technology

Indian culture of the past was not geared to an optimistic faith in human beings, nor did it have as its goal the creation of a more efficient and gratifying world for most of the population. The elites came from the top three castes and were almost entirely concerned with the welfare of their immediate families. Their goals were geared to the hereafter and to a culture that took for granted its domination by the supernatural world. Each Hindu saw life as a never-ending series of transitions from a lower form of life to a higher one, or from a higher to a lower one, for the soul went through a number of transmigrations at each death until it received the status to which its previous lives entitled it.

It was considered far more important to have a metaphysical point of view toward life than a realistic one based upon studying man as he actually was. Deprivation of desires was considered more socially useful than finding satisfaction for them through a richer life. Early in India's history, men learned to turn their eyes to avoid seeing the intense poverty that existed in the villages rather than to try to do something about it. Human beings were plentiful; and there was no cultural need to make life pleasanter, richer, or more satisfying for everyone.

The holy men preached poverty as an ideal in order to encourage taking the reality of it for granted. They considered that riches lay not in men's attempts to use nature more efficiently, but in the ability to escape one's environment, fellowmen, and life by retreating into a cultural world where one received direction, guidance, satisfaction, and eventual happiness through ignoring the physical world.

Hinduism permitted little room for nontraditional thought or even for dissent. Even if an individual could succeed in seeing the world as it actually was rather than through the colored glasses of metaphysics and religious beliefs, his influence upon the rest of the community might be virtually nil. Science and dissent, like religion, require converts in order to grow. Cultural change, which is the essence of scientific thought, could take place in India only within the approved culture brought by the British, in which specific entrepreneurial, managerial, and scientific skills were approved and rewarded. These skills were not rewarded in Akbar's day because they posed a threat to the traditional way of life. Akbar himself was as traditional mentally as his subjects; and so no Indian equivalents of Roger Bacon, Isaac Newton, or Robert Boyle would have been sought out or encouraged.

India was no wealthier in the seventeenth century than she had been in the tenth. There were no printing presses (these came in with the British) and no formal schooling—not even for one percent of the population. In the past, India attempted to meet its shortages by urging each individual to cut down on his wants. India was not ready culturally for a point of view that sought to create new forms of wealth and an abundance of goods and foods, or to try to solve man's age-old problems. In the past, supply kept pace with desire, and desire was consciously kept down by the Indian philosophers and the holy men.

In the sixteenth and seventeenth centuries, little incentive existed for the type of civilization that developed later in England, France, Germany, and the United States. In any forced industrialization, only the trader castes and non-Hindu Parsis could have participated in establishing new factories. Only the lower castes could have worked the machines because the artisan castes would have felt a loss in status if they had done so. But industrial stimuli did not exist in India then, nor did they begin to develop until the middle of the nineteenth century when a few Parsi merchants and some families of Hindu trader castes accumulated the capital to hire a few Europeans to build small textile mills and modest consumer goods industries.

The Indian managers, technicians, and engineers first had to be trained in the technical schools and universities established in India by the British and by the British and American religious denominations. Later on, during the first half of the twentieth century, tens of thousands of Indians were trained in England, Germany, France, and the United States to be industrial initiators.

Great Britain was responsible for giving an overall national consciousness to the subcontinent of India, even though the divide-and-rule tendencies of a good many British administrators encouraged antagonisms between the Moslems and the Hindus. The Moslems were descendants of both lower and upper Hindu castes since there had been a good deal of voluntary conversion to Islam in North India from the eighth century on. Most of the new Moslems, however, were peasants and artisans; few were educated scribes or former priests.

Great Britain, in governing the subcontinent, developed and paid for railroads, communication lines, printing presses, schools, and universities. It also spent large sums in building hospitals, in creating sanitation facilities in the cities, and in training modern physicians and nurses. Although Great Britain taxed the population for the costs of running the administration, army, police force, public services, transportation, and schools, most of village India was much too poor to pay its way. Even today, after more than three Five-Year Plans, the annual per capita share of the average Indian in the gross total of the nation's industries and services comes to less than $75. It was closer to $20 before 1914, but World War I and World War II spurred Great Britain to encourage local investment in the creation of industries that could supply the Indian army and the local administration with the goods they needed. The money India earned in supplying the British army during World War II laid the basis for the industrialization that took place after Independence.

Independence in 1947 partitioned India between the Moslems and the Hindus, with the Moslems creating their own state of Pakistan, which was divided into West and East and was separated by over 1,000 miles of India. Half as many Moslems, however, as lived in Pakistan remained in India. Partition brought communal riots, millions of refugees, and at least two million dead. Partition also brought an enduring enmity between the two neighboring nations and thus solved no problems.

Since 1947, India has carried on a series of Five-Year Plans to industrialize and raise the standard of living of the entire country. Her problems are enormous. Almost 80 percent of her present population are illiterate peasants living in some 550,000 villages. Although a Community Development Program was started in the 1950's, the number of villages that have been reached by the *Gram Sevak,* or Extension Worker, is still a small percentage of the total number. There are not enough trained agricultural agents, social workers, teachers, and handicraft instructors to make more than a feeble impression in India's hundreds of thousands of villages with their illiteracy, apathy, disease, and low standard of living. Although a number of villages have been able to build their own schools, construct dirt roads, erect bridges, and develop sanitary facilities, the overwhelming majority remains untouched.

India is potentially a rich nation for a small population, but not for a large one. Her 450 million people are almost untrained at present. Less than one percent of her inhabitants lives mentally in the Secondary civilization or possesses skills that can be used in administering, managing, or building an industrialized society. The Five-Year Plans have created a technical and scientific base, but the work done thus far is only a minute part of what needs to be done. More than a century of industrialization is needed before India will be able to increase her standard of living to levels equivalent to those of the poorer European nations. In the meanwhile, however, her population will have increased almost as rapidly as the number of industrial plants, schools, or new sanitary facilities. By the year 2000 if present population figures are projected, India will have a population of over 1 billion, which could then increase to 2 billion by the year 2025, and to about 16 billion within a century. Neither her soils nor her industrial resources could support a population that large; such a population requires a highly industrialized base with huge resources of scientific and technological skills to help compensate the nation for its lack of land and materials.

Although more than 80 percent of the population are directly dependent upon agriculture for their living, most of the peasants have neither enough fertilizer nor adequate tools to increase their yields. Some improvement has been effected in agricultural production since 1950, but the increase has been barely enough to feed the population, which is increasing at the rate of more than 12 million each year. India is a food importing country; and although famines such as the extensive one in Bengal in 1943 are now a thing of the past, there is still not enough food grown or even imported to feed the population adequately. Most of the people suffer from vitamin and protein deficiencies, and malnutrition in most parts of the country is chronic. Most of the farms are small, and the plots are not sufficient to grow enough food even for the peasant's immediate family.

India has the largest cattle population of any country in the world, but religious traditions stemming from the Indo-European invaders prohibit their use as food. Old cattle are removed to "Cattle Homes" or are left to die on the land, whereupon they are removed by the Untouchables. Most of the cattle are used to pull wooden plows or wagons; few of them are milked. The average per capita consumption of milk from both cattle and water buffalo comes to less than five ounces per day. Plans call for a 30 to 40 percent increase in milk production in ten to twelve years, but this will require substituting modern breeds of milk cows for the scrub Brahma cattle owned by the peasants and the religious temples. The cattle eat fodder, which could be used for better purposes; and their chief value seems to be to supply manure cakes for fuel. (There is neither enough timber nor enough coal available for the tens of millions of peasant families to cook their daily meals.) Cattle manure cannot be used for fertilizing the land as long as there are no other sources of fuel for the villagers, most of whom live great distances from railroads and important highways. Even if coal were available, it is doubtful that most peasants could afford its use.

India is deficient in regular rainfall. Most of the rains in the greatest part of the country come from the summer monsoons, which last from one to three months. (When they fail to come, famine is near.) During the rest of the year in northern and central India average rainfall is not enough to provide the moisture needed for growing crops. In the northern part of the country, sufficient underground water comes from the Himalayas to warrant digging artesian wells; and a certain amount of irrigation of dry land can be done with these wells. A large part of northern India is arid; and even if the monsoons come regularly, not enough moisture falls to prevent large areas from turning into desert. The green tropical rain forests of India are found only in the southern part of the country.

India has adequate natural resources for moderate industrialization. She possesses extensive iron ore and coal reserves, large deposits of manganese, and radioactive sands in large enough supply to enable her eventually to use nuclear power for many of her industrial needs.

Compared with present-day China or with pre-Communist Russia, India has a larger network of railways and paved highways—a valuable heritage from the British. Her numerous universities have educated Nobel Prize winners; and the quality of her scientists, technologists, and mathematicians equals that of the more industrialized nations. Unlike Africa or South America, India has enough individuals trained in the skills of Secondary civilization to guide its industrialization without too much outside assistance.

A large part of present-day funds is being devoted to training engineers, technicians, and scientists. By 1966 India expects to be turning out at least 50,000 more engineers from its more than 100 engineering schools, 75,000 more technicians from the 200 polytechnic schools, 45,000 more scientists with bachelor's degrees and 7,000 with master's degrees than she educated in 1961. By 1971 India hopes to have all the engineers, doctors, scientists, and technicians she will need.

But on the whole the newly trained carriers of the Scientific and Industrial Age in India will add only another fraction to the less than one-tenth of one percent who have been trained to manage a Secondary civilization. More than 95 percent of the population remains on the outside, competent to carry on in an agrarian peasant Primary civilization but not in a rapidly advancing Secondary one. Although an increasing number of individuals will be trained in the thought and the culture of the Scientific and Industrial Age, an equally increasing number are becoming obsolete, as machines and new skills make work and cultivation more efficient. The problems that India faces are thus social as much as economic. She can educate enough individuals to become the scientists, the engineers, the managers, and the innovators of an advancing industrial organization of society; but even in fifty years she cannot educate enough peasants to become farmers, technicians, and local problem solvers to help the population adjust to the Industrial Age with as little discomfort as possible.

A recently organized common educational system has not yet been able to take the diverse elements of the 450 million people who live in India and weld them into a people who can communicate with one another in one language that all can understand or who can articulate goals that all can share to some degree. Caste, regionalism, and linguistic nationalism act as separatist tendencies in isolating large elements of the population. The vast majority of Indians have not accepted the nation-state of India as one to which they owe loyalty. Caste, region, language, and low levels of education still act as barriers to the advance of the new morality of science, with its emphasis upon understanding those who are different. Moslems and Hindus continue to view one another with deep distrust, and both are suspicious of the Sikhs and the Christians. In the South, the Untouchables have created an underground political movement whose target is the *Brahmin* caste. Each region of the country feels put upon by the other regions, and each insists upon its right to use its own language as its official one and to be free of molestation from the Federal Government.

Through education the upper castes are today rapidly changing, and their daughters enjoy greater freedom in choosing careers and in specifying the kind of husband they want their parents to provide for them. The great problem for India, however, is that social conditions are changing through urbanization, industrialization, education, and science far more rapidly than the population can adjust to the changes. Unquestionably, the transitional stage that India is experiencing will produce growing pains of severe intensity during the next fifty years; but the path leads to a much greater participation by the rest of the population in the Secondary civilization of industry and science. The problems of India are enormously complex, and the Secondary civilization is arriving at a time when her small number of educated personnel are incapable of helping her adjust easily and peacefully. There are over 40 million permanently unemployed who need to be given work, at least 200 million peasants who are only employed during three to four months of the year, and an illiterate and unskilled population that is growing much faster than it can be cared for. India needs to educate large numbers of problem-solving scientists and social scientists, for she is today creating more problems than she can competently solve. Her urban problems today are beyond her capacity to handle. Her slums may not be removed for at least a century or more. India also needs masses of educated individuals to help guide her through the maze of human problems that have been accumulating for thousands of years. The late Prime Minister Nehru told this author in 1957 that all he could hope for was that the vast majority of Indians would be able to eat at least one good meal per day by the end of the twentieth century.

JAPAN

While India represents a developing country, Japan has today become one of the world's greatest industrial nations. The poverty that one sees in India is absent in Japan, which takes its place within Secondary civilization. India is still dependent upon the outside world for many of its industrial skills, but Japan has arrived at self-sufficiency in this area. The demand for technicians, engineers, and scientists increases each year; and Japan is in the fortunate position of being able to satisfy her own needs from her educational resources. Japan has had compulsory elementary school education since the third quarter of the nineteenth century, and her state and private universities have been in existence for the better part of the twentieth century. (Her leading universities—among them the Imperial University of Tokyo—were established during the latter part of the nineteenth century.)

When the first settlement of Englishmen landed at Jamestown, Virginia, in 1607, there were more than 300,000 Christians in Japan, where they had been persecuted as traitors for more than ten years. By the time the Dutch had settled New Amsterdam in the New World, the Tokugawa Shogunate had expelled the Roman Catholic missionaries, condemned all converts to death unless they recanted (many upper-class Christians preferred to go underground), and banned all travel abroad by the Japanese.

Although relations with Europe came comparatively late, Japan has still had a longer and more intimate contact with the civilization of Western Europe than India and China, which helps somewhat to explain the rapidity as well as the eagerness with which Japan adopted various aspects of Secondary civilization after 1868.

Christian missionary activity in Japan began in 1549 with the arrival of St. Francis Xavier and his Jesuit priests. From the beginning the Christians seemed to be eminently successful in winning converts to Roman Catholicism. Among the reasons for this were (1) the rough similarity between some of the teachings of the Pure Land Sect of Buddhism (which had a far larger following in Japan than in China from whence it came) and Roman Catholicism; (2) the attractiveness of the material culture that the Portuguese and the Jesuits brought with them; and (3) the political chaos and feudal separatism in Japan, which encouraged many of the Daimyos, or feudal lords, to become Christians, when they saw in their conversion an opportunity to obtain Portuguese weapons and technical guidance in building fortified castles against the Shogun and the other lords. Throughout most of the sixteenth century, European goods, foods, and ideas became the rage among the lords and warriors.

By the beginning of the seventeenth century, a clan general by the name of Tokugawa Ieyesu was able to defeat the Samurai soldiers of the other clans and thus unify the nation, making himself the actual military ruler and the figurehead Emperor the sacred source of temporal power. The civil wars and the political chaos that had existed in Japan from the thirteenth through the sixteenth centuries had inaugurated feudalism and the age of the Samurai, or the warrior-knights. The Shogun was the military ruler who controlled the person of the Emperor and all temporal power. Beneath the Shogun were about 250 feudal lords, each with his territory, fortified castle, and warrior-retainers. The retainer owed loyalty to his lord, who in turn owed loyalty to the Shogun. The Shogun could keep the loyalty of the lords by giving them gifts of fiefs. The lords passed some of this land, along with the peasants, to their retainers. The lords also owed protection to their vassals and serfs. Tokugawa Ieyesu was the first Shogun since the thirteenth century who was able to win and keep a commanding control over the feudal lords who owed him allegiance. He did this by impoverishing them through taxation and special levies, and by demanding hostages from their immediate families to live in the Shogun's city of Edo, or Yedo (present-day Tokyo), while the lords remained on their fiefs.

Tokugawa feared that Christianity might continue the divisive tendencies of past Japanese life by encouraging the lords to become self-sufficient politically on the assumption that they could get weapons and technical assistance from the Portuguese. He also feared that a Christianized Japan might lead to its occupation by the Portuguese. As a pious Buddhist, he saw Christianity as a dangerously competitive religion to Buddhism. By 1603 he ordered all missionaries to leave the country, all converts to recant, and all ports to be closed to both the incoming Portuguese and the outgoing Japanese ships. At the same time, competition between the Dutch and the Portuguese offered the Shogun an alternative supply of weapons and goods. By permitting the opening of a Dutch trading post at Nagasaki in 1609, the Shogun strengthened his hand against the local Christians, for now there was no danger of his being cut off from Western technology by antagonizing the Portuguese. In fact, the Japanese during the seventeenth and eighteenth centuries were closer to the sources of European science and technological achievements through the Dutch than they had been with the Portuguese. By 1637 most of the feudal lords who had been publicly baptized renounced their Christian faith. Many of the Japanese lower classes and Samurai, who were smarting at the inability of the older culture to give them the respect and sense of identity they wanted, continued to fight the Shogun's orders with arms. It required more than a year for the Christian forces to be crushed, and from that time on Christianity was forbidden as being a treasonable movement.

The Pure Land Sect of Buddhism came from China to Japan in the eleventh century, and its following became greater than in China. The original teaching of Buddhism that peace can be gained by divesting oneself of all desire could win converts only in a culture that continuously reaffirmed individual guilt. In a shame culture such as that in Japan, where one could not retreat from one's social group and where shame was a much stronger force in making the individual conform to the group than guilt, which encouraged retreatism, the doctrine of Nirvana, or the divesting of human desire, had little appeal. In the Pure Land Sect, Nirvana was replaced by heaven (the Pure Land); and the many reincarnations were replaced by a simple doctrine of heaven and hell to which one went after death. Salvation, then, came from belief and faith in the Buddha as one's personal savior. Individuals were rewarded with an eternal life in heaven for their unswerving faith and good works. By calling on the name of the Amida Buddha, one could achieve salvation for oneself as well as for the group. In Japan, then, Buddhism became a group religion in which rituals and conformity brought rewards in the afterlife. In India it had begun as an individual retreat from the group. The Japanese found the Christian belief that Christ died to save mankind for a heavenly existence not too different from what they had previously been taught.

There were other factors in Japan that paralleled the growth of the Secondary civilization in Europe. As a result of the civil wars beginning in the thirteenth century, many who were defeated (numbers of them were former Samurai) lost their lands and became merchants. Chinese weakness on the seas encouraged these Samurai-merchants to turn to trade and piracy in order to increase their wealth and personal status. Large fortunes were made through attacking Chinese merchant ships that traded with Korea, the Philippines, or the Malay regions (just as later fortunes were made by the British knights-turned-merchants in piracy against the Spaniards). From the fourteenth to the sixteenth century, as the merchants increased their trade and piracy, the handicraft industries expanded enormously, agricultural production was tripled, and a class of wholesale and retail merchants developed. A peaceful trade was also carried on with China, Korea, and East Asia as far as the Malay Peninsula. In the fifteenth century, sailors and merchants brought home a good deal of information about the Europeans; and thus, before the arrival in Japan of the Portuguese in 1543, curiosity about the Europeans and their technology was greater than in India at that time. In Japan, wealth brought as much status to the individual as it did in England; and when one could not achieve status by acquiring land as a warrior, one could obtain it by building a large house in town and living as the merchants did in the towns and cities of Europe. From the fifteenth through the seventeenth century, other parallels existed between Japan and Europe, including a growing intellectual interest in the physical world and an optimistic belief that a better human society could be built with the material at hand.

The Portuguese from 1543 to 1603 brought new plants, such as tobacco, potatoes, and European wheat; beef cattle; milk cows; simple agricultural implements; clocks; spectacles; hats; trousers; chairs; artillery; and fortifications. The Dutch at Nagasaki after 1609 introduced the Japanese to European shipbuilding, navigation, advanced artillery, astronomy, medicine, art, and scientific thought. At no time during these centuries was Japan really isolated from European technology and science. For example, the techniques of European brickmaking, iron smelting, and handicrafts came in during the seventeenth century. Dutch words, along with Portuguese and Spanish, entered the language; and many educated individuals learned Dutch in order to read the books that were imported clandestinely after 1609. In 1720 the Shogun permitted books to be imported from Europe freely; and this led to a considerable trade in books, maps, globes, and instruments between the Dutch and the Japanese (similar to the trade between the European monasteries and the Moslem world before the thirteenth century).

Although the Shogun's policy was one of impoverishing the Daimyos so that they would not have the funds to revolt against him, the Tokugawa Period (1603-1868) was one of peace and prosperity for most of the nation. The merchants in the towns waxed rich; and although trade and travel abroad had been prohibited, a great many merchants and young Samurai traveled secretly abroad for trade and education. Towns and cities grew in population, and the merchant and artisan classes stimulated an urban culture during the eighteenth century. The theater played as important a role in Osaka and Edo in the eighteenth century as it had in London in the sixteenth and seventeenth centuries. The Kabuki theater flourished, as did new forms of art and music. Although the merchants were consigned to an inferior social status by the Shogun, they became so wealthy and powerful that many of their children married into the impoverished Daimyo families. The merchants became more restless in their desire to compete for status with the landed warrior and feudal classes (as the same group had done in Europe a few hundred years before). The children of the merchants were the ones most attracted to European science and technology. The severity of control by the Shogun, the Daimyo, and the Samurai over the peasants, artisans, and merchants caused the latter to escape by turning toward entertainment and religion as forms of retreat and solace.

By the eighteenth century Japan had become a money economy. The Shogun minted gold, silver, and copper coins; and paper money was issued by the Daimyo. The money changers early played the role of bankers by lending money, receiving deposits, and issuing checks and letters of credit. Some of the great financial houses of modern Japan were started by the descendants of the money changers in Osaka and Edo during the seventeenth and eighteenth centuries. Many of the great department stores of today started as small retail shops at that time. For example, the great Daimaru chain started as a dry-goods store in Kyoto in 1727. As the merchant-trader family became more prosperous, new retail outlets were established by sons and sons-in-law. Merchants amassed capital and carried on an extensive trade in supplying goods and services to the Shogun and his retainers, the Daimyos, the court at Kyoto, and other well-to-do merchants and artisans. New cottage industries in handicrafts were established with techniques borrowed from the Dutch, who in turn had taken them from Flanders and Italy. (Holland at this time was the leading shipbuilding country of the world. Peter the Great and others came to Amsterdam to learn Western techniques of building ships and making cannon.)

At the beginning of the eighteenth century, Japan was almost as urbanized as England. Edo, or Tokyo, had a population of about 600,000, as compared with 500,000 in London and 800,000 in Paris. Osaka had a population of 400,000 in 1779; Kyoto had over 70,000. During the eighteenth century, at least seven towns had a population of from 20,000 to 70,000, most of which were the castle towns of the Daimyos such as Nagoya and Hiroshima. Nagasaki, the site of the Dutch trading post, had more than 50,000 inhabitants throughout most of this period. The towns did a thriving business in selling foreign goods and books and in supplying credit to the Daimyos and their retainers, who were then being severely taxed by the Shogun. The town merchants, or Chonin as they were called, plowed back their earnings into more cottage industries and into a higher standard of living for themselves.

Unlike India, but again like England in the seventeenth century, elementary education spread rapidly in the cities and towns. Schools were opened to teach the three R's to the children of the merchants and artisans, who needed sons to read, write, and use the abacus. Girls were also taught to read, write, and use the abacus and were in addition given lessons in needlework, flower arrangements, and the behavior connected with the tea ceremony. The widespread literacy in the towns led to the rapid development of printing; novels, books of poetry, philosophy, and art forms were published in editions of thousands. During the eighteenth and nineteenth centuries, puppet shows, samisen music, and the theater were the three chief forms of entertainment among the merchants, the artisans, and their workers. The eighteenth century also saw a flowering of realistic art in the cities; and one can easily visualize the urban life in the eighteenth century by studying the paintings of Korin, Moronobu, and Utamaru. The early nineteenth century is represented by such urban artists as Hokusai, Hiroshige, and Goshun.

The rise of education during the seventeenth and eighteenth centuries also encouraged many of the Daimyos who had been humbled by the Shogunate to obtain intellectual ammunition against that institution. The Lord of Mito, for example, from 1661 to 1700 encouraged historical research which showed that the Imperial Family had been weakened by the usurpation of its power by the Shogunate. The Mito family continued to finance and support studies designed to weaken the legitimate power of the Shogunate, though not to increase that of the Imperial Family. From 1830 on, the Lord of Mito issued an appeal for the abolition of the Shogunate and the introduction of political as well as social reforms in the country. The Mito branch was supported by various other feudal lords, who felt that both they and the peasants had been impoverished by the oppressive taxation of the Shogunate. The peasants were suffering a series of bad rice harvests; and the lords felt that unless the Shogunate were removed, Japan would be taken over by Russia, England, or France. The outbreak of the Opium War in 1840 [2] convinced many of the younger feudal lords, and their elders as well, that steps must be taken

[2] See following section on China for an explanation of the Opium War.

to prevent Japan from being humiliated as China had been. The younger and poorer Samurai, who formed the majority of the students in the higher schools at that time and whose learning had given them an important voice in the councils of the various clans, insisted that Japan had to learn from the West. To weaken the Shogunate, they supported efforts to back the Emperor. The more powerful clans backed attempts to do away with Japan's exclusion policies; they believed that only by opening her ports could she save her economy and defend herself against the West.

Contrary to stories on television or in the movies, the arrival of Commodore Perry at Uraga Bay in 1853 did not account for the opening of contacts between Japan and the West. Japan had been in the stream of Western education, science, and technology from the seventeenth century on. Commodore Perry merely hastened the overthrow of the weak Shogunate and the beginning of the modernization of Japan.

Those who plotted the destruction of the Shogunate were the lords who had never forgiven the Shogunate for having humiliated them by cutting down their power, and thus their status. It was not they, however, who led Japan to become a modern industrial state. The Government of Japan in the period immediately after 1868, when the Shogunate was overthrown, was in the hands of young intellectuals who had been students of the West. Many of them had even been abroad, although this had been expressly forbidden by the Shogunate. They helped create modern Japan, but they could do so only with the tacit approval of their elders and their clans. (At no time during the nineteenth century was the structure of authority within the clans ever challenged.)

In the period between 1868 and 1914, Japanese statesmen ranged far and wide for their institutional forms. From Germany came their constitution and concepts of law. From France came the educational system of elementary and secondary schools. From Great Britain and the United States came their business and industrial structure.

From 1868 to 1912 in the early years of the Meiji Restoration (named after the emperor under whose auspices Japan was reformed), the Government would build an enterprise and staff it with foreign technicians and managers or with Japanese who had been abroad. When the plant was running smoothly, the Government would sell it at a low subsidized price to the new Japanese industrialists, who came from the merchant, the Samurai, and the Daimyo classes. In the early formative years of Japan's industrialization, emphasis was placed upon those industries and means of transportation that could be used to build up Japan's military strength.

The new government officials, military officers, financiers, and entrepreneurs came from the wealthy peasant class in the villages, from the families of the powerful Daimyos, from court nobles, and from the merchants in the cities. The largest number, however, came from the Samurai. More than 67 percent of government officials, 83 percent of the new army and navy officers, 44 percent of the new entrepreneurs, almost half of the corporate executives, and over one-third of the financiers were sons of Samurai. The Samurai managed Japan for their clans after 1868 and gave themselves and their sons the leading positions in government, in the military services, and in the new industries. The reforms of 1868 were carried on by the younger Samurai of lower rank on behalf of their elders, who accepted this complete transformation of Japan. (In Japanese fashion, the decisions were made by the younger men and passed up to the elders with the request that they approve.)

Within twenty-six years after the decision of the powerful feudal clans to make Japan into a modern state, the reorganized navy defeated China in a short war and annexed Formosa (Taiwan). Ten years later, the navy severely damaged the Imperial Russian fleet off the coast of Japan, while the army fought the Russians to a standstill on the plains of Manchuria. Between 1905 and 1918, Japan took over the southern Manchurian ports, Korea, and South Sakhalin, the former German concession of Shantung, and assumed control over the German Marianas and Caroline Islands in the South Pacific. During World War I, Japan became an important industrial supplier to both the United States and Great Britain.

Japan was achieving a position as one of the great military powers, but other currents were at work besides those of militarism and the nationalist desire to make Japan the leading power in Asia. Even in the latter part of the nineteenth century, many young Samurai wanted Japan to become intellectually rather than militarily great. Many were afraid that a large military establishment would bring back the Shogunate with its repressions and lack of respect for the dignity of the individual. Japanese students and scholars were also influenced by the waves of pacificism, democracy, liberalism, and socialism that came from other parts of the globe. Christianity had been permitted to propagate its beliefs after the Meiji Restoration, and hundreds of thousands of converts were made among the middle and upper classes in the population. It was considered more progressive to be a Christian than to be a Buddhist or a Shintoist.

The older generals in Japan during the nineteenth and early twentieth centuries had come from the Samurai class, with its close links to businessmen, government officials, and educated elites. In the 1920's the new officers began to come from peasant and small-town merchant and artisan backgrounds. For the sons of peasants, the army offered opportunities to rise in the social scale and to acquire economic security as well. The new products of the military schools reflected the peasant prejudice against the businessman in the cities and against the intellectual in the universities. When universal male suffrage was inaugurated in 1925, the aristocrats and Samurai lost out to the peasants, artisans, and small-town merchants and officials, who gave their support to the more authoritarian nationalist groups in politics and supported the bid of the younger army officers to power. The new class of businessmen, who came from the Samurai, Daimyo, and wealthy merchant classes, were more interested in profits and domestic status than in militarism and the expensive acquisition of a colonial empire; politically, they were anti-militarist.

Totalitarianism of the Left as well as of the Right increased steadily among the frustrated members of the lower classes, who wanted a higher standard of living, a greater recognition from those with power, and political channels through which to vent their discontent. Better health facilities in the rural areas had led to overpopulation. Unemployment increased in the cities as millions of unskilled and semiliterate individuals who were displaced from the farms found few opportunities for their labor. As a result, the assertions of the extreme militarists and nationalists that it was necessary to create a new co-prosperity sphere in Asia found a receptive ear among many in both rural and urban areas. Assassinations, terror, and mystical appeals to the Emperor cult helped bring the nationalists to power. Gradually, the liberal elements among the businessmen lost out or acceded to the will of the new totalitarians.

Japan After 1945

When World War II ended, Japan was in the unenviable position of being completely dependent upon the country that had defeated her. During the closing months of the war, incendiary bombs had burned most Japanese cities to a fine ash, excepting the ancient capital of Kyoto, which was spared because of its irreplaceable architectural treasures. Two atomic bombs had turned Hiroshima and Nagasaki into holocausts in which few buildings or people survived. In Tokyo, Osaka, Nagoya, and Kobe, the blackened, roofless shells of ferroconcrete buildings stood like rigid corpses in the destroyed business sections. Surrounding them were empty spaces stretching for miles in every direction—only a few charred boards remained of the tile-roofed, unpainted, and flimsy houses, which had sheltered millions inside their paper-thin walls.

The goals of the American military occupation had been to remake Japan into a democratic country, with the yardstick for democracy generally being that which existed in the Scandinavian countries, Great Britain, and the United States. The American occupation fitted unknowingly into the pattern of the Shogunate. The seven years of the American occupation became known as the "MacArthur Period," as one speaks of the Heian, the Tokugawa, or the Meiji Period. In the minds of tens of millions of Japanese, General MacArthur was the new military Shogun, whose powers came from the Emperor. (After Japan's defeat, the Emperor exercised his theoretical right—the first time that it had been used since the fourteenth century—to advise the nation in its peril. He urged the people to put the war behind them and to obey the country's new military authorities.) Women were given the vote; civil rights were promulgated; labor unions were organized (they had never been free in the prewar period); the school system was reformed; Shintoism was separated from the state; the rigid family system was modified; large-scale industry and commerce, which had been in the hands of the Zaibatsu, or family cartels, were parceled out; and a land reform was initiated that made millions of farmers out of former tenant-peasants.

The reforms effected by the American military became part of Japanese political culture. Education was opened to all, and university enrollment today has increased to more than fifteen times its prewar figures. An opposition political party exists in Japan. Academic freedom is widespread, and the pacifism that was initially encourged by the American military is still strong enough to prevent any great growth of the military spirit. With all of its faults (the chief one being that of arrogance), the American military occupation did succeed, by authoritarian means, in bringing the Japanese back to their prewar path of liberalism and parliamentarianism. As a result, the totalitarian extremes of Communism and Fascism have had only a minute following in recent years.

Despite the American occupation, which lasted over seven years, traffic still moves on the left side of the road, as it did before the war and as it does in Great Britain and as it did until 1963 in Sweden. The introduction of apple pie and doughnuts does not offset the fact that most recent influences in food have come from France, Germany, and the Scandinavian countries rather than from the United States.

The right-wing labor unions look to Great Britain rather than to Germany or the United States for ideological inspiration. The Socialist party is a strange conglomeration of followers, somewhat as if the British Labor party and the French Communist party were to combine in a single political unit. The Liberal Democratic party is more tradition-minded than either the American Democratic or Republican parties, and in its conservatism it approaches the British Conservative party rather than the self-styled conservatives of the United States. The socialism of the Japanese left-wing labor unions, such as Sohyo, comes close in point of view to that of the Communist-dominated French General Confederation of Workers, although Sohyo is not actually under Communist control. The political attitudes of the Japanese intellectuals are much closer to the French than to their American, British, or German colleagues. As in France, the belief has existed among the educated Japanese elites that the Left represents progress and humanitarianism, while the Right symbolizes reaction and obscurantism. Again like the French, most Japanese intellectuals see America more as a danger to their cultural interests than a help. One can say that most intellectuals in Japan are socialist in political orientation, anti-American, pro-Chinese mainland, and antagonistic to the Soviet Union. France is looked upon as their intellectual home.

In general, most Japanese tend to see themselves as more similar to the British than to the Americans. British virtues appeal strongly to the Japanese. Both countries have traditions of feudalism as well as of mobile aristocracies. Both need to export to live since both are islands with few important mineral resources. Both have been industrialized by the same poorer relations of agricultural yeomen. Both have felt a need to turn to the continents that face their shorelines to seek a sense of identity. And both are extremely conscious of the existence of the United States as a force they must live with but which they would like to influence.

Transitional Japan

Japan is going through a transitional stage wherein old loyalties are breaking up, and two separate cultures exist in the minds of the youth. There is the sense of obligation that one owes to parents, family, neighborhood, peer group, and those in positions of authority. In the past, there were various categories of obligations; and those to a parent were considered somewhat different from those to one's teachers, employer, or temporal authorities. The individual owed a lifelong debt to those who made him what he was. In Japan in the past, the individual's own merits did not matter; what did matter was the family to which he belonged. Individuals received positions and favors on the basis of family friendships, influence, and class. The top positions in government and in industry for a long time have gone to the graduates of the Imperial Tokyo University (to which only one in eight applicants was admitted) whose families were influential enough to pull strings for them. Children of less fortunate parents were at a great handicap in entering the more favored universities or industries after graduation for they had no one in high places to speak for them or to write necessary letters of recommendation.

On the other hand, a new culture is arising in which adolescents are being encouraged by their peer group to consider their own personalities and interests first and to decry loyalties to superiors as well as to families. Formerly, the individual felt himself completely subordinated to his family, his neighborhood, his superiors, and finally to the Emperor as the sacred embodiment of the nation. The older generation, especially in the rural areas, still feel these loyalties strongly; but the younger people, particularly in the cities, are forging new identifications and loyalties to their labor union, occupation, political party, or association.

Women have gained immeasurably from the social revolution that has taken place since 1945. In a poll taken in 1963, 49 percent of the men questioned said that they would prefer to be women if they could be born

again, while only 44 percent of the women said that they would like to
be men if they could be reborn.[3] The wife's role within the family is by
no means a submissive one, except formally to her husband, whom she
must respect as the head of the family. She is expected to give in to her
husband; but she has her own ways of getting around him, as do women
in other parts of the world. Although women in rural areas still ask their
husbands for money to buy even the smallest and least expensive items,
in the cities workers' wives handle the finances for the family and even
dole out allowances to their husbands. Few women in Japan would care
to take over the responsible male role; most enjoy being wives and mothers. Even the relationships of the sons are closer with mothers than with
fathers. In general, women in educated middle-class circles use their rights
more than their sisters in the rural areas. Today women take their places
in public and professional life as social equals to men. Like American
women, however, most prefer to make their careers in the home.

The Standard of Living

The Japanese housewife suffers from a low standard of living and poor
facilities. Even though the per capita income in Japan has more than
tripled since the war, most of the added income has gone into the purchase of appliances rather than into better housing. Under the primitive
conditions of most Japanese kitchens, it takes at least two hours to prepare a simple meal.

Despite the industrialization that has come to Japan during the past
100 years and the changes that have taken place in the physical aspects
of the business sections of the cities, the Japanese home has undergone
little change during that time. Even in the cities of Tokyo and Osaka,
with their millions of inhabitants, most of the houses are small frame
ones of flimsy construction on tiny plots of land. With the exception of
having electricity, they are little different in appearance from the houses
of 1868. Flimsy construction will continue to be employed until the
standard of living doubles and triples again, as it undoubtedly will by
the end of this century. Incomes need to be higher to allow the purchase
of those building materials necessary in the construction of houses that
are warmer in winter and more convenient for cooking, bathing, and the
entertainment of visitors. For the workers, apartments in large-scale developments offer more efficient use of land than the individual building
of tiny houses on small plots in cities of a million or more inhabitants.
Until now, the increase in real wages has gone into more varied food;
television sets; motorcycles; and recreation, including tens of thousands of
coffee houses, an equally large number of bars, and numerous pinball

[3] *The Des Moines Register,* July 17, 1963.

machine parlors, where hundreds of thousands stand glued throughout the day before their machines in the hope of winning one of the prizes offered. Tomorrow, the increased standard of living will result in better housing, improved social services, and more consumption in appliances and equipment of all kinds.

Future Trends

Japan is now the fifth most highly industrialized country in the world (after the United States, the Soviet Union, Great Britain, and Germany), with a steel production of over 40 million tons (even larger than that of Great Britain or Germany), an expanding electronics industry, and shipbuilding yards second to none. She educates all the engineers and scientists she can use, although the numbers are still not high enough for future needs; and she has an ample supply of managerial and entre-preneurial skills. Japan is handicapped, however, by the fact that only one percent of her industries are large enough and wealthy enough to afford continuous research on future products. Because the nation is de-pendent upon the outside world for most of her raw materials, she must work continuously upon improving her competitive position in world markets. Although Japan has been able to move away from production that requires an intensive use of cheap labor, she needs to expend more effort in developing new products to compensate for her lack of raw ma-terials. During the next twenty-five to thirty years, Japan will be com-pelled to fall back on her own ingenuity to develop a new technology that will make her independent of her present need to import and export.

Productivity in the modern world is a combination of management and technological skills made operational by ongoing research dealing with everyday problems. Productivity is geared to attitudes that assume continuous improvement in management skills as well as technological changes in production. Japanese industrialists have identified themselves with this point of view. They know that they must automate, using much higher levels of skill than they have used thus far and emphasizing origi-nality of design and product, efficiency, and low cost.

The labor unions are pessimistic because they do not know where they are going, and neither do the literary intellectuals who are seeking purpose and goals. The scientists and industrialists, on the other hand, are the most self-confident and optimistic groups in Japan today. Both are certain that Japan can reach her goals of higher educational levels and of a relative and gradually obtained absence of deprivation. (Pov-erty is still present among large numbers of the old, the unskilled, and the rural inhabitants.) The scientists are convinced that the chemistry of synthetics will enable Japan to meet her basic needs, including an adequate food supply supplemented by the common elements found abundantly in and around the country.

The industrialists, scientists, and government officials who are concerned with the future of Japan know that their problems can be solved only through intensive research and increased management skills. Japan is three times the size of New York State with six times the population. Only 18 percent of the land surface is cultivable; the rest of the country contains mountainous slopes and poor soil, most of it more suitable for forests than for crops. A moderate climate plus intensive fertilization make possible two to three crops per year. On a one-crop basis, this means the equivalent of double the cultivable land surface. The seas are a rich source of protein food, and they are insufficiently utilized at present to supplement protein deficiencies in the Japanese diet.

Despite the enjoyment of the highest standard of living in Asia, the Japanese are still undernourished. Their diet is deficient in protein, vitamins, and calcium. Their average caloric intake is 2,000 units per day, compared with more than 3,200 in the United States. Milk consumption is very low; and the diet is poor in meat, eggs, and even fish. Meals consist mostly of rice, with beans, a little bit of fish, seaweed, and vegetables.

Japan is now self-sufficient in rice despite a population of over 95 million. (This figure has become stabilized, because Japan has one of the lowest birthrates in the world. The natural increase in population is less than one percent per year as compared with over 1.7 percent for the United States.) A good part of the peasantry has slowly been transformed into farmers, who have been able to increase their output by at least 5 percent per year. Although their land averages little more than two acres, it is cultivated so intensively that even on a tiny plot of this size, a farmer in the plains can earn more than $600 per year—a far higher productive average than in any other country in the world. Such a farmer owns a radio and perhaps even has a telephone. He probably belongs to a rural cooperative which rents out machinery to its members. On a plot of about 3.7 acres, a farmer with an income of about $1,500 per year may own a television set and a tractor, harrows, and plows, which he can then rent to his neighbors. More than one-third of the farmers own at least one simple farm machine; most have two or more. At least one-third own television sets. All the farmers have had enough schooling above the fourth grade to be considered literate. Only one son will stay with the father; the others will need to make their way in the city.

The agricultural revolution continues as some of the small farmers buy out neighboring lands, and as the latest agricultural techniques are used in conjunction with large amounts of chemical fertilizer and improved seeds. As time goes on, more chickens and milk cows will be raised, although production of beef will always be on a small scale because of the shortage of good grazing land.

With an overpopulation (millions of repatriates returned at the end of World War II from Korea, Manchuria, and China) that has become stabilized, with few natural resources, with inadequate capitalization (Japanese industry is spotty in its development), and with the necessity of looking to other countries to make up for the deficits in food and raw materials for industry, Japan views her future through somewhat blurred eyes. Her standard of living can rise only by greater industrialization (in the past fifteen years, the industrial growth rate of more than 8 percent has been one of the highest in the world), and a large share of the profits must go into intensified scientific research necessary if Japan is to become less dependent upon others.

The industrial managers know that Japan cannot survive as a low labor-cost country, because as the standard of living rises labor will become progressively more expensive and automation will become as important for her mass industries as it is for those of the United States. Thousands of small family-owned industries, now dependent upon big industry for their business as well as their specialization, must be transformed into efficient producers of new products, able to meet competition for markets in all parts of the world. (Basically, the largest market for Japan—as for India and China—is the internal one, the export market being tied up with Japan's overdependence upon other countries for too many of her needs.) Japan's present role is that of a manufacturing country, transforming raw materials she buys abroad into finished goods that she must also sell abroad in order to buy enough raw materials for further needs. She depends upon the goodwill of the rest of the world to stay in business; she cannot afford to antagonize any of her present or potential customers. For this reason, Japan needs to become more self-sufficient in order to acquire more self-confidence and pride in her world role. At present, Japan has not been able to develop a role commensurate with her industrial power and her large population.

Japan has left her past behind her. In the future, she will become an even more urbanized industrial society, with a small percentage of mechanized farmers growing the food that the country will need for its stable population of a little over 100 million. There will be a high degree of technological and scientific sophistication and a standard of living much higher than she enjoys today. Beyond this, few Japanese care to look, except to agree that some sort of welfare state will undoubtedly be established.

The transitional phase that Japan is experiencing was expressed so well by a famous Japanese editorialist in an interview with the author in 1958 that little can be added to it:

We stand today half and half between Asia and Europe. Historically and geographically, we are part of Asia, but industrially and culturally we are part of the Western world. Our assimilation of European culture has been extremely rapid, and has been increasing in a crescendo fashion during the past sixty years. The Japan of the past—with its Geisha girls, rickshaws, and paper lanterns hanging from quaint doorways—is gone and it can never come back. In its place is a Japan which lives in two worlds and sees no contradiction between either.

On one side is the world which is still Japanese: our religious sentiments, our family feelings, our attitudes toward our children, our mentality, our personality, and so on. No matter how modern our young people may be, they still have their marriages arranged for them by their families. Our houses are slowly becoming Westernized, but they are still the last physical remnant left to us of our Japanese past.

On the other side is the modern world of Western-type office buildings, the latest electrical appliances and cars, modern clothing, television, and advanced means of communication through which the scientific and technological world comes rushing into our Japanese homes. Our music and literature are now in a transitional phase, half-Western and half-Japanese. More and more we are becoming part of the West.

You can't take in industrialization and the spirit of science and technology without taking in the thinking which goes with them. Other things are coming in from the West too. Our political thinking, our hopes, and our dreams are all tinged with Western overtones.

We are now in the middle of our transitional period. We do not know what sort of future we will have. We do know, however, that we feel more helpless than at any other period in our history. We are worried about the nuclear future because we see no means of defending ourselves against possible atomic fallout if there is a nuclear war elsewhere. We can only be passive spectators as horror after horror may be developed for future generations to deal with. We know that our defense efforts will not influence the course of history, which is why there is so little enthusiasm for an army in Japan. What good will it be?

There is a yearning for something better in Japan. We are lonelier at present than we have ever been. Urbanization is now part of the fabric of Japan. We are becoming detached from our families, from the extended group which gave us a sense of security in the past. We must now live for ourselves, and yet we are still confused by our past teachings which insisted that we must live for others, that we must think of the family rather than of ourselves, and that our sense of belonging came from being attached to Japan. All these are now going.

Despite the changes, we still feel optimistic about the future. We believe that people are good, and that they did not fall from grace in the dim past. We accept the principle that man is innately kind and considerate, but that his thinking is faulty and he creates evil conditions out of his own lack of knowledge. We are convinced that in principle the nature of man is not bad.

We need a purpose, a sense of idealism as well as a higher economic standard for the future. We shall get the latter, but we hope that we shall get the former in cooperation with other nations so that together we can build a world in which there is freedom, peace, and a sense of security for the common man and his children. This is what we would like to see in a future in which Japan is a friend to all and an enemy to none.

CHINA

Social Life in China of the Past

Although great inventions had been made sporadically in China during the more than 3,000 years of its existence, there had been no organized attempts to build upon them. Printing, for example, was known to the Chinese centuries before it was reinvented in Western Europe, but it led to no diffusion of literacy to the lower classes. The knowledge of gunpowder and cannon in the thirteenth and fourteenth centuries did not lead, as it did in Europe, to the improvement of mining techniques and the growth of more efficient foundries.

China until recently was a self-satisfied nation, where more than 95 percent of the population were self-sufficient villagers, tilling their lands efficiently but in roughly the same manner as their forefathers. Above them was a large population of land-owning gentry, out of which the ancient mandarins, or administrative officials, were recruited by examination. The top administrative positions were not hereditary, as they were in India and Japan, for both theoretically and actually the ministers who advised the emperors in the past were selected from the mandarin class of administrative scholars.

Although comparisons have been made between ancient Rome and China, China in fact has been like no other power or civilization. Her villagers were not warriors; carrying arms was never given the status it had in Japan, India, or even Rome. The scholarly gentry represented the highest level of social status next to that of the emperor, who ruled with a mandate from heaven (which meant that revolution was permissible when the emperor was unable to rule benignly). China had no city like Rome with its large slave population and elements from other urban centers and from the far corners of the Empire. With the exception of the small handicraft centers around the court and those situated in the various regional capitals (none of these was large in population), most of the artisans of China lived in villages, where they were usually part-time peasants. The merchants lived in the regional administrative centers from whence they traveled to the villages to purchase their goods. The traders were domiciled in the larger villages, making purchases for the merchants from the peasants and artisans. The Chinese privileged gentry cannot be compared with the Roman senators, for though both were landlord farmers, the Romans were more interested in the actual tilling of the soil. The Chinese gentry felt that all physical labor, or even supervision of the fields, was socially degrading for them.

Land in China was privately owned rather than cooperatively shared as in India. Since the peasant through his taxes and rent bore the burden of supporting the administration, the scholars, and the gentry, he had to learn to farm with more intensive hand labor as his family grew more numerous and available plots became restricted by their high price. Throughout Chinese history the peasants have angrily rebelled against their high taxes and rents when a series of bad harvests made their food supply precarious. At such times, the peasant and his family had to live on starvation rations until the next harvest in order to squeeze the heavy taxes and rents from their small food production. Many peasants in the past sold their children into slavery to the gentry or even practiced infanticide in order to cut down on the burden of feeding too many mouths in hard times. (Old parents were given more considerate treatment than children.)

The lot of the peasant in China was hard, though no more difficult than that of his brothers in Japan or India. He was illiterate and lived in a world of his own which contained his folk religion, medicine, and implements. His mental horizon was limited to the corners of his tiny plot, his family, and his village. The vast majority of the peasants never traveled more than five miles from their home villages at any time; distant places did not concern them any more than the doings of the court of the mandarins in the regional centers. The dream of every peasant was to save enough from the sale of his produce, after taxes had been paid, to buy another small adjoining plot. Land represented wealth and security; a landless peasant was considered little better off than a beggar.

Population

Even in Neolithic times China had a relatively large population for its habitable area. As the peasants became more industrious, the increase in population kept up with the increase in food, until finally the land became so subdivided that only tiny plots remained. There were no urban centers to drain away the surplus population, and the younger sons of poor peasants with no land of their own were compelled to become outlaws or soldiers seeking their fortune through force of arms. Chinese population experts have estimated that by 1700 China had over 150 million inhabitants and that by the end of the eighteenth century the number had doubled to over 300 million. By 1850 the population of peasant China had reached over 430 million,[4] far more than the country could handle comfortably with its antiquated agricultural techniques. The lack of roads and cheap transportation meant that certain regions would have famines while others a few hundred miles away might have a surplus.

The shortage of land, periodic famines, and high taxation caused the peasants to lead many a bloody revolt against the gentry in the hope of seizing their lands. They were crushed time and time again, but as poor

---

[4] See, for example, Ho, Ping-ti, *Studies on the Population of China, 1368–1953* (Cambridge, Mass., Harvard University Press, 1959), pp. 281–282.

harvests followed one another in succession and the peasants were still squeezed for their taxes, frustration would lead to blind revolt, which again would end in defeat. The peasants could not organize themselves or their efforts for any sustained defense against the troops from the regional centers. The presence of troops meant an increase in taxes to pay for them, and this led again to a smoldering discontent, which was never very far from the surface.

The Influence of Christianity

After the eleventh and twelfth centuries, China had been somewhat influenced by Islam. Large numbers of Turki-speaking inhabitants living in the far west of the country were converted to that religion, although people in the more heavily populated parts of the country were scarcely affected. Christianity first entered China with the Nestorians from Persia in the seventh century, but its influence was minimal. Roman Catholicism came with the Jesuits in the middle of the sixteenth century, but unlike Japan where Christian missionary efforts encountered a good deal of receptivity, the number of converts in China was small and mainly among the lower classes. The Pure Land Sect of Buddhism played far less of a role in China than it had in Japan, with the result that little parallelism with Roman Catholicism existed in China.[5] During the sixteenth century in Japan, many Daimyos and Samurai had become fervent followers of Roman Catholicism, but in China the gentry and the scholars held themselves aloof from the movement. The Manchu emperors were somewhat tolerant of the Jesuits and used them to build fortifications, palaces, water fountains, and even clocks. In the court, however, few mandarins felt the need to exchange their Buddhism-Confucianism-Taoism for Christianity, which initially was exclusive and refused to let itself be joined to other beliefs, although the Jesuits maintained that family rites honoring ancestors and public ceremonies to Confucius were civil occasions which did not conflict with Christian belief. (At the instigation of the Dominicans, this was denied by the Pope in 1715, and the Jesuits were forbidden to hold such a position.) At no time was Christianity a threat to Chinese traditional beliefs, as it had been in Japan.

The Impact of European Technology

China in the eighteenth century influenced European art and design with its porcelain, paintings, furniture, and techniques, but Europe had

---

[5] Ancestor worship doubtless precluded a need for a religion of salvation.

little that the Chinese wanted in return. The Chinese scholars and administrative officials were convinced that Europe had nothing superior to offer them; they had no desire to have the cheap textiles or clocks of Europe when their own artisans could furnish them with much finer brocaded silks and furniture. Unlike the Japanese, who saw European technology and science as important answers to many of their puzzling questions, the Chinese asked no questions, had no curiosity about the outside world, and were quite convinced that their Celestial Civilization could not possibly learn anything from the European barbarians.

During the seventeenth and eighteenth centuries, trade was concentrated at Canton, which was the only port that the Imperial Manchu Government permitted foreign merchants to use. For most of the seventeenth and eighteenth centuries, trade was a one-way street, with tea, fine Chinese silks, porcelain, bronze, delicate scrolls, and artwork going to Europe, but with little coming back except cheap textiles and cotton for the lower classes. Unlike Japan, there was no interest in scientific books dealing with, for example, comparative anatomy, astronomy, navigation, mathematics, or any of the fields that the West had developed by this time.

The Interest of the West in China

As the population increased during the eighteenth century, the plots of land tilled by the Chinese peasants became progressively smaller. Taxes and rents went up as the families of the gentry and the administrative mandarins also became numerous and more money was needed for their support. The administrative officials attempted to squeeze as much as they could from the peasants and from the merchants engaged in exporting Chinese goods through Canton.

The mandarin system encouraged the system of "squeeze." Each lowly official had to offer tempting gifts to the officials above him, who, as "sons to fathers," would, it was hoped, treat their "sons" with affection, promote them, and see that they obtained land cheaply to support their families and provide an adequate income for them after retirement. The mandarin system could not countenance change, for change would upset its oligarchic bureaucratic power and balance of existence in which all change and decisions had to be made by the ministers on top and percolate downward. This was in contrast to the Japanese system whereby decisions were made by the middle groups of officials and administrators and sent upward for the top to approve as its policy, a procedure that largely operates in Japanese business and industry even today. The mandarins had no desire to legislate themselves or their system out of power. Change, if it did come, would have to come at the top.

Trapped by the worsening conditions in China, which brought an increasingly oppressive environment, the peasants and artisans could either withdraw by taking opium, which was native-grown and had been used by the Chinese for hundreds of years, or revolt against the gentry in an outward gesture of defiance. Although many chose the second outlet (peasant revolts disturbed the peace of the Chinese countryside throughout the eighteenth and nineteenth centuries), the large majority took to opium to help them forget their daily frustrations, the low quality of their lives, and their lack of self-confidence.

The rise in opium consumption created a shortage of that drug in China. The English merchants at Canton, who had been unhappy that trade with China was a one-way street, were now able to do something about importing a commodity that was in short supply and for which there was a demand. Large plantations in India were planted to the poppy, and refined opium sent to Canton brought back large amounts of Chinese silver in return. Opium and cotton from India now tipped the scales, and the Chinese merchants became debtors to the British and other Europeans. Although the Manchu Government ordered a stop to the import of opium and even confiscated 30,000 chests of that drug in Canton, nothing was done to cut down the quantity of opium grown in China by important segments of the gentry. In consequence, Great Britain considered this an affront to her "natural" right to trade freely; and in a short war in 1840 she defeated the poorly trained, equipped, and led Chinese troops. As reparations, Great Britain received Hong Kong and Kowloon, and suzerainty over Burma and Nepal, which had been tributary vassals of the Chinese Emperor. (The Chinese authorities had a value definition of the role of a tributary vassal: any country trading with China was felt to be paying tribute at the same time. As a consequence, the extent of the Chinese Empire in the nineteenth century was based more upon China's assumed right to it—much as Spain and Portugal claimed huge areas for their monarchs in the early sixteenth century—than upon any actual physical occupation of that land.)

China now became a prize for the other European powers, and later for Japan, to capture and divide up. France and Great Britain received rights of sovereign settlement along the coast and even in the interior. Czarist Russia took over Manchu territory extending eastward from the Amur and Ussuri rivers to the Pacific (including the area of present-day Vladivostok) and pushed forward her claim for ports in Manchuria. Later on, Germany demanded and received a long lease on the peninsula of Shantung. France invaded Indo-China in the 1860's, and in 1883 replaced China's weak suzerainty over that territory with its own. In 1894 the ineffective Chinese navy was badly defeated by the new Japanese fleet, and as reparations Japan insisted upon the annexation of Formosa and upon her right to participate in extraterritorial settlement in the coastal and inland cities of China. (Under the principle of extraterritoriality, nationals of other countries had the right to live under their own laws and to be tried by their own rather than Chinese courts.)

The Taiping Rebellion and the Boxers

The occasional peasant revolts led to an extremely bloody one in 1850 when a Chinese convert to Christianity led a rebellion against the Emperor, under the slogan of "Heavenly Peace," or Taiping. The revolt lasted for more than fourteen years, and at least 40 million people are estimated to have died as a result. Under their leader, who called himself a younger brother of Jesus Christ, the rebels besieged the gates of Peking and laid waste to countless homes of the gentry and the mandarins. Land was redistributed to the peasants; slavery, prostitution, the binding of feet, polygamy, and arranged marriages were all declared abolished; and all sale of opium was prohibited. The rebellion was finally put down by Western mercenary soldiers led by British and American officers. Its result was to shake the foundations of Chinese civilization as they had never been shaken before.

Within forty years, or in 1899, the seeds of the Taiping rebellion, carried by various anti-foreign secret societies, led to another full-scale attack, this time against the European, American, and Japanese embassies in Peking. The fighters went under the name of I Ho Chuan (Righteous, Harmonious Fists), or Boxers. Secretly supported by the Chinese Empress Dowager and fighting with primitive weapons, these military groups of peasant background were defeated by the soldiers sent in by Great Britain, France, Italy, Germany, Austria, Russia, the United States, and Japan. China was now forced to pay a high indemnity and to agree to the stationing of foreign troops in Peking to protect the various foreign embassies there. American marines, for example, remained in Peking until the beginning of the Second World War. The United States used its share of the Chinese Boxer indemnity to pay for scholarships in American universities for Chinese students.

The Beginning of Republican China

By 1912 the Manchu dynasty fell, having long outlived its usefulness. It could not unify the country against the foreign invaders who had taken over the coastal ports and who regulated traffic into the interior, nor could it transform Chinese resentment at the country's humiliation into a nationalism strong enough to drive the foreigners out. China was too poor and too much of a preindustrial anachronism in a world where

European powers were using technology and science as weapons to keep themselves strong against those who were weak.

The Chinese nationalist revolution against the Imperial Regime was led by a Western-educated Chinese, Sun Yat-sen; but he had neither the force of arms nor a strong enough following to be able to weld the country into a united whole. As a result, China after 1912 was controlled by foreigners and warlords. Although China entered World War I on the Allied side, she was given no rewards for doing so; instead of being permitted to win back the concessions held by the defeated Germans, the Germans' privileges were given to Japan. Only a tiny handful of educated Chinese who had a knowledge of the technological and scientific civilization were on hand to initiate the transformation of the hundreds of millions of peasant Chinese and the few million poverty-stricken urban dwellers into the builders of an industrial age in China. Although thousands of Chinese students had been sent abroad after 1901 to learn the technology, the weaponry, the business, and the science of the West, they were too few in number to make much of a dent upon the rest of the population. Although dozens upon dozens of mission schools and colleges were opened after 1914 by the Americans, the British, and the French, their products filled only part of the intellectual vacuum that existed in China.

In the meanwhile, China was divided into foreign concessions and military warlord fiefs as various generals, brigands, and local administrators attempted to take advantage of the chaos that followed the fall of the Manchu dynasty to consolidate their own local rule. Combinations of warlords or single strongmen covered China from one end to the other, destroying those who stood in their way or who refused to accept their rule. The warlords conscripted the sons of the peasants as their soldiers, confiscated the peasants' surplus food and stock to feed their marauding armies, and exacted tribute from gentry and merchant alike. One rule they all observed, or attempted to observe, was not to molest the missionaries and priests from Europe and the United States lest they bring punishment from these countries down upon themselves. It was easier for the adventurer-lords to fight Chinese than foreigners.

Meanwhile, British, French, Japanese, Russian, and American capital financed the opening of factories in the coastal cities and the construction of railroads, roundhouses, and railroad shops for the maintenance of the locomotives and rolling stock. The British took over the customs for the almost nonexistent government of China; and the Japanese took the place of the Russians in Manchuria, where they opened numerous coal and iron ore mines to supply their steel mills and blast furnaces both in Japan and in Manchuria. The South Manchurian Railway, which had been taken from the Russians, was modernized; and branch lines were opened to all regions rich in soil and minerals. Manchuria, which had been virtually empty in the 1860's, began to fill up with Chinese peasants migrating from the north in search of land they could till. By the turn of the century, the Chinese migration had risen to millions as Chinese in other parts of the country left to escape the chaos and deprivations of their villages.

During the latter half of the nineteenth century, Chinese from Canton began to migrate to the United States (Chinese laborers helped build the Central Pacific Railroad between 1865 and 1869), the Philippines, Indonesia, Singapore, Malaya, Thailand, and Burma. In the United States, the Chinese were restricted to a few occupations. In the countries of Southeast Asia and in the islands of the South Pacific, they became the shopkeepers, the traders, the merchants, and even the artisans. The Overseas Chinese slowly accumulated fortunes, which enabled them to educate their sons in Western universities and sometimes to build small plants in the safe settlements of foreigners in the cities of Shanghai, Hankow, or Tientsin. These Chinese became more literate than those who had stayed behind. As marginal people living among strangers, they became very sensitive to the humiliations that they and their fellow countrymen received as Chinese. It was the Overseas Chinese who, with funds and even manpower, supported the Nationalist movement of Sun Yat-sen until his death in 1925.

The Struggle Between the Communists and the Nationalists

Despite the previous existence of a Nationalist party, Mao Tse-tung and twelve others, with assistance from the Soviet Union, founded a Communist party in Shanghai in 1921, with initial strength coming from students and middle-class young people. In an attempt to gain support from the young Union of Soviet Socialist Republics, Sun Yat-sen in 1922 supported an alliance between the Communist party and his Kuomintang, or Nationalist party. The Soviets gave their support to the Kuomintang the following year on the theory that a burgeois nationalist revolution had to precede a proletarian one. Since the Chinese population at that time was still rural, the Russians felt that there were too few workers upon whom to base a future Communist state. They believed that it was preferable to stimulate a nationalist revolt against the European and foreign powers who were then a threat to the Soviet Union and that with a nationalist victory, it would be possible to build a moderate capitalist state that would create enough workers out of peasants to make Communism eventually triumphant.

The Kuomintang at that time was centered mainly in the Canton area, since most of the Overseas Chinese had come from this region; the rest of China was in the hands of the various independent warlords. The Russians sent arms, money, military advisers, and political experts to assist the Kuomintang; and the Communists were ordered to join that movement, even though the Communist party still kept itself separate. A young follower of Sun Yat-sen, Chiang Kai-shek, who had been educated in Japan, was sent to Moscow for military and political training and upon his return was put in charge of the Russian-organized Whampoa Military Academy in Canton.

At Dr. Sun Yat-sen's death in 1925, there was a cooling off between Chiang Kai-shek and the Communists, although a definite break between the two did not occur until 1927. Chiang was convinced that China could not afford two competing political parties and that the first need was to unify the country by eliminating the warlords and the Communists. Believing the Communists to be the weaker, he started with them. Membership in the Communist party was made a criminal offense; by 1928 Chiang had caused four-fifths of the Chinese Communist party's membership to be killed, and the remainder, in order to escape extermination, went underground in the cities and rural regions of Hunan.

Chiang Kai-shek believed that it was more important and useful for him to cooperate with the rural gentry and the urban middle classes than to permit the Communists to destroy the nationalist movement by antagonizing the local Chinese elites. By 1928 he broke with his Russian advisers and expelled them, thus effectively destroying Communist strength. By attacking the Communists, Chiang found that his campaign to unify China had become easier. He used the Kuomintang to create a political machine loyal only to him, and he encouraged the various cliques within the nationalist movement to fight one another. Within ten years, or until the Japanese took the city of Peking in 1937, Chiang had been fairly successful in making himself the undisputed leader of Nationalist China.

In the meanwhile, the remaining Communists went underground in the rural areas and created guerrilla bases from which they could harass the troops of Chiang Kai-shek. They received no help from the Soviet Union, for the latter remained convinced that a successful Communist movement could not be developed out of peasants alone.

By 1929 the remainder of the Communists in South Central China had collected their small forces together, organized a minor "Soviet Republic," trained a tiny "Red Army," and instituted major land reforms in the areas under their control. It was at this time that Mao Tse-tung formulated his four rules for carrying on guerrilla warfare: (1) "When the enemy comes forward, we withdraw; (2) When the enemy withdraws, we go forward; (3) When the enemy settles down, we disturb him; and (4) When the enemy is exhausted, we fight him." By 1934 there were six separate "Soviets" with a total population of more than 9,000,000, but they were highly transitional in character. In that year, Chiang Kai-shek threw 300,000 troops against them and succeeded in driving them out of their rural-held areas. With 90,000 surviving soldiers the Communist leaders attempted to get out of the trap set for them by making a retreat of over 6,000 miles through backcountry and over high mountains to northwestern China. In 1935, after suffering great losses of men and animals, they made their new headquarters at Yenan. Here they stayed until the end of the Second World War. Then with the help of augmented forces and equipment captured from the Japanese and the Kuomintang armies, they mounted an offensive against the troops of Chiang Kai-shek and were able to drive him and his followers out of China in 1949. After that, under the the leadership of Mao Tse-tung a Communist party dictatorship was organized over the entire population.

China Leaves the Primary Civilization

The system of examinations for entrance into the bureaucratic class of mandarin administrators had been abolished in 1905, but no alternatives were organized within Chinese culture after that date to permit the hundreds of thousands of young men from the rural and urban gentry to advance themselves through education. A few thousand were sent overseas to study in the universities of Europe and the United States; a good many (like Chiang Kai-shek) were sent to Japan to study; but the overwhelming number were given few outlets for study in China.

The colleges and universities of China were not organized until after 1900, but almost immediately after their establishment they became agents of change. Reared in traditional families, the young Chinese were sent to middle (secondary) schools and to colleges, whose instruction and textbooks were in English or French and whose curricula had no room for the traditional Chinese classical learning. The schools and colleges trained young people to live in an industrialized and technological world that barely existed in China of the Civil War period. The values the young people developed led to a distaste for the Chinese world from which they had come and to a reaction against the European and American worlds for treating them as social inferiors. Being in rebellion against both their worlds, they were attracted to those radical plans for the transformation of their Chinese society that would enable them to become the intellectual equals of the Europeans, though without the physical presence of Europeans on Chinese soil.

Europe, the United States, and Japan were not wealthy enough to build up a country as populated as China. By the beginning of the twentieth century, there must have been at least 400 million people in China itself. There was little known wealth in China proper [6] and few skills that could be used to create export goods. Most of the country was agricul-

6 Oil, iron, and coal resources are now known to be enormous.

tural; illiterate but efficient peasants tilled tiny plots of land with intensive labor, few animals, and only simple tools. Any surplus food was quickly absorbed by taxes, rents, payments to moneylenders, and the increase in population.

The medical schools, colleges, technical schools, highways, railroads, industries, and communication media were financed in large part by foreign capital. More than 7,000 miles of railroad track were built by English, French, Russian, and Japanese capital. From an initial investment of some $500,000,000 in 1900, imported foreign capital came to more than $1,000,000,000 by 1904; by 1930, it had doubled again to more than $2,000,000,000. But these investments were only a drop in the bottomless bucket of China. Russian capital before 1905 and Japanese technicians, machines, and funds after that date opened up the coal and iron ore mines of Manchuria and built settlements, railroads, and industries in the central and eastern parts of the province. British and Japanese textile mills were concentrated in Shanghai. British, French, American, and Swiss capital poured into the extraterritorial settlements of Shanghai, Tientsin, Hankow, and Peking after the First World War; and American, British, and French funds opened up and financed countless colleges, technical schools, and medical schools for training Chinese students.

With the Japanese invasion of Manchuria in 1931, foreign capital, except from Japan, declined to a trickle. By 1937 the Japanese had annexed Manchuria and invaded northern China. In the next five years the Japanese occupied the entire eastern part of the country. Numerous technicians and engineers and large amounts of machinery were sent into the cities of occupied China in order to utilize Chinese labor in helping Japan fight its Pacific war. The Chinese carried on a perfunctory guerrilla war against the Japanese troops, but the Communist Eighth and Fourth armies and the Nationalist armies under Chiang Kai-shek were building up their effectives each with an eye to the destruction of the other once the war ended. Neither the Communists nor the Nationalists had any desire to weaken themselves by fighting the better equipped Japanese. Between 1943 and 1945, the Communists and the Nationalists observed a truce; but neither side trusted the other. Although the Japanese occupied the cities, railroads, and main highways, the Chinese Communists infiltrated the rural areas, which the Japanese could not control, and there laid the foundations for their eventual capture of power.

The Communists Gain Control

Unlike Chiang Kai-shek, whose main appeal was to the gentry, urban traders, merchants, financiers, and regional warlords, the Communists made the peasants their psychological target. They attempted to follow the paths laid by the peasant revolts of the past, especially the bloody Taiping rebellion. Land reform and moral puritanism went hand in hand as the local Communist units attempted to construct an organization that would appeal to the poor and landless peasants, and thus split the villages into Communist and Nationalist supporters.

Between August and October, 1945, the Communists and the Kuomintang jockeyed for position, both knowing that neither could rule a united China without completely destroying the other. Although American Marines occupied Peking and American planes ferried Kuomintang forces to the cities that the Japanese evacuated, the Chinese Communists were able to infiltrate the entire countryside, even though most of the important cities were held by the Nationalists. By 1949, Communist forces had defeated the Nationalist armies one after another and taken over the entire mainland. Chiang Kai-shek and 2,000,000 of his followers escaped to Taiwan, where they set up their Chinese Nationalist Government and vowed that they would soon return to the mainland.

When the Communists took over China in 1949, they took over one of the least industrialized nations in the world. Despite the partial industrialization of Manchuria and Shanghai, most of China was in a preindustrial stage of growth. There were only a few thousand engineers, scientists, and managers whom the Communists could use to build up their country. War, civil war, and the chaos attending both had destroyed much of the railways, rolling stock, and industry. The Soviet Union in its war of one week against Japan in Manchuria had looted that province of all the electric motors, generators, machine tools, rolling stock, and machines that its armies could transport back to the Soviet Union. (Some of their replacements were returned as a loan in the early 1950's when the Soviet Union was helping China both to fight the Korean War and to industrialize at the same time.) Compared with India in 1949, China had fewer railways, roads, communication facilities, colleges, technicians, engineers, and scientists. Although India was certainly not an industrialized country two years after her Independence in 1949, she had a much greater basis upon which to erect an industrial society than China possessed.

Even the Soviet Union had a better industrial base with a larger technical and managerial population in 1921 than China did in 1949, though both countries had been ravaged by war, famine, and civil war. It took the Soviet Union seven years after the end of the Civil War to regain its prewar industrial production; China did it in three years because the prewar base was less. Real income had been at least four times as high in the Soviet Union in 1928 (or in 1913) as it was in China in 1952. The industrial output of China in 1952 was less than that in czarist Russia during the 1890's. The Soviet Union in the early 1920's had a surplus of grain, timber, gold, and furs that could be exported to other countries for machines, technicians, engineers, and industrial plans. China had less agricultural land, a more overcrowded population, and fewer individuals trained in science and technology or equipped to direct industrialization. China began her drive for industrialization in 1952 with a per capita income of a little more than $35 per year (which indicated that most Chinese peasants lived on a subsistence level, producing very little in goods and services for the market), or less than India ($50), Nigeria ($80), or Haiti ($45).

In the Soviet Union the Five-Year Plans after 1928 actually saw a diminution in the amount of grain the Russian peasants produced. Despite mechanization the Russian peasants grew proportionately less food in the early 1960's than they had in 1913 or even 1928. The Soviet Union could make up this deficit by exporting gold, timber, furs, or manganese in return for grain. The Chinese had few reserves; and if a harvest was poor, they had to dig down into their slim reserves of luxury goods to get the foreign currency needed to pay for the imports of grain.

The Chinese Five-Year Plans

In the first Five-Year Plan, between 1953 and 1957, the Chinese Communists expected that the Soviet Union and its satellites would help their industrialization by sending them large numbers of technicians, engineers, and managers as well as factories, tools, machines, and raw materials. The Russians had supplied the Chinese Communists with weapons, tanks, and planes during the Korean War, but these were sent on loan rather than as gifts. The technicians and engineers came in large numbers, but nowhere near the figures that the Chinese wanted. Although the leadership had developed plans to make China become a great industrial nation within a couple of decades, the lack of technicians, the shortage of food supplies, and the growth of population (increasing at the rate of 15 million each year) soon forced the Chinese to slow down their industrial expansion. Bad harvests during the second Five-Year Plan, from 1957 to 1962, coupled with the withdrawal of Russian technicians and supplies in 1960 and the Soviet demand for immediate repayment of the loans made to the Chinese from 1946 to 1962, soon caused the lumbering Chinese industrialization drive to come to a halt. While many foreign observers felt that China was industrializing more rapidly than India, or even the Soviet Union in its two initial Five-Year Plans, the fact remained that China was industrializing only as fast as the Soviet Union would let her. Without Russian resources and with only her own efforts, the Chinese Communists would make progress, but not nearly as rapidly as had been originally supposed.

There is little doubt that in the ten years between 1952 and 1962,

China built more railroads than had been built in the fifty years before, more steel mills and coal mines than had been built or opened by the Japanese, more factories than had been built in the past by all the foreign powers on her soil, and more schools than had been built by missionaries, government, or private foundations. The Russians sent China over 11,000 experts, and the satellite states sent some 1,500 technicians and engineers; more than 7,000 Chinese students were sent to the Soviet Union for advanced study in its institutes and universities, and over 7,500 skilled workers were sent to Soviet factories to acquire experience that would equip them to be foremen and production supervisors. The Soviet Union supplied plans and generators for large hydroelectric plants, plus electronic equipment consisting of computers and a medium-sized atomic reactor pile and rotating accelerator, a facility in which the few Chinese physicists trained abroad were concentrated. Altogether, the Soviet Union assisted in building more than 156 large plants in heavy industry, including plants for the production of trucks, automobiles, tractors, and planes.

Although the Soviet Union and the members of its bloc helped China begin its industrialization campaign between 1952 and 1959, most of the essential and basic capital for industrialization had to come from Chinese efforts. In fact, the Chinese complained that the Soviet Union was sending as much technical assistance to India and other non-Communist nations as to her; and much of the aid to other countries was being given on interest-free or low-interest loans. Although the Chinese complained that Soviet assistance was not enough, the greatest spurts in industrialization took place when this technical assistance was made available. The Chinese had planned upon producing 18 to 20 million tons of steel a year by 1964, but actual tonnage was no more than 10 million in that year, or a little more than the steel production in India, less than one-eighth that of the Soviet Union, and one-twelfth that of the United States.

To procure even this limited help from the Soviet Union, China had to export special food and luxury goods to the Soviet Union and its bloc. For example, to get textile machinery from East Germany, the Chinese supplied that country with canned goods, cigarettes, rice, and tea. In supplying the Soviet Union and other countries with meat, rice, eggs, soybeans, edible oils, and canned fruit, China was in fact cutting down on the consumption of goods among her own peasants. In the period of the second Five-Year Plan, the Communists attempted to place the Chinese peasants in communes, thus skipping the stage of collectivization that had taken place in the Soviet Union during the early 1930's. For two years, tens of millions of peasants were made to live in large, poorly constructed dormitories, eating in mess halls and keeping their children in nurseries. The local Communist officials exaggerated agricultural production in order to please their superiors, with the result that the Government committed a larger proportion of the future grain and food production for export than actually existed. The beginning of droughts in the winter of 1959–60, followed by a series of crippling floods over large parts of China, followed again by excessively dry weather, forced the Government to give up its attempts to mechanize agriculture. Although food production was greater than it had ever been, even with the droughts and floods, the population of China was growing at a faster rate than ever before and the Government was exporting more of its agricultural production to the Communist nations to get machines and tools in return. The result was a severe shortage of food in the cities and the new industrial centers. To increase food production even more, the Communists finally decided to abolish the communes; the peasants were permitted to move back to their homes and till their land cooperatively through "work brigades." The construction of new factories was curtailed while millions of workers were furloughed to return to the villages to help increase the yield of crops.

Between 1952 and 1960, industrial production increased at an average annual rate of a little over 6 percent, which meant a doubling of output every twelve to thirteen years. But the annual increase in population is more than 2 percent, which means that if the present birth and death rates continue, China will double her population to over 1,200,-000,000 by the year 2000. To raise her educational levels as well as her technological and scientific standards to more than subsistence levels, China must triple her food production and at least quintuple her industrial plants during the next thirty years or so. But even if she is able to increase her production to these levels, China will still not be a rich nation. By the year 2000, she will have reached the industrial and scientific levels of Japan in 1970, but with a population twelve times as great.

Communist Education

Education has increased the influence of Communism in China enormously since 1952. Elementary, secondary, and higher schools have been established all over the country; and the numbers who have graduated from them have been quantitatively impressive. The number of openings in the university and technical schools is far less than the number of applicants. As in the pre-1905 past, more than 200 regional examination centers have been established where students of middle, or secondary, schools can take their tests for entrance to the higher schools. During the early 1960's, more than 80,000 middle school students were unable to find places in the higher schools, even though technical schools, teachers' training schools, and colleges were being expanded at a rapid rate.

For example, compared with the two dozen colleges and universities of various kinds existing in 1949, there were in 1962 more than 62 general universities, 271 engineering schools, 142 medical schools, 174 normal schools, 99 agricultural colleges, and a scattering of colleges specializing in finance, art, and economics. The educational standards for these schools, however, were much lower than in the pre-1949 colleges.

In 1949 when the civil wars ended and the Communists were in complete control of the country, more than 90 percent of the population was illiterate. In 1949 the primary grades contained 13 million pupils. In 1961 there were over 95 million in the elementary schools; more than 13 million in the middle schools; and 820,000 in the colleges, technical schools, and institutes.

In Communist China, the emphasis in education is upon applied technology and teacher training for the elementary and secondary schools; almost 60 percent of the students fall in these two categories. As in the case of the Soviet Union, from which the Chinese adopted many features of their educational system, education in the engineering and applied technological fields is much narrower than in the United States, with a great deal of specialization at an early stage. At the present time, there is little encouragement given to the physical and natural sciences or to the social sciences. Again, as in the Soviet Union, the Chinese Communists need engineers and technicians for specific industries, which they plan to open when the students are graduated. The students are not free to pick and choose their courses of study, but are directed into their fields of specialization through subsidies and scholarships.

Academic freedom is virtually unknown both in China and in the Soviet Union. Instead of encouraging universities to feel free to explore new horizons of knowledge or to develop new theories to explain their data, the Chinese Government makes certain that all research is based upon those theories of mankind, society, and the physical world that the leaders in authority happen to hold at the moment. The theories are a mixture of ideas derived from Chinese pragmatism; European and Russian nineteenth century socialism; Soviet experiences from 1917 to 1953; emotional reactions to European colonialism in China; thoughts of the Chinese Communist leadership, especially in the underground rural period from 1928 to 1948; and conceptions of the technological and scientific world as they have filtered from university students trained abroad to those educated at home who wanted a more satisfying society.

The planners of the Communist society of the future admire and would like to live in the Secondary civilization of technology and science. The leadership feels optimistic that man can remake himself, and it has faith that science and technology can definitely help the Chinese solve their age-old problems and bring the country up to the levels of the United States and the Soviet Union. The Chinese leadership is convinced that through the technology of Secondary civilization, China can regain her former civilizing role and can bring new ethics in interpersonal relations and moral behavior to the rest of the world, especially to the developing areas. The Communist ethics and morals are theoretically based upon the individual's using his efforts and thoughts for the good of society and mankind. Society and mankind, however, are restricted in usage and include only the following: members of the Communist party in good standing, the leadership itself, the Red Army of China, the poor peasants, and the workers. Society and mankind are not meant to include Chinese enemies of the Communist party, formerly wealthy landlords, the gentry, capitalists, the Nationalists in Taiwan, or the enemies of the Chinese Communists abroad even though they may call themselves Communists.

Chinese Communist Relations with Others

The Communists in the mid-twentieth century are in complete control of all of China, and their government is the strongest and the most centralized that China has ever known. The Communists possess the strongest army that China has ever had; and although China cannot be compared industrially to the nations of the industrialized West or to Japan, there is little likelihood that other powers will treat her as she was treated in the period after 1839 (mainly because the world has also changed since then).

The leaders of present-day China are convinced, however, that they stand alone against all other powers. They have not forgiven the United States for intervening in the Civil War by flying Kuomintang troops to the territory evacuated by the Japanese at the end of 1945. Although the United States feared the Soviet Union in 1950 rather than Communist China, the Soviet Union manipulated North Korea into fighting a war against the United States, which unwittingly brought in Communist China as the antagonist rather than the Soviet Union. Since the Korean War, the Communists have felt their belief confirmed that the United States stands at the head of the imperialist countries who hope to rewin China as a colony for them to exploit. Great Britain is considered a lackey of the United States, as is India since the latter is a member of the British Commonwealth. Even before they took over power in 1949, the Communists had given to the United States the propagandistic image of a grasping foreign landlord. American wealth and power made them aware of their own lack of wealth and power. At the same time, American hostility and American efforts to exclude the Chinese Communists from the United Nations and other international organizations, as if these were clubs to which the aspiring members could be blackballed, only intensified the sense of isolation and rejection that the Communists felt they had been subjected to by the outside world (both as Communists and as Chinese) since 1928.

Toward the Soviet Union the Chinese have nothing but bitterness for the way in which their "comrades" have treated them since 1921. In 1923 it was the Soviet Union that insisted that the Chinese Communists could not create a revolution and take over power as the Russian Communists had done in 1917 because their urban base was too weak. The Chinese Communists were ordered instead to cooperate with the Kuomintang to harass the British, the French, and the Japanese (especially from 1921 to 1932 when these three were considered to be threats to the sovereignty of the Soviet Union). Between 1924 and 1927 the Soviet Union helped the Kuomintang with weapons, military advisers, and funds; and in 1927 when the Kuomintang turned against the Communists and wiped out four-fifths of the Party effectives within a year, the remnants received neither sympathy nor weapons from the Soviet Union. After 1934, when the Communists regrouped their forces in Yenan in northwestern China as a base from which they could strike again at Chiang Kai-shek, they again received little help from the Soviet Union. In 1936 the Soviet Union considered Japan her chief enemy; and by encouraging the Nationalists to fight the Japanese, Stalin hoped to pit one of his enemies against another.

During the Second World War, mountains of equipment went to the Kuomintang armies, mostly from the Americans. In 1946 Stalin was convinced that it would be impossible for the Chinese Communists to defeat the Kuomintang for control of China; since the United States had now become an enemy of the Soviet Union, it was therefore in the Soviet interest to support the Kuomintang against the United States but not to help the Chinese Communist party assume power. A good part of the equipment used by the Chinese Communists in the Civil War between 1947 and 1949 came from Japanese stocks captured by the Soviet Red Army, but most came from the Nationalist armies that surrendered to the Communists bringing their American arms with them. Much of the more than one billion dollars worth of military equipment that the United States supplied to the Nationalists eventually found its way into Communist hands.

The mutual dislike that existed between the leadership of the Chinese Communists and of the Soviet Union was kept hidden during the first few years after the Chinese Communists gained complete power. Although the Soviet Union helped the Chinese with large quantities of military equipment during the Korean War, she sensed early enough that the Chinese were competing with her for the leadership of the Communist world and that the Chinese wanted all the technical help they could get in order to achieve status as a great power as quickly as possible and thus become independent of the Soviet Union. She also suspected that China could easily turn into a hostile neighbor if China no longer had any need of the Soviet Union.

For their part, the Chinese had not forgotten that the Russians were the first to annex Chinese territory in 1858 and 1860, even though that territory was then Manchu, with no Chinese living there; that the czarist regime ran with the pack in wanting to divide up mainland China; that the Soviet Union in the 1920's had taken over the suzerainty of both Tanna Tuva and Outer Mongolia, both of which were at one time possessions of the Chinese Empire; or that the Soviet Union in 1945 demanded and got from the Kuomintang the old czarist concessions in southern Manchuria, including the harbor facilities of Port Arthur and the main railroads across Manchuria (which the Soviet Union operated jointly with the Chinese Communists until forced by the latter to give them up in the 1950's). Although the Soviet Union had supplied technicians and materials to the Chinese, they had insisted upon being paid back with food and agricultural resources. At the same time that the Soviet Union niggardly helped the Chinese, she was building steel mills and large-scale industries in India and other non-Communist countries.

From the Chinese point of view, the Communist leadership in the Soviet Union was as indifferent to the buildup of socialism in China as the United States had been in the development of democracy and technological change during the era of the Kuomintang. The emotional enmity between the two Communist powers was rationalized as differences in theory; from the Soviet point of view the Chinese were challenging traditional Communist experiences in the Soviet Union, and from the Chinese point of view the Russians were revising Marxism-Leninism by coexisting with the imperialist world rather than cooperating with the Chinese to challenge everywhere the authority of the American "paper tiger" through supporting Communist revolutions in the underdeveloped areas.

Chinese Building of Socialism

The Chinese Communist leadership sees a definite value in the kind of socialism that it is attempting to create in China. The leaders see themselves as bringing into existence a new civilization even greater than that of some 3,500 years before. The leaders cannot accept a secondary position to the Soviet Union in creating this future socialism because they are convinced that anything the Soviet Union has done, China can do better. Once the technological foundation has been laid through education and an increase in agricultural and industrial productivity, then the future ideal society can be constructed on top of it. To reach this Communist goal, men must be oriented from childhood toward the Communist party and its authority. The path to the future Communist society is thought to be thorny, difficult, and long; and various temptations will be present to induce individuals to think of their own gratifications first, and thus "betray" future generations of men. It is believed that only by getting the Chinese to obey implicitly the directives of the Party can the difficult problem of building a better society be partially solved. From the Chinese Communist point of view, if there are too many opinions, too many differences, too many views of what the future society should be, then the result will be confusion and an inability to achieve the future goal. The Communist state cannot permit such confusion, for no matter how high the price, the chief priority for the nation is the building of socialism, to which all other goals and virtues must be subordinated. The Chinese Communist leaders fervently believe that only they can lead the Chinese on the correct path to socialism. Any other leadership would cause the people to stray from this goal and into the hands of those who would harm China and thus, by extension, mankind.

Since the Communists view the goal of socialism as an important one, they consider that all individuals have only one duty; and that duty is to work under Communist direction to achieve socialism. If individuals falter or fall by the wayside, then they must be made to see the danger that their actions present to the eventual realization of the rewards that future generations will enjoy. Men must not think of themselves but only of others. Men have obligations and duties to perform, and they must do them willingly and happily. Those who do not do so are, in fact, traitors to the present China as well as to the future society. Strong police actions are necessary to make them admit their guilt, selfishness, and inability to cooperate for the benefit of all. Here, briefly, is the police technique of brainwashing, which is the traditional fear of betrayal of the family interests projected and magnified to make it embrace the nation. The Chinese police have learned, as the czarist and Soviet police forces discovered many years before them, that most individuals whom they interrogate have hidden feelings of inadequacy, guilt, and worthlessness that must be voiced to give relief—especially when those arrested are ashamed of having failed, as evidenced by their having fallen into the hands of the police.

Through the countless members and minor officials of the Communist party located in every village, factory, school, and police station in China, the centralized State can have its wishes, thoughts, plans, and orders known to almost all individuals in the country within a short period of time. By concentrating their efforts and employing the labor and thoughts of the tens of millions who are affiliated in some way with the Party, the Communists have been able to accomplish more in the years since 1949 than was accomplished by a weak series of governments after 1840.

Despite the advantages of the Communist political organization and of modern media of communication, Communist China still lacks the technical, scientific, and managerial skills that are needed to develop the socialist goals of "nationalism, scientism, and popularism" over the next thirty-five years. To the Communist leadership, these three terms imply confidence in being Chinese, an awareness of the culture that must be learned in order to make China great, and a need to transform the illiterate peasant and the semiliterate worker into future carriers of the new civilization of technology and science. Literacy and narrow specialization by technicians and scientists will not decrease the huge gap that exists between the highly industrialized states that have already entered the Secondary civilization and such developing nations as China. Thrown on her own resources, as the Soviet Union was in 1928, China has much further to go than that country in order to reach a comparable standard of industrialization and power. China needs more than the 600,000 to 700,000 narrowly trained students that she has in the mid-1960's in her higher schools; she needs countless millions if she is ever to catch up with the Soviet Union or the United States.

Summary

There is little doubt that China will become more industrialized as time goes on; that her agriculture will become more productive; that her technicians and scientists will multiply (China feels that the arts and the social sciences are not as important as the applied sciences because the Government knows of no problem that cannot be solved by the talents already possessed within the Communist party); and that her standard of living will eventually rise. There is little doubt that the population in the cities will double, triple, and quadruple within the next twenty years and that the country will eventually be self-sufficient in almost all important raw materials, in manufactured goods, and even in the supply of governmental directors, factory managers, and scientists.

It is questionable that the loyalty of the individual to his family can be displaced within the near future by substituting the Party; that fulfillment of the goals set by the State will be carried out faithfully by the vast majority of the population; or that the Communists will be able to carry out the Party's far-reaching social and cultural changes by the end of the twentieth century. Many problems will arise during the next twenty to thirty years both for the people and for the rest of the world because China is changing, but one fact is clear: the Communist leadership is taking the Chinese people out of Primary and into Secondary civilization. With all of her growing pains, China will continue to travel this route in the future.

Like the Africans, the Chinese Communist leadership is impatient to show the rest of the world what it can do; but unlike the African states, it is in no hurry. Time, the Party leaders feel, is on their side. Sooner or later, despite the problems involved in trying to build a modern industrial structure on the backs of peasants, China will reach a level that will enable her to plan for a new civilization, which will merge into others in the distant future. Because China is determined to build a better socialism than either the Soviet Union or the African states, competition between her and the rest of the world will continue rather than diminish. Ethnocentrism, totalitarianism, and planned scientific experimentation will be combined with a type of education that will encourage common goals and obedience to centrally determined policies. Freedom to explore intellectual horizons or to dissent from traditionally established policies will have little place in China during the next fifty years. Technology and scientific agriculture will be highly developed, but there is little likelihood that the pure sciences will be encouraged at the same pace as the applied ones.

China's greatest problem is population growth. Unless she can develop the education and technology to limit her numbers, her efforts to increase agricultural yields will end in surpluses being used to feed extra mouths rather than to pay for foreign machinery or industrial plants. The Chinese Communist leadership has recognized this challenge and is now making efforts to restrict the number of births by encouraging later marriages for both men and women. Birth control information is being disseminated, and a slogan has been coined that *re*production must take second place to *pro*duction.

It is difficult to know how much of the peasant culture still survives in China in the last third of the twentieth century. For people older than fifty, the way of life continues roughly as it always has. Most peasant families today are small, and sons are still preferred to daughters. Relatives are more important than the strangers living in distant administrative centers.

At the same time, the standard of living has increased somewhat for the peasant. He is now able to send his children to school. Even though medical care is still fifth-rate when compared to that of the other industrial powers of the world or with countries in Western Europe, it is still far better than it was in the past. There are too few trained physicians, and Western medicine still competes with Chinese acupuncture and herb doctoring, though antibiotics have been accepted by all.

The clan is not as important as it was, and the extended family is now a thing of the past. The gentry have disappeared from the village, partly with the arrival of Communism and partly because of the blood-bath that the Communists encouraged in the late 1950's, when at least a million former landlords were executed by Communists in the villages at the instigation of the Central Government.

Women are freer than ever before. They can no longer be married off at an early age to men they have never seen before, nor "adopted" by a family to become the wife of a small son. They are free to take any sort of employment, leave their husbands if they wish, or sue for divorce. They have the same theoretical rights as the men and can compete with them in education and the professions. As in the Soviet Union, the women are equal with the men only in the lower income and unskilled occupations. They are expected to work, take care of the home, and rear the children with little assistance from their husbands or the State. Consumer goods are in short supply, as are efficient kitchens, shops, and mechanized laundries. Over a period of time, this apparent equality of women to men may lead to a period of actual equality, with all the cultural change within the family that this would entail.

The Communist leaders have ambitious plans for China, but the fulfillment will require a highly educated population with a high level of technological achievement and the same attachment to future goals as the leadership. Communism, however, has been the agent of change in moving the vast population of China from the age of the donkey and the wooden plow into the age of technical schools, railroads, paved high-ways, hydroelectric plants, and urbanization.

The Communists have had and will continue to have a more lasting influence upon the thinking of the peasants and the new technical classes of workers, technicians, and professionals than the past dynasties had. China will be cajoled, pushed, and driven into the Secondary civilization by a leadership that will brook no opposition. Much of past Chinese culture will gradually wither away as new concepts and values are incorporated into Chinese society as a consequence of the enormous number of schools, newspapers, radio stations, movie houses, and clubs which the Communists have established in all corners of the country. Few villages are isolated from the directives and plans of the Communist leadership, and scarcely anywhere is there not at least one Party functionary or follower to acquaint the local population with centralized Communist thinking.

With only 35 million out of 750 million who are non-Chinese minorities, the Communists have succeeded far more than the Indians in creating a unified political nation-state with a political culture to go with it. Since the leadership is firmly convinced that its goals must be the only ones for China to follow, there will be little tolerance of dissent, apathy, or refusal to conform to the wishes of the leadership. Technical values will continue to be encouraged in the near future, but human values will be subordinated to the task of making China first among equals of the technological and scientific nations in the world.

Selected Bibliography

India

Basham, A. L., *The Wonder That Was India* (London, Sidgwick & Jackson, 1956).

Beals, Alan R., *Gopalpur, A South Indian Village* (New York, Holt, Rinehart and Winston, 1962).

Dube, S. C., *Indian Village* (Ithaca, Cornell University Press, 1955).

Griffiths, Sir Percival, *The British Impact on India* (London, MacDonald, 1952).

Hsu, Francis L. K., *Clan, Caste and Club* (Princeton, N.J., Van Nostrand, 1963).

Marriott, McKim, *Village India* (Chicago, University of Chicago Press, 1955).

Nehru, Jawaharlal, *The Discovery of India* (Garden City, N.Y., Doubleday, Anchor Books, 1960).

Sinai, I. R., *The Challenge of Modernization* (London, Chatto & Windus, 1964).

Wiser, William, and Wiser, Charlotte, *Behind Mud Walls, 1930–1960* (Berkeley, University of California Press, 1963).

Japan

Benedict, Ruth, *The Chrysanthemum and the Sword: Patterns of Japanese Culture* (Boston, Houghton Mifflin, 1946).

Borton, Hugh, ed., *Japan* (Ithaca, Cornell University Press, 1951).

Embree, John, *Suye Mura: A Japanese Village* (Chicago, University of Chicago Press, 1939).

Reischauer, Edwin O., *Japan: Past and Present* (New York, Knopf, 1953).

Sansom, G. B., *Japan: A Short Cultural History* (New York, Appleton-Century-Crofts, 1944).

——, *The Western World and Japan* (New York, Knopf, 1950).

Vogel, Ezra F., *Japan's New Middle Class* (Berkeley, University of California Press, 1963).

Ward, Robert E., and Rustow, Dankwart A., eds., *Political Modernization in Japan and Turkey* (Princeton, Princeton University Press, 1964).

China

Barnett, A. Doak, *Communist China and Asia: A Challenge to American Policy* (New York, Random House, Vintage Books, 1960).

Chai, Ch'u, and Chai, Winberg, *The Changing Society of China* (New York, New American Library, Mentor Books, 1962).

Clubb, D. E., *Twentieth Century China* (New York, Columbia University Press, 1964).

Fremantle, Anne, *Mao Tse-Tung: An Anthology of His Writings* (New York, New American Library, 1963).

Granet, Marcel, *Chinese Civilization* (Cleveland, World Publishing, Meridian Books, 1958).

Hsu, Francis, *Americans and Chinese* (New York, Abelard-Schuman, 1953).

Levenson, Joseph R., *Confucian China and Its Modern Fate* (Berkeley, University of California Press, 1958).

Li, Dun J., *The Ageless Chinese* (New York, Scribner, 1965).

North, Robert C., *Moscow and Chinese Communists* (Stanford, Stanford University Press, 1963).

Peffer, Nathaniel, *The Far East* (Ann Arbor, University of Michigan Press, 1958).

Snow, Edgar, *The Other Side of the River* (New York, Random House, 1961).

Redfield, Margaret, ed., *China's Gentry* (Chicago, University of Chicago Press, 1953).

Welty, Thomas, *The Asians* (Philadelphia, Lippincott, Preceptor Series, 1963).

Yang, C. K., *The Chinese Family in the Communist Revolution* (Cambridge, Mass., Technology Press, 1959).

Yang, Martin C., *A Chinese Village* (New York, Columbia University Press, 1945).

22

The Soviet Union: Communism and the Secondary Civilization

Today the Soviet Union is engaged in both forced industrialization and compulsory education in order to bring tens of millions of its inhabitants into the Industrial and Scientific Age as quickly as possible. Since 1917, the Soviet Union has been governed by a small group of middle-class leaders who have dedicated themselves to changing the population through totalitarianism. They have used their authority to transform illiterate, inefficient peasants with narrow values into an industrialized population with a new culture and Communist values. To do this, the people have been brutalized, severely disciplined, and forced to accept the changing picture of themselves as the Communist party leadership visualized it. To prevent dissension from arising, Medieval concepts of heresy have been resurrected and broadly applied. Like many of the great religionists of the past who ferreted out dissent as a crime against the salvation of humanity, the Communist leadership views heresy as sinful and negative. It brooks no interference with attempts to realize its vague dreams of a twenty-first century in which an educated population will lead the world in creativity, standard of living, and moral and ethical values.

The Soviet Union must be viewed as a nation very much in a hurry. It feels that it has an appointment with destiny to lead the development of human society to even higher levels than it has reached thus far. The Soviet Union looks upon itself as struggling painfully to give birth to a new civilization in which all men will receive the goods and services they need, and in turn will be able to utilize their uninhibited creative talents for the good of society. The Soviet Union represents a frenzied twentieth century attempt to move a whole population into adopting the mental habits of a presumed scientific and technological twenty-first century. To achieve this goal, the methods of a totalitarian state are utilized to control the lives of the citizens and their children.

The citizens are offered little choice or opportunity to decide the forms and content of the future Communist culture. Decisions concerning those concepts and goals that will be part of it are determined in an authoritarian fashion by the Party leadership, whose decision makers run into the thousands. The Communist goal aspires to break with the irrational past and to develop a rational and scientific way of life, with a series of values all its own, in which all individuals will theoretically be given opportunities to develop whatever talents they possess by means of encouragement and free educational facilities. In return, the educated individuals must use their creativity for the good of society (at the present time, this good is the welfare of the Party) and for the service of the State, which is the instrument of the Communist party.

It is difficult to see the steps by which the Communists expect to achieve their goals because they are pragmatic about them and do not discuss them in any specific detail. Their first task has been to erect a technological and scientific base for the creation of social wealth, and this they have done since 1928—with time out for war and reconstruction.

The Industrialization of the Soviet Union

Unlike the United States and Great Britain, where the presence of heavy industry, such as that in steel, machine tools, and engineering equipment, went hand in hand with a rapidly growing consumer goods industry (the Industrial Revolution in England was associated as much with the textile industry as with the improvement of blast furnaces and steam engines), the Soviet Union gave first priority to developing a technological base for heavy industry in order to become self-sufficient in supplying its future industrial and military needs. The Soviet Union concentrated most of its efforts in a few key industries and trained large numbers in highly specialized schools so that in certain technical areas it could catch up to the highly industrialized countries in the shortest period of time. The Communists were not concerned with the efficiency of the plants they built or the individuals they trained, for they looked upon all their preliminary efforts as the necessary social costs of industrialization. The leadership was more concerned with training a population that could eventually run a highly complex technical and scientific civilization than with giving it direct benefits from the greater industrial yields. The Communists were willing to run at a deficit for decades in order to achieve their industrialization.

Although the leaders paint glowing pictures of the eventual benefits of industrialization, which will accrue to the children and the grandchildren of the present generation, they have made their population pay a very high price for this rapid industrialization. The problems involved in transforming a largely untrained and illiterate peasant population into industrial technicians have been enormous; and the Communists have been somewhat successful, although the educational process will continue for decades.

The Communists were also faced with the task of discovering and educating managerial talent for the large number of new plants that they erected. In the beginning, they used their educated Party membership and whatever non-Communist managerial talent had not gone into exile. As time went on, the Party pushed to the top as rapidly as possible those Communist workers and clerks who showed skills in organization, innovation, and resourcefulness. Some of the Party membership had received at least a secondary education, but large numbers had been semiliterate when the Party came to power. The more literate ones were used as teachers to educate and train the less literate because Party leaders trusted literate members or individuals sympathetic to their aims more than they did dissenting intellectuals or those who disagreed. During the 1930's, whenever production schedules fell the dissenters became scapegoats; and many either paid with their lives or were punished continuously for the inefficiency of the workers and the chaotic system of distribution of raw materials.

The Totality of Communist Controls

Industrialization and the applied sciences underwent a forced growth; and the leadership made no effort to temper its harsh controls with any eighteenth, nineteenth, or twentieth century concepts of humanism. To the Party, with its police controls, the privilege of being human was not a right that every individual should normally enjoy. The leadership treated as "human beings" only those who slavishly, willingly, and at a good deal of personal sacrifice obeyed Communist party directives. Those who dissented or were definitely opposed had their "humanness" taken away, which meant that the Party as executioners could destroy them without any twinge of conscience. Only the Communist party leadership could confer human dignity upon its subjects; those who did not belong to the Establishment received their individual dignity only at the sufferance of the Party leadership. (The terror of the 1930's and of the Second World War tended to be more strictly controlled after the death of Stalin in 1953, though dissent and opposition were still banned.)

Life was no harsher under the Communists than it had been under the repressive authoritarianism of the czarist regime. The Communists justified their totalitarianism by insisting that "an omelet cannot be made without breaking eggs," and a revolution cannot be carried out without cracking skulls. What they considered a moral end result was the important thing for the Communists, not the unethical means used to achieve it. If millions were sent to labor camps, if arbitrary arrests affected scores of individuals in influential positions, if police terror killed countless numbers, if people were afraid to express their thoughts for fear of reprisals from the security police, the regime and its followers rationalized all this as a normal and necessary adjunct to rapid social and cultural change. Few members of the leadership could put themselves psychologically in the place of those who became the victims of their forced cultural change; from their point of view, people were expendable in the urgent task of building socialism. Those who were not with them became automatically against them, which meant that no sympathy was to be wasted upon those who could not qualify for the honorary title of "human being," as judged by the Party leadership.

Communism as practiced in the Soviet Union is thus a mixture of the old totalitarianism practiced by the tyrant (and by the religious zealot) and the new efficiency of a modern police state working to push a large population into the age of applied science, industrialization, and technical efficiency within the shortest period of time. In the Soviet Union, the creation of wealth takes third place to building socialism and training people to live in a socialist society; but there is little doubt that by the end of the twentieth century the Soviet Union will become a rich and highly industrialized nation. There is also little doubt that within the next thirty to forty years, a large supply of creative, innovational personalities will be encouraged to lead the population from Secondary to Tertiary civilization. But there is little evidence thus far to indicate that a more humanitarian and ethical society, emphasizing the importance and dignity of the individual, will arise in that same period of time. For a truly scientific culture to develop within the Soviet Union, an ideological break with the past mythology and orthodoxy of the Communist party and a willingness to see the tactics of the police state as an admission of inefficiency in carrying through a program of industrial change will be required.

Perhaps the leadership of the Communist party has handicapped itself by its inability to trust anyone else to give the directives. Instead of getting other innovational personalities to cooperate in the tremendous task of achieving cultural change in the Soviet Union, the Party has insisted upon its sole right to control all forms of thought that might, if left undisturbed, weaken Communist party ideology. Since theoretically all individuals outside the influence of the Communist party are enemies, no one but a trusted leader within the Party can be permitted to make any decisions that might have theoretical implications in shaping the new cultural world that the Communists are attempting to bring into being.

The Communists are so anxious to prevent the iniquities and irrationalities of the past from influencing future generations that they are unaware of how much they themselves represent this continuation of the conditions they are attempting to eradicate. The leadership has reflected the attitudes of eighteenth and nineteenth century Russia toward both the outside world and their fellow Russians.

Although the Soviet Union in 1936 went through the forms of promulgating a constitution, which the leadership called the most advanced in the world, few of its provisions guaranteeing human freedoms were ever put into practice. Individuals are still sentenced without trial to long terms in prisons or labor camps on the assumption that the prosecutors and the secret police would not arrest them if they were not guilty. Even today the individual has no protection from arbitrary arrest. Anyone arrested is presumed guilty rather than innocent, and he possesses no rights that must be respected either by the police or the courts, both of whom serve the Party. No writ of habeas corpus exists to force the release of the individual from imprisonment without trial and proof of guilt. Individuals can be guilty through association, and the sins of the parents can also be visited upon the heads of the children.

The regime rewarded those who stuck with it through thick and thin, however. In the past, these favors included a share of whatever consumer goods were in very short supply for the rest of the population; a three to four room apartment, when the vast majority of the urban population lived in one room or less, sharing a bathroom and a kitchen with three to seven other families; a summer log house, or *dacha;* vacations in the Crimea or the Caucasus; and other special privileges.

Those who dissented or who were in opposition found themselves the targets for the harsh police measures reserved by the Soviet Government for those whom it judged as obstacles in the way of achieving Communist goals. Dissent from official standards was not permitted in the sciences, literature, the arts, music, or the humanities. In all these fields, the guidelines were promulgated from the top; and all instruction, all writing, and all activities had to be measured by the values set by the Communist leadership. Although this state of affairs may slowly change during the next thirty years, in the past the Communists have felt too insecure to give freedom to the intellectuals. In no phase of human endeavor could an individual make his own decisions if he in any way contradicted the directives of the Communist leadership.

In the last third of the twentieth century, the Soviet Union is in a transitional stage. On the one hand, it cannot return to the harsh, repressive purges of the Stalinist era; but on the other hand, the leadership fears that too much permissiveness toward the young intellectuals might lead to a violent outburst against past and present governmental restrictions, which might end in modification of Communist party doctrines. In fact, the subordinate Communist states of Czechoslovakia, Hungary, Poland, and Romania are gradually shifting away from close adherence to the past experiences of the Soviet Union. Since it is no longer able to use the severe repressions of the past, the Communist leadership today is being forced to give way slowly to the pressures for more freedom. But those intellectuals who want more freedom will need to fight every inch of the way for it because the leadership is aware that every step of freedom it allows must lessen its own freedom to enforce its decisions.

The Russian Past

Until the eighteenth century, Russia was limited to a landlocked area stretching from the White Sea in the north to the Sea of Azov in the south. The country was made up of small principalities that had been united only in the latter part of the sixteenth century. Sweden still controlled the Baltic states and Finland; Turkey controlled Moldavia, the Crimea, and part of the Caucasus. The Don and Volga cossacks had lost their freedom to the Muscovy czar in the seventeenth century even though some of their numbers had, for the Russian czar, explored Siberia from the Urals to the Pacific Ocean between 1583 and 1620. Stopped from moving eastward and southward by Chinese arms at the Amur and Ussuri rivers, they turned north and went by sea to the peninsula of Kamchatka, which they reached by the beginning of the eighteenth century.

Russia was a land of illiterate, inefficient peasants, ruled by equally illiterate and inefficient feudal lords. Byzantine Christianity had come to Kiev in the latter part of the tenth century, and then moved northward during the eleventh and twelfth centuries. Kiev was not Russia, but an independent Slavic principality centered around an old trading post that had been used for hundreds of years by the merchants who used the Dnieper River as the pathway from the Scandinavian peninsula to the Greek settlements along the Black Sea. Fifteen hundred years before Byzantine Christianity came to Kiev, the Iranian-speaking Scythians occupied the area south of Kiev. Gold vessels made by Greek artisans along the Black Sea give us a picture of Scythian warriors, dressed as the Russian peasants were until the beginning of the twentieth century, wearing tunics, baggy pants, and shoes and leggings made of bark strips. On their heads they wore pointed leather caps.

North of Kiev were countless villages of peasants, each village ruled by the elders of large extended families with the land owned in common. Village houses had changed little since early Neolithic days; they were still thatched and made of notched logs with small openings in the roof for smoke and small apertures along the side for windows that could be boarded up in winter. Further north the houses were semisubterranean, with exit by way of a ladder leading to an opening in the roof. More than two-thirds of the house was underground so that its inhabitants could keep warm in winter, when most of the village hibernated from the first severe cold wave till the first thaw. In villages situated near lakes, the peasants fished and farmed. The population was fairly sparse; and land for growing crops had to be cleared from the thick forests, which extended almost solidly from an area south of Kiev to the port of Archangelsk. The rivers and lakes provided the chief means of travel, though paths led from one village to another through the thick pine forests.

By the early fourteenth century, the peasants had been converted to Christianity; but their faith remained a mixture of old folk beliefs and their interpretations of Christianity gleaned from various traveling monks. Rituals, in which magic played an important part, and religious icons (pictures of Christ, the Virgin Mary, and the saints) formed the basis of their beliefs. The Devil was everywhere and the purpose of the icons was to furnish magic protection against molestation from the Evil Spirit. Happiness was negative rather than positive: it was an absence of disease, famine, and war and of the work of the Devil and his countless willing helpers. There were good spirits who protected the hearth and home, to whom one could appeal for help, using roughly the same appeals that one made to the saints of the icons. The icons and the Cross, plus holy water blessed by a priest, formed an important part of the peasants' defenses against the cruel unknown, which plagued them continuously with pain, hunger, and death. The peasant also needed protection against the minor evil spirits, who roamed the woods, dried up his cow, killed his pig, and even prevented his crops from growing.

Besides the protection that the peasant needed from spirits he could not see, he also needed safeguards against those whom he could see, those who killed or enslaved his sons, captured his daughters, took his supplies, and burned his hut. From the ninth century on, the Varangians (merchant-warriors from Scandinavia) gave some protection to the peasant villages of both the north and the south against the Tartar, Scandinavian, and Finnish raiders. From the twelfth century, after the Mongols had overspread the land, new rulers arose to act as intermediaries with the fast-moving Mongol hordes. By the end of the thirteenth century, a new feudal principality developed around the small trading town of Moscow, a settlement that had been made by Finnish-speaking peasants. These were conquered sometime between the sixth and the ninth century A.D. by Slavic-speaking bands who intermarried with them.

A few monasteries and churches were built in the small towns, where merchants came once a year with horses loaded with packs of goods, which were displayed before the monastery and church walls for periods of one week to a month. To these settlements came the peasants and their elders to exchange furs for swords, axes, kettles, needles, and cloth. The monasteries farmed the surrounding area and engaged in various artisan activities. There was not enough wealth, however, for the monasteries to become centers of learning. The main intellectual activity for the monks was copying and recopying Biblical texts in the Cyrillic script. This alphabet had come to them from the first missionaries and was based upon the Greek script that Saints Cyril and Methodius first developed for the Slavic-speaking peoples in central Europe—present-day Czechoslovakia—whom they had converted to Christianity at the end of the ninth century. The Russian monasteries became sterile as centers of learning when rituals and icon making became their two chief pre-occupations. They brought no literacy to the people, and they were not even the means whereby the ancient artisan culture of the Greeks and Romans could have been taught to the Russians.

From the sixteenth century on, northern Russia became a market for English merchants, who came seeking furs. The English aristocracy at that time lived in unheated stone halls, in which the temperatures equaled those outside during the months from December to March. It was difficult to entertain guests at banquets when the temperature in the large hall hovered around the freezing mark. The shivering merchants in the city of London were also good customers for fur cloaks, as were their wives.

The English were followed by the Dutch and within a century by the northern Germans. Soon small settlements sprang up around Moscow, Novgorod, and Pskov, where the foreigners lived in isolation from the Russians. The British ships that traded with Archangelsk put factors on shore to buy the furs from the hunters, who came to barter for the knives, guns, kettles, needles, tools, and cloth that the foreigners brought.

Russia by the seventeenth century was ruled from Moscow, where the family of Romanovs had founded a dynasty. The feudal lords and their retainers were used by the czars as part-time armies, and soon Western arms and cannon were bought from the Venetians. It was not long, however, before the art of cannon making was learned from the foreigners and accurate copies were turned out in a small foundry near the czar's palace. The foreigners also became the architects for the new churches and palaces built by the czars and the nobles, for they were artisans as well as merchants.

The foreigners lived as they did in their homelands with their own taverns and shops. They even farmed nearby plots of land, where they could grow the crops to which they were most accustomed. Though the Court used them increasingly, the nobles and the peasants ignored them because they could not speak Russian well and did not have the same cultural frame of reference as themselves. Although at this time the Russian peasants and nobles rarely took baths and found it difficult to free their dwellings of bedbugs, fleas, and beetles, they still looked down upon the foreigners as "dirty." During the eighteenth century, the Germans came in large numbers to be the artisans, teachers, and merchants for the peasants and nobles and to act as instructors for the czar. Although they bathed frequently, wore clean clothes, and lived in white-washed cottages, the Russians also considered them dirty. The term *dirty* did not have the same meaning to the Russian that it did to the German, the Dutchman, or the Jew. It had nothing to do with cleanliness of person, clothes, or home (which the Russian along with the French and most Europeans lacked at that time), but was based upon the foreigner's inability to understand Russian religious practices with their distinctions as to what was ritually impure. The fact that the foreigner washed everything he used was enough to make him dirty, since certain utensils could never be clean no matter how often they were washed. The sanitary facilities also made the foreigner unclean, since he kept definite vessels for that purpose rather than using the great outdoors as the Russians did.

This ethnocentrism prevented the Russians from learning new techniques from the foreigners who came to live in their midst. They considered what they did or had far superior to anything the foreigners did or had. If the foreigners were disciplined, as the Russians were not, or if they were willing to work to earn money to save for future enjoyment, then they had an eccentric weakness, which, according to the Russians, made them willing to "sell their souls for money." Many Russians in the eighteenth and early nineteenth centuries boasted that they would rather work for nothing on a voluntary basis and be free than work for money, which would enslave them.

Both the nobles and the peasants looked through ethnocentric glasses at the way of life of the Germans, the Dutch, the Scots, and the English whom they saw in their foreign settlements. There was no motivation for the Russians to be changed by the culture of the outsiders any more than there had been for the Indians or the Chinese in the eighteenth century to be changed by their initial contacts with the West. They had all been reared traditionally to believe that what they were told as children or what they learned from their parents as adolescents represented common sense and the only concepts that a decent and Christian human being could possibly accept.

In India and China, acculturation to European ways came because of influences from the top down. In Russia, acculturation to the superior technology of Western Europe also required determined pressures from the top to make a large part of the population change. This pressure and use of force in Russia made the gap between the values of Western social institutions and those of Russia even greater, as the technological and scientific culture continued to develop in the West during the following two centuries. The force exerted by the czars led to the authoritarian conviction that the people could not know what was best for them in the long run, that they had to be led by the nose and forced to do what the authorities decreed was in their interest.

The Age of Peter the Great

During the latter part of the seventeenth and the early part of the eighteenth centuries, Peter the Great recognized the military advantages of Western European technology and used it as far as he could to build a navy and an army that subsequently enabled him to defeat the Swedes. Sons of nobles were ordered to study in Holland and England; and even the Czar himself, in the disguise of a corporal, went to Holland and England to learn how to build naval ships. Although his uncouth behavior shocked the English, Peter learned early that Western technology was an absolute necessity if he wanted to win both battles and the respect of other European monarchs. Upon his return, he was not satisfied with merely the introduction of a new technology, but insisted that his nobles dress, live, and behave like Western Europeans. With his own hands he cut the beards of his nobles; but later he permitted them to pay a "beard tax," since like the Orthodox Jew and the Moslem, the Orthodox Russian could not suffer the indignity of going to heaven clean-shaven when all the saints and even God were believed to wear long flowing beards.

Peter the Great invited German mathematicians and technicians to come to Russia as instructors and ordered the sons of nobles to spend a certain amount of time studying in the schools of the West. Peter had learned a good deal as a youngster from the Dutch, Germans, Scots, and Swiss who were quartered near Moscow and who had taught him much about war and the technology of waging war. Peter had no interest in educating the vast illiterate masses of Russians, for he had little education himself. He was interested only in the education of officers and administrators, whom he recruited wherever he could find them, although most came from the nobility.

Russia during his reign reached the Baltic Sea. St. Petersburg (present-day Leningrad) was established as his capital so that he could have quicker access to the West by sea. He established a civil service with fourteen ranks, in which all started at the bottom and through promotions rose to the top. Since promotion was based upon pleasing one's superiors, this system led to the officeholder's taking action only upon orders from the top; individual initiative, originality, and imagination were all stifled. Schools were organized with foreigners as instructors. For five years, from ages ten to fifteen, the sons of nobles learned mathematics, military engineering, and foreign languages, subjects that would enable them to take their places as future officers and administrators. No learning was encouraged that would not lead to practical benefits for the Czar's military forces and government. Peter also encouraged foreigners and Russians to establish workshops to manufacture the supplies that the army and navy needed.

The lot of the peasants, on the other hand, was adversely affected by Peter's drive for Westernization. On their work-worn backs fell the ultimate financing for all of his projects. They were made to pay greater taxes; and as rewards to his favorites, serfdom was extended to include free peasants as well as those who farmed state lands. As additional rewards to his officers and administrators, whole villages of peasants and their lands were often handed over to them as gifts. Few of the peasants escaped this harsher serfdom. To make sure that they did not try to flee to the border regions, a system of internal passports and strict controls over travel was introduced, which was enforced by both the army and the noble landlords (the latter were given the power of life and death over their serfs). What little freedom the Russian peasant had before the eighteenth century was taken away from him by a czar imbued with the goal of national rather than personal equality, that is, of making Russia the military equal of both the Swedes and the English.

Despite his inhumane treatment of the peasants, Peter did set in motion a series of changes in Russian culture that had far-reaching effects upon the nobility. New academies for technical learning were established; a newspaper was printed for the first time in St. Petersburg; women were freed from their forced seclusion in the home; and rewards were given to the few families with a smattering of Western education, thus encouraging them to ignore the disapproval of the Church and other noble families for their foreign ways. Russia under Peter's regime became a great European power and began to shift away from her isolated Byzantine past to an awareness of Western European directions. The overwhelming majority of the population did not benefit, however, from the changes. Despite the greater exactions now demanded from them, neither Peter or the new proprietors of the land attempted to help the serfs become more productive. Peter wasted little sympathy upon the peasants; he looked upon them as existing largely to help him make Russia into a great military power. Peter was not concerned with people whom he considered not quite equal to himself. They had to be forced to obey—by the whip if necessary.

The Eighteenth Century

In the second half of the eighteenth century, a university was established in Moscow. The aristocracy learned to speak French among themselves, and the technicians and engineers developed a facility in German. But at that time in Russia, no movement existed that was equivalent to the democratic and humanist trends of France and England, which were beginning to influence large numbers of educated individuals in their countries, the German states, and the American colonies. Schooling was reserved primarily for children of the aristocracy, though after Peter's death the curriculum dealt more with literature for the upper-class pupils than with technical subjects.

In the meanwhile, the Russian population increased threefold during the eighteenth century. It had been only 11 million at Peter's death in 1725. By the year 1800, it had grown to some 36 million. Although part of this increase was due to conquests by Catherine's armies and the partition of Poland, the largest part came from the natural increase among the Russians themselves. Agriculture was still the Medieval three-field system, in which one field lay fallow while two crops were grown in the other fields. Land was plowed in long, narrow strips with a wooden plow that merely scratched the surface of the earth instead of turning the soil over. The heavy plow, which had been used in Western Europe for centuries, was unknown among the Russian peasants, who used primitive agricultural implements that had changed little during two thousand years.

The Russian hut, or *izba,* was generally one room with a dirt floor and a large clay stove on one side of the room, upon which the parents or the grandparents slept. Although chimneys of a sort had come in during the seventeenth century, the room was generally filled with smoke from the wood, which burned with poor combustion. The walls were filled with bedbugs, lice, and beetles; and it was customary for the peasant at least once during the winter to put out the fire in the clay stove and open the door and windows to the sub-zero weather outside in order to kill the insects. The insects returned in a short period of time, however, in the clothes of the family after they had stayed in other peasant huts.

Glass was unknown during the eighteenth century and a good part of the nineteenth, and oiled cloth or wooden shutters were used to keep out the cold arctic air in winter. Clothes were generally worn until patches could no longer be sewn over other patches; the wool was generally homeshorn, homespun, and often woven on a primitive loom. Only later were artisans in nearby villages employed to make the things that the peasant could not make for himself.

The Beginnings of Industrialization

Russia turned from agricultural serfdom, which differed little from actual slavery, to industrial serfdom during the latter part of the eighteenth century and the first half of the nineteenth century. Industrial plants employing serf labor were set up in the cities; the workers were not permitted to leave their barracks without permission, and were expected to put in long hours of efficient labor for subsistence and no other motivation. The only escape from serfdom was to enlist in the army for twenty-five years, but the harsh discipline of the army made it no place for a peasant to escape his hard life. During the second half of the nineteenth century, the peasant escaped his poverty-stricken lot (the institution of serfdom had been abolished in 1861) by moving to Siberia where he could often buy land at a low price from the State.

The workers in the industrial plants that were being established during the nineteenth century, many of them employing thousands of workers, could only look forward to a life of deprivation, living five or more to a room on little better than a subsistence level. The free public schools were not available to their children, but only to the offspring of the city's middle classes and the petty aristocracy. The worker, like the peasant, was considered "dark" in his ignorance and subhuman status. Unlike his peasant ancestors, however, he could not be bought and sold at public auction. ("Souls" had formerly accompanied the sale of property, and some were even sold for factory work.)

The czars and czarinas, for all their reading of French eighteenth century enlightened thought, had no interest in improving the lot of the illiterate masses. One educated aristocrat who had spent a good many years abroad returned to write a book on the depths of poverty and the evils of serfdom which he had witnessed in a trip from St. Petersburg to Moscow. Upon reading the book, Catherine the Great ordered the author deported to Siberia for life. Other writers who harbored "dangerous thoughts" were imprisoned in fortresses or deported to Siberia. Even with the new education, individuals were not free to see the world as it was around them. Official censorship intervened between them and their small reading public (as it would later under the Communists).

The Nineteenth Century

The czar's power derived from the nobility and its officers in the army who supported him. The autocrat could not rule alone, but only with the assistance of others. The fear of peasant revolts and of rebellions led by peasant pretenders to the throne made most of the aristocrats support the autocratic czar, for few other alternatives were open to them. A small group hoped for necessary reforms that would eradicate serfdom, raise the levels of education, and bring Russia closer to the West; but almost none dreamed of a democracy that would wipe out the hereditary privileges of their group or that would raise the social classes beneath them to their level. Dreams of reform were still placed within a framework of czar, nobility, and landlord. Even the merchants were given little status; they were looked down upon as being too prim, disciplined, and concerned with advancing their own security. They had little appeal for the peasant or the noble, both of whom assumed that drunkenness, fighting, and the use of obscene language were far more commendable in men than restrained behavior.

Out of the contrast between Russian and North German merchant behavior arose those early nineteenth century Russian nationalist writers who felt that there was a special Russian soul whose mission it was to secure the approval of educated public opinion for the uncontrolled and undisciplined emotional behavior of the Russians. With this defiant, juvenile delinquent subculture as a frame of reference, they often referred to the Czechs as the "Prussians of the Slavs," since they neither fought in public, shifted from one mood to another in a matter of minutes, nor sold all they owned for a wild spree of almost unconscious drunkenness. Such behavior was considered to make the Russian free, for if he knuckled under and became a disciplined individual like the German or the Czech, then it was felt that he had sold his birthright to become a slave. This single-minded urge to discipline the unruly Russian masses has been carried on in the police tactics and the distrust of their own populations by successive czarist and Communist governments. Undisciplined and independent individuals were as much the targets of the czarist police as of the Communist ones. Whether they wanted to be or not, Russians have over the centuries been molded into the images decreed by their rulers.

The fear of rebellion against the cruel autocrat kept palace revolutions stillborn; the identification of the tyrannized sons with the despotic father was too strong to let them make a gesture of independence by severing the strong ties of dependency that kept the nobility and the small but growing intellectual class identified with the autocracy. Although Alexander I played with democratic and constitutional reforms, he ended by brutalizing the peasants. Through permanent military camps located in the rural areas, the peasants were forced to produce a certain number of soldiers for the Czar's army; even their wives and children had to serve the military. The penalty for the slightest infraction of discipline was revolting and sadistic brutality on the part of the visiting officers.

In the first half of the nineteenth century, Nicholas I was known as the "gendarme of Europe," for he repressed revolutions against tyranny outside his borders as severely as he did in his own country. In Poland in 1830 and in Hungary in 1848, Russian troops broke the back of insurrection against Russia and Austria. (Soviet troops would play the same role against the East Berlin workers in 1953 and in the Hungarian rebellion in 1956, and as they would threaten to do against the Polish strikers in 1956.) Although the Russians entered the Balkans presumably to pro-tect the Orthodox Christian Greek, Romanian, and Slavic populations from the Islamic Turks, they ended by encouraging obscurantist reaction in the states that received autonomy.

During the thirties and forties of the nineteenth century, industry slowly expanded; but the factories were worked by serfs, who were often owned by the plant owners themselves. Russia could not escape the strong technological winds coming from Western Europe. Railroads were built by American, British, and French engineers; and capital for new enterprises came from all the industrial countries of that time. Wheat became important as a Russian export item, along with timber and furs, thus providing the means with which to purchase the foreign skills and machines that were needed. After 1842 the peasants were permitted to buy their freedom; and finally in 1861 the serfs were freed of their past obligations, though few were loaned enough funds to enable them to buy sufficient land to till for themselves.

In effect, the liberation of the serfs did little to solve their economic problems. Many of them found themselves deeply in debt to their former masters for the small plots of land that they were given. Although 40 million serfs were freed in 1861, few of them possessed even half as much land as they had previously tilled for themselves while working for the landlord. The land prices were overinflated to include all the possible future earnings that the landlord felt he would lose. The land, though paid for by the peasant, was still not his own private property. It was vested in the hands of the village council headed by an elder, or *starosta,* who was elected by the wealthy peasants (those peasants who had been free even before Emancipation). They taxed the land and made them-selves the village administrators, though even they were subject con-tinually to the will of the larger neighboring landowners. The peasant had no civil rights. He could not leave the village without permission from the Elder, and even with permission he still had to apply for a pass-port. In case of minor infractions, the village council and the Elder could order him beaten. And even when the peasant received permission to move to the city, he had to promise to pay all his future taxes to the vil-lage from his new residence.

Despite his hardships, the peasant was not ready for revolution, as the young students from the universities and secondary schools discov-ered when they came to the villages after 1861 bringing their messages of Populism and Rural Socialism. Most often the students were turned over to the czar's police representatives for punishment, after being reported to the village council by the peasants themselves. Nevertheless, enough of the new ideas persisted to make the peasant aware that he was being mistreated and to make him believe that someday his lot would become better. The small allotments of land, never averaging more than thirty acres, became divided and subdivided as the children claimed their rights of inheritance. With the rapid rise in population the plots became too small to support even one family. Agriculture was still backward (as it would remain until the middle 1960's); and the peasants were still illiterate, knowing only what their parents had known. There was an absence of machinery, almost no use of fertilizer, and only scrub stock. As the population grew during the second half of the nineteenth century, the surplus rural population had no place to go. Industries were still small, and not until the late 1880's was there a demand for unskilled factory labor.

The Background for Communism

The frustrated need for reform soon led to a preoccupation with revolution. In the 1870's and 1880's, a movement called the *Narodnya Volya* (People's Will) stressed the future reconstruction of Russia through the peasant, who would be used to inaugurate a new type of socialism based upon the old village commune. Others turned to Nihilism (complete destruction of the existing regime) and, like the anarchist Bakunin, believed that the world could progress only when society was first "cleansed" of past "obstructions," such as social classes, government, and institutions. By the early 1880's the revolutionary groups organized by students soon became both conspiratorial and insurrectional. The conviction spread among the newly educated groups, who saw a contradiction between the democratic ideal in Western Europe and the absolutist tyranny in Russia, that the elites had an obligation to organize the rest of the population against the regime. In many ways the revolutionary fervor among the students of Russia was similar in tone to the nationalist ardor in the twentieth century among the returning African students (whom we have already discussed) who organized their political following across tribal lines in reaction to the colonial powers. In both nationalist movements it was necessary to raise the rest of the population up to the students' standards and goals. In Africa, the nationalist parties had been organized in relative peace and often with the blessings of the colonial administrators. In czarist Russia, however, organization was dangerous, for police spies spent their time infiltrating groups and ferreting out the students who were leaders. The students answered these arrests with assassinations and bombings.

A great many students were arrested and imprisoned, but popular imagination was fired by their deeds, and more sympathy developed for them among the rest of the population than for the police or the administration. Among those students executed in 1887 for an attempted plot against the czar was one Alexander Ulianov, the son of a district school inspector and the older brother of Vladimir Ilyitch Ulianov, whom the world would know later as Lenin, the architect and father of the Communist party.

In the latter part of the nineteenth century, Russia had the fastest growing population in Europe. Industrial expansion was pushed by the Government with large amounts of credit at its disposal. Russian bonds were sold throughout Europe; in France, for example, many peasants dipped deep into their stockings for money to buy bonds for the building of steel mills, railroads, and harbors. Although the number of factories declined, the workers doubled as more capital went into building some of the largest engineering works in Europe. By 1890, more than 1,000,000 workers were employed in the industries around St. Petersburg, Moscow, the Donets basin, and Kiev. The Trans-Siberian railroad was begun in 1891, and twelve years later its single track reached the Pacific Ocean at Vladivostok, whose surrounding territory the Russian czar had annexed from Manchu China between 1858 and 1860.

In this period of industrial growth and railroad building, the press was gagged; the universities had their original autonomy taken away; the district schools were placed under the police; and the rural areas were put under the direct control of the local petty nobility, who accounted only to St. Petersburg for the measures they took to keep discontent from blazing into rebellion. The national minorities were persecuted, but none was oppressed as much as the Jews, who were made to live in poverty within the areas annexed to Russia after the eighteenth century. Only a few wealthy Jewish merchants received permission to live in the cities of St. Petersburg and Moscow. The Jews were restricted in the number of places they could fill at the universities; none could enter the civil service or the army; and the police encouraged a harsh official anti-Semitism. This still continues in varying degree among the top Communist leadership and a large part of the population. Its virulent forms were brought to Germany in the 1920's by Russians escaping from Communism; and it played an important role in making anti-Semitism an integral part of Nazism, in addition to its uses by reactionary fringe movements in the United States and elsewhere.

Many of the Russian students who had been attracted to a vague form of socialism after the 1860's went abroad to escape police surveillance and to write, study, and make plans for a more efficient revolutionary movement. By 1882 Marxism had been discovered by a Russian scholar named Georgi Plekhanov, then living in Switzerland. In 1883 he founded the Federation of Labor in Geneva to give a new Marxist orientation to the Russian socialist movement-in-exile. With many of his fellow exiles, Plekhanov believed that Russia had to go through a capitalist industrial revolution before it could create the basis for an eventual socialist state. The peasants, he believed, were too backward to be used as the foundation of a new commonwealth. Plekhanov also felt that terror could have little value in attracting the population to socialism; only political education could be used to train followers for the new struggle to organize the workers within a Marxist Social Democratic party. Plekhanov and his followers in the 1890's were convinced that a socialist party was needed to exert political pressure in order to win universal suffrage and free elections. Through these methods socialism could eventually win and control the government of Russia.

The chief socialist competitor to the Marxist Social Democratic party organized in 1898 was the Socialist-Revolutionary party, established as a secret organization between 1901 and 1902 and having as its aims the socialization of ownership of all land and the governing of Russia by the entire population, including the national minorities. The Socialist-Revolutionaries saw the peasant as the backbone of their future socialist society; they emphasized the use of terror in order to draw attention to their movement; and they created a special fighting group to direct the activities of the Party. Though ostensibly a peasant organization, the Socialist-Revolutionaries, like the Social Democrats, received little support from the peasants. Their strength came from the educated elements within the national minorities, who wanted an identification with the Great Russian majority rather than actual separation. The czarist regime rejected them, but the Socialist-Revolutionaries and the Social Democrats gave them a chance to be part of a future government and society. (In fact, this was also what the intellectual elites wanted in Indonesia and Africa; but they were not given such a chance.)

Neither the Social Democrats or the Socialist-Revolutionaries were very numerous before 1917. The Social Democrats had been organized in 1898 out of previously independent Marxist groups; but within a short period of time their ranks had been infiltrated by the czarist police, and most of their leadership was arrested. Even in 1903 when the Social Democratic party met in London, since they could not meet at home, their numbers were still tiny. The Party split on the proposal made by Lenin to restrict party membership to a small, dedicated group of professional revolutionaries. The majority (*bolshinstvo*) of the votes went to Lenin, and thus his followers became known as Bolsheviks, or those of the majority; the minority became known as Mensheviks (*menshinstvo*). The small number of delegates of both factions did not reflect equivalent strength in Russia.

Between 1900 and 1902, the czarist police attempted to organize the industrial workers in order to control them; but the wave of strikes that were led by police agents upset the Ministry of Interior so much that the latter quickly dissociated itself from these pseudo-revolutionary tactics. The organized workers, however, soon fell into the hands of the socialists, who used them to drum up popular support for their political demands. Although Russia until 1928 was still a peasant country, industry was expanding during the first decade of the twentieth century around the large cities of European Russia and in the coal and iron ore areas of the northern Ukraine. Steel, machine building, and oil received a good deal of capital from abroad. From 1890 to 1914, the industry of Russia expanded over 10 percent per year, or at the same rate as during the Communist Five-Year Plans.

In 1904 Japan declared war upon Russia because the latter was poaching in Japanese spheres of influence (though the Japanese Government had repeatedly suggested that they should divide equally the spoils of Korea and China). The Russians were completely unprepared for war. With the Japanese destroying the Russian navy off Japanese shores and stalemating the Russian army in Manchuria, the war soon came to a close. Although the Russian losses were minimal, revolution soon broke out in reaction to this national humiliation; and both the middle classes and the revolutionary groups insisted upon far-reaching political reforms in the government. Again, the police organized a controlled demonstration in St. Petersburg led by a Russian Orthodox priest, but it got out of hand and before the day was over the cossacks had killed more than 1,000 demonstrators.

Communism Takes Over

Although political reforms were promised and a Duma, or parliament, was established, the Czar gradually withdrew his political concessions; and by 1908 the Duma became an empty gesture. In 1914 World War I broke out, for which Russia, despite her recent industrial growth, was as unprepared as for the war in 1904. By the early part of 1915, widescale bungling by the military, bureaucratic inefficiency, and unimaginative leadership coupled with the breakdown of the weak railroad system brought Russian fighting to a standstill. Although offensives were carried on briefly in 1915, the Russian army was already beaten; and the morale of the Russian soldiers indicated that they knew it. Many of those on the front lines could obtain rifles only from men who had fallen. There were few cannon with enough shells to fire for more than a few minutes per day. The Czar at this time assumed command of the armies and turned his decision-making powers over to his wife. The Empress, a fanatically religious woman, in turn sought advice from an illiterate Siberian "holy man" named Rasputin, who had no connection with the church. Rasputin was assassinated in December, 1916, by a group of noblemen, but both the Czar and Czarina had already lost the loyalty of the vast majority of the educated members of the population, including most of the nobility and the industrialists.

In early 1917, the distribution system disintegrated completely, and severe food shortages developed in the large cities. Consumer goods became almost unobtainable as the weak industrial structure attempted to produce supplies for an army of more than 13 million men. Railroad rolling stock broke down because of lack of parts for replacement, and the blockade of the few Russian ports by the Germans and Turks prevented the import of necessary weapons and goods. Revolutionary propaganda carried on among the soldiers at the front and in the rear encouraged a desire for peace.

On March 9, 1917, strikes broke out among the workers in St. Petersburg; and the police were called out to drive the mobs of workers from the center of the city. For the first time in Russian history, the cossack soldiers refused to assist the harassed police and instead turned against them. Soon the cossacks were joined by disgruntled soldiers, who poured out of their barracks to join the demonstrators in the streets. On March 12 two regiments of the elite guards went over to the revolutionaries, an arsenal was seized, weapons were distributed to the demonstrators, and the prisons and police headquarters were occupied. On March 14 the Duma took over power from the Czar; and a provisional government under Prince Lvov, an agrarian leader, was formed. The following day the Czar abdicated under pressure; and the provisional government, which at that time had no mass following and was representative only of the upper classes, assumed complete power.

The Petrograd Soviet (the German-sounding St. Petersburg became Russified at the beginning of the war into Petrograd, or Peter's City) had reluctantly given its backing to the new provisional government under the latter's promise that a new election would be called soon to determine the permanent form of Russia's future government. The Petrograd Soviet at this time had a majority of Menshevik and Socialist-Revolutionary delegates, with few Communists. On April 16 Lenin arrived from Switzerland; he had been preceded by the Communist leaders who had been freed from exile in Siberia. Lenin immediately issued a call for a socialist revolution in which land would be redistributed to the peasants (the peasants had already done this themselves by taking over the large estates of the nobility and the Crown), bread would be given to the hungry, and peace would be presented to the war-weary. The Bolshevik party, under Lenin's leadership, immediately fought for the control of the Soviets, or Councils. But as late as July, 1917, the Communists represented less than one-fifth of the membership in the Soviets of Russia; the overwhelming majority were still Mensheviks and Socialist-Revolutionaries, with the latter having a clear-cut majority. In the beginning of April, 1917, it was doubtful that the Communists could muster more than 25,000 members, although their numbers doubled by July. Nevertheless, by having a determined program and a fanatic and dedicated leadership, the Communists were able to take over power in Petrograd on November 7, 1917, even though their following was a minute fraction of the population. The Communists made peace with the Germans in January, 1918; but Russia was immediately plunged into a Civil War, with the Communists and non-Communists fighting for power, which lasted almost three years and was as bloody as the previous war against the Austrians and Germans.

The Union of Soviet Socialist Republics

By the beginning of 1921, the new Union of Soviet Socialist Republics had been pushed back industrially to where Russia had been in 1890. Seven years of war had seen millions of dead, innumerable houses destroyed, most railroad equipment worn out, and the majority of factories closed for want of machine tool parts. Although in 1919 and 1920 there had been a good deal of organized military opposition to the Communists, the Communists won because they were better organized, had an appealing political program based upon an improved human society, and had definite goals. The opposition, on the other hand, had no idea where it was going. The Communists were determined and ruthless, even though they feared that they could hold power only temporarily. In February, 1918, Lenin was jubilant that the Communists had already held power as long as three months (or longer than the Paris Commune of 1871). By 1921 the Red Army had driven the opposition White Armies out of Russia; and in 1920 it had crushed various revolts against its rule. The defeat of Germany by the West in November, 1918, permitted the Bolsheviks to regain the Ukraine, which had been conquered by the Germans. The Baltic states and Finland proclaimed their independence, as did Poland, which in 1919 had resumed sovereignty over the territories that had been partitioned by Austria, Prussia, and Russia in the 1790's.

Communist Problems Between 1921 and 1928

In 1914 when World War I began, more than 85 percent of the Russian population was peasants. The cities were few and far between, although an industrial base had slowly been built up which produced 5 million tons of steel per year (the United States produced more than 32 million tons in that year), mined 32 million tons of coal, and obtained 11 million tons of oil from its Caucasian deposits along the Caspian Sea. The quality of the small educated class in Russia compared very favorably with the rest of Europe, but the illiteracy rate in the country was still more than 90 per cent. A large part of the educated class had escaped with the

White Armies between 1918 and 1920, but enough stayed behind to help rebuild the truncated industries. The Communists themselves, using as many non-Communist educated individuals as were available, initiated a crash program to produce technicians, engineers, and managers out of their more promising Party material. Nikita Khrushchev was one of the illiterate workers who was given an education and managerial responsibility during this period.

To increase domestic production at a time when no capital was willing to come to Russia and when trade had almost ceased (the victorious European powers did not recognize the Communists until 1924, and the United States did not do so until 1933), the Communist leadership modified the wartime requisition of food from the peasants by force and the nationalization of all plants. Private owners were now permitted to reopen small factories, and well-to-do peasants were encouraged to produce as much as possible for profit. This "taking one step backward in order to take two steps forward" was referred to as the NEP, or the New Economic Policy, and lasted until 1928 when the first Five-Year Plan began.

The seven years between 1921 and 1928 represented a period of reconstruction. Steel, coal, and oil were brought up to 1914 levels. Thousands of schools were built to educate new Communist managers since the old non-Communist intellectual groups were not trusted by the Communist leadership. By 1928 the standard of living had surpassed that of 1914.

Lenin died in 1924, and for three years a jockeying for power took place between Trotsky, Stalin, Rykov, Tomsky, and Bukharin, with Stalin finally capturing the Communist party apparatus and thus making himself the sole dictator of the Party, which was the Soviet Government. By the end of the 1937 purges, most of the original leaders of the Party had been executed by Stalin's orders. The Central Executive Committee was rid of all possible opposition to Stalin; his men were placed in all important positions of authority. Marshal Bulganin once said of the period that he never knew when he was asked to see Stalin on official business whether he would be permitted to walk out of his office a free man.

The Five-Year Plans

Between 1929 and 1941 the Soviet Union desperately attempted to industrialize in a hurry. As Stalin expressed it in 1931, Russia had been beaten time and time again by the Mongol, the Tartar, the Swede, and the German because she was weak; she would be beaten again in the future unless she became stronger; and she had less than ten years in which to gain the necessary strength. It was prophetic of Stalin that the Soviet Union was attacked within ten years, in 1941, because the Nazis had been convinced that the country was weak and could be defeated, although the Soviet Union would prove to be the graveyard of the Nazis.

Beginning in 1930 the well-to-do peasants, who had been the Communists' strongest opponents in the rural regions, were now treated openly as enemies. Their lands were confiscated and attempts were made to force them into collective farms under Communist control. The well-to-do peasants, or *kulaks* (from the Russian word meaning tight-fisted), killed their livestock by the millions to prevent them from falling into the hands of the Communists, and burned their crops, their hay, and their barns. Hundreds of thousands of these *kulaks* were driven from their homes and placed in labor camps in those regions of Siberia where it was impossible to get voluntary labor. They were put to work under severe climatic conditions felling timber, constructing railroads in desert regions, and building canals and industrial complexes.

The Communist leadership considered the *kulaks* as expendable labor that was cheaper to obtain than machines. They received little else but black bread and porridge and were forced to live under conditions worse than those suffered by the serfs before 1861. They were even more exploited than the nineteenth century Russian factory owners had exploited their serf labor.

After 1930, tens of millions of poor peasants were forced into collective farms and a good many into state farms; but little capital was expended to provide them with the education, the tools, the machines, and the fertilizers that the American farmers had at that time. Most of the skills, machines, and managerial talent went into heavy industry: steel, machine tools, coal, oil, munitions, aviation, and railroads. There was little left for the peasants or the consumers (few consumer goods industries were built during this period).

The cities expanded enormously as millions of poor, unskilled, illiterate peasants poured into them from the impoverished countryside. The collectivization of agriculture offered little to the agricultural laborer or to the sons of the small peasants, for the overpopulation of the rural areas and the forced sale of most grain to the State at low prices meant that there was little left for the peasant. The cities and new industrial centers grew from 15 percent of the population in 1928 to more than 50 percent by 1960, although the construction of housing, shopping facilities, and transportation did not keep up with the flood of new arrivals. In the new industries workers were housed in flimsily-built frame dormitories. Even the apartment houses for the staff needed repairs within a few years after construction.

The vast majority of urban workers in the older cities had to double up in houses built before 1914, sharing bathrooms and kitchens with at least three or four other families. Few workers had the luxury of even one room for their families. Living conditions sank to pre-1890 standards, as the cost of living rose steadily with little done by the Communist leadership to ameliorate the harsh living and working conditions. By the end of World War II the standard of living of the Russian industrial worker was little better than that of the factory worker in the underdeveloped countries of the world. Although the standard was somewhat higher than that of the Indian or Chinese worker, the real wages were from one-tenth to one-twelfth of the American average for workers. Although the Russians paid little for rent and received free medical care, the purchase of simple food items took most of their monthly income, leaving little for clothing. A pair of shoes, for example, took a month's pay for an unskilled worker; a suit of clothes where available cost three to five months' pay.

The Communists looked upon the Five-Year Plans primarily as educational experiments aimed at industrializing the country and raising the level of skills among the urban population. The inefficiency of both work and plant and the wastage of raw materials were accepted as normal risks involved in bringing about this cultural change. Through the Five-Year Plans the Soviet Union was changed from an underdeveloped peasant country to the second most highly industrialized country in the world. From 1929 to 1937 the Soviet Union increased its industrial production by an average rate of over 12 percent per year. (This does not mean that the quality of industrial production was raised proportionately, for the quality has been quite low even in recent years.) The concentration of effort was on heavy industry and transportation. Consumer goods, housing, and agriculture were given no priorities of any kind.

The Five-Year Plans for all their brutality, their slave labor camps (which were abolished only in the 1950's), their lack of freedom of movement for the workers, peasants, and even teachers did succeed in bringing the Soviet Union into the Secondary civilization. Where only 15 percent of the population were literate when the Communists took over power, one could say that the entire population had become literate by 1965. Where the universities and the higher research institutes graduated only a few thousands during the last years of the czarist regime, the Communists were graduating engineers and scientists by the hundreds of thousands. Although the education was narrowly specialized and emphasized the applied aspects of both technology and science, a small number were permitted to become research scientists. Hundreds of thousands of physicians were trained, but the education of most left much to be desired. The majority of the physicians were women who received a salary little higher than that of the workers. The so-called free medicine of the Soviet Union has been at the expense of the women physicians, who have received far less than the technicians, engineers, or other professionals.

While 974,000 technicians had been trained in the technical schools by 1940, the number increased to over 2 million by 1962. In 1940 there were over 800,000 students in the universities and higher schools, but by 1962 the number had increased to more than 2,500,000. The Soviet Union by 1964 was training more engineers than the United States, though the engineers of the Soviet Union were trained more narrowly than those of the United States.

The social sciences, as they are known in the United States or Western Europe, are relatively unknown in the Soviet Union, although there is a trend whereby some of the statistical methodologies of economics and sociology are being adopted. Psychiatry is relatively unknown, as is most of American academic psychology. A good many of the fields of anthropology are studied, such as physical anthropology, archaeology, linguistics, and ethnography. Cultural anthropology is relatively unknown in the Soviet Union, since its theories and methodology conflict with those of the Communists. The earth sciences are taught, as are the natural sciences, with the single exception of genetics, which fell on hard times under Stalin since it held that physical characteristics are inherited, whereas the Communists insist that anything can be changed through Communist research efforts. A good deal of theoretical work is being done in chemistry, physics, and mathematics; but the stress in the Soviet Union, as in the United States, is generally on the applied rather than on the pure sciences.

The Communists through their Five-Year Plans have been able to show that industrialization can take place in a noncapitalist society. Industry had developed in the United States and in Great Britain through private efforts; the state, however, was the major initiator of industrialization in Japan, Germany, Russia, and partially in the United States. Factories are built in the same physical way in all countries of the world, and engineers and technicians are trained in roughly the same manner. In fact, industrialization has no more to do with Communism than with capitalism. It has more to do with a social climate that encourages the development of entrepreneurs, technicians, and innovators. The Soviet Union had its entrepreneurs in the Government and in the State Planning Commission. Although the Soviet Union has not thus far encouraged the growth of consumer industry or an efficient scientific agriculture, there is no reason why these two could not grow if given the opportunity.

Scientists and Managers

Academic freedom did not accompany industrialization in the Soviet Union. No scientific inquiries can be undertaken without initial approval from the Soviet National Academy of Sciences, and emphasis has been placed mainly upon those technological and scientific disciplines that do not contradict Communist philosophy. Physicists, chemists, mathematicians, physiologists, bacteriologists, virologists, and biologists are given a great deal of academic freedom and large sums of money for laboratory equipment and research. Even the earth sciences are encouraged in mapping mineral and oil resources. In many ways, one can say that the scientist who is working on projects that will benefit industry and the military has more individual freedom, higher social status, and more monetary rewards (such as a large new apartment, a country cottage, an automobile, and vacations in the luxurious spas) than the rest of the population.

The managers also receive a good deal of individual freedom, within the limits of the Communist structure. Although they receive their orders from the Planning Commission and the regional offices, they are permitted a certain amount of leeway in planning the production of their own plants, in making private deals with other managers of other plants for raw materials or finished goods, and in running their own plants. The average factory in the Soviet Union is run in as authoritarian a manner as any American one. The Soviet Union calls itself a Party dictatorship for the benefit of the workers and peasants, but neither of these two groups participates in any decisions that concern them. In the typical Soviet factory, no one speaks for the worker or represents him. The Communist-run factory council, the local trade union, and the Communist party cell have as their function supporting the director in all decisions that aim at an increase in the productivity of the plant.

According to David Granick,[1] the average Soviet factory manager is better educated than his American counterpart. In the Soviet Union, a college education is a virtual requirement for an industrial management post. In 1960 all Soviet plant directors were college graduates, as compared with almost 60 percent of the industrial executives in the United States. Although many of the initial managers in the early days of the Five-Year Plans were self-educated Communists, the present trend is to give the posts to graduate engineers, for only those with a highly specialized technical education are promoted to the top managerial positions. In the United States, on the other hand, more managers come from a liberal arts college background than an engineering background.

The Soviet engineer is often encouraged to take business administration courses to equip him for the financial and managerial aspects of factory life. Some business schools educate for economic planning, others specialize in personnel work and pricing, still others train individuals for work as bankers, comptrollers, and accountants. A new type of engineering-economics school has been organized in recent years whose graduates are placed in junior executive positions.

[1] *The Red Executive* (Garden City, N.Y., Doubleday, 1961), pp. 46–47.

Although the factory managers are extremely well paid by Russian standards, their way of life would be considered very Spartan by their American colleagues. Few of them receive more than a four or five room apartment. If an individual is the manager of a large factory, he may live in factory-owned housing, which may give him a better quality apartment than he would get in government-owned buildings. The manager's standard of living is going up and will in time doubtless be equivalent to what he would enjoy if he worked in the United States or Western Europe.

As a manager, he is also an important member of the governmental and Party apparatus. Most factory managers are members of the Communist party, factory cells, and the local industrial unions. As in the United States, the factory manager in the Soviet Union is a member of the Establishment. He is not an outsider governed by a hierarchy of Communist bureaucrats, but a member of the organization itself with his "contacts" going all the way up into the industrial ministry, of which his factory is part.

Although the Soviet Union is considered to be a bureaucrat's paradise, the number of clerical and administrative workers is less than in the United States. In 1963 in the United States, the percentage of white-collar and administrative workers was greater than that engaged in production. As industries become more complex, the number of individuals required to furnish the top managers with information about their plants also grows larger. The Soviet Union today is behind the United States in this respect; but as it becomes more industrialized and as services increase to what they are in the United States, the personnel problems will also be roughly similar.

The Soviet Union as a New Industrial State

The Soviet Union is still going through a transitional stage of industrialization and education. Although the brutality attendant upon industrialization has been lifted, the Soviet Union is still a totalitarian culture, where only those freedoms approved by the leadership are permitted to the people. The individual innovator is encouraged only in those fields that the Party considers important for its future. The individual is rewarded when he conforms and is punished severely when he does not. (Some of this also exists in the United States, but not to the extent that it does in the Soviet Union. There are important qualitative as well as quantitative differences between the two countries in the amount of freedom offered to the individual.) Although authoritarian patterns of behavior exist among Soviet scientists and those in academic domains, still there is the hope that the critical frame of mind and the questioning of theories that do not explain known facts may help in changing the totalitarianism of the Soviet Union within the next generation or so.

There is no doubt that the speed of industrialization in the Soviet Union has been spectacular, although the social and human costs have been tragically high. The Soviet Union was able to increase its annual industrial yield about 7 percent from 1937 to 1940, even though much of her industrial energy was going to the increase of armaments during that time. World War II was even more destructive of property and lives than World War I, the Civil War, the Volga famine, in which untold millions died, or the collectivization campaign of the early 1930's, in which hundreds of thousands, or even more, may have died of hunger after the State took its allotments. The Soviet Union itself admits that more than 25 million of its citizens died during the last war, of which some 6 million were soldiers. Millions of civilians perished as a result of hunger, bombings, disease, or execution by the Nazis. All told, some 45 million may have died in the Soviet Union from war, hunger, disease, and execution from 1914 to 1945. Although the Communists were responsible for a large number of these deaths, the deaths of a still larger number were caused by circumstances beyond their control.

The Soviet Standard of Living

Today the Soviet Union has become the second greatest industrialized nation in the world, if one considers mainly heavy industry as the basis. Her steel production is more than 85 million tons per year, as compared with 125 million tons in the United States. In the extraction of oil, in the mining of coal, and in the construction of railroads, the Soviet Union has made spectacular progress. She has competed with the richer United States in the manufacture of hydrogen bombs and space missiles; and she is educating a larger number of individuals in the technical fields and the sciences than any other country, including the United States.

On the other hand, the Soviet Union has not been able to solve her housing problem, for the shortage is so great that even by using mass-production methods in the construction of apartment houses, most urban families are still housed in one room, sharing both bath and kitchen with other families. Her consumer goods industries cannot compare with those in Western Europe, Japan, or the United States. Every family does not have the opportunity to have an electric refrigerator, enough good quality clothes, and a varied assortment of foods. The diet is still heavy in carbohydrates and fats and deficient in vegetables and fruits. A good deal of the meat consumption is in the form of sausages that contain a high percentage of fat and water mixed with cereals. Although her agriculture has made some strides since 1914, in general her peasant-farmers cannot compare with those of Western Europe, Israel, the United States, or Japan.

Because the Soviet Union is so much further north than the other agricultural nations, she has special problems of frost, a short growing season, and an erratic rainfall, which can only be solved by a greater concentration of her technicians and scientists working on the problems of agriculture. Even though the Soviet Union has developed a large industrial base, it is interesting that she still exports very few of the more than 200,000 machine tools she makes each year. Her exports are roughly what they were in 1914: timber, furs, gold, and oil. Her grain exports have ended because a larger population and poor agricultural techniques have made previous surpluses a thing of the past. Most experts believe that if the Soviet Union developed a more complex industrial structure, she could export her industrial products for agricultural imports from those countries that have a much better soil and climate.

The Soviet Union has been starving agriculture and her consumer goods industries in order to build up heavy industry. Considering all the goods and services that a modern industrial nation can produce, the Soviet Union still has a long way to go. Despite the claims made by its leadership, it is doubtful that the Soviet Union can "overtake and surpass" the United States in its standard of living before the end of the twentieth century, if then. There is no doubt that the Soviet Union will be a rich nation in the twenty-first century, but it seems unlikely that it will have a standard of living higher than that of the United States in the twentieth century.

Soviet Communism has placed emphasis upon creating an industrial and agricultural base for a future organization of society in which a floor would be placed under the needs of all people below which no one would theoretically be able to sink, but in which no ceiling would exist upon the individual's right to be both creative and innovating. To create the wealth for this future, the Communists have been willing to be totalitarian, anti-humanitarian, anti-intellectual, and unethical in their everyday dealings. The goal of this perfect society of the future has motivated the leadership so much that many among them feel that any means, no matter how amoral or unethical, are justified if they can hasten the day when this form of Communism can come to the Soviet Union.

Although the Soviet Union will undoubtedly undergo a good deal of cultural change in the future and may even realize parts of its goals during the next 100 to 200 years, it has thus far in its fifth decade of existence not had the time or the incentives to develop a new altruistic cultural personality with strong identifications with one's fellowman. The frustrations of living under Communism have been so great that the average citizen feels a good deal of aggressive dislike toward the minorities in his country, toward those who may not disagree with the goal but do disagree with the means employed in achieving it, toward those whom he feels are not pulling their weight, and toward non-Communist nations and powers. Humanitarianism, or an understanding and identification with human beings, has not been stressed, either in the Russia of the past or in the Soviet Union of today. A humanitarian outlook requires security of personality and a sense of individual importance which most of the Soviet population has lacked thus far. The test of how successful Communism will be in the Soviet Union will come when its citizens develop a greater identification with one another and with others outside the country.

So far, the Communists have been too busy developing the economic base for their future society to build up a sense of security for their population. It has not been very many years since a dread knock at the door at three o'clock in the morning meant arrest and removal to a labor camp or even execution. It has not been very many years since released Russian and Ukrainian prisoners of the Nazis were afraid to return home lest they be punished harshly because they had been taken prisoner alive. The leadership has thus far led the population by using both the carrot and the stick. As the educational levels rise, as the Communists themselves get away from their legends and mythology, and as a more critical spirit is born, then there is hope that Communism and the Soviet Union may change for the better.

Marxism-Leninism

During the past forty-eight years, the new culture that has developed within the Soviet Union has been a mixture of technological thought with eighteenth and nineteenth century concepts about man, his history, and his future, a combination which has been termed Marxism-Leninism. Marxism represented the ethical reaction of eighteenth century humanitarian and democratic hopes against the reality of the early nineteenth century Industrial Revolution in England and against the distressing poverty of the masses of people—both peasants and urban dwellers—in France and Germany at a time when wealth was increasing in the hands of a few. Leninism represented the reaction of the Marxist socialist tradition upon educated individuals against the authoritarian, inhumane obscurantism that went under the name of Russian autocracy. Both movements represented the emotional impatience of those who compared what could be new with what was old and obsolete.

Marxism was an attempt to bring a more humane and just society out of the indifferent dog-eat-dog class system that existed in England and on the Continent. Marx did not invent the class system; it existed thousands of years before he was born, and its reality was apparent to the underdogs living in Western Europe at that time. Contemporary economics had held open no hope for the workers to improve their conditions; they were told that little could be done to improve their lot because as soon as wages went up for them, they would bring them down again by having too many children, thus increasing the future supply of workers over possible demand. Even the concept that labor gave a value to the product it made which it did not receive back in its wages, was not new to Marx; Ricardo, the English Classical economist, had discussed it in detail long before Marx was even aware of the Industrial Revolution.

Leninism was a reaction to the czarist autocracy; it was the nineteenth century educated mind in Russia taking a hard look at the fossilized autocracy and class structure that prevented that country from becoming a counterpart of Western Europe, and especially of Germany and France. Much of the nineteenth century reaction to czarism and the Orthodox Church came from the educated noblemen who had lived abroad; from the children of half-German marriages; [2] from those who had identified with the educated Westerner and thus saw Russia from the latter's point of view; from the small group of entrepreneurs who were attempting against great odds to industrialize Russia; from the enlightened children of the ghetto who would like to have been treated as Russians, but who under czarist law and Russian culture felt that they never would be; from Polish intellectuals who viewed czarism and Orthodoxy as their two enemies; from Georgians and Armenians who wanted the Russians to be better than they actually were; from Letts who were torn between two worlds and who wanted to be above both; from Ukrainians and White Russians who wanted unity on equal terms rather than upon the unequal terms of the Russians; and so on. All these individuals had an emotional need to change Russia from the poverty-stricken country that it was, with an ineffective czar and a formalized church, to a country in which all could share equally. After 1861 too many insecure personalities were growing up with an inability to identify themselves with the Russia that then existed. They wanted to change a culture in which they did not feel at home and in which they found little satisfaction or recognition into a culture in which they believed they could participate with some meaning.

Karl Marx was born in Trier in the German Rhineland in 1818. His father was a lawyer who had become identified with the eighteenth century French enlightenment. A neighbor and close friend of the family, a Baron von Westphalen, who was a Prussian civil servant and whose daughter Marx later married, was also a product of the French libertarian enlightenment. Marx went to the university at Bonn and later to the university at Berlin, which was at that time the intellectual center of the

---

[2] Lenin's mother came from the Volga German community, and it is quite possible that she may have looked with contempt upon the unkempt masses of Russia.

German states. At Berlin, he was influenced by the Young Hegelians, David Strauss, Moses Hess, Bruno Bauer, and Ludwig Feuerbach, who were all then reacting against Hegel's idealism (that is, that forces other than man are the explanation of man's behavior). Early in his career, Marx became a materialist, which does not mean that he was an egoistic hedonist interested only in pleasure, but rather that he thought that man and his society could best be understood in terms of themselves. Today most of us are materialists in this sense (there has been a good deal of fuzzy confusion in the use of these philosophical terms). At no time was Marx a follower of Hegel, although he accepted a good many of Hegel's concepts and ideas since that could not be avoided in the intellectual climate of the day.

Marx became a newspaper editor when he was twenty-four, but his criticisms of the Prussian government soon led to the suppression of the paper. In Paris, he met Friedrich Engels, the son of a German textile manufacturer, with whom he developed a lifelong friendship and collaboration. In many ways it is difficult to separate the contributions made by Marx from those made by Engels. From 1849 to 1883, Marx lived in London. Friedrich Engels had come earlier to Manchester, where he was a partner in a textile mill owned by his father. Engels died in 1895. When the term "Marxism" is used, it is understood that the intellectual contributions of both Marx and Engels are meant, since Engels was neither a rubber stamp for nor a passive disciple of Marx.

Marxism as a System of Thought

Marx had no use for any theoretical explanation of the world that man lived in, although a good deal of his own interpretation turned out to be theoretical. He had said that it was no longer important to interpret the world, but rather to change it. It was as theoreticians of social change, then, that Marx and Engels made their great contributions.

Neither Marx nor Engels was deterministic, although they have been accused of being so. Both felt that man was very much influenced by the environment, or culture, in which he was born, but that he could change this if he were conscious of his own ideas and their influence upon his actions. All men, Marx and Engels said, require food, clothing, and shelter. Without production, men would be like wild animals. Because men have organized their efforts to develop agriculture, and later, manufacturing, they have changed their interpersonal relationships as a result. Once there are governors and governed, there are classes. New classes emerge as warriors become landlords who are supported by the peasants; and then new classes of priests, government clerks, and artisans emerge. Social classes are founded by one class' "exploiting" or living off another.

As artisan production in Europe became more complex, a new class came upon the scene whom Marx called the *bourgeoisie* (originally, those individuals who lived in fortified towns). These were the entrepreneurs and capitalists, and they inaugurated more revolutionary changes than any other previous class in history. But in doing so they brought into being a new class of workers called the *proletariat,* whom they exploited.

The bourgeoisie, who are both merchants and manufacturers, compete with one another, with the strongest tending to wipe out the weakest, thus creating monopolies for their goods. Because the less strong are afraid of defeat and amalgamation, they spend a good deal of time trying to make a cheaper and better product through improved machines, tools, and processes and in general trying to stave off a dog-eat-dog cataclysm through the use of advanced technology and superior management. Unfortunately, in the field of technology the little manufacturers cannot compete with the big ones; and they eventually sink to the level of the workers after losing their factories and wealth. Since the big manufacturers still do not feel secure, they do everything they can to encourage the invention of laborsaving machinery; and at the same time they try to make a large profit by paying the workers the lowest wages possible consistent with keeping them adequately fed so that they can work the machines. In the long run, according to Marx and Engels, when the majority of the population have sunk to the level of the lowest paid workers, they will revolt against the "big capitalists" who control the government. By means of a general strike or even a revolution, they will topple the minority of bourgeoisie, confiscate their plants, and develop a new form of society in which production will be for the use of everyone rather than for the profit of a few. Marx believed that the motive for past historic cultural change was caused by the clash between classes rather than by conflicts between nations. The class struggle was fundamental in Marx's and Engel's thinking as it became later on in that of Lenin and the Communists.

Marx and Engels developed no new school of economics. Both of them were followers of Smith, Ricardo, and Malthus, the founders of the Classical school of economics. Even Marx's assertion that the workers would get poorer with time while the owners would become wealthier was what both Ricardo and Malthus had also claimed. From Smith and Ricardo, Marx took the concept that labor is the basis for all value in the manufacture of a commodity; this concept was made into a justification for socialism. Marx's argument for a change in societal structure was ethical in tone rather than "scientific"; since the wages that the workers received were less than the total value that they created, the difference between what the worker received and what the employer got for his product represented the latter's profit, which was the appropriation by the employer of what actually belonged to the worker. According to

Marx and Engels, the workers did not need the capitalist; they could create a form of society in which they would be able to run the factories and the transportation systems themselves, thus keeping for their own use the full value of what they produced and thereby giving themselves a higher standard of living.

Men, according to Marx and Engels, make their own history, which means that if one form of society becomes obsolete, a new one can take its place only after many individuals have thought it out in detail and have organized themselves into a political movement with common aims to push it through. According to Marx, nothing is inevitable by itself; each new stage of economic society requires the conscious efforts of dedicated men to make it work. This was how capitalism arose.

Marx and Engels said that capitalism could not stabilize itself or survive for long because of its internal contradictions. The motivation for capitalism was profit, and to make a profit the capitalist had to prolong the working day. Or if this was impossible, he had to introduce new tools, speedups, or more efficient processes. Under the pressure of competition, the capitalist must expand by putting more capital into plant and machines than into labor. The capitalists by their large-scale investment cause a boom, which is soon followed by a depression because a large number of workers cannot purchase the goods they make. And so the factories cut down on production, and the workers lose their jobs. This causes a few of the more efficient capitalists to invest new capital into more efficient production in order to attract new markets. In doing so they create another boom. The less efficient manufacturers, on the other hand, have to close their factories and dismiss their workers, thus creating still another depression. Such crises were normal to capitalism because the workers who formed the bulk of the population were not receiving their just share of the value they put into their commodities, and as a result their wages were not large enough to enable them to buy back the goods that they themselves produced. Because the internal markets could not absorb the goods that were being increasingly produced in huge quantities by each manufacturing country, the capitalists had to seek markets elsewhere. This meant a cutthroat competition not only between leading capitalists but also between industrial countries. The industries became larger but remained in fewer hands; the rich became fewer but richer, while the poor became even poorer.

Such was the picture Marx and Engels drew to describe the development of capitalism. The conclusion that they and others reached from this depressing picture was that if capitalism could not benefit the majority of the population and if the developing sciences and technologies could not be used for the general welfare of the inhabitants, then capitalism as an inefficient, reactionary system of societal organization must be abolished. It was necessary to use technology and science to plan a better society in which all individuals would be employed, in which the benefits of labor would return to labor, and in which men would be manufacturing for a society where all would have the commodities they wanted. At the same time, all would be giving their labor gladly in building up such a society. This was the reasoning that provided the rationale for "scientific socialism."

According to Marx and Engels, it was necessary to plan ahead for such a socialist form of society. The workers must be organized; and the leadership must be educated to understand what the defects of capitalism were, why it could not work, and how to achieve a more just socialist society. Socialism, however, was not inevitable. Even though capitalism was weak, no revolution could take place unless the socialists were well organized and intelligently led.

The workers had to become the nucleus of the socialist movement, according to Marx, Engels, and Lenin, because they were numerous, were in a strategic position to paralyze an economy by striking, were disciplined because of their work habits, and were unable to compromise their sharp differences with their employers. The workers could solve the conflict between themselves and the capitalists only by expropriating the plants and operating them under their own direction. Marx and Engels both believed that socialism might be achieved peacefully in a democratic country, but that in a nondemocratic country it undoubtedly would require violence in order to take over power.

The workers were considered to be the future dominating class, but Marx and Engels were also convinced that the workers could not create a new society without the intellectual socialists' organizing, educating, and showing the way. Neither Marx nor Engels had any interest in the "exploited" peasants, for they were convinced that the latter were basically petit bourgeois at heart, that they could not be organized, and that they had no desire to live in a socialist state. Both Marx and Engels felt that the peasants had to be transformed into landless laborers before they could be led into the lush pastures of socialism.

At no time did Marx and Engels describe the path to socialism; they could only describe the future socialist society in very vague terms. What they did emphasize was the organization of a political party to educate and train the workers to work for the establishment of a new economic order. In Western Europe and in the United States, Marx and Engels thought that the socialists could come to power via parliamentary democracy. In autocratic countries such as Russia, they felt that violence would be necessary for the workers to dispossess the ruling groups.

On the other hand, no matter how democratic the country, the expropriation of the capitalists required some continuing form of social and economic dictatorship by the workers over them. In a political democracy, Marx and Engels believed, the capitalists exercised a social and economic dictatorship, for the small number of owners controlled the livelihoods of the many and in fact dominated their lives as well. As the dominant class, the capitalists controlled the state and its police powers to keep the organized workers at bay. Under socialism the dominant form of political behavior would be that of a workers' democracy, in which the workers control the means of production and use the power of their state to prevent the organization of the private means of production. Under a democratically run society, the workers would be able to create an industrial system that would produce an abundance for their needs, a system in which they would have a voice and an opportunity to share in its growth.

Such in brief were the main points of the theories developed by Marx and Engels. Both stressed the importance of ideas in bringing about cultural change. But both also insisted that economic interests were paramount and that workers and employers would find it impossible to share the same interests because the many conflicts existing between the two could be resolved only by creating a society in which one class could not exploit another. The history of mankind, according to Marx and Engels, was a history of class conflicts, which were resolved by the exploited class taking over power. But in time it also developed a subservient class, which it also exploited, and thus continued the circle of conflict.[3]

Lenin's Contributions

The above ideas were taken over in the 1890's by the Russian intellectuals who organized the Russian Social Democratic party, which split in 1903 into the Bolsheviks and Mensheviks. These ideas about man, history, and the world were also taken over by Lenin in the period between 1895 and 1917 as authoritarian truth. He added little to the ideas, although he added a great deal to the theory of how a party of workers can take over power.

Lenin made his greatest contribution in the organization of the Communist party. Marx had used the term *communist* to differentiate his "scientific" thought from that of the romantic Utopians who called themselves socialists; in the latter part of Marx's and Engel's lives they used the term *socialist* more frequently than communist. Lenin had taken over the early Marxist term *communist* to differentiate his party from those whom he had accused of revising Marx, that is, of rejecting the theories of class conflict and violence, and who called themselves

---

[3] Marx's theory of class conflict makes poor history. In Roman days, though slaves were exploited, they never took power away from their masters to become the new rulers themselves. Capitalism did not develop out of feudalism, but out of the trader-merchant-artisan complex.

socialists or Social Democrats. He had gone one step further than Marx in insisting that the political party must be run mainly by the educated class, or the intellectuals. The latter would be the dedicated revolutionaries who would spend their lives planning how to take over power. Marx had believed that the workers would become revolutionary because of their worsening situation and would organize themselves into a political party to take over power; Lenin sensed that there were not enough class-conscious workers in Russia to make such a party meaningful. Lenin believed that it was necessary to have a small and dedicated group of socialists (Marx and Engels had also believed that the leadership must come from the educated socialists), who would be an educated elite paid by the party to devote its energies to organizing the workers, educating them, and acting as their consciences. The Communist party, from Lenin's point of view, could not be a loose collection of many individuals but must be a tightly disciplined elite, or a "vanguard of the workers," which would know far better than the workers or the peasants what had to be done since the workers and peasants were too uneducated and not politically oriented or class-conscious enough. Like Marx and Engels, Lenin believed that the Party's chief function was to educate the workers in the Party's ideas and point of view.

Where Marx and Engels had little interest in the peasants, Lenin believed that the peasants and the workers together needed to form the mass base for a Communist party, though neither could be permitted to fashion its structure. Lenin believed that only a tightly organized political party with a definite program could educate the peasants and workers and thus transform them. (Education was a fundamental tenet in Lenin's Communist party.)

The rise in the educational level of czarist Russia encouraged the sons of middle peasants to become interested in bettering the living conditions of the rural areas. The revolutionary role of the peasants in taking the land from the landlords during the Revolution of 1905 led Lenin to believe that the peasant when properly directed could be a force for change. Lenin was realistic enough, however, to know that one could not take over the power of the state in a peasant Russia with only a few million workers and a small, educated Party elite. As a result, the Communists after 1905, unlike the Social Democratic parties of Western Europe who concentrated upon trade unions and the urban workers, spent as much time working with the poor and middle peasants as with the workers. During the Civil War period, or the counterrevolutionary era of 1919–1920, it was the active or passive support of the poorer peasantry that enabled the Communist Red Armies to win their victories. (Most of the Red Army soldiers still come from the peasantry.)

Lenin also modified Marx's theories on capitalism. In an attempt to prove to his following that evolution from a capitalist to a socialist state could never be accomplished peacefully, but only through war and revolution, Lenin developed the concept that rivalry existed not only between individual capitalists, but also between monopolists of one industrial nation competing for markets with monopolists of other industrial nations. Although the workers in the more advanced capitalist countries share some of the wealth of their employers, according to Lenin, their advantages are gained, nevertheless, from exploiting the colonies and the underdeveloped areas of the world. As the competitive need for outlets becomes intensified, the colonies become even more exploited, which ends in the natives' organizing their own movements for national liberation. Before the colonies can achieve national freedom, however, the conflicts between the various advanced capitalist countries become so intensified that wars are almost always inevitable between them. Thus, from Lenin's point of view, capitalism not only leads to crises but also to war.[4]

Although the workers in the capitalist nations appear to be economically better off, their advantage is only a temporary one; and sooner or later they will pay the price in a successive series of depressions which will throw millions out of work and cut the wages of the others to a little above subsistence. Capitalism, according to Lenin, finds it impossible to develop internal markets because, as was shown by the Marxian theory of surplus value, more goods are produced than can be bought by the workers. To keep production up, the capitalists are compelled to dump their goods in other countries or in their colonies.

As the colonies rise up against the imperialists, Lenin believed, their markets are closed to the capitalists. Sooner or later as the various national independence movements take colony after colony out of the hands of the imperialist nations, the capitalists will find that their markets have shrunk so much that economic depression is the natural consequence. Therefore, although the workers in the capitalist nations appear to be better off temporarily under capitalism, in the long run they will be much worse off than those in the Communist camp. From the Communist point of view, then, even independent nations are considered colonies of the imperialists if they are small and weak. They too will in time rise up in arms against their exploiters; and this will lead the capitalist nations not only to become embroiled with one another in never-ending conflict, but also to fight the various national liberation movements of the weaker nations and dependencies.

Lenin, in his desire to be the true heir of Marx and Engels, reacted violently against those who were trying to revise Marxism with their claim that socialism could evolve from capitalism within a democratic society. In Germany, Great Britain, and the Scandinavian countries, Social

[4] From the Communist point of view, this is why Americans are automatically imperialists or warmongers, while the Communists are peace-loving and anti-imperialist.

Democratic movements had arisen whose emphasis was upon getting enough electoral strength in parliamentary elections to influence the nation's laws. The Social Democratic and the Labor parties believed that socialism could evolve slowly and peacefully. The Communists denied this and decried the socialists as betrayers of the working class because they tried to give its members the impression that revolution was not necessary. Until the advent of Nazism in Germany in 1933, the Communists considered the Social Democratic party as their chief enemy, for in being socialist they competed with the Communists by "pretending" to be for socialism, while the Conservative and Fascist parties at least made their positions clear as class enemies. In Germany the socialists were the target of the Communists, and in Berlin in 1932 the Communists joined forces with the Nazis to destroy the Social Democratic Transport Workers' Union. In this period, the Communists referred to the Social Democrats as "Social Fascists."

The Communists under Lenin could tolerate no opposition to their political programs. If the European socialists differed with them, they did not look upon this as any ordinary dissent in political fields where no one knew what the future would bring, but as "criminal behavior," "revisionism," "betrayal of the working class," "slander of the Communist party," "paid lackeys of the capitalists," and so on. The Communists were convinced that they were always right and all others were wrong. From the Communist point of view, it was foolish to waste one's time arguing with those whom one already knew to be wrong; all one could do was to prevent innocent individuals from following the "wrong-headed" lead of one's opponents. As a result, the Communists engaged in various emotional campaigns to label any opposition to them as enemies of progress, supporters of capitalism and imperialism, fascists, and members of other movements the Communists considered unsavory. In their attempts to destroy the image of the opposition by any possible means, the Communists engaged in card-stacking (taking words out of context), guilt by association, unfounded accusations, wild assertions, and other unethical devices.

In the Soviet Union after 1918, opposition became virtually impossible; and after 1924 when Stalin came to power, it was extremely dangerous. By the 1930's any opposition to Communist decisions often meant execution. This moderated somewhat after Stalin's death in 1953; but opposition to fundamental Communist party tenets is still not permitted in the Soviet Union, although the death penalty is no longer demanded as a punishment.

Marx and Engels thought that socialism could only come in a highly developed capitalist society. Russia in 1917 had been in transition from a peasant economy to an industrialized one. To make Russia fit the model suggested by Marx and Engels, the leadership decided to telescope the capitalist and the socialist revolutions through Five-Year Plans. In the first five years of power, Lenin and his followers hoped that the workers in Germany would revolt so that Germany could provide the industrial base to help Russia become an industrialized nation. Lenin had been willing to sacrifice Communism in Russia for its success in Germany. He was convinced that it would be very difficult to create a socialist base for society out of a poor and isolated Soviet Union. Although he had predicted that "imperialism was the last stage of capitalism" and that the more advanced industrial countries would fight one another for markets, by 1920 Lenin was convinced that the weak Soviet Union would be the victim of another attempt at intervention.

In 1919 the Communist International, with its fifty-odd member parties, was organized to spread the Communist revolution so that the Soviet Union would not be isolated in a world of non-Communist states. In 1923 help was given to the Kuomintang of Sun Yat-sen so that a national revolution could drive the "imperialists" from China and at the same time prepare the way for a future Communist revolution. In 1923 Lenin and his followers were convinced that Germany would soon join them as another Communist power. Inflation, unemployment, and the occupation of the Ruhr by French troops had encouraged the Soviet Union to believe that a revolutionary situation had been building up in that country.

After 1924 these optimistic hopes fell. Nowhere in the world did it seem that Communism had much of a chance for success. Trotsky, at that time fighting with Stalin for his political life, insisted that the Soviet Union was too weak to exist alone, that she had to support revolutionary movements everywhere in order to increase the number of Communist states. Stalin, taking another tack, insisted that socialism could be and had to be built in one country. As a result, Stalin used the Communist International and the various Communist parties to strengthen the Soviet Union's defenses in international affairs.

The slogan "Defend the Soviet Union" became the chief function of every Communist party, including those in the underdeveloped areas. The assumption was that the Soviet Union as the fatherland of the workers had to survive in order to prepare the industrial base that was necessary to enable other Communist parties to come to power later on. If the Soviet Union were defeated, that would be the end of the Communist experiment. Therefore, each Communist everywhere in the world owed his first loyalty to preserving the Soviet Union.

During the 1930's, although the turnover in Communist party membership outside the Soviet Union was extremely high, the individual leaders kept their parties close to the existing policies of the Soviet Union. A sense of guilt had been built up among Communist party leaders that any Party that attempted to go off on its own was in fact betraying the Communist cause and preventing untold future generations from enjoying the benefits of Communism. Any criticism of the Soviet Union, no matter how mild, was considered slander; any attempts to make the Communist party mirror local and national conditions was considered a sell-out to the enemies of the Soviet Union and Communism. The Soviet Union was identified with everything that was progressive and beneficial for the working classes, and the mention of the existence of slave-labor camps, police terror, and an extremely low standard of living was denied as slander emanating from the enemies of the Soviet Union. In the past, the Communists have viewed the world as filled with plots, hostilities, and deviant conspiracies aimed at preventing the Soviet Union from achieving its socialism. (The Communists believe that Communism as a system of society will not come into existence before the end of the century. Under Communism each individual will receive from society what he needs; and in return he will devote his energies, talents, and creativity to the development of a better society.) Socialism is thus a transitional stage in creating the industrial wealth that will make possible the egalitarianism of a future Communist society.

Contemporary Soviet Society

After almost fifty years of power, interrupted by civil war, famine, forced collectivization, and the widespread destruction of World War II, the Soviet Union has been raised from a peasant society with little industry to one of the great industrial and scientific nations of the world. It is difficult to draw up a balance sheet, for although industrialization and technical education have made impressive gains, the Soviet Union is still far from satisfying the needs of its population. The standard of living in the 1950's went up for the first time since 1917, but there is no doubt whatever that the average citizen, say, in Norway commands more services, more varied and superior quality goods, better medical care, and more of the elements of the welfare state than does his equivalent in the Soviet Union. The Communists have developed no new shortcuts to an industrialized society; what they have shown is that there are many ways in which a country can become industrialized and that technology and science have nothing to do with the ownership or nonownership of the means of production. In this sense they have broken away from the traditional conviction that industrialization can take place only with private investment capital.

In the past five decades the Soviet Union has educated large numbers of its citizens. Although technical education is becoming broader and is moving away from the narrow specialization of the 1930's and 1940's, few opportunities have been offered the intellectual and academic communities to develop the types of curricula that would help the Soviet student adjust to changing conditions in 1980 and 1990. Although the Communists talk a good deal about socialist humanitarianism, very little has been done thus far to bring it into existence. There are few of the freedoms for the individual or the safeguards to protect him from the arbitrary power of the State that exist in the Scandinavian countries, the Federal Republic of Germany, Switzerland, Austria, Italy, the Benelux countries, France, Great Britain, Canada, the United States, Australia, New Zealand, or even India. In the Soviet Union the individual is not presumed innocent until proven guilty, and no courts exist to which the individual can turn for protection from the despotism of the State. No media of communication are available to permit him to criticize the Government's policies. The Communist party is *the* Government, and it monopolizes all media of communication to present its point of view.

Until a few years ago, the Soviet citizen found it difficult to listen to radio stations in Western Europe because of official jamming. Nowadays the Soviet Government permits its citizens greater freedom to listen to certain outside radio stations. The Soviet citizen cannot read what he pleases. He can read selected literary classics of the nineteenth century, but he cannot read the social philosophy of that period if it is in opposition to the tenets of Communism. He can read the Communist view of itself, but not critical reviews of Government policy. He cannot travel within the Soviet Union without a passport (as the serf could not in czarist days), and it is almost impossible for him to obtain permission for personal travel abroad. His picture of the world has been presented to him through the media of Communism; even the view of world history is screened through the official theories of the Communist party.

Nothing is permitted to develop that will threaten the image of the Communist party as the repository of the most accurate knowledge about the past, the present, and the future. In this sense, the Communist party leadership is both authoritarian and totalitarian. It is authoritarian in the sense that its leadership alone makes the decisions that affect the lives of more than 225 million Soviet citizens. It is totalitarian in the sense that it permits no opposition to its decisions and to its culture. It has no sense of humanity for those who oppose or who are dissenters; these have voluntarily removed themselves from the human race by such acts and therefore can be treated as if they had no human rights. In this meaning of the term, Communism in the Soviet Union, in the Bloc states, and in China and its adherent states is as totalitarian as Nazism. In many respects, the totalitarian mind is to be found more in the authoritarian states than in the democratic ones. In the democratic states the individual has a good many personal rights guaranteed to him by the courts, possesses considerable safeguards against arbitrary arrest and harassment, and is permitted by law to dissent and to disagree even with the majority. Majority rule is not the mark of democracy. Quite often it can lead to group authoritarianism and even to totalitarianism. The chief political characteristic of democratic societies is the right guaranteed to the individual by law and the courts to dissent and to belong to minorities.

Thomas Masaryk, the first president of Czechoslovakia, insisted that the State had to be as moral as the individual. Using this yardstick, one can say that the Communist State has often been immoral, and most times its behavior could be termed amoral. The Party and the Government have distorted facts to fit whatever theory they were developing at the moment. History has been rewritten and often falsified, and the quest for the truth has not been a value or goal of either the Party or the Government.

The Communist party has created many hostilities toward it among its citizens. A good many peasants are implacable enemies who have long memories of decades of Soviet mistreatment. The national minorities, especially those in Central Asia, have resented the forced Russification that has taken place and the use of Russian as the chief language everywhere. Moslems have found themselves discriminated against; and the prejudice against Jews has kept many of them out of the universities, the foreign service, and the military officer corps. The Great Russian has been set up as the model of what the behavior, language, and culture of the other minorities should be.

And yet, in any balance sheet one must agree that, although most of the citizens in the Soviet Union would like to see many needed reforms introduced into the Communist system, most of them may undoubtedly back the regime because they may be convinced that in the long run their children and they will benefit. They may disagree with many of the decisions made by the Government and they may want more freedom for themselves, but they will insist that Communism as such is a better system of economic society than that which they refer to as capitalism. Even if the Communist party were overthrown, which is very unlikely at this stage, few citizens of the Soviet Union would want to return to what existed under the czars. The private ownership of the means of production could never come back, any more than it could in the other countries that have adopted Communism since 1945. Communism as an economic system is here to stay; Communism as a totalitarian movement and form of government may not be. In this latter sense, a good deal of cultural change may take place in the Soviet Union during the next fifty years as pressures in the country bring greater freedom for the individual and for the thoughts he can express. Although authoritarianism will remain in the Soviet Union for some decades to come, totalitarianism may not. Democratic forms of governmental behavior as we know them are still far in the future.

Soviet "Democracy"

The differing interpretation placed upon "democracy" in the Soviet Union can be seen from the following editorial in *Pravda* dealing with "socialist democracy":

The Soviet people understand the term "freedom" to mean freedom from exploitation, from the horrors of unemployment and poverty, from racial, national and social oppression; freedom is the right to a dignified life and genuine political equality; it is the right to enjoy all the benefits of science and the arts.

During his visit N. S. Khrushchev said to an American statesman: "You say that the prime mover of man's energy, mind and initiative is profit or, to put it your way, business. We say: The prime mover is man's consciousness; his awareness that he is free; that he works for himself, for his family, for his society; and that the means of production belong to society, and not to an individual who profits from the exploitation of someone else's labor."

The advantage of socialist democracy lies in that the working people themselves own the means of production, and they themselves exercise state power through the organs of genuine democracy, the Soviets, elected by secret ballot. . . . At present, 1.8 million persons are deputies to the Soviets of our country. . . . Soviet democracy is permeated with a profound concern for man, for his labor, for his welfare and happiness and the all-around development of his personality. Soviet democracy guarantees all citizens the right to work, to recreation, to education, to old-age insurance and other democratic rights and freedoms. Ever new measures are taken to raise the Soviet people's living standards and improve their living and working conditions on the basis of a steady growth of the social wealth . . .

The Party educates all the people in the spirit of collectivism and industry, in the awareness of their social duty, in socialist patriotism and internationalism, and in the spirit of the observance of the lofty principles of the new society.[5]

Communist Ethnocentrism

Perhaps the greatest delusion of the Communists is their tendency to take their words at face value. Words of the Party become reality in the Soviet media of communications. They tend to confuse historical periods of time. In viewing the two different economic systems of the United States and the Soviet Union, the Communists tend to compare what they believe the Soviet Union will possess in the twenty-first century with what the United States had in 1900. Despite the official definition of "socialist democracy," few citizens of the Soviet Union enjoy the specified freedom from poverty, from national and social oppression, or the right

[5] *Pravda*, Moscow, December 5, 1960, as translated by the Soviet Embassy, Washington, D.C., Press Release No. 15, January 14, 1961.

to a dignified life and genuine political equality. Comrade Khrushchev and the peasant on the collective farm were not equal politically; neither are the factory workers and the factory director. Although 1.8 million delegates to the various Soviets are elected, no opposition slate is permitted, and only one list of names is given. The deputies are expected to approve automatically all the decisions made by the Communist party leadership.

Equality is as far from being an ideal in the Soviet Union as it is in the United States. Despite the existence of the Soviet Constitution of 1936 with its rights for the Soviet citizenry, not a single one of the rights dealing with personal freedom has ever been implemented. Freedom in the Soviet Union means the right to agree with the Communist party leadership, not to disagree with it. The Soviet citizen is not free to explore on his own the horizons of knowledge. He is free only to do what he is told and to believe that what the Party has told him is the truth. He does not have the right to be openly skeptical of past Party pronouncements, or to point out publicly how often the pronouncements have been in error or how often the Party leadership has been unable to see the near future clearly or rationally.

The Soviet teacher or professor is not free to point out to the pupils or students in his classroom that, although Marx and Lenin had some truth to their assertions, they also had a good deal of error and that Marx's interpretation of history explains very little. Instead of the middle class sinking to the level of the more numerous impoverished workers, just the opposite has occurred. The technical middle class, even in the Soviet Union, has become more numerous and more affluent, while the workers have become fewer as automation and modern technology make the unskilled and semiskilled workers almost obsolete. Instead of becoming impoverished, the mass of workers in the advanced industrial countries have seen their standard of living raised innumerable times in this century as a result of the increase in productivity caused by improved technology and scientific research.

Even Lenin made a series of errors in judgment. His theory of imperialism neither explained war nor correctly predicted future conflicts. During the Second World War, it was a so-called capitalist nation, Nazi Germany, that fought the Soviet Union, Great Britain, and the United States—three odd bedfellows from Lenin's point of view. Neither Marx nor Lenin properly understood the importance of nationalism, even in assessing the worker's role. The 6 million Germans who voted Communist in 1932 were more identified with a nationalist Germany than with an equally nationalist Soviet Union. Workers outside the Soviet Union have more in common with their own middle classes and farmers than with the Communist party leadership in the Soviet Union.

As embryonic social sciences, both Marxism and Leninism are very much out of date. Marx was a brilliant observer of his day; but he died in 1883, and much has gone on since his death, including a large accumulation of knowledge and more valid theories about man's behavior. Lenin, who died in 1924, was an outstanding organizer and manager, but he viewed the world through his nineteenth century Marxist and Russian cultures. He had a compulsion to make the facts of reality fit his theories, rather than the other way around. Although Marx considered his analysis of the world scientific, it was nothing of the sort. It was a good analysis containing many insights; but it was also polemical, argumentative, and prophetic in tone. It did not lay the foundation of any scientific analysis of human society.

Marx was wrong as often as he was right. He was wrong about the role of labor in increasing productivity; in fact, it is management and research that initiate an increase in the wealth of nations. The roles of unskilled and semiskilled labor are passive compared with the role of skilled research in increasing the worker's hourly output. Marx's great contribution was in the study of the crises under capitalism, although many of his insights in this area have become somewhat obsolete.

Both Marx and Lenin overrated the importance of the worker as a new class. The class that has superseded the "capitalist" has been the new managerial and technical middle class, whose members have made the twentieth century revolution. It is they who reflect the society of the future far more than the less educated workers or the illiterate peasants. Lenin had more insight than he would openly admit when he sensed that the new Communist party had to be led by the new managerial class and the educated, dedicated professional revolutionaries rather than by the less self-confident workers and peasants.

It was the intellectual party organizer who took over from Marx, not the worker. Unfortunately, most intellectuals had insufficient self-knowledge to sense how prone the educated man is to authoritarianism and to deciding what is best for others. This has always been true of the intellectual, from the prophets to the religious organizers and teachers. Authoritarianism has also been the mark of trade of the manager, the visionary, the military leader, the organizers of men, and the seers who have attempted to peer into the future. Capitalism, socialism, communism, and nationalism all suffer from this authoritarianism. The religious leaders who are convinced that only they possess the truth are brothers in spirit to the Communists who are certain that in their hands lies the welfare of future humanity. In this respect, the Communists are continuing a tradition that goes back even before the beginnings of civilization in ancient Sumeria.

Instead of creating new theoreticians of the caliber of Marx and Engels in order to understand the society being created, the Communist leadership brought about a good deal of cultural change, but their theoretical understanding of what it was they were trying to do was based upon the insights of more than a century before. No one attempted to improve upon Marx and Engels; instead, as men of action, the Communist leadership from 1917 to the present day have not let one part of their minds understand what the other parts were doing. Communism is still being led toward the future by the ideas of men who have long been dead.

Trends in the Soviet Union

Despite the great increase in industrial production that has taken place since the end of World War II, the Soviet Union is still floundering. Her agricultural production, which in 1965 was less than half that of the United States, is not sufficient to absorb the shocks of drought for more than a year or so; and the inefficiency of farming can be seen from the fact that 100 million people still live in rural areas in the Soviet Union, compared with less than 15 million in the United States. Soviet industrial wages and living conditions are not high enough to attract the surplus rural population, which still lives off the inadequate agricultural production of the collective farms without adding its labor to the urban production of goods and services. Unemployment may not exist in the Soviet Union, but the underemployment of at least 50 to 60 million indicates that unemployment has merely been hidden. Although the key industrial indices are impressive, it will still be a good many years before the increased production in a few fields will mean a plentiful and varied supply of goods for the consumer.

The 1961 Program of the Communist Party is more a wishful propagandistic piece of writing than an actual blueprint or guide to the future. To the Communists, words, instead of mirroring action, have a reality of their own. The leaders do not know where they are going. They merely aspire to continue past production increases in the hope that something new will come of them. The guidelines for the future are still the thoughts of Marx, Engels, Lenin, and Stalin, none of whom was able to see the future clearly or even think about it. The future to the Communists is cloudy and not even dimly seen. Communist ideology is of little help in deciding what values must be stressed in the future to develop the ideal society where each individual receives what he needs and spends his time working for the good of society.

This does not imply that the Soviet Union will not have a high standard of living for its inhabitants in the next twenty to thirty years; the evidence indicates that it will. But the higher standard of living will be based upon the degree to which the technological and scientific culture will be incorporated by the largest number of people within the

Soviet Union. Thus far, the percentage of those who are participants in this culture is relatively smaller than in the United States. That the numbers will increase both in the Soviet Union and in the United States no one can deny. In both countries it is technology and science that have brought about the change, not the outward forms of ownership. And in both countries, technology and science will grow and develop guidelines and values for the future.

In the Soviet Union, Marxism-Leninism represents much obsolete intellectual baggage, just as folk theology does in the United States. Both countries will need to develop their guidelines and values for the future through the careful study of what reality actually is, rather than what most laymen think it is. Some steps have been made in this direction with the development of the social sciences, but many more need to be taken since the social sciences have still not moved much further than their bare foundations. As time goes on, a better understanding of men and their works will go hand in hand with the managerial, educational, and governmental decisions that affect them.

Selected Bibliography

Barghoorn, Frederick C., *Soviet Russian Nationalism* (New York, Oxford University Press, 1956).

———, *Soviet Foreign Propaganda* (Princeton, Princeton University Press, 1964).

Bereday, George, and Pennar, Jaan, *The Politics of Soviet Education* (New York, Praeger, 1960).

Bergson, Abram, *Soviet Economic Growth* (New York, Harper & Row, 1953).

Charques, R. D., *A Short History of Russia* (New York, Dutton, Everyman Paperbacks, 1958).

Curtiss, John Shelton, *The Russian Revolution of 1917* (Princeton, N.J., Van Nostrand, Anvil Paperbacks, 1957).

Ebenstein, William, *Today's Isms* (Englewood Cliffs, N.J., Prentice-Hall, 1961).

Fainsod, Merle, *How Russia Is Ruled* (Cambridge, Harvard University Press, 1963).

Granick, David, *Management of the Industrial Firm in the USSR* (New York, Columbia University Press, 1954).

———, *The Red Executive* (Garden City, N.Y., Doubleday, Anchor Books, 1961).

Hook, Sidney, *Marx and the Marxists* (Princeton, N.J., Van Nostrand, Anvil Paperbacks, 1955).

Mehring, Franz, *Karl Marx* (Ann Arbor, University of Michigan Press, Ann Arbor Paperbacks, 1962).

Meyer, Alfred G., *Communism* (New York, Random House, 1960).

Mills, C. Wright, *The Marxists* (New York, Dell, 1962).

Mongait, A. L., *Archaeology in the USSR* (Baltimore, Penguin, Pelican Books, 1961).

Moore, Barrington, Jr., *Soviet Politics* (Cambridge, Harvard University Press, 1950).

Pares, Sir Bernard, *A History of Russia* (New York, Knopf, 1953).

Redl, Helen B., *Soviet Educators on Soviet Education* (New York, Free Press, 1964).

Ritvo, Herbert, ed., *The New Soviet Society* (New York, New Leader, 1962).

Rostow, W. W., ed., *The Dynamics of Soviet Society* (New York, New American Library, Mentor Books, 1954).

Whiting, Kenneth R., *The Soviet Union Today* (New York, Praeger, 1962).

III

Where
We Are Going

23

Transition to the World of Automation: The World of Tomorrow

Secondary civilization, which has played such a role in changing the world after the eighteenth century, is itself being transformed in the latter third of the twentieth century into a new stage of industrial and scientific development. The new Tertiary civilization, which may not burst into full bloom in the United States, Western Europe, Japan, and the Soviet Union for another century, is at present visible only in its unannounced infancy. (The Secondary civilization in the United States and the technicians and scientists of the world seem to be its parents.)

Primary civilization was based upon sheer backpower and physical energy, and its tools represented extensions of the human arm and leg. Men's skills were necessary to direct the work in which the tools were used. Secondary civilization developed new mechanical forms of energy, along with complex tools that took the places of man's finger and tweezer dexterities. Although the machines were complicated and even semi-automatic, they could not displace the human skills required in utilizing them; skilled mechanics and operators still had to control their movements and regulate their work.

The man at the wheel of a truck, the engineer at the controls of a diesel locomotive, and the airline captain skillfully landing a huge jet transport reflect the mechanical symbols of Secondary civilization. Tertiary civilization will be represented by machines that control themselves, locomotives that pull trains of cars without human presence, as the self-service elevators do today, and planes that get off the ground and land themselves automatically.

The Tertiary civilization of the twenty-first century will be an automatic one, in which man for the first time in his existence will be able to tame the countless electrons of the universe to be his personal slaves. Primary civilization used the labor of human beings and domesticated animals; Secondary civilization employed the far greater energy derived from steam, electricity, and petroleum; but Tertiary civilization will exploit the tiny unseen electron in its many various forms.

Primary civilization added little to the standard of living that men had already enjoyed during the Neolithic period. A few on the top made use of the luxuries that were then available, but the overwhelming majority lived on a subsistence level. Secondary civilization raised the living standards of the many even higher than those enjoyed by the fortunate few in the ancient past. During this period in the United States and Western Europe, hunger was abolished, bacterial diseases were eradicated, housing standards were raised, and entire populations were made literate.

Tertiary civilization may doubtless see poverty abolished, along with the wide gaps existing today between rich and poor. It may see education and living standards raised to ever higher levels, as men adjust their social culture to their new technological and scientific skills. Perhaps it may even give way within a century or so to a new Quaternary civilization, the outlines of which we cannot dimly perceive today.

Unless men one day blow themselves off the face of the earth by expensive weapons systems that have got out of hand, there is a likelihood that cultural and technical change will continue at an accelerated pace during the next few centuries. Despite the cultural lag in mental capability which most individuals bring to their age, it is possible that men may one day solve their problems almost as quickly as they create them. Their mental ingenuity may open up vistas of service to mankind that can only be dreamed about today. Despite the existence of totalitarianism as a cultural lag in our present-day world, men are freer to think than they have ever been before; and although originality of ideas is still not prized as much as it needs to be, freedom of expression and intellectual exploration are more encouraged than in past centuries. In terms of man's possible future, mankind has barely begun to develop and grow.

As organized thus far, Secondary civilization can use only a small number of innovators and creative personalities (though these are increasing from decade to decade). Possibly Tertiary civilization may find it necessary to have at least one-third of its population in this special category. Secondary civilization was built through the labors of the illiterate and the semiliterate; Tertiary may require a college-educated population, with a more specialized training for the top 10 to 20 percent.

Our Changing Secondary Civilization

One-fifth of the American people are classified as living in poverty with an annual income of less than $3,000 in the year 1965. Such a classification has meaning only when this group is compared to the other four-fifths of the population who are more affluent, or the top 5 percent who are well-off. Compared with the man who lives in a $100,000 house, owns two or more cars, sends his children to private schools and universities, and takes a month's vacation in Europe, the unskilled factory worker who pays $50 a month for an unpainted two-bedroom house and who earns only $250 a month is poor. So are the elderly couples who live on $100 a month Social Security income, and the uneducated Negro, Indian, and Mexican. But when compared to the standards of the rest of the world or to those of a century ago, the American poor eat more varied food, wear better quality clothing and shoes, and live in larger houses with better beds, linen, furniture, and appliances. The poor often have running water, a bathroom, gas stove, electric refrigerator, electric lights, a radio, a television set, and, if they live in small towns, an automobile, which, though old, still runs and takes them to visit relatives and friends. Only the aged are generally without cars.

Although his standards of taste may differ, as well as his relative standards of cleanliness, orderliness, and aesthetic appeal, the unskilled worker shares more of Secondary civilization with the affluent middle classes than he does with the unskilled worker in the factory of 1865. Although he has little to do with the way civilization works, he knows its benefits and wants as many of them as he can get. Although inequalities do exist in the social systems of Secondary civilization, they are not as great as those that existed between the aristocrats and the peasants in Primary civilization, nor as small as they may be in Tertiary civilization. Qualitatively, little comparison in social equality can be made between the lot of the slave in Primary civilization and the fate of the unskilled worker drawing unemployment compensation or welfare payments in the Secondary. During the past two hundred years, a social conscience has slowly been created among people, which makes those living today less indifferent to human suffering than was true in seventeenth century Western Europe or nineteenth century India or China.

Secondary civilization in the United States still discriminates against those over 65. Age has taken on some of the discriminatory characteristics that were at one time reserved for differences in social class and color. Compulsory retirement between 65 and 70, with accompanying cuts in living standards, has been arbitrarily legislated in the United States Government and in most corporations over the past two or three decades. Only the chairmen of the board and the superannuated congressmen and senators escape this classificatory discrimination, which is based upon chronological rather than physiological age. There is also discrimination toward the Negroes, the American Indians, the Mexicans, widows, the uneducated, the unskilled, and those who happen to live in certain underdeveloped areas.

Most of those who make the decisions for Secondary civilization were reared during the end of the nineteenth or the beginning of the twentieth century when the cultural vestiges of Primary civilization were still strong. Their parents and their teachers had grown up just as Secondary civilization was beginning to show itself (although the technical aspects of the new age were accepted earlier than the scientific ones). The nineteenth century placed greater emphasis upon the theological and classical values it gave to the young in its schools than it did upon the technological or the scientific. The twentieth century was thus dominated by those who received their values during the nineteenth.

Since most of those who made the important decisions were educated in fields that had little to do with production, social growth, or science, they were more aware of problems that affected the generation immediately preceding their own, that is, their parents, teachers, and the parents and teachers of their friends and colleagues, than with the possible problems to be faced by the generation they were rearing, which would come into control after they were gone.

The cultural lag actually consists of looking at today through the eyes of yesterday, of not sensing reality as it exists today but as we believe it to be through the symbols given us in our earlier years. Viewing today or tomorrow through the experiences of yesterday means that we are always behind the times in trying to take stock of what faces us. In an era that has changed as rapidly as ours has, a lag of thirty to fifty years in becoming aware of our problems can mean the difference between being confused by the signals we receive and being able to do something about them.

There is little doubt that the technological and scientific changes that took place in the past have influenced our values as well as our mutually agreed upon goals. We bring to the greater affluence and awareness of the physical and social worlds of today the values developed in past ages. As an example, the nineteenth century reintroduced the ancient world of the military into the new world of the factory. Again, as the nineteenth turned into the twentieth century, the company became the private domain no longer of the entrepreneur but of the corporation, a common enterprise of a self-perpetuating oligarchy. In its influence upon the lives of the millions in its employ and the tens of millions consuming its products or services, the corporation had become a powerful private government, responsible to no one but its top decision makers.

By 1965 two-thirds of the nonagricultural economically productive assets of the United States were owned by a group of less than 500 corporations, which were in turn controlled by no more than 20,000 men. More than nine corporations enjoyed greater income than any state government.

In a society that stresses the role of citizen participation in those decisions that concern him, private corporations are in a position to affect the lives of tens of millions of individuals, directly and indirectly, without in any way being answerable for their deeds to the general public. Although federal and state bureaucrats are always in fear of being investigated by legislators of the opposition political party, private bureaucrats are answerable only to the chairman of the board and the board of directors.

The large corporation in its public image, however, insists that it takes its final orders from John and Jane Doe, consumers, whose purchasing power determines the success of the corporation. In a society of apathetic individuals reared in the values of their parents and teachers, the large corporation generally leads rather than follows public taste. The reins of power are not in the hands of Jane and John Doe, consumers, for rarely do they know where to go to complain of corporate abuses. There is no built-in protection in the law that shields them from fraudulent packaging, advertising, or obsolescence of products. And yet, when compared with the conditions of the 1890's, the consumer has far more protection than he had then; and his influence, although minor, is still great enough to make the large corporations at least try to create a favorable public image of themselves.

The corporation is still in the process of growth, and decentralization is no more characteristic of corporate behavior than of government. Both believe they need to be highly centralized to offer adequate services. Government in its development, however, has become somewhat less authoritarian than the corporation, for some minor choice is open to the voters to select an opposition every four years. The large corporations are not influenced as much in this way by their myriad shareholders or by the public to which they supply goods or services. In neither government nor business is freedom of choice actually present; the limitations of law derived from the past have cut down the number of independent choices that the knowledgeable voter or stockholder can make.

The transitional stage between Secondary and Tertiary civilizations is still in the process of painful growth. Institutions develop and are given content by the thoughts and experiences, generally based upon the past, of their leadership. Men cannot visualize a future that they have not seen; institutionalized precedents are generally the spur-of-the-moment pragmatic results of past decisions. Institutions tend to grow in size when the need for managerial actions to handle continuing problems increases in intensity as men attempt to adjust their worlds to the chaotic conditions brought about by technological and scientific change. Instead of accepting the concept that all institutions change as men's ideas and experiences about them develop, the initial thoughts of those who established them become symbolized as traditional or sacred. The precedents developed in the past then become the basis for thought and action in dealing with the developing problems of the present and the future. Authorities are educated in the precedents of the past, so that they become its defenders as well as its managers. Although changes occur in the technological and scientific spheres, they are followed by little change in the social and institutional worlds, as defenders of the latter attempt to transform the thoughts they learned as children and adolescents into safe havens from a confusing and apparently chaotic world of adults.

Secondary civilization had to develop new institutions of its own when problems of urban living, factory life, the rise of the middle classes, the increase in the aging population, and international affairs made them necessary. For a good many decades after the rise of Secondary civilization, however, governments attempted to continue the institutions developed when most of their populations were still self-sufficient farmers or peasants under the control of a few wealthy landlords.

Even today in the United States, when 70 percent of the American people live in metropolitan areas of more than 100,000 inhabitants and less than 7 percent of the population live on farms, Congress hesitated to create a Department of Urban Affairs, although one existed for agriculture. Until 1965 it was easier to get funds to subsidize the inefficient marginal farmer than to provide mass transportation to cities choked by the traffic of the automobile age. The traditional thinking of most American congressmen assumed as late as 1965 that the country was divided into farmers, laborers, and businessmen; but not into technological middle classes, urban slum dwellers, white-collar workers, and service employees, with most of the last four groups living in the metropolitan areas that supplied most of the goods, income, and education for the American people. It is difficult for congressmen born in rural areas in the late nineteenth century to realize that the United States is a new urban country with technological and professional classes that did not exist fifty years before and with problems that originated with technological and scientific change.

The Automobile as a Symbol of Secondary Civilization

The automobile is the symbol of Secondary civilization at its best and worst. The railroads united all sections of the country and permitted the new industries and the expanding agriculture to find markets. The steamship permitted inland waterways and oceans to be used as "sea railroads." The automobile, on the other hand, drastically changed the social life of both rural and urban areas and became the keystone of American industrial prosperity. At the same time, it made the large urban center almost obsolete. The social and economic effects of the automobile upon

American society have still not been properly understood, and the problems that it brought into existence have become intensified during recent years.

The changes that have taken place with the introduction of the automobile have also adhered to the traditional forms of the past. In the early years, the horseless carriage was just that. As it took on a different form in the first decade of the century, the engine was kept in the front as the horse had originally been. Although space could have been conserved by putting both the engine and the luggage space beneath the car, automobiles today are still being made in roughly the same forms as in the 1920's. The engine space has been made to appear longer and the rear has been extended as far as technically possible to give a feeling of affluence to its possessor.

From the beginning the automobile was primarily a means of easily available transportation that could go where streetcars and trains could not. The automobile has never been inexpensive, for mass transportation was and still is cheaper. But the auto gave its owner a sense of independence from railroad and streetcar timetables. This feeling of independence led the automobile industry to develop into the largest in the United States, employing directly or indirectly in production, supplies, and services at least 10 million of the 70 million in the labor force.

The early automobile manufacturers made cars, but once their products were sold they had nothing more to do with them. They were not in the business of supplying roads for the cars they built; but the public clamor for better roads led the states and the Federal Government to spend their tax money to build the roads, which in turn encouraged more people to buy more automobiles, which in turn enabled the few large automobile corporations to become even larger in size and wealthier in resources.

As in the case of the nineteenth century railroads, private enterprise was not sufficient to make the automobile industry the prosperous one that it is today. Without paved roads, the automobile would have been a rich man's plaything, used only in the large cities where municipal enterprise had started paving streets during the second half of the nineteenth century. (Actually the paved street is a seventeenth century rediscovery of an ancient invention.) The paved roads, which started increasing immediately before 1914, made possible the extensive use of the Model T and other less expensive cars.

Rural-dominated legislatures spent a good deal of tax money raised from the new automobile owners during the 1920's and 1930's for farm-to-market roads, some of which were paved, but most of which were graded with gravel. Tens of billions of dollars have been spent on building roads and superhighways. The more roads that were built, the more cars were sold, until finally General Motors became the symbol of big business at its very biggest. During World War II, General Motors was able to produce an astounding amount of tanks and weapons. It had by that time become an industrial government in its own right, employing hundreds of thousands and governed by a self-perpetuating oligarchy who, though it owned little stock, made all the important decisions.

Although paved roads helped the rural areas become urbanized, they brought little but headaches to the large cities. Paved roads encouraged the more affluent members of the middle classes to move to the suburbs, leaving the city to the very poor and the very rich. The suburbanite created traffic chaos for he still had to come back to the city to work, and his tax dollars did not pay for the facilities he used in the city. The cities were not built for the masses of automobiles that poured into their streets each morning and evening, nor could they spare the space that these commuting cars demanded. The streets consequently became clogged with cars, and mass transportation suffered losses in revenue. Hundreds of millions of dollars were spent to cut wide swaths across the large cities so that armies of suburbanite cars could carry their single occupants to and from work, though their local taxes went to the suburbs (and their Federal taxes to the subsidizing of agriculture, weapons research, air travel, and numerous other enterprises). The creation of hundreds of millions of dollars of new superhighways funneled even more traffic into the cities.

The suburbs, with their concentration of middle-class families, represented a consequence of the mass use of the automobile. Around 1900, suburban families lived in convenient areas of transportation near the metropolitan centers so that they could commute by streetcar, interurban, or railroad. After World War I the suburbs offered each man his own middle-class house at a manageable price, which enabled him to get away from the noise and dirt of the cities, which had acquired huge sprawling slums through the expansion of commerce and industry. After World War II this dream of a house surrounded by grass and trees became a goal for almost all white-collar workers and skilled technicians. After 1946 the ease with which a house could be financed caused even more individuals to depart from the cities, leaving the cities to the new migrating applicants for the diminishing unskilled and semiskilled jobs to be found there.

The growth of suburbs meant an increase in property taxes for the homeowners to pay for paving the new streets, putting in waterpipes and sewers, and building schools for the children, whom the younger postwar families were producing in increasing numbers. Huge fortunes were made by speculative builders, who created mile after mile of sprawling suburbs out of $100- to $500-an-acre farmland or out of bulldozed scrub woodland. The houses were often built hastily, with a few shrubs and empty lawns, some on curving but most on straight streets whose pavements were filled with cars in the early morning as husbands went to work and children to school, and again in the afternoons and evenings as they returned. The growth of the suburbs meant an increase in new appliances and backyard cooking, for the good life as it was lived by the suburban affluent middle-class junior executive, technician, or organization man (salaried employees of the huge corporations) was depicted in advertisements showing bright green lawns, barbecue pits, and men in sport shirts standing around with glasses of beverages in their hands.

The suburbs did away with the urban lodges and organizations and created new ones, such as the parent-teacher associations, various clubs, and the social church with its de-emphasis on theology and its stress upon fellowship. Neighbors invited one another to backyard feasts; and wives spent their time visiting, chauffeuring, baby-sitting, and dreaming of new household furnishings. This was the suburban way of life, made possible by the enormous growth of industry, the proliferation of automobiles and highways, and the tremendous wealth created by the Technological and Scientific Age.

In general, not enough time elapsed between the post-World War I variety of suburbs and the post-World War II varieties for new values to follow the changing way of suburban life. Technologically, the new suburbanites of the post-World War II period had the benefit of labor-saving gadgets, mechanical appliances and tools, a wide variety of foods, and spacious housing. Their educational levels were higher, their children were better cared for, their wives were more attractive, and husbands and wives had a better knowledge of the world about them than the preceding generations; but their values were in many ways still closer to those of a leisured aristocracy than to those of a new technological and scientific middle class. They looked neither back nor far ahead. Their concern was with the present, to earn enough money to retire at sixty-five with enough income to let them spend their "Golden Years" as they had begun their lives—by playing.

Leisure-time activities were nonintellectual and were largely devoted to forgetting daytime tasks in an attempt to escape into the nonpractical world of childhood. Yet, new values were slowly emerging—piecemeal, incomplete, and contradictory—as the suburbanites adjusted their traditional social views to the realities of a changing Technological and Scientific Age. They were slowly beginning to rear their children to believe that each generation must create its own values and that childhood learning must be superseded by knowledge of and insights into the world that are gained through increased maturity and understanding.

The Steady Trend Toward the Automatic Age

Secondary civilization came of age in the United States only after the Civil War. In 1865 the energy required on the farm and the motive power needed for transportation in the small cities were still carried on by horse and cart. Over 80 percent of the power used on most farms and in most cities was supplied by animals. Only 6 percent of all production, both farm and factory, was carried on by machine. Steam was still the main motive energy, but many textile and machine shops in New England obtained their power from water. Until 1850 in the United States, water-power was more important than steam. Men and their muscles were used to supply more than 15 percent of the needs for energy in production. And as late as the 1930's, most farm work was still accomplished with the energies of both horse, or mule, and man. Even the factories existing in 1865 were closer in spirit to the artisan workshops of the eighteenth century than to the semiautomated plants of a century later.

The Era of the Laborer

In 1865 the demand for men of brawn was greater than that for men of brains. Immigrants were needed to supply the labor for the growing industries. All that was required of them was that they understand simple instructions and have the muscle power to do the unskilled tasks that were necessary.

Only in New England was there a demand for skilled mechanics and machinists to fashion the machine tools needed by the growing factories that would dot the country from north to south and east to west. The railroad industry required labor mainly to build track, shovel coal, tighten hand brakes on freight cars while the train was still moving, and in general do tasks that required little training though a good deal of imagination and resourcefulness. There was little opportunity or place for the highly trained scientist and engineer; few in industry knew what to do with them. Most found employment in the new scientific and engineering schools that crisscrossed the country as a result of the Morrill Act of 1862, which set aside lands for the support of agricultural, technical, and engineering schools. The bright young men of 1865 entered finance, law, medicine, or the ministry. Even the new industries preferred the self-made man of action to the educated managerial visionary.

The Agricultural Revolution

From 1815 to 1865 farming changed little. After 1840 the number of farms increased as the lands stretching from Indiana to Nebraska were quickly taken up and as railroads after 1860 were built from Chicago to the midwestern grain fields to bring the surplus grain and hogs to market. The farmer had become urgently aware of the importance of having cash for his new consuming needs. In 1865 large herds of longhorn cattle were slowly driven from Texas to the temporary railroad terminals in Kansas. After 1870 many railroads were built almost side by side from St. Louis in a southwesterly direction to tap cattle and grain sources to supply food for the burgeoning populations of the United States and Europe.

The age of improved seed, chemical fertilizers, and mechanical implements would wait until after World War I, when the American farmers began to increase their agricultural productivity enormously. In 1865 half the population was still needed on the farms to support the other half in the expanding cities and industrial towns. Agricultural productivity increased even more as the Industrial Revolution inched its way to the agricultural regions of the Midwest and the West. By 1940 one farmer fed 15 others besides himself; by 1965 he grew food for 25 others. By the end of the twentieth century, one farmer aided by his machinery would be feeding at least 60 others.

From 1865 to 1920 the farmer was restricted in area by the distance that his horse and cart could cover in one day on poor dirt tracks—as a rule hardly more than twenty miles. This measure also became the distance that separated one county seat from another. The county seat was where the farmer bought his supplies and where he sought loans from the bank. The county seat also became the seat of the Agricultural Extension Agent, who collected information from the new land-grant agricultural schools. Until long after World War I, however, less than 5 percent of the farmers bothered to visit the Extension Agent to find out what was new in farming methods.

Surrounding the farms of the Midwest and the East were small villages paced five to ten miles away. Here were the depot, or station, if railroads ran through the territory; the local hotel; two or three restaurants; two or three general stores; the blacksmith; the local church; the veterinarian; two or three medical practitioners; one or two dentists; and the local academy, or secondary school, which was taught by one or two male teachers who had had some college education. Many villages might also have had a local bank and a weekly newspaper.

Halfway between the villages were the crossroads general stores, the one-room schoolhouses, and the rural churches. There was at least one of these schools in every four square miles of farmland, taught by farmers' daughters or wives who had little more than an eighth grade education. In many ways the rural areas of the United States were midway between Primary and Secondary civilization. The men tilled their farms roughly as farms were tilled a century before both in the United States and in Europe. In the tools, clothing, and hardware that they bought in the nearby village general stores, however, the farmers had access to the machine-made goods of Secondary civilization.

This age ended with World War I, when the former isolation of the farmer was destroyed by the automobile (especially the Model T Ford) and the new farm-to-market roads. The first to suffer from this transportation change were the small crossroads stores; then the artisans in the villages; the general stores; the small hotel for the commercial travelers coming by train; the country physicians and dentists, most of whom had limited formal training; and finally the one-room schools, as buses picked up farm children and brought them to consolidated schools. The village retained its function of supplying the farmers with their daily necessities, and after World War I it became the center for the area's consolidated elementary and secondary schools.

On the other hand, the county seat also became more important to the farmer since he depended more and more upon government assistance and subsidies to help him meet the problems of a market that was organized against him.

Frequently the farmer drove even to the industrialized small cities for the goods and implements he needed. In the 1930's and 1940's through the cooperatives sponsored by the government-supported Rural Electrification Administration, the countryside became electrified to the point of enabling the farmer to increase his standard of living to that approaching urban levels; and he became a customer for appliances, canned food, and specialized delicacies. His investment in machinery rose each year, as did his expenditures for improved seeds, better quality farm animals, and fertilizers.

In 1916 over 32 million persons lived on farms in the United States. By 1964 this number had been cut down to a little less than 15 million. If the present trend continues, more and more marginal farmers will be pushed off the land; and the large-scale family operator with a large investment in machinery and land, along with the corporation operator with its oversize holdings, will become the main farmers. In 1965 a farmer in Iowa could run a 400-acre corn, soybean, and hog farm with the help of a son on shares. Fourteen- to eighteen-year-old sons received part of the crop for plowing forty acres a day by tractor.

The farmers' children are now sent by bus to the nearby county center for both elementary and secondary school education. Half go to colleges and universities for further education; few of them remain on the land. A rising standard of living for the farmer has made it imperative that farms be larger and that more money be invested in machinery. Farming in the United States in 1965 is no longer a way of life but a business. Few young men can start farming in the Midwest without an initial capital investment of at least $25,000 and an opportunity to rent the land he will need. Purchasing a farm would run from $100,000 to $200,000 and more.

As the farmer enters the transitional stage to Tertiary civilization, mechanization has become almost semiautomatic; and the automatic farm is not too far in the future. The 15 million on farms may soon be cut to 10 million and finally to 5 million as larger and more mechanized farms, aided by numerous mechanical and chemical industries and dozens of agricultural research stations, gradually take over the task of feeding a population growing at the rate of 4 million per year. Surpluses rather than scarcities now plague the more efficient farming countries of the world. And in industrial farming countries, a good many of the technical and managerial middle classes are the sons or grandsons of farmers.

The Rise of Metropolitan Centers

In losing her predominantly rural population, the United States needs to change her traditional image of herself. No longer is the small town typical of the "real" America. New York City with its metropolitan area of 15 million inhabitants, or more than all who live on the farms of the country; Megalopolis, or the strip city from north of Boston to south of Washington, D.C., with its 40 million; Chicago with its 7 million; and Los Angeles with its 7 million in their respective metropolitan districts are far more typical of the new United States than Mount Pleasant with its 8,000 or Centerville with its 7,000 citizens.

The small town has become atypical of the new America, even though a good many Americans, including some of those living in the metropolitan areas, still have a nostalgic memory of the small towns of their childhood. The small town legend dies hard; and as America enters the last stage of the Secondary civilization and the beginnings of the Tertiary, she is slowly surrendering the Jeffersonian dream that the small town and rural America were the chief repositories of all the democratic, self-reliant virtues that elevated the dignity of man to new levels.

More and more it will be the prosperous suburbs that will supply the moral and intellectual leadership of America in the future. Even the large metropolitan cities will in time become obsolete unless they can recapture the flavor and pleasure of urban living that they once possessed for the middle classes. Even the suburbs, however, cannot continue growing as they have in the midst of a continuing population expansion, spreading their one-family houses up hill and down dale throughout the country, hesitating only when this insatiable expansion of house and lawn meets the new obstructions of the superhighways connecting suburbs to cities.

Soon agricultural land will be swallowed up as house sites and wide limited-access superhighways take first priority on their space. This may well lead to our food's being produced synthetically in gleaming, hygienic automated factories so that land can be used for more efficient and useful purposes.

For Selected Bibliography, see end of Chapter 24.

24

The Age of Automation Begins

The age of automation has not arrived like a flood sweeping everything before it, but rather like a quiet brook starting with droplets and covering only a small area. Because it has grown very slowly over the past 70 to 80 years, its impression has been felt only in this decade. Its total effect, however, may not be sensed for another thirty to thirty-five years, and our social adjustment to it may not take place for possibly fifty years beyond that.

Automation involves the mechanization of work processes; previous industrialization required that the machines duplicate the work of the human being faster and more efficiently. Automation goes further. It promises to free man from routine tasks and to spare him for the work that no machine can do: the ability to think and to solve problems creatively. What man can do routinely, the automatic machine can do better. Any task requiring repetition can be performed by automated machines with greater speed, more efficiency, and less error. The possibilities that automation opens up for benefiting mankind are endless, and its uses can make possible the worldwide eradication of abject poverty, illiteracy, and traditionalism. Unfortunately, as the world is presently constituted, automation may be a mixed blessing that brings more problems than benefits. But seen against the perspective of the future, automation could well be the answer to all of man's prayers and dreams.

Because automation is very expensive to install and because its possibilities have been only partially explored, its absorption into the fabric of American industry will be relatively slow, with only a few plants automating at a time. For years to come, most industries will still operate with semiautomatic machines, much as artisan handicrafts existed side by side with mass-production industries until a few decades ago in the

United States and as they still do in France, Germany, and Great Britain. In most service industries and many consumer goods industries, automation will be slow in displacing workers, although machines may be introduced into larger industries within the next few decades, displacing even skilled employees.

Through the slowness in adopting automation, American society, as well as Western European, Japanese, and Soviet, has gained some time in which to think about the implications of automation and to adjust the population to its inevitability. Automation represents the new age of tomorrow. When it has been incorporated in most production processes and in most services, even in mass transportation, education, and entertainment, one will be able to say that Tertiary civilization has arrived (although it too may be replaced by a new civilization—perhaps one where creativity is universally organized).

Automation is a more efficient industrial system than the old system, for it preserves unusual human skills indefinitely. Under the past industrialization of Secondary civilization, the skills and experiences of the highly trained technician, engineer, or scientist died with them. Under automation the skills can be taped and transferred to machines to perform indefinitely in the future what these men had done in the past. Until new skills arrive on the scene, past skills can be produced endlessly on an extremely high level without the moods and the ups and downs of ordinary daily production by people. Highly qualified human skills can thus be preserved for posterity, as they are being saved today on film or on tape. Under automation, even the technical skills of the unusual craftsman or engineer can be used in industries all over the world, much as hi-fi records can display the talents of the performer even in the most isolated hamlet.

Although automation will initially be used in mass-production industries, the introduction of tape-controlled, multipurpose machine tools will permit small shops, where there is a production of ten to twenty items, to switch quickly from one product to another by utilizing different tapes. One automated machine tool in use in 1965 can interchange thirty-one different cutting tools and can handle hundreds of operations in proper sequence without any human hand regulating any part of the work performed.

It is fortunate for us that automation is being introduced into American industries and offices at a fairly slow rate; otherwise the adjustment problems would be much greater than our American society or government could handle at the present time. No one knows yet what to do with the individuals who are displaced by automation, for even retraining requires that some idea be held as to what to train unskilled and uneducated workers for. No attempts have been made to visualize those employment possibilities that may be open to them now or in 1975 or 1980. Even the schools continue in their traditional ways, educating young people for a society similar to that of the immediate past. Our colleges tend to duplicate one another in the proliferation of courses that have little to do with the society of the United States or of the world as it may exist during the next ten to twenty years (which is a very short time in the life of a twenty-year-old, who would only be forty in twenty years, with still another forty years of life expectancy ahead of him).

Technological progress in productivity, or the output per work hour, as a result of recent automation and improved machine tools, now permits the discharge of more than 2 million workers per year, but with output still increasing.[1] During the next ten years, at least another 1.8 million young people will be leaving schools annually to enter the labor market. During the 1950's, when the number of jobs displaced by automation was far less than it will be in the 1960's or 1970's, less than 1.3 million young people had to be absorbed into the labor market.

During the past fifteen years, automation has slowly been eroding the number of jobs in industry held by the unskilled and semiskilled; and it is now reaching out for the work done by the skilled workers. In 1950 almost 50 percent of the labor force was still employed in the production of goods, but by 1964 the number of industrial workers had fallen to less than 40 percent of the country's wage earners. Today, in the United States the number of individuals employed in services or as white-collar workers exceeds the number working in various industries. In 1947, 26,470,000 individuals worked in production and 26 million in services. In 1962 production workers had declined to 25 million, and service employees had increased to 35,670,000. If the present trends continue, there will be more than 50 million in the services in 1975, as compared to a little less than 25 million in production. But by 1975, there will be at least 85 million in the labor force.

In 1947 the automobile industry needed 649,000 production workers to turn out 4.8 million cars. In 1962 it turned out almost 7 million autos with 37,000 fewer workers. In 1951 the steel industry required 540,000 men to produce 96.8 million tons of steel. In 1962 it produced the same quantity of steel with 79,000 fewer men. As a result of mechanization, rather than automation, in the mining regions, employment dipped from 344,000 to 174,000 in ten years. In the hard coal, or anthracite, mines, employment dropped from 70,000 to a little over 12,000 during the past fourteen years; yet productivity per miner doubled.[2]

In the beginning of the industrial era, most labor in the United States was unskilled. Today less than 5 percent of all employment is unskilled. In the meanwhile, professional and technical positions increased

---

[1] Ackley, Gardner, "Automation: Threat and Promise," *New York Times Magazine,* March 22, 1964.

[2] Bill Francois, "The Fear of Tomorrow," *The Progressive,* March, 1962, p. 16.

by more than 50 percent in the past twelve years and will jump another 40 percent during the remaining 1960's. More steel, more cars, more appliances, more of everything, are being produced with fewer workers. Our problem is no longer scarcities but surpluses that continue to accumulate. Even the automobile manufacturers must come out with glamor models every six months to increase the sales of their products, which are now inching up to the goal of 10 million cars each year. Every year almost 5 million cars have to be junked, and a mounting problem for large American cities is what to do with the cars that are abandoned on public streets since there is little demand for the metal even in steel mills. To keep production going, industry is faced with the need to make its objects obsolete in a few years so that no surpluses will develop.

In agriculture a cornpicker, which costs a little over $4,000, can cut 100 tons of ears from their stalks in one day, work that required the labor of twenty men in the days before the machine. A beetpicker, which costs a little over $5,000, can dig up two rows of beets at a time, shake off the dirt, cut off the tops, and drop the rest onto a conveyor belt that loads them onto a truck, replacing fifty agricultural laborers in this operation.[3] Soon all the fruit and vegetables will be plucked or picked by mechanized steel fingers and hands, and then hundreds of thousands of migrant laborers will be displaced.

The number of white-collar workers has increased enormously in the past twenty-five years as banking, financing, insurance, record-keeping, and credit have become bigger than ever before. Installment debts alone increased from $15 billion in 1947 to over $45 billion by 1962. Although the numbers have been increasing absolutely, however, the rate of increase has been dropping relatively. For example, almost half of the white-collar workers are composed of clerks and related workers, of whom two out of every three are women. Between 1940 and 1950 the number of women clerks, bookkeepers, secretaries, and related workers increased by more than 80 percent. During the 1950's the increase was only 57 percent. By the early 1960's the rate of increase had dropped to a little over 10 percent. As another example, the average annual increase of clerical workers from 1950 to 1957 was 280,000; from 1957 to 1960 it had dropped to 150,000; but by the end of 1962 there had been only 25,000 more women employed than in 1961. This gap will become narrower during the next few years.

At present, the spread between demand and supply of white-collar workers is being filled by electronic processing systems, or clerical automation. Despite the ever-rising amounts of paper work, the new data processing systems have enabled the businessman to do more work with relatively fewer employees. By 1962 almost 90 percent of the banks, insurance companies, public utility firms, and large credit houses had

[3] As quoted in the *New York Times*, October 5, 1961.

installed electronic processing equipment. In businesses employing between 100 to 1,000 employees, some 80 percent by the end of 1962 had installed automatic clerical and bookkeeping machines.

The rising costs of white-collar workers have made many businesses believe that the machines are now cheaper, despite their high initial cost, than the clerks, bookkeepers, and other related employees. Automation has affected the production worker considerably, but its influence on the white-collar worker has been minimal so far. The latter will not be affected by its innovations for at least another ten years; but when it does come, it will hurt him as much as it has the industrial wage earner. Neither the white-collar worker nor the industrial worker can be retrained successfully, for the techniques of automation have gone much further than the understanding of its effects upon the working population or of the jobs that could possibly be opened up to take care of the displaced worker. Despite an increase in population, the trend is toward the displacement of jobs in the traditional industries. The railroads, for example, employed two-thirds fewer in 1960 than in 1920, although new employment was created in the trucking industry and in the construction of highways. As productivity increases in those industries that can be automated, the number of employees will become even fewer. The petroleum industries are good illustrations of this particular trend. The Standard Oil Company of New Jersey, for example, employed 160,000 in 1950 and 140,000 in 1960; but its total revenue increased from a little over $5 billion in 1951 to almost $9 billion in 1960. Wages and salaries rose from $677 million to more than $940 million, and the cash dividends paid to stockholders went from $250 million to $500 million.[4]

As automation becomes more developed, it will affect services and trades as much as clerical and industrial fields. There will be an increased trend toward automated self-service retail establishments, self-repairs, and sales such as insurance, travel, and banking. As time goes on, appliances and cars will be repaired by removing whole units and replacing them. This trend will mean a definite attempt to simplify parts and engineering designs. Most cars, machines, and appliances at the present time have far too many parts that can go out of repair.

Construction can also be automated by having printed electrical circuits; mass-produced walls, floors, kitchens, bathrooms, and recreation rooms; and built-in electronic devices that heat, cool, clean, and light the inside rooms automatically. At the present time, the average housewife in suburbia puts in a long week cleaning, cooking, and baby-sitting. The first two can easily be taken care of by new electronic devices that require little human control. The social question for educators, parents, and legislators to answer is what will women do with their spare time in a more automated future?

[4] As indicated in the Annual Report for 1961.

The few rivulets of job displacement may become a roaring torrent within the next fifteen to twenty years. Between 1962 and 1964, for example, more than 10,000 "back office" clerks were fired from their jobs in brokerage houses. In 1963 the Chase Manhattan Bank cut down the number of its staff positions by more than 300 by using computers to take over many of middle management's decision-making functions.

The role of the computer in making decisions was illustrated by its use in planning a warehouse for the Union Carbide Company in 1963. Instead of asking its trained executives what the size of the building should be and what chemicals it should stock, the computer was asked to give its decisions through a process called simulation, whereby the various alternatives given to the computer are cross-checked in great detail at great speed. In a matter of minutes the computer calculated the movement of chemicals out of different sized warehouses, each time with different rates, shipping methods, and inventory levels. The computer next considered hundreds of ways to stock the various chemicals, and then from all these computations selected the one that was most efficient and economical. Union Carbide built its warehouse as suggested by the computer; and after completion within a matter of months, costs were cut, sales increased, and labor saved.[5] At one time, such decisions were the prerogatives of top management, working with large staffs and having less information to base their judgments on than the computer does at the present time.

The computer does not make these decisions by itself. It must be fed the information that it needs by highly trained, specialized individuals, who collect the data and store it in the "memory" of the computer. Because the electrons can travel at the speed of light, they can tap their memory cells faster than man and do in a short period of time tasks that could not be done at all without them. Problems that would have taken thousands of years to solve by ordinary mathematical computations can be done today in a matter of minutes with the aid of electronic computers.

The electron was first discovered in 1896; but the technology that has been developed to utilize its power stems from DeForest's invention of the triode tube in 1907, which permitted the amplifying of the weak electronic impulses in both wireless and long distance telephony. For a long period of time, electronics was used primarily in communications.

The computer uses mathematical principles that have been known for almost 200 years. The problem of using the electron to take advantage of known mathematical principles, however, was not solved until after World War II. In the Bell Telephone Laboratories, the invention of the transistor with its small size and almost indestructible forms made possible the development of huge computers with extraordinary memories.

[5] Thomas O'Toole, "White Collar Automation," *The Reporter*, December 5, 1963, p. 24.

(Lest the computer be overrated as a mechanical device, it needs to be pointed out that the normal human brain has the energy equivalent of some 5 billion transistors; so far most brains have been operated below capacity by their owners.) Although computers began growing to a gigantic shape, recent trends have indicated that the computers of the future may be made in miniature sizes.

The computer, or the "electronic brain," cannot think or engage in creative thought. It can only operate in simple ways. The operator of the computer must break down a problem into its simplest binary forms; this is called programming. The questions asked must be in simple yes or no forms, and they must be presented in simple formulas that the computer can understand, which is to say that a computer can only operate in terms of the information that has been presented to it. It is the information presented to the computer that enables it to act or to control other machines.

The electronic computer operates in terms of closed and open circuits; and when this is combined with a self-regulating mechanism, which is called feedback, automation is the result. The feedback again is as old as the mathematical principles used by computers. Watt's invention of the governor to regulate the amount of steam entering the cylinder head is the first modern use of feedback; the governor is self-regulating and is based upon the amount of steam the engine is generating. A closed circuit is also a self-regulating device. The ordinary thermostat in a room is a good example of the closed circuit. As the heat rises, the mercury in the thermometer goes up, thus triggering a metal point that shuts off the furnace.

The automated machine, using the computer as its memory and motivator, can control other machines in addition to regulating itself. It can do what it is programmed to do efficiently, quickly, and without any human error. It does not get tired, moody, or bored. As a series of machines, it does what it is made to do or told to do. It begins to imitate the human brain in its memory of electron transistors and its ability to control more than one machine at a time. Because electrons work much faster than the human brain, it can tap its stored amount of information in a fraction of a second; and through its punched tapes it can make decisions or carry on certain action. (The punched tape is a modification of the punched card, which is an eighteenth century French invention. Its principle was used in the mechanical player piano of the early twentieth century.)

The automatic elevator, which has displaced thousands of operators all over the country, is a good example of how a data processing device, similar to a computer, works. It registers in its memory which buttons have been pressed on which floors; it knows where it is; and it decides whether to go up or down and where to stop. It has all sorts of safety devices built into it; for example, it cannot start if any door is open and if there is any danger, it stops and buzzes an alarm (for like the computer upon which it is patterned, it operates through open and closed electronic circuits).

The knowledge that has been built up for one industry can be transferred to another industry, much as the early mechanical principles were applied to a series of machines having similar functions. For example, the punch card machines, which were reinvented for the Bureau of the Census in 1890, were adapted to insurance and other business needs around World War I. The theories worked out for firing weapons during World War II became the basis for automating oil and chemical plants. A good deal of the spurt in automation came from the computers developed for the government in tracking missiles, in creating new weapons systems, in designing rockets and supersonic planes, and in generally solving the problems raised by a complex government that subsidizes most of the scientific and applied technological research being done in the United States today. Without the research done on computers during World War II, modern-day automation would not have progressed very far. And without the billions of dollars spent on research for weapons that may never be used by a government that spends almost half of the tax dollars on preparing for a war that may never be fought, contemporary automation could not be as advanced as it is. Preparations for war since World War II have saved industry billions of dollars in research on computers, which industry itself might never have spent, and have pushed the American economy much closer to becoming an automated industrial society than would have been the case if these defense funds had not been appropriated. Even today many of the computers used in the United States are owned by the Federal Government. In 1961 there were 9,000 Federal employees running electronic computers, and it has been estimated that there will be around 16,000 working with computers in 1966.[6]

Computers in the government, in insurance companies, in banks, and in industries have taken over a great deal of clerical, accounting, and auditing functions. They write checks, issue bills, and credit sums received to individual accounts. They operate machines through transfer devices, and they can do tasks in a short period of time which cannot be duplicated by human beings. In state highway departments, computers now study rights-of-way for new highways, add up the estimated property values, and pick out the land that combines low cost with ease of construction and directness of route. Computers tell commercial bakeries how

[6] On the other hand, one of the reasons for the decentralization of industry in the Soviet Union is that it would take about one million computers to furnish the Centralized Planning Board with all the information it would need to make efficient decisions.

many rolls or loaves of bread they should leave at various supermarkets at certain times of the year. They determine the most economical use of garbage trucks in large cities. They may even be used in the near future to operate diagnostic machines that will determine the various illnesses of patients.

Computers are today divided into four categories: (1) *Information,* which store data; (2) *Detroit Automation,* which link machines of production as an integral line through automatic transfer devices; (3) *Process Control Systems,* which utilize a computer to integrate a control system for continuous operation of oil, chemical, or even atomic plants; and (4) *Numerical Control,* which employ punched tape and automatic control devices to direct the operation of a series of machines.

The importance of automation in the above categories is not the mechanical aspects of connecting machines together but the supplying of information and control systems. Automation is not the machine, but the combination of principles under which self-correcting systems operate. It is an upgrading rather than a downgrading of talents. In its theory it opens up widespread application in all fields of human endeavor. Any routine decision, day-to-day task, or continuous operation can be done far better by automated machines that have captured the skills of the most diverse middle managers, technicians, and highly trained craftsmen. Automation thus offers to mankind a vista of a civilization in which only a few will be trained for production, while the larger number of individuals will be able to devote themselves to the accumulation of knowledge and the development of creativity.[7] No other civilization has been able to promise as much as the Tertiary, once it replaces Secondary civilization in man's thoughts, goals, and values.

An example of Detroit Automation is the assembly line 1,545 feet long which since 1951 has been turning out six-cylinder engine blocks for the Ford Motor Company. Rough castings, which are produced in an automated foundry, are fed into this line. From then on, 42 automatic machines, linked together by transfer devices, automatically move the blocks through 530 precision cutting operations and borings. Formerly it took nine hours to fabricate a rough casting into a finished engine block; in the Ford plant in Cleveland it takes a little over fourteen minutes.[8] The expensive installation of machines of this type prevents their introduction in large numbers, for there must be a large savings in manpower before they can be considered a worthwhile investment. General Motors has been automating a little faster than Ford in recent years, but even it is a long way from completely automated factories.

[7] Creativity is here used to indicate the problem-solving innovator rather than in the conventional use of this term, which refers to those with artistic aptitudes.

[8] Congressional testimony by John Diebold, as quoted in *Automation: Implications for the Future,* Morris Philipson, ed., (New York, Vintage Books, 1962), p. 30.

Automation as an industrial system may not take over until at least the end of the twentieth century.

The automated factory is not the beginning but the end result of automation. Automation is only a by-product of a new point of view toward production which implies a radical redesigning of machines, factories, and ways of production as well as ways of doing business. Automation requires the complete rethinking of both production and business so that more efficient methods of solving complex problems will result. For example, instead of creating large wings that flap as birds' did, man learned to fly by taking advantage of the different air speeds both over and under a wing. Instead of creating a mechanical appliance that walked like a man, early men created a round wheel that rolled over comparatively smooth surfaces. Automation in its turn will necessitate rethinking about manufacturers, manufacturing, and services.

Automation makes its greatest contribution when it permits man to carry on new tasks that were previously unattainable. Many companies have discovered that automation helps them produce a better product with less waste and that its savings are more in increasing the efficiency of production than of labor. Automation can help mankind do tasks that could never have been done at all, and it can assist in doing them efficiently and well.

At present, automation is in its infancy because it has not developed a language that computers can use without translation by programmers. The future automated machine will need no programmers as intermediaries. The truly automated machine may be invented within the next ten to twenty years and will permit a man to dictate into a machine that will then type out his letters in clean, even type. The automatic typewriter of the future will use an automated type of English with more logical spellings, and perhaps it might even correct the errors made by the one using it.

Within the next twenty years, attorneys may be connected with a central repository, which could contain all the laws, rulings, regulations, procedures, and commentaries on legal subjects. By using his hookup to this central repository, the attorney could get information on any query he made to the central computer. The huge central repository will be able to give its answers in a matter of seconds, and the amount of research time for lawyers will be cut down enormously.[9] Scholars may have hookups to central repositories in their fields, which could supply them in a matter of seconds with the information, footnotes, and bibliography that would previously have required months if not years of research. Physicians practicing in county seats may get diagnoses of their patients' illnesses in a matter of seconds, as well as suggestions for treatment. Such

---

[9] David Bergamini, "Government by Computers," *The Reporter*, August 17, 1961.

computers could change the structure of the world's health needs immeasurably.

The electronic computers of today are still in their infancy. They can be compared to the machines in the first stages of the Industrial Revolution. Someday these machines may be equal to huge superbrains in the information that they will be able to store, and within the next century computers might also be able to think electronically.

At the same time, the industrial trend is toward both greater centralization and greater decentralization. The centralization will occur as large centers find themselves in a better situation to make intelligent overall decisions for national policies than do the local centers. The decentralization will take place when small urban centers become more self-sufficient than they are today through miniature computer systems hooked up to large centralized ones.

It may be possible to make goods and supply services in decentralized areas much more efficiently than in huge centers that may become too unwieldy to manage. In a society of surpluses, even the concept of international or interregional trade will make little sense when each area can supply its own needs, including its own synthetic foods and raw materials. Trade might lie in the realm of intellectual ideas and systems rather than in goods. It is quite possible that in the centuries ahead, countries (or what will then pass as countries) may prefer to exchange creativity rather than goods that after all can only duplicate what each could easily make in its own workshops.

It is not at all unlikely that within the next two to three decades daily censuses of knowledge of national decision-making purposes may take place by having every inventory computer in industry, government, business, banking, and services connected to a large analyzer in central cities. The central analyzer would then tabulate information on every transaction and every item made; on the energy used in each home, factory, and business; on the products of every farm; on the oil pumped; on the ores mined; and on the sales made and wages paid all over the United States. Instead of managerial decisions being arrived at without adequate information, the huge analyzers could perhaps be connected with other computers to make the routine decisions that are made today by the various agencies in the Federal Government. The important decisions could be made after all alternative possibilities had been analyzed and the best choice had been presented. A common input language could easily take the place of the intensive calculations required to prepare the instructions for the coded magnetic tape. This task may be simplified in the coming decades, thus making the computers even more efficient by doing away with the intermediaries of present-day programmers.

At present, there is a trend for district or regional plants and offices to make the decisions that cannot be made in the central headquarters because of their separation from the scene of day-to-day facts and operations. In the next few decades, centrally located computers could easily receive information quickly and accurately on every phase of a corporation's activities. This will enable the top executives to make decisions with the aid of computers, which can then be used for administrative guidance by the various regional plants. Within a few decades after that, even the top management decisions may be made by a new type of electronic computer that will be able to draw upon greater experiences, insights, and judgments than are possible to the average top manager today. The element of human error in far-reaching managerial decisions may well be a thing of the past.

It is also quite possible that the future top manager will require a far different training and education than he has today. He may not need to become knowledgeable about the techniques of production. His position may be that of a creative planner for the future; he may be responsible for coordinating the information fed him by the information-gathering computers and the data of the decision-making computers and drawing them into administrative guidelines for the future. Instead of having to devote much time to obtaining an overall picture of the company's production, sales, possibilities, and future trends, he will be able to get this information quickly in intellectually digestible forms, thus giving him more time to be the creative leader rather than the administrative head.

Automation and the use of computers in decision making may lead to an increase in creative top management, and at the same time to a decrease in the functions of routinized decision-making middle management. Supervision over production or even management of warehouses may be taken over by highly developed information-receiving computers. Any task that can be done day after day with little variation can be done more efficiently by computer, because judgment in this case may be much closer to the data than most decisions that are made on a routine daily basis. A good deal of middle management may possess traditionalist ways of thinking that have been learned from predecessors and are continued because others in the same position have made the same decisions, rather than because the decisions made are the most efficient or the best solutions.

The decisions in future management will be made by a new type of manager with an entirely different educational background, who will be trained to see more of the alternatives than present-day executives see. The decisions will be made with the assistance of computers that utilize the most complete variety of experiences and of past and present judgments. A great many corporations both in the United States and in Europe are even today turning over many of their middle management functions to computers because computers use the accumulated knowledge of middle management in much greater variety and intensity than would be possible for one or two individuals working in isolation. Automation requires a new point of view in looking upon both business and production. (Production should be viewed as an integrated system rather than as a series of individual steps.)

In the future, top management will have to become much more creative than it is today, for automation carries dangers as well as advantages. Its chief danger is that it may cause industrial decisions to become stabilized and fixed and thus lead to a form of managerial fossilization. Automation can lead to a society of leisure where thinking is left only to a few, and these few may get into the habit of making noncreative decisions for fear of disturbing the escapist reactions of the many. It can lead to a society where individuals are guaranteed a minimum standard of living just for existing, and it can lead to an oligarchic society where the few may make all the decisions for the many. In a self-satisfied society filled with material surpluses of all kinds, life can be pleasant and unexciting, and can fall into the traditional tyranny of a few over the many. An automated society puts the main burden of getting the society to function on a very tiny percentage of the population, who become its leaders, innovators, and creative thinkers. For an automated society to be successful in the future, the values of our contemporary Secondary civilization must be superseded by new values that emphasize participation, equality, and extremely high standards of civic behavior, standards made even higher by continuous competition among most individuals to be creative and socially responsible.

The problems brought by automation will affect most of the advanced countries of the world, including the Soviet Union and the United States. Automation can increase the standard of living innumerable times; it can open up new fields of endeavor; it can challenge the industrial society to produce with much higher standards; and it can revolutionize the entire world of knowledge and greatly increase the theoretical understanding of the social and physical worlds. It will conserve human energy to do the things that could not be done when individuals had to spend all their waking time working to keep themselves alive. Automation means new sights, visions, and aspirations. An automated society with high levels of scientific understanding cannot permit billions of human beings to vegetate in other parts of the world. There are too many talents to be uncovered, too many discoveries to be made, and too many insights to be disclosed. An automated society will be highly mechanized, using human labors for the creative tasks and the willing electron for the dull and routine.

On the other hand, an automated society operating within our present concepts and values will mean high unemployment and a large number of uneducated and untrained human beings. An automated society that displaces labor without turning laborers into useful and creative individuals can lead only to its chaotic breakdown, for products must be consumed and services must be used. Individuals cannot live on relief checks without losing confidence in themselves; they must be able to give something of themselves in return for the security that they expect to receive from an automated society.

We cannot have a nation made up only of passive consumers, for then the promise of a creative future will be difficult to attain. We cannot have a society in which individuals are pensioned off at the age of twenty and given a gold pass to all the ball games, all the bowling alleys, and all the cars-and-boats-for-hire agencies, without producing a mass society composed of individuals who do not carry their intellectual and moral weight. Man's great promise in the past was that he alone was able to symbolize, to think, to make of himself whatever he set out to be. Slowly and with much difficulty he has tried to keep the goal of being a creative human ever before him. Until now, only a few persons have worked toward this aspiration; and in doing so they have immeasurably benefited the rest of the population. Today and in the future, these few must be augmented by the many, otherwise the road will be thorny and beset by many obstacles of apathy, traditionalism, and authoritarianism. Men should be freed from their arduous labors so that they can become more creative, not to become vegetative and to while away the days until death comes for them. Over the past two million years men have raised their sights from mere animal levels of satisfying their hunger and sex impulses to the development of values that emphasize new goals that will provide more satisfaction to later generations.

Slowly and somewhat uncertainly, mankind is moving toward Tertiary civilization. In Primary civilization, only a few benefited directly from the creative talents of man; in our Secondary civilization the vast majority have had their elemental needs satisfied, although differences in opportunity still exist. In Tertiary civilization, men's dreams of equality with the wealthy, with the well-born, with the psychologically secure, will have a much better chance of attainment. Mankind has slowly moved from the levels of the hunter, of the peasant, of the industrial worker, and now in the next stage to the standards of the prosperous middle classes.

The Need for More Research

Automation uses mechanization, planning, and intense research activity, all in equal amounts. As a result of its spread, new occupations and professions have arisen, of which those engaged in research are basic. Research in itself as a profession is not very old in the United States. It has been said, for example, that 90 percent of all the scientists the world has ever known are alive today. Government expenditures for research have been climbing to over $15 billion per year, more than is being spent on private research by all the private corporations combined. Most of the government research funds, however, are spent in only a few industries, with atomic energy, defense, and space exploration receiving the lion's share. Private industry spends most of its research money on computers, petroleum products, and drugs; but compared to government funds, its efforts are minute. The oil companies spend the most, but this comes to only $100 million per year. Very little research is done today on transportation equipment, foods, electric motors, machinery, or chemicals. The steel industries spend very little money for research, for they put out more money on replacing worn-out equipment than on increasing productivity.

An example of how valuable research can be in increasing productivity in steel is the new method of using oxygen directly in the smelting of ore. As recently as 1955, almost fourteen hours were required to run a 150-ton "heat" of steel through a furnace. In 1960, by injecting oxygen directly into the furnace to increase the temperature of the molten mix, 300 tons of steel were run through in less than seven hours, a 400 percent increase. In 1963 the United States Steel Corporation announced the installation of two new oxygen converter furnaces, which could turn out a 300-ton "heat" of steel in 52 minutes. Two of the new furnaces can produce as much steel as the 14 unused open hearths, with one-seventh the number of men.

During the past ten years, steel has spent less than $0.015 in research for each $1.00 invested in new plant equipment. As a result, it has increased its productivity at a rate of only 2 percent per year. In the same period, $11 billion was spent on new equipment. By neglecting research and the investigation of its production problems, American steel now faces stiff competition from Japan, Germany, and Italy. In 1952 American steel men scoffed at foreign competition, insisting that their "know-how" then made the production of steel in the United States much cheaper than was possible elsewhere. Within ten years foreign producers were exporting steel and steel products to the United States, since they could undersell the American producers in their own home market.

The Products of Research in Other Industries

It is estimated that American business spends $11 on advertising for every $0.90 spent on research. Altogether, industry spent more than $11 billion on advertising of all forms in 1960 and a little more than $1 billion on research in order to raise its productivity. If the more than $3 billion that is spent each year on preparing to send a man to the moon could be devoted to research for the increase of productivity, our annual output could be increased by at least 50 percent.

As an average, it takes more than ten years for research results to be translated into production, which means that production for 1975 and later has already been decided upon. The small current of clerks and workers being displaced by automation will become an angry torrent in the 1970's unless greater creativity in new products and jobs is carried on now. The millions leaving school during the late 1960's will be demanding work. Our labor force will increase to over 88 million by 1975 from the 70 million in 1965, but no conspicuously new products have been developed and no new markets have been opened.

In addition, American urban areas need to be renewed, housing must be made cheaper and more efficient, mass transportation must be changed from previous conceptions of fixed forms to one that offers the flexibility to accommodate the lack of stationary radii in the chaotic development of modern suburbs. More than two-thirds of our productive plant is now obsolete, as are our cities, factories, schools, colleges, and universities. Our societal values need adjustment and change; and most important of all, we need to emphasize the continuous creation of new wealth if our expanding population is to be kept employed and off the welfare rolls. More than this, we need to upgrade skills, values, and standards. We need to give greater dignity and importance to the individual than he has enjoyed thus far. We need to give him the right to enjoy a sense of independence that only millionaires have at the present time. Thus, there is a need for enough research and creative work to occupy tens of millions for countless generations to come.

Tertiary civilization will require masses of creative individuals—certainly at least one-third of the population—whereas previous centuries had only a small handful concentrated in certain urban centers. Civilization has become far too complex to operate chaotically through trial-and-error methods or through chance. Tertiary civilization requires that an ever larger percentage of the population be employed in educating the young to higher levels of skills and accomplishments and in carrying out the research that permits an automated society to function. Research will carry on analyses of American industry in order to encourage an even greater automation of its administrative and productive functions. Research will be required to study more efficient means of educating those whose home backgrounds have given them little motivation for study. Research will enable us to see what is needed to raise the bottom third of the population to the standards of the top third. Above all, we need to spend more research time on our entire educational system in order to make it more efficient and less traditionalist than it is today. Even the concepts of teaching itself must be better understood in order to make their practice more meaningful and rewarding. There must be more pleasant and more effective ways of learning than sitting quietly in classrooms from three to five hours a day. The human brain in succeeding decades must learn more and more; education must be far more integrated than it is today. Obsolete courses and instruction represent inefficiency and make adjustment to the near future difficult.

The Need for New Values

An automated society needs to be an extremely responsible one. If the routine decisions in school, factory, and government are to be made by computer on an impersonal basis, then the individual citizen must be reared to exercise self-discipline as a citizen and responsibility in the governing of his school, factory, or government. Education must be used to train individuals to participate far more than they do today in the decisions that concern them. A complex civilized society requires a citizenry aware of its responsibilities and conscious of its need to behave creatively. An educated population requires less passivity and more awareness of necessary innovations. The values of society need to give social prestige to innovational and creative personalities rather than to sports stars, glamor girls, and unscrupulous individuals. All these needs require far more research on man and his behavior than we are carrying out today. We need to be led by those living today who are conscious of the problems of the population being educated now to live in the future.

Research will be needed to lead us into tomorrow and to tell us for what jobs and professions we need to train today's children, what products they will manufacture, what wealth they will create, and what education they must have to become more responsible participants in society.

In the beginnings of today's automated age, the poorest one-third of Americans own one percent of the wealth of the United States. The next 23 percent own 5 percent. This means that over half of the American population own only 6 percent of the country's wealth. The richest 1.6 percent own nearly one-third of the country's physical assets. This small percentage owns 80 percent of the corporate stock, almost all of the state and municipal tax-free bonds, and over 90 percent of the corporate bonds. The goal for the future is not to take away from the top one percent of the population the possessions that it now enjoys, nor even to tax most of it out of existence (this is a nineteenth century proposal rather than one that has meaning in the twentieth century). The goal should be to raise the top two-thirds of the population to the levels now enjoyed by the top one percent and to raise the bottom one-third to the affluent levels enjoyed by the middle classes today.

The next century will require tremendous creations of new wealth in order to support the education, the research, and the cities that will be needed. Research and education will in turn develop even more wealth than has been invested in them. As we have seen from the past, a proper perspective for the role of the future requires that we devote even more of our energies to the organizational, innovational, and managerial needs of the future than we have spent on them in the past. We must encourage the education and the creativity of as large a proportion of the population as we can. Ideas have created our civilizations thus far, and ideas will create new variations in the future.

We need to be more aware than ever before that parents tend to relive their own traditionalist childhoods in rearing their children, who thus tend to accept the values of previous generations. This means that a child born in 1980 will be reared by parents who received their thoughts, behavior, and values from parents reared in the 1950's and 1960's; the parents, in turn, were reared by parents who acquired their patterns in the 1920's. There is thus a lag of at least three generations in acquiring values that determine decision-making action for the future. Social science and educational research must take this into consideration in planning a more efficient and viable educational system for the future.

Selected Bibliography

Bazelon, David T., *The Paper Economy* (New York, Random House, 1963).

Bendix, Reinhard, *Work and Authority in Industry* (New York, Harper & Row, Harper Torchbooks, 1963).

Bining, A. C., and Cochran, Thomas C., *The Rise of American Economic Life* (New York, Scribner, 1964).

Drucker, Peter F., *The New Society* (New York, Harper & Row, Harper Torchbooks, 1963).

Dunlop, John T., ed., *Automation and Technological Change,* An American Assembly Symposium (Englewood Cliffs, N.J., Prentice-Hall, Spectrum Books, 1962).

Gallup, George, *The Miracle Ahead* (New York, Harper & Row, 1964).

Markham, Charles, ed., *Jobs, Men and Machines* (New York, Praeger, 1964).

Michael, Donald N., *Cybernation: The Silent Conquest* (Santa Barbara, Calif., Center for the Study of Democratic Institutions, 1962).

Philipson, Morris, ed., *Automation: Implications for the Future* (New York, Random House, Vintage Books, 1962).

Scientific American, eds., *Technology and Economic Development* (New York, Knopf, 1963).

Theobald, Robert, *The Challenge of Abundance* (New York, New American Library, Mentor Books, 1962).

Walker, Charles R., ed., *Modern Technology and Civilization* (New York, McGraw-Hill, 1962).

Weeks, Robert P., ed., *Machines and the Man: A Sourcebook on Automation* (New York, Appleton-Century-Crofts, 1961).

25

The Future as More Than the Traditionalist Past and Present

In an age strongly influenced by the beginnings of an electronic revolution, which promises to give man a dignity of person that he has never known before, a greater freedom for creative expression, and the means to satisfy most of his dreams, we still seem to think within the context of a traditionalist past. We look upon the future as a continuation of the past rather than as something that may be drastically new. We find it difficult, for example, to conceive of a future human society in which the normal way of life does not require tens of millions of individuals to work on routine tasks which they may dislike and which may even numb their minds. At the same time, we can only assume a future society similar to that of the past, in which creative individuals still compete with one another in extraneous factors for the few posts that confer social prestige and monetary rewards.

Despite the enormous benefits of the Industrial Revolution and the Scientific Age that immeasurably raised the previous low standards of living of the majority of people, most individuals still cannot conceive of higher levels of affluence. It is difficult for people reared in past environments containing relative deprivation or few of the good things of life to shift over to an optimistic belief that it is possible for all individuals to have equal opportunities to achieve their goals of status, independence, and self-confidence. We are still part of a mental age that does not let us really believe that all individuals are endowed with potential skills of various kinds; that in any group of 500 to 1,000 individuals anywhere in the world, we might find roughly the same gamut of talents that we would theoretically discover at random in the more highly developed industrial countries.

We still cannot accept the common humanness of all individuals who share the same capabilities of thought, speech, and behavior. We still evaluate individuals intrinsically into good, better, and best, on the basis of their past performance in achieving traditionalist middle-class standards of success. People are poor, some say, because they lack ambition. (Even the poor themselves generally believe that being poor is mostly their own fault, a belief that only adds to their lack of self-confidence.) We often hear or read that those who drop out of high school should be encouraged to learn trades, a statement that overlooks the fact that the motivation for learning vocational education may be as lacking as it was for secondary school classes. (Education is a strong cultural factor in the Secondary civilization; but if one is reared to believe that schooling will bring few rewards in self-satisfaction, the incentive will be to withdraw from painful interpersonal experiences with teachers and other pupils.)

We theoretically believe in equality of opportunity, but there is not the equality of opportunity for the Negro born in the slums of an industrial city that there is for the son of a multimillionaire; nor even between one college graduate and another if one comes from a municipal college and the other has graduated from an Ivy League college.

Children who come from professional homes in large urban centers have far more intellectual opportunities available to them than do the sons and daughters of industrial workers. The former have verbal advantages; they are motivated to discipline themselves in schoolwork; they are given goals which they have the self-confidence to believe that they can achieve. The sons and daughters of the unskilled and semiskilled, on the other hand, have less self-discipline, have vague or unvoiced aspirations (generally in terms of the acquisition of material objects), and are less confident of their ability to compete successfully with middle-class children.

The Need for a New Education of the Future

If contemporary society is to develop a higher percentage of innovational and creative individuals, we need to develop compensating substitutes in school for those who come from intellectually deprived family backgrounds. It is necessary that the children of apathetic or withdrawn parents learn the new values of the middle-class schools without too much difficulty and without being forced to run into conflict with the contradictory values of their fathers and mothers. The children must be imbued with a sense of optimism that they can become politically and economically responsible when they are adults. How this can be done efficiently represents a problem to be solved by research in human behavior.

Tertiary civilization will require large numbers of highly educated and creative individuals, not only to solve the technological problems that an automated society will develop, but also to make decisions concerning the values that will go along with this new civilization. As automation becomes a more important part of our production methods (perhaps during the 1980's and 1990's), more and more individuals will be displaced from traditional forms of work. On the other hand, skills will be upgraded, and new creative positions and professions will be developed. The hidden talents among the poor must be tapped for social use; to do this will require new approaches both to education and to social integration. Not enough is known about educating the creative personality let alone educating what appears to be the noneducable.

Many of our present ways of rearing children, including their education both at home and in school, are oriented more to the past (but without learning from its shortcomings) than to the future. This traditionalism is evidently reinforced by the child's peer group, who also have been oriented to the values of their parents' childhoods. How this works was described and summarized by Christopher Jencks:

. . . In my observation the most important single factor in shaping an alumnus of a school is neither the physical facilities, the content of the curriculum, the erudition or imagination of the teachers nor the size of the classes, but the habits and values of the pupil's classmates. Students learn most of what they know informally rather than formally, and they learn from one another rather than from their elders . . .

If, as often happens in the slums, the school is dominated by the "hoods," it doesn't seem to matter how small the classes are: the most ambitious and often the most gifted students will concentrate their attention on learning how to jump the wires on a car rather than on learning the theory of electro-magnetism. If, as may happen in the small town, the school football team is the focus of the whole community's chauvinism—its patriotic representative in competition with neighboring towns—the most talented students will become athletes no matter how many Ph.D.s the school board hires. And if, as increasingly happens in prosperous suburbs, attending school is mainly a way of getting into a competitive big-name college, the ambitious pupil will become something of an intellectual no matter how dim most of his teachers may be (of course, every school has individual pupils who defy its norms, who go to Harvard despite attending a "football school") . . .

The quality of education depends largely on the spontaneous interplay of habits, interests, and ideals which each group of classmates brings from its homes, partly on the ingenuity of teachers and administrators in controlling this interplay, and hardly at all on the quality of the formal instruction offered by the teachers. It seems to follow, moreover, that if you want to improve the education available to a child from the slums, the most important thing to improve is the attitude of his classmates toward adults, toward "brains," and toward work in general.

Slum children come to school with a pattern of habits and values which even the most tolerant teacher can hardly approve. They are usually obsessed with physical prowess, contemptuous of ideas and books. They are also likely to be infatuated with the outward symbols of success—money, ostentation and publicity—without any apparent respect for the technical skill and craftsmanship which make success possible for most people. Perhaps because their parents live up to neither lower class ideals of strength and loyalty, nor to middle class standards of respectability, most slum children regard not only their parents but all adults as knaves and fools.

The only way to keep such a child from growing up into another of the unlovable and unemployable adults he scorns is to make him change in fundamental ways. He will not do this simply because his teachers urge him to do so. The teacher's approval isn't that important to most slum children. The thing that counts—that makes his day-to-day life either intolerable or tolerable—is in the opinion of his classmates and more especially of the popular and omnicompetent children who are the cynosure of all eyes. In effect, these children are the teacher's unofficial self-appointed deputies. Even in the best cases, where they have been brought up to share most of her future-oriented "bourgeois" values, they short-circuit many of her efforts. When these young tastemakers and opinion-molders are hostile to the school and the teacher, her hope of converting lower class pupils to her sedate values is almost nil. To put it another way, a lower class pupil is unlikely to become middle class unless he has potential middle class friends in his class; friends who will support him when his streetcorner playmates make fun of his respectability . . . [1]

If we have difficulty in educating large numbers of our present population to middle-class behavior and thought, consider the difficulties involved in educating a majority of the population to be innovators, original thinkers, and creative personalities in twenty to thirty years from now.

The nineteenth and twentieth centuries have seen a tremendous increase of interest in education for cultural change, although much of it has taken place among groups that have traditionally given approval to education as a means of social mobility—for example, among the Scots, among those living in the northern United States, among the European Jews, or among the rising new urban populations in the various industrial countries of the world. Education is perhaps a twentieth century phenomenon, for the nineteenth century academies and colleges educated only a small proportion of the population in the United States.

In the United States today, 70 percent of the young people graduate from high school, 50 percent of the adults have graduated from secondary school, and the percentage of those going to college increases each year. A generation ago most Americans finished their education with elementary school; the generation before that had less than half their schooling. Before World War I, there were less than 200,000 students in the colleges and universities of the United States, for the demand for college graduates was small at that time. Most elementary school teachers, for ex-

---

[1] Jencks, Christopher, "Slums and Schools, II," *The New Republic,* September 17, 1962.

ample, were normal school graduates, the equivalent today of junior college. In 1965, there were more than 5,000,000 going to the colleges, universities, technical and professional schools in the United States. By the end of this century, perhaps more than half of the American population will be college graduates. In 1965, 30 percent of the high school graduates went to college; the percentage may double by 1975.

The fact that half of the American adult population are now high school graduates indicates that the problems of the unskilled, uneducated, and untrainable could be solved during the next two generations, since it has taken less than two generations to train the large number of technicians and scientists we have in the United States today. Although the present generation of unemployed, displaced, unskilled workers may be expendable, the conclusions are not lost upon them that education is an important means of social mobility and that an educated person not only earns more money but also commands more respect. While these motivations may not stimulate originality or creativity in their children, they may at least encourage the children to graduate from high school and perhaps even from college.

Part of the incentive for creativity and innovation may come out of the need for children to prove themselves more worthy of commanding respect from the outside world than their parents did. For example, the marginal individuals who have been hurt by the changing world about them—such as the displaced coal miners of the Cumberland Valley, the slum dwellers of the metropolitan centers, the Negroes, the American Indians, the Mexicans, and the rural whites of the South—may eventually accept the middle-class assessment of themselves and consequently spur their children on to prove themselves as good as the middle classes in terms of middle-class standards of values. Perhaps an awareness of themselves as judged by others will encourage cultural change not only in the United States but also in the poor nations of the rest of the world. Perhaps it takes a generation of stirring up the embers before the fires begin to burn.

A huge investment in both research and education will be needed during the next twenty-five to thirty years. The relationship between research and education is similar to that between the chicken and the egg; it is difficult to say which comes first. Although the word *education* has become a hackneyed term, a cure-all for all the problems that beset us, it cannot be employed in this usage in the future. Tertiary civilization will require an integrated educational system that embraces learning as a means of understanding, adjusting to and utilizing efficiently the knowledge about man and his universe that will continue to accumulate in mountainous proportions. Education must train individuals to be of service; it must advance the funds of knowledge that will make for greater insights into the most efficient ways of satisfying man's needs for security, creativity, dignity, and identification. Education must assist in pinpointing and encouraging the talented child and adolescent to make their most creative contributions.

We have much to learn in advancing and improving the teaching of necessary integrating techniques. Perhaps the future elementary schools will find it easier to teach the basic tools of learning, including a more consistent spelling and grammar, in a much shorter period of time and with greater zest. Perhaps the secondary schools will play a more important part in teaching students about the universe and the world of man than the colleges do today. Perhaps future basic education may teach the fundamentals of scientific learning in a much shorter period of time, with the principles possibly being learned in elementary school.

The Educability of Mankind

During the Neolithic period and Primary civilization, most men learned easily to be peasants, just as previously most of them had learned to become hunters and fishermen. The differences between one man and another were mostly a matter of family backgrounds that emphasized certain personality characteristics. Most women learned to be wives and mothers, and again the differences between them were small and based upon slight cultural differences existing between families. In the Industrial Age, most workers were responsible and learned their tasks equally well. In the past 100 years the evidence has become conclusive that what one group of people can do in Western Europe, another can do equally well in China, Japan, India, Africa, or South America; that talents and aptitudes for learning are spread equally in all human beings over the face of the earth; that what in the dim past was developed in one part of the world spread to strangers thousands of miles away; and that the barriers were not lack of human skills, but obstacles of isolation or absence of incentives.

No evidence has ever shown that the creativity of man follows geographic lines. The story of mankind thus far has been a story of human beings sharing the same qualities of humanness, which have enabled both civilizations and knowledge to grow. Ethical and moral standards are universal, as are strivings for brotherhood, peace, and goodwill. Educated American and African Negroes can theoretically win Nobel prizes in the sciences, invent new products and processes, and manage highly efficient enterprises, just as any group of American or European whites can, since all of these activities are part of man's cultural learning. On the other hand, we cannot expect peasants to become self-taught physicists and chemists or innovators in new industrial efficiency, since their receptivity to learning does not include the adoption of a culture that is completely isolated from them. There is no way in which they could learn these new forms of thought without formal schooling.

Industrialization, as we have seen, is a complex culture that must be learned not only in schools but also through informal instruction in the plant. Engineers, production men, and managers learn a good deal of tacit industrial behavior on the job; and one of the problems of diffusing this culture to the developing or poor nations is that those who have been the carriers of the new culture have often failed to articulate it through writing and formal instruction, or by summarizing its ways of thinking, its cues, and behavior. To learn this industrial culture of management and entrepreneurship requires a basis of formal learning that gives the individual a receptivity to concepts of efficiency, innovation, and change.

The industrialized nations have created their industrial cultures out of the thoughts and experiences of those who built their industries and laboratories. In exporting machines, for example, the technology is sent but not the culture that goes with its operation. This is why we need research as well as education to codify, simplify, and amplify this technological and scientific culture so that it can be taught not only to the more unskilled third of the American population, but to the two-thirds of the rest of the world who are today receptive to learning it.

The Problem of Poverty as an Obstacle to the Future

More and more of mankind is finding that it cannot afford poverty because it is too expensive. The social capital required to take care of the poor, the uneducated, and the unskilled is far greater than the latter's contribution to the mounting fund of societal wealth. Slums do not pay their way in taxes, either property or income, or in the energies that a complex civilization requires of its adherents and supporters. The poor do not pay for the cost of their children's education or for their municipal costs, which are much higher for them than for the more affluent middle classes. Even the police are required in large numbers to protect the affluent from the disorganized behavior of some of the poor. (Although there are middle-class criminals, they tend to be less violent than those of the lower classes.) The poor have more mental illness and require more subsidized social welfare, medicine, and old-age care. Even the slum buildings in the metropolitan centers need more visits from the inspectors of health and sanitation than do the middle class residential blocks.

Unless concerted efforts are made during the next twenty to thirty years to transform the uneducated and unskilled urban and rural poor into educated, technical middle-class individuals, their needs and numbers will swamp the abilities of welfare, social, and police agencies to care for them. Although the cost today of supporting the poor is small, it can reach magnified proportions by the end of this century, when automation and scientific innovations will have displaced large numbers of the un-educated and the unskilled. The costs of unemployment and poverty are much higher than any possible sums that could be invested in education and research to discover ways to make the displaced poor into self-support-ing contributors to the industrial welfare of the rest of the population.

The poor and uneducated function in a never-ending circle, for they lack self-confidence and can only do tasks that require little training, or those jobs that automation and improved technologies are eliminating. New positions are being created in the professional, educational, and technical fields for which the unemployed or displaced poor are com-pletely unsuited. Yet, it is their children who are dropping out of high school before they graduate (over 40 percent of the total in 1963) and who then seek the jobs that their fathers are losing in large numbers to the more skillful and impersonal machines. The poor are in fact sur-vivors of a previous age when their labor was in greater demand. They need help in order to change and in order to let their children become members of the more affluent elements in the population.

Pilot studies indicate a drop in employment during the next two decades for the unskilled and the uneducated. But few studies have been started that will help the authorities in 1985 solve these problems. A ran-dom study done in Chicago of 684 able-bodied relief recipients, 16 to 64 years of age, found that more than 50 percent could not pass the fifth grade reading and vocabulary tests and that more than half of the adults on relief were functionally illiterate, even though 95 percent had gone beyond the fifth grade. The study ended by stating that "the problems of public welfare are not due to newcomers in the community, but stem from unemployment and economic and technological displacement, and, most important, from the lack of basic educational skills of relief recip-ients which are essential to compete in our modern society." [2]

The Need for More Educated Women

In an age that increasingly requires creative and innovational personali-ties, the mothers who will rear the next generation of scientists, entre-preneurs, and managers must also be highly educated themselves. Unfor-tunately, most young mothers do not have the education or the skills that they need if they are to rear children who will function creatively in the future. To educate children for 1975 and 1985 requires some awareness of the type of society that might exist then. To prepare their children for

[2] *New York Times,* September 22, 1962.

the world ahead, mothers need to motivate their offspring to think and behave differently than they do themselves. The problem lies in the fact that mothers, or fathers for that matter, who do not read are expected to encourage their children to do so. Mothers or fathers who spend their evenings watching television or entertaining friends with small talk are asked to motivate their children to become socially responsible and creative. Mothers whose mental horizons embrace only housework and physical child care are urged to prepare their children to develop new values for the industrial and scientific world in which they will live. Mothers who assume no better goal for their daughters than to get married as early as or earlier than they did cannot be expected to turn out a generation of skilled mothers who in turn will motivate their children to be innovational, intellectually curious, and efficient in the use of their mental powers.

The Demand for the Research Oriented

Because of the problems that beset us, we need to develop human personalities that have the skills to solve them. But to do this, we need more specialized research to help us learn to utilize the talents and creative personalities that girls and boys share in common. Until now, the demand for creative individuals has been slight. Although their results are welcomed, more encouragement has been given to those who are traditionalist than to those who are creative. Until recently, most colleges and corporations steered clear of the creative individual for fear that he would not be able to adjust to their routines. Today the demand for creative individuals, at least in the physical and biological sciences, has been growing.

The demand for educated and innovational individuals has steadily become greater since World War II; but not so long before that war, the educated found it almost as difficult to find positions as the uneducated. During the 1930's, American colleges had only about one-quarter the number of undergraduates that they do today, and the number of graduate students was less than one-fifth. But the number of positions for the graduating PhD's was comparatively less. The huge expenditures during World War II and afterward created an unsatisfied demand for engineers, physicists, and chemists. Today the increased amount of money for medical research has created a demand for those trained in the biological sciences. The demand for social scientists has also been steadily increasing, with a greater demand for economists, psychologists, political scientists, historians, sociologists, and anthropologists, roughly in that order.

As the decades pass and as the economy demands even more research men, educators, and coordinators of the research and educational fields, the number of the highly educated may double, triple, and perhaps quadruple. Over a period of decades, or perhaps centuries, the ratio of the educated to the uneducated will be similar to the proportion of urban to rural inhabitants in the United States today. The cultural change that will take place in the future will be increasingly fashioned and carried on by the growing percentage of the population going to four-year colleges and graduate and professional schools.

As research and education gradually become two of the greatest industries in future America, especially in the numbers of individuals employed and in the amount of production that will come from their efforts, more study will be needed to make both more efficient. Perhaps we may even need a new group of researchers to study research and perhaps another group to study education, so that both research institutions and the schools and colleges can become ever more efficient and less wasteful of human resources. Perhaps we may even need a third group of researchers to tell us how to turn the children of the intellectually deprived into creative and innovational personalities in the same period of time.

The Problem Presented for the Future by the Untrained and the Uneducated

It is not the sheer number of individuals on this earth that creates problems, but the mass of untrained and uneducated men and women who have been frustrated in their simple desires for human dignity and social respect. It is quite possible that the earth could support a population of 40 billion far better than it does the less than 4 billion today if the vast majority were highly trained and creatively educated. Intelligent and educated men can create their own substitutes for the natural resources or the climates that are lacking.

It is even possible that humanity and the future Tertiary civilization could use even 50 to 60 billion highly educated, creative individuals. Perhaps the future could use those numbers much more easily than it could, say, 10 billion unskilled and untrained ones. We can see that the problem, then, is not so much numbers (although a crowded world would have its problems) as the level of education, the skills, and the quality of the inhabitants.

On the other hand, if the world's population continues to expand as it has during the past one hundred years with the poor, the uneducated, and the untrained reproducing themselves to become even more numerous during the next century, the social, cultural, and economic problems brought about by this type of overpopulation can be grave indeed. Even today, less than 5 percent of the world's population are its managers, skilled technicians, entrepreneurs, and scientists, which means that 95 percent of the world's inhabitants are probably unequipped for life in the future Tertiary civilization. If this percentage is not cut down to less than half during the next thirty years, the majority may prevent the creation of those values that can lead to a less frustrated and more secure human existence.

The future automated civilization could be a great boon to humanity if a culture is developed that can utilize its benefits to the maximum. There is no need to waste human resources by employing them in factories doing routine, boring tasks (a French worker the author interviewed in 1955 thought that there was nothing more "idiotic" than doing work that was "brainless," which repeated day after day the same motions and tasks), which the machine can do better and more cheaply, and with less drain on human emotions.

If automation leads to replacement without educating those who have been removed, then the very high costs to society for unemployment payments and relief will have made it the worse loser. Automation to be successful should lead to rising skill levels, with more employed in creative undertakings and in the more important services. Automation should free men from arduous and monotonous labor so that they can devote their mental and physical energies to more self-satisfying tasks.

During the period of Secondary civilization, the literacy rate in the United States and England rose from less than 20 percent to more than 95 percent. During the twenty-first century, it is quite possible that the common standards of literacy will need to be raised to those of today's technologically and scientifically literate. Future centuries may raise their standards (as well as levels of teaching) even higher.

Research must start to tell us very soon how we can raise the educational and technical levels in the United States and in other industrial countries, and how we can transform the children of the majority into technicians, scientists, and administrators within the next twenty to thirty years. Unless we do so, there may be no Tertiary civilization that can use science and technology to make our way of life richer and more personally rewarding.

Government, economists, and sociologists point up the need to do something to eradicate the pockets of poverty still remaining in the United States; but few of the social scientists are prepared today to recommend what to do or where to begin, although all agree that the children of the poor must be aided first. We need to know what to do about the areas in the United States that lack entrepreneurial, technical, and scientific skills. In many ways these areas are facing the same problem as the developing poor nations, that is, just how it is possible to get the widest participation of entrepreneurial, technical, and managerial skills in the shortest period of time.

The Importance of Creative and Innovational Persons

A great many towns and small cities in the United States could be called deprived in terms of entrepreneurial, technical, and managerial talents. Like the Cumberland valley, they are dependent upon outside skills, capital, and entrepreneurial ability to tell them what they must do; all they can offer the outside world is more unskilled or semiskilled labor. Can these towns and cities find within themselves the creative resources to develop services or new products that could educate and employ its population? Could they establish research bureaus which, by utilizing local talents and ideas obtained from the outside, could create services or products that would raise the living standards?

For example, it is quite possible that a reservoir of one percent innovational and creative personalities in a town of 25,000 might be able to increase the work possibilities of the town and offer its citizens better medical, educational, and recreational facilities than they enjoy today. Such a small reservoir of highly trained innovators, subsidized in the beginning, could make a great dent in the present economic and social stagnation of most of the towns and small cities in the United States that are isolated from the large metropolitan centers. A city of 50,000 with one percent of its population creative and innovational personalities could have a total of 500 highly trained persons doing the planning and thinking for the rest of the population.

But even a one percent reservoir of creative personalities may represent a very small proportion of the creative innovators we shall perhaps need during the next 50 to 100 years. One percent may be a far higher number than we have today; it is doubtful that the average city of 500,000 has as many as 5,000 trained creative and innovational personalities, or that a city of 5 million has as many as 50,000, or even that the United States with a population approaching 200 million has as many as 2 million. It is difficult to estimate the number of individuals who are in a position today to solve problems or develop new products or create new services, but it seems unlikely that we have trained as many as one percent of the population in these fields.

Undoubtedly, future technicians, engineers, and physical scientists may be able to develop a civilization that can use scientific principles more efficiently than ever before and thus create a way of life that would be more comfortable for the rest of the population who would be its recipients. There is considerable doubt, however, that we could develop a culture that would adjust to the new civilization in the same amount of time required to create it. The consequences would be tragic if, side by side with a growing technical and scientific civilization, the number of displaced unemployed were to grow by leaps and bounds or if their children were not trained at their various levels of ability to contribute actively to such a civilization.

A culture adjusted to a scientific civilization requires large numbers of educated individuals who are sensitive to what their problems are. Perhaps in such a culture the qualifications for teaching would be raised to levels higher than the conventional PhD, with its traditional conformity to the set borders of the various segments of human knowledge. The promise of automation for teaching is that routine decisions and monotonous tasks would be taken out of the hands of teachers and administrators, who could then spend more time solving the problems of training the young for the technical and scientific civilization that lies ahead.

Unfortunately, today many individuals are being retrained for services and trades that may have little opportunity for growth. It is extremely difficult for educators to decide what training must be given to students if few specialists have any idea what the economy may require five to ten years from now. Perhaps we need a new group of professionals who can work on the trends for the future so that they can give guidance to our educators, economists, and administrators. After all, we have more indications today of what may happen in the future than we know of what happened in antiquity. But the shortage of knowledge of the past has not stopped the archaeologists, the prehistorians, and the paleontologists from working on the past. At the same time, a lack of evidence should not handicap the professional in working on the future.

The poor, the uneducated, and the unemployed normally feel humiliated by what has happened to them. Although society has learned to eliminate the pains of hunger, disease, cold, and fear for most people, it has done little or nothing to abolish the pains of social humiliation, one of the greatest tribulations that human beings undergo and perhaps the most severe of deprivational feelings. As long as any man is continuously humiliated by the actions of others, he has little human dignity. Cultural and economic change humiliates those who are compelled to bear its burdens and its risks.

The Narrowing of Class Divisions

The number of the very wealthy may increase and proliferate as children and grandchildren inherit large portions of paper wealth, but we can expect the influences of the wealthy upon the economy and political bodies to decrease in future years. As more individuals go to college and graduate school, the differentiating marks may no longer be the possession of wealth but the degree of knowledge that people possess. Highly trained scientists, innovators, and managers in the future will not feel socially inadequate when rewards will be coming their way doubtless in larger amounts than at present.

As social pressures begin to emphasize education rather than consumption or leisure, the descendants of the new oil and real estate multimillionaires may find that a sense of accomplishment may become as important to them as the possession of money. Even today, a certain percentage of the millionaires are finding that a life of leisure can become monotonous unless one has other goals to accompany it, that wealth must be used as a floor rather than as a roof.

Income, education, and occupation are important determining factors in an individual's social identification; but differentiating class lines have become somewhat blurred as the educated middle classes have expanded their participation in big business and big government. Such broad social categories as upper, upper-middle, middle-middle, lower-middle, and so on, come down to the conclusion that the higher the education, income, and authority, the higher is the individual's social position. However, as scarcities in both education and income become comparatively less, the concept of class will play far less of a role than it does today.

With the trend toward greater wealth, position, and education for the technological middle classes, social status may shift somewhat during the next twenty to thirty years. Conspicuous wealth would have little meaning when most people share roughly the same standards of comfort. Although the multimillionaire may continue to have greater privacy, space, and services, the new groups of professionals may find themselves enjoying the same luxuries in smaller amounts.

All this means that a complete change in our social relationships may take place during the next 50 to 100 years. Although hunger, disease, and illiteracy with their shriveling of the human spirit may still exist in most parts of the world, and although social indifference to man's psychological and physical suffering continues to be the norm in many countries, the trend is nevertheless toward a world in which age-old scarcities will become a thing of the past. Humanity for the first time in its history is entering an era of great abundance and creativity. This means that man's past concepts about production, money, and arduous work may eventually become as irrelevant to the world of tomorrow as ideas about the permanency of previously existing social institutions.

Since mankind will be able to turn out mountains of surpluses in every field of production during the next twenty to thirty years (though this is not to say that it will), some conception of another series of goals must be developed in which production is geared to man's needs rather than to despoilment of resources or of human beings. If the production of food and material goods can be handled by fewer individuals, new goals should be developed to shift the emphasis from working in order to earn money to a concept of work for the benefit of the individual and society. Future society needs more services rather than fewer, more education, more research, more problem solving, and even more creation of social wealth. Men do not need more leisure, 10-hour work weeks, or bigger and better sports events; but they do perhaps need more involvement with the problems of mankind as well as greater self-realization. Although our values have changed greatly since man first became aware that he had the ability to make life easier for himself, our concepts of recreation and leisure-time activities still seem to assume that the end result in achieving scientific and technological breakthroughs is not to satisfy man's deep intellectual curiosity about himself and the universe he lives in, but to enable a large number of individuals to live their short lives gratifying their senses and emotions rather than their intellects.

As we look back to where mankind started, we can see that we have not reached a plateau beyond which we cannot go. Rather, we have barely begun to climb in our feeble attempts to leave our animal existence behind us and to realize our human potentialities. Even if it turns out that mankind may have a future life-span only half as long as that of the Earth, we must still conclude that we have barely begun to grow. Though we have some 2.5 billion years of life behind us, we may have from 5 to 10 billion years or more of life ahead of us. The preservation of human life for the future becomes an important obligation for those who have within their power the ability to destroy all of mankind with the new weapons of war.

We have passed through 3 million years of human evolutionary development, and we have an endless future unwinding before us. Only a few thousand years have passed since Primary civilization began, and a little over two centuries since the Secondary came on the scene, and it is possible that the next stage of civilization, the Tertiary, may be in full operation within the next hundred years. Then it will be anyone's guess as to what will happen two hundred, three hundred, or five hundred years from now. We cannot visualize what the twenty-second century will bring to humanity, let alone the twenty-seventh, or the thirtieth.

We may all be able to agree that Secondary civilization does continue a rational development that seems to go back to man's first attempts to make himself secure, efficient, and self-confident through tool making as a projection of his mental strength and as a compensation for his physical weaknesses. As more and more of the earth's population is swept up into the wake of industrialization and scientific development, new social problems will certainly arise. There is no doubt that man can become more creative, secure, and efficient. But if no means are found to help those displaced by the machine to develop their more human potentialities, then those made to feel inadequate can become sullen, conflict-creating drags on the future.

As the industrial and scientific culture changes through increased participation of the thought processes of every one of us, new values may be created that could enhance the common humanity of all men. Men have taken giant steps from the time when they spent their days seeking only food. Now the amount of time spent on earning enough to buy our food has become minimal. Even shelter and warm clothing are within the reach of each individual in the industrial countries of the world. Men now need to raise their sights higher, to think of what they can build in the future.

These new values may come as more and more individuals are able to obtain a better perspective of themselves as part of a mankind that has come a long way, but that still has a long way to go. Men need to be modest and unassuming when they see themselves in the beginning of a movement that will go on for hundreds of thousands if not millions and perhaps tens of millions of years after they have gone. Their immortality will also remain in what they do to make life easier and pleasanter for all those who survive them, for each of us is an ancestor of the future.

Since a lag always seems to exist between recognizing research needs, obtaining funds or permission, and training personnel, we should identify today the emerging social and economic questions that future political decision makers may need to answer. This means that we also need to discover what knowledge future administrators must have if they are to make decisions that are meaningful. In order to help our descendants understand their world of 2000 and later, we ourselves must try to understand what it is that we are bequeathing them. In doing so, perhaps we can help the creative leaders of mankind take time out to see where they are before they resume their blind plunge into the uncharted future.

Selected Bibliography

American Assembly, *Goals for Americans,* Report of the President's Commission on National Goals (New York, Columbia University Press, 1964).

Bazelon, David T., *The Paper Economy* (New York, Random House, 1963).

Caudill, Harry M., *Night Comes to the Cumberlands* (Boston, Little, Brown, 1963).

Dunham, Barrows, *Heroes and Heretics* (New York, Knopf, 1964).

Galbraith, John Kenneth, *The Affluent Society* (Boston, Houghton Mifflin, 1958).

Henry, Jules, *Culture Against Man* (New York, Random House, 1963).

Myrdal, Gunnar, *Challenge to Affluence* (New York, Random House, Pantheon Books, 1963).

Roche, John P., *The Quest for the Dream* (New York, Macmillan, 1963).

Theobald, Robert, *The Rich and the Poor* (New York, New American Library, 1961).

———, *The Challenge of Abundance* (New York, New American Library, 1961).

Whyte, William H., Jr., *The Organization Man* (New York, Simon and Schuster, 1956).

Index